Book of Enoch

Volume II

Son of Man

Michael B. Rush

Section One – Analysis of Book of Enoch Chapters 39.1 to 71.17

Chapter 1: Parables

This is the second volume of the Book of Enoch series. Volume one of this series analyzed the portion of the Book of Enoch commonly known as the Book of the Watchers. In that volume, Enoch gave an account of the corruption of the prediluvian world, which was caused by two hundred men who came to this world from elsewhere. It spoke of the disastrous consequences of their interference with humankind anciently. Enoch prefaced his account by stating that he was sharing it to benefit those who would live upon the Earth in the last days, during the days of trial, when the wicked would be purged. Enoch explicitly stated that the Watchers would return in the last days and that the Earth would become as it was before the flood. In that volume, I shared much evidence that Enoch's prophecies in this regard are being fulfilled before our very eyes.

This volume will focus on the second portion of the Book of Enoch, commonly called the Book of Parables. The Book of Parables is considered the most controversial section of the Book of Enoch. The reason for this is its messianic nature. This volume introduces the world to the messianic title, Son of Man. As such, this volume contains many prophecies concerning the life and mission of the Savior. Indeed, of all the ancient biblical texts, no other book comes close to describing the life and mission of Jesus Christ in greater detail than the Book of Parables. Furthermore, as we conduct our analysis of these writings, it will become clear that the mortal ministry of Jesus Christ was greatly influenced by this book, more so than any other Biblical text.

Nephi, the great prophet from the House of Joseph, saw that many plain and precious things would be removed from the Bible. As such, we must understand that such prophecies had not been removed from the holy writings in Nephi's day. The editing of the Old Testament narrative is believed to have occurred after the Babylonian exile. As was discussed in volume one of this series, both the Northern Kingdom of Israel as well as the Kingdom of Judah were destroyed as a result of their worshiping false gods of the Canaanites– see Jeremiah 7:8,13-20 and 44:1-3,9,15-19,24-29.

After the Jews witnessed the destruction of the Northern Kingdom of Israel and their own captivity in Babylon, there was a movement to purge all aspects of polytheism from their writings. Because Lehi's family left Jerusalem before the Kingdom of Judah was destroyed by Babylon, the Brass Plates were never purged. This is one reason that the Brass Plates are described as containing more records than the Bible. As a result, the people of the Book of Mormon spoke openly of the trinity, the Father, Son, and Holy Ghost, while the post-Babylonian Jews did not.

As a result of this doctrinal purge, the pivotal roles of the Son of God and the Spirit of God became veiled. Only hints and shadows of the coming Messiah survived the post-Babylonian polytheistic purging of Jewish Biblical texts. However, despite the revised text of the Bible, it was clear that the Jews were still looking for a promised Messiah. This can be seen in the following dialogue between the masters of the law and Jesus at the temple.

> And Jesus walked in the temple in Solomon's porch. Then came the Jews round about Him, and said unto Him, How long dost thou make us to doubt? If thou be the Christ [*the Anointed, Elect, or Chosen One*], tell us plainly.
>
> Jesus answered them, I told you, and ye believed not…Then the Jews took up stones again to stone Him.
>
> Jesus answered them, many good works have I shewed you from my Father; for which of those works do ye stone me? The Jews answered Him, saying, for a good work we stone thee not; but for blasphemy; and because that thou, being a man, makest thyself God.
>
> Say ye of Him, whom the Father hath sanctified, and sent into the world, Thou blasphemest; because I said, I am the Son of God? If I do not the works of my Father, believe me not. But if I do, though ye believe not me, believe the works: that ye may know, and believe, that the Father *is* in Me, and I in Him. (John 10:23-25, 31-33, 37-38)

The above interaction cuts through all of the monotheistic editing of the Bible. It lays bare the polytheistic nature of the Godhead: God the Father has a divine Son, and His Son was the promised Messiah. What is not obvious from this conversation is how the Jews retained the knowledge of a coming Christ if all polytheistic references had been removed from their core writings.

This is where the Book of Enoch comes in. For some reason, the Book of Enoch survived the Old Testament Purge. Perhaps the Jews did not dare edit a document handed down to them by Abraham himself. Perhaps too many copies of the Book of Enoch existed for them to control. Regardless of the reason, the parables within the Book of Enoch are now highly controversial because they bridge the monotheistic gap of the Old Testament. They do this through the repeated usage of titles such as the Elect

One and the Son of Man. The title "Elect" or "Chosen One" could just as easily have been translated with another synonym: "the Christ."

The Son of Man is another curious messianic title in Enoch's writings. This phrase is often used in the Old Testament without messianic connotations to highlight the difference between mortals and God. However, the Book of Enoch clearly uses the title Son of Man messianically. Therefore, the Jews would have been familiar with these titles. Indeed, the only two examples of such titles that remain in the Old Testament have themes that link them back to the Book of Enoch. Consider the first example from the writings of Daniel:

> I saw in the night visions, and, behold, *One* like the Son of Man came with the clouds of heaven, and came to the Ancient of days, and they brought Him (the Son of Man) near before him (the Ancient of Days). And there was given Him dominion, and glory, and a kingdom, that all people, nations, and languages, should serve Him: His dominion *is* an everlasting dominion, which shall not pass away, and His kingdom *that* which shall not be destroyed. (Daniel 7:13-14)

In this passage, Daniel uses his own language to describe his vision, but these are not the words of his angelic guide. What would have sparked Daniel to see a divine Being in the clouds of heaven, watch that Being come to the earth to speak with Michael and take the governance of the Kingdom of God and, as a result, say He is like the Son of Man. The way Daniel phrased his wording suggests that what he saw in his vision reminded him of another account that he was already familiar with, an account concerning the Son of Man. What account would have existed in Daniel's day to which he could have compared his vision? The only account I know of is found in the Book of Enoch. Consider the following:

> And there I saw One who had a head of days, and His head was white like wool, and with Him was another being whose countenance had the appearance of a man, and His face was full of graciousness, like one of the holy angels. And I asked the angel who went with me and showed me all the hidden things, concerning that Son of Man, who He was, and whence He was, (and) why he went with the Head of Days? And he answered and said unto me:
>
> This is the Son of Man who hath righteousness, with whom dwelleth righteousness, and who revealeth all the treasures of that which is hidden, because the Lord of Spirits hath

chosen Him, and whose lot hath the pre-eminence before the
Lord of Spirits in uprightness forever. (BoE 46:1-3)

Daniel's vision is obviously reminiscent of Enoch's vision, which would have occurred some two thousand years earlier. In both examples, the Son of Man is seen with a man named the Ancient of Days and the Head of Days. In both instances, the Son of Man also correlates with a Messianic figure to whom the Father has given the kingdom. This can only be referring to the Lord Jesus Christ. In addition, Daniel's vision of the Son of Man coming in the clouds of heaven has strong Enochean undertones. Therefore, Daniel did not spontaneously make up the phrase Son of Man; rather, he used it because what he had seen in his vision reminded him of what he had read in the Book of Enoch.

Enoch was given the title Son of Man in conjunction with the Lord Jesus Christ from his angelic guide. This is the source of the title, Son of Man. In this context, only one other messianic usage of this singular phrase survived the Old Testament purge. This phrase is found in a verse of an ancient biblical song. Consider the following:

> Let thy hand be upon the man of thy right hand, upon the
> Son of Man whom thou madest strong for Thyself. (Psalms
> 80:17)

The psalmist's usage of this messianic title is in complete harmony with the other two usages of the title above. The title refers to God's condescension in all three of these passages. It refers to Jesus Christ, the Son of the Most High God, who subjected Himself to His Father's will and descended below everything.

In the restored scriptures of the restoration, we have additional curious usages of this title that provide further insight. According to Abraham 1:31, Abraham had a copy of the records of the original fathers. He used the phrase "Son of Man" to describe a being he had seen in vision. Consider the following passage:

> And the Lord said: Whom shall I send? And one answered
> like unto the Son of Man: Here am I, send me. (Abraham
> 3:27)

In this passage, Abraham described the individual who volunteered Himself to do the will of the Father as being "like unto the Son of Man." The phrase "like the Son of Man" or "like unto the Son of Man," used by Daniel and Abraham, promotes familiarity through an external source. People often describe the taste of different meats by saying they taste like chicken. "Like chicken" and "like unto the Son of Man" are used similarly. That is to say, both Daniel and Abraham are likening the person that they saw in their vision to the Son of Man spoken of in Enoch's writings. For this to be the case, the Book of Enoch would have had to have been very common amongst the ancients. The Dead Sea Scroll gives us the best sampling of ancient scriptural libraries of the House of Israel known to man. All of the Old Testament books, except the book of Ester and Nehemiah, were found amongst these scrolls. It is, therefore, very telling that one of the most prevalent books recovered among the Dead Sea Scrolls was the Book of Enoch, suggesting it was common knowledge at the time, which would have been why Daniel and Abraham would have linked what they had seen in vision to the Son of Man spoken of within the Book of Enoch.

Abraham understood what Christ was volunteering to do, so the title Son of Man seemed to apply so readily. Christ, the foremost in Heaven, second only to His Father, condescended to subject Himself to the most horrible things imaginable. In my mind's eye, I hear an extended version of the conversation Abraham might have witnessed.

> Here am I, send Me. I will do thy will, and the glory be
> Thine. I will go down and take upon Myself the sins, pains,
> sicknesses, and sorrows of thy people, that I might know
> how to succor them. I will tremble because of pain, and bleed
> from every pore, and suffer in both body and spirit that My
> life might be a ransom for their souls. This I will do that
> through the shedding of My blood the bands of death and
> Hell may be broken, that they might come again into Thy
> presence as Thy begotten sons and daughters, having been
> born again through Me.

Christ's willingness to come to the earth and do all these things is embodied in the messianic title – Son of Man. As such, the title Son of Man perfectly embodies His life and mission and is even more expressive than Christ's. Perhaps this is why Jesus often referred to Himself as the Son of Man rather than Christ. All those who heard Him do so would have linked this title and the writings in the Book of Enoch. It would have been from the context of the Book of Enoch that they would have attributed meaning to this title. The familiarity of the ancient world with this text is evident in the writings of other New Testament authors, such as Peter, John, and Jude.

Consider the following bold usage of this messianic title by Christ, which had the Jews scrambling over one another for stones with which to kill Jesus.

> For the Father judgeth no man, but hath committed all
> judgment unto the Son: That all *men* should honor the Son,
> even as they honor the Father. He that honoreth not the Son

honoreth not the Father which hath sent him. And hath given him authority to execute judgment also, because He is the Son of Man. (John 5:22-23, 27)

Now consider the following passage from the Book of Enoch, which the Jewish scholars would have surely been familiar with, that states the same thing:

And the congregation of the elect and holy shall be sown, and all the elect shall stand before Him on that day. And all the kings and the mighty and the exalted and those who rule the earth shall fall down before Him on their faces, and worship and set their hope upon that Son of Man, and petition Him and supplicate for mercy at His hands. (BoE 62:8-9)

There can be no doubt that Christ claimed Himself to be the Son of Man, written in the Book of Enoch. All the Jews who heard Christ use this title would have known the title's source – the messianic prophecies within the Book of Enoch.

Christ's usage of this singular title was deliberate. There are over eighty such examples in the New Testament alone. Indeed, Christ seems to use this title to place specific importance upon the subject matter He was teaching. A stunning pattern arises by studying Christ's usage of this singular title. This pattern focuses on preparing the saints for the last days' events. Furthermore, beyond accompanying prophecies of the Great and Terrible Day of the Lod, His usage of this title seems to accompany some of the most astounding doctrines in all scripture. I will lay this pattern out within the pages of this book.

It is also important that I highlight the relevance of this term in the book of Moses, particularly regarding the extracts on the life and teachings of Enoch. Joseph Smith received these revelations in 1830. Here is an example of one such reference.

And there came generation upon generation; and Enoch was high and lifted up, even in the bosom of the Father, and of the Son of Man; and behold, the power of Satan was upon all the face of the earth. (Moses 7:24)

Joseph's revelation concerning the life and experiences of Enoch includes eight usages of the title Son of Man throughout eighty verses. I consider this to be an astounding validation of Joseph's prophetic mantle. How would Joseph have otherwise associated this title with Enoch's writings, as Richard Laurence's American edition of his translation of the Book of Enoch would not be available until 1838? As such, Joseph would have had no way of knowing of Enoch's pervasive usage of this messianic title but for the power of God.

The Book of Enoch fell into obscurity when the early church fell into apostasy. When it resurfaced almost two thousand years later, the messianic titles within the Book of Parables became an obvious point of contention among orthodox Jews. Indeed, Jewish orthodoxy adamantly contends that the parables of Enoch could not have preceded the coming of Christ and must have been written by the Christians of the first century. However, these statements are at odds with the chief editor of the Dead Seas Scroll project, Dr. John Strugnell. Indeed, Dr. Strugnell claims to have handled four Aramaic copies of the entire Book of Enoch that were discovered in Qumran cave eleven. Dr. Strungnell stated that one of the scrolls was in excellent condition and had been entirely microfiche. He offered the scrolls owner one million dollars for one of the scrolls, but the owner would not sell them.

The caves at Qumran, where the scrolls were originally discovered, were located in Jordan at the time of their discovery. As such, the Jordanians discovered and sold the scrolls to the highest bidder. Often, the highest bidders were individual investors, not the Dead Sea Scrolls team. However, after the six days war, Israel claimed the land upon which the scroll had been discovered. According to Dr. Srugnell, after the six days of the war, an Israeli archeologist by the name of Yigael Yadin began confiscating, rather than purchasing, scrolls from the Jordanian people who had discovered them. As such, the four complete Aramaic copies of the Book of Enoch went underground and remain in private hands to this day.

This kind of behavior made everyone highly suspicious of the Jews. The orthodox Jews, in particular, were kept at arm's length from the project. Apart from concerns about confiscation, Dr. Strungnell stated that the Jews were kept at arm's length because the team was also highly suspicious of the agenda of the Jewish orthodoxy. Dr. Strugnell made his concerns public in an explosive interview with Avi Katsman, a reporter for Ha'aretz - a Jewish newspaper. In the interview, Dr. Strugnell was challenged that Christian scholarship could not deal impartially with the subject matter of the scrolls and that the task should fall to the Jews instead.

Dr. Strugnell's response was raw and unfiltered. He vigorously refuted the reporter's claim by stating that it had been the radicalized Jewish orthodoxy that persecuted the Qumran sect into hiding the scroll in the deserts of Jordan in the first place. He stated that Jewish orthodoxy was the true enemy of the scrolls and that he highly doubted that the scrolls could survive the Jewish orthodoxy unedited. As it is, none of the many

Aramaic fragments of the Book of Enoch that are in the possession of Israel have been translated into English.

Dr. Strugnell brazenly went on to state that if it had not been for the corruption of the Jewish orthodoxy, the religion of Judaism would be extinct. He said that the same Jewish orthodoxy that persecuted the sect at Qumran was also responsible for causing the Jewish people to reject the God of Israel when He came among them in the flesh.

For obvious reasons, Dr. Strugnell's remarks brought down an antisemitic firestorm that resulted in his dismissal and removal from the Dead Seas Scroll project. Not long after this explosive interview, ownership of the Dead Seas Scrolls shifted from Dr. Strugnell's team to the Israel Antiquities Authority. However, this transition did not take place until after many of the original translations that Dr. Strugnell's team had made were released to the public.

Today, the Book of Enoch remains highly controversial. However, I find that most of the controversy stems from those who either have a vested interest in the Book of Enoch being a Christian fabrication or those who know next to nothing about the book's content. It is my sincere desire that this book will help you form your own well-studied opinion on the parables of Enoch as expounded upon in this book.

Hugh Nibley made a study of the Book of Enoch and wrote the following:

> For his work, Enoch is endowed with power – the power of the priesthood. He had but to speak the word of the Lord and mountains shook and rivers turned from their courses. He is the king who is given power from on high to organize and lead the people of God in their migration and in the building of their city and in the great missionary program that went from it. He is their leader as both priest and king, the founder and director of their sacred society on earth.

> Enoch is the epitome of a great high priest. Enoch is a great advocate, the champion of the human race, pleading with God to spare the wicked and refusing to be comforted until he is shown just how that is to be done. He feels for all and is concerned for all. He is the passionate and compassionate, the magnanimous one who cannot rest knowing the others are miserable. He is the wise and obedient servant, the friend and helper of all, hence the perfect leader and ruler.

I could not agree more with Hugh Nibley's assessment. One of the readers of the first volume of this series sent me a copy of a book that a family member had received from Hugh Nibley. Upon the inside cover, Nibley had written a meaningful but cryptic statement. "It is all about the Book of Enoch." As you continue within this series, I hope that you will be able to arrive at the same conclusion. The Lord told Nephi six hundred years before the mortal ministry of Jesus Christ that He had spoken directly to all the nations of the earth and that they had written His words. This statement of the Lord has prompted me to pour over the ancient documents of the world in search of the Father's message to the ancient kingdoms of the earth.

There can be no doubt that the Book of Enoch is foremost among such writings. If such were not the case, why would the Lord tell the restored Church in modern times that the truthfulness of the Book of Enoch would be testified of in due time? (See D&C 107:57) Furthermore, if the Book of Enoch was nothing more than a spurious work, why would Christ call Himself the Son of Man, a title which originates within the Book of Enoch? Why would the two foremost leaders of the early Church, Peter, and John, both cite the Book of Enoch within their teachings?

I have been asked many times before, if the Book of Enoch is true, why hasn't it been canonized? Such a question is symptomatic of a dangerous paradigm that blinds many within the church today. This is the belief that others will highlight everything we need to know; if they do not, we need not concern ourselves with it.

If this were true, and all the knowledge that we need to obtain could be found exclusively within the biblical canon, then why would the God of Israel give us the following commandment:

> I give unto you a commandment that you shall teach one another the doctrine of the kingdom. Teach ye diligently and my grace shall attend you, that you may be instructed more perfectly in theory, in principle, in doctrine, in the law of the gospel, in all things that pertain unto the kingdom of God, that are expedient for you to understand; of things both in heaven and in the earth, and under the earth; things which have been, things which are, things which must shortly come to pass; things which are at home, things which are abroad; the wars and the perplexities of the nations, and the judgments which are on the land; and a knowledge also of countries and of kingdoms— That ye may be prepared in all things…Therefore, [you] are left without excuse, and [your]

sins are upon [your] own heads. He that seeketh me early
shall find me, and shall not be forsaken. (D&C 88:77-80, 82)

In the Lord's commandment above, He uses strong language so that we might know we are responsible for our spiritual education. We should not need to be commanded in all things. We should educate ourselves about the world around us. We should understand what is happening above the earth, under it, and within its seas. We should understand the history of the Lord's interactions with the ancient world. Those histories are more complex than we have been led to believe. Having been thus commanded by the Lord, our ignorance will be upon our heads if we do not heed His council. From the Lord's council above, we should not seek ways to limit our understanding but to broaden it. I hope that the readers of this series will understand just how important a tool the Book of Enoch can be in this process.

I, for one, have developed a great love for the Book of Enoch and the profound words of council contained within it. I have also found it to be a doctrinal treasure trove and an unbelievable resource for preparing for the pending events of the last few days. I believe that the Book of Enoch is what it claims to be and that the days wherein its truthfulness will be proved are now upon us. However, as in all things, we must decide for ourselves. Choose wisely – what can I say more?

Chapter 2: The Holy Race

Volume one's analysis of the Book of Enoch concluded with the chapter titled The Holy Race. You will recall that Enoch was teaching of the day when the Lord's chosen people would be restored to the Earth in a miraculous event rivaling the Exodus of Egypt. To their detriment, the world has forgotten much of its history. It is woefully prepared for the supernatural nature of the events that are about to unfold upon its surface.

These supernatural events will include the miraculous restoration of the House of Israel. We learn of the scattering and gathering of Israel from the writings of Zenos, as found in the Brass Plates. Zenos was a prophet the Lord called to preach unto the Northern Kingdom of Israel just before they disappeared from our recorded history. According to Zenos, as recorded in the fifth chapter of Jacob in the Book of Mormon, the original House of Israel was regrafted into the far reaches of the Lord's vineyard. Zenos described the scattering of Israel as taking place in three separate grafting events, the first, the second, and the last, see Jacob 5:39. The first grafting corresponds with the first group of Israel to have been scattered, namely the Northern Kingdom of Israel. The last grafting corresponded with Joseph, who was grafted into the vineyard's most chosen location.

In volume one, I proposed a theory about the first of these grafting events about the lost ten tribes of Israel. Zenos taught that the grafting of the lost ten tribes would actually be comprised of two separated bodies, see Jacob 5:20-23. Zenos taught that one of these two groups would be grafted into the worst place in the vineyard, and the second body would then be taken to a second location described as even worse.

I proposed a theory for how the ten tribes were broken into two separate groups after leaving Assyria together in one body. In 2nd Esdras 13:39-48, Ezra describes the departure and journey of this large host. This journey took them a year and a half and covered a pathway that stretched from Turkey to Scandinavia. The further this group traveled north, the less desirable the landscape became. These traveled until they reached the ends of the earth, somewhere near the modern-day North Cape, Norway. It was upon those rocky fridged shores that I theorized that the faith of this group then splintered. One group continued onward with faith in boats built with their own hands further northward into the frozen Arctic Sea, and the other remained in Scandinavia and migrated from their southward into northern Europe.

I postulated that those who braved the fridged Arctic Sea eventually made it to the former landmass that existed at the Earth's North Pole. There, like with the city of Enoch, the Lord lifted this group, together with this mighty landmass, into the heavens, where they disappeared from recorded history. This theory is supported by a careful analysis of Revelation 12:13-17 and the teachings of the Prophet Joseph Smith, who explicitly stated that this occurred, the account of which has been reviewed in volume one of this work. The records of the Lost Tribes of Israel will be needed to fill in the missing gaps in this account. Nephi prophesied of the day when this would occur (See 2 Nephi 29:13-14).

This explains the first two parties that comprised Zenos's first grafting event. Therefore, the second and third grafting events had to pertain to the Jews and the House of Joseph. Regarding Joseph, we know that before the Lord grafted Joseph in America, He removed the remnants of the wicked Jaredite nation that had begun to cumber the choicest land of His vineyard. The Jaradites, who had become the most powerful nation in the world, destroyed themselves in a terrible, bloody civil war. After their destruction, the Lord performed two grafts that we know of in North America: the Mulekites in the north and the children of Lehi in the south. The Mulekites represented a mixed bag of Israelites, including Mulek, a descendent of the royal lineage of the Kingdom of Judah. These, however, did not bring any record with them and, in short order, began to forget themselves and the God who delivered them.

The children of Lehi brought with them the Brass Plates, which was an account of the history of the tribes of Joseph. Joseph led the Northern Kingdom of Israel from its capital city of Samaria. Just as Israel had been divided because of wickedness in their original lands of promise, shortly after the sons of Lehi arrived in America, they also split into two separate people, the Lamanites and the Nephites, with the Lamanites ultimately destroying the Nephites. Zenos spoke symbolically of these things in Jacob 5:43-45.

Therefore, by elimination, the second grafting spoken of in Zenos' writings must pertain to the Jewish nation. As such, we understand that the order of Zenos' graftings, the first, second, and last, correspond with the order in which these nations were destroyed. Therefore, the first graft, which is that of the Lost Ten Tribes of Israel, corresponds with the destruction of the Kingdom of Israel in 720 BC. The second grafting, the Kingdom of Judah, began with the Babylonian diaspora of the Jews and ended with the complete Roman destruction of the Jewish nation. The third, or last grafting, pertains to Joseph in America, who was the last to be destroyed, and destruction occurred on the hills of Cumorah in 420 AD. However, as I discussed in volume one, I believe that the Lord preserved the posterity of Nephi by sending a large host of Nephites into the lands of the North, led by Hagoth. This group became absorbed into the Germanic tribes of Europe, which I postulated were comprised of the hosts of Israel that stayed behind, not braving the fridged Arctic Sea, but who nonetheless had become a seafaring people themselves.

Thus, when the scriptures speak of the first being the last and the last being the first, I believe they are prophesying that the House of Israel will be restored in the reverse order in which their destruction occurred. Therefore, as Joseph was the last to fall, he would be the first to be restored in the last days. As the Lost Tribes of Israel were the first to fall, they will be the last to be restored. It was the restoration of the lost ten tribes of Israel that Enoch referred to in the closing passages of our analysis of volume one. Those passages read as follows:

> **39.1**. [And it †shall come to pass in those days that elect and holy children †will descend from the high heaven, and their seed †will become one with the children of men.

> **39.2**. And in those days Enoch received books of zeal and wrath, and books of disquiet and expulsion.] And mercy shall not be accorded to them, saith the Lord of Spirits.

We have reviewed at length how the restoration of this mighty host will result in the purification of the Americas and the liberation of the captive saints that will be found there. These will be glorious days, and they lay at our door. As we have now reviewed the closing subject matter of volume one, we are now in a position to continue with our analysis of Enoch's incredible commentary:

> **39.3**. And in those days a whirlwind carried me off from the earth, and set me down at **the end of the heavens**.

> **39.4**. And there I saw another vision, the dwelling-places of the holy, and the resting-places of the righteous.

The verses above immediately remind me of Ezekiel's vision of the return of the Lost Ten Tribes given in the first and tenth chapters of his writings. In those chapters, Ezekiel described burning whirlwinds of fire enfolding upon themselves. Wheels then emerged from these burning whirlwinds, moving upon their four sides like Frisbees. The outer rims of these wheel-shaped crafts were filled with eyes. Ezekiel stated that these wheels moved as fast as lightning and carried with them strange symbolic beings with four faces: a lion, an eagle, an ox, and a man. These faces correspond with the four ensigns of the four armies of Israel that camped around the tabernacle of the congregation while Israel sojourned in the wilderness for forty years.

Enoch now describes himself as being caught up in a heavenly whirlwind that lifts him off the face of the earth and takes him to the end of heaven. This is clearly a biblical description of interstellar travel. I propose that Enoch is retracing the travel path of the Holy Race, meaning his whirlwind has taken him to where the lost ten tribes now reside. You will recall that Moses told Israel that a portion of their numbers would be taken to and restored from the ends of heaven. He was not the only one to do so. Consider the following examples:

> If *any* of thine be driven out unto the **outmost *parts of heaven***, from thence will the LORD thy God gather thee, and from thence will he fetch thee: and the LORD thy God will bring thee into the land which thy fathers possessed, and thou shalt possess it; and he will do thee good, and multiply thee above thy fathers. (Duet 30:4-5)

And

> But *if* ye turn unto me, and keep my commandments, and do them; though there were of you cast out unto the **uttermost part of the heaven**, *yet* will I gather them from thence, and will bring them unto the place that I have chosen to set my name there. (Neh 1:9)

Given the first two verses, **39.1** and **39.2,** spoke of the Holy Race coming to the Earth to dwell among humankind in the last days, I believe that it is from this perspective that we are meant to understand the location to which Enoch's whirlwind took him. In another way, I believe Enoch was taken in vision to the off-world location where the main body of the Lost Ten Tribes has been residing for the last 2,700 years. If this is true, we will now understand what the society of the Lost Ten Tribes of Israel is like in the subsequent passages of Enoch's writings. Consider the following:

> **39.5**. Here mine eyes saw their dwellings with His righteous angels, and their resting-places with the holy. And they petitioned and interceded and prayed for the children of men, and righteousness flowed before them as water, and mercy like dew upon the earth: thus it is amongst them for ever and ever.

According to the passage above, the whirlwind took Enoch to "their dwellings." From the context of verses **39.1**, **39.2**, and **39.4,** we must understand that these dwelling places belonged to the Holy Race spoken of in the opening verses of the chapter. The Holy

Race will arrive on the Earth via the whirlwinds described by Ezekiel, and Enoch traveled from the Earth to their current dwelling place in a similar whirlwind. Curiously, Enoch witnessed righteous angels amongst the Holy Race. In addition, Enoch heard intercessory prayers being made for the children of men. This passage immediately reminds me of 3 Nephi 17, one of the most spectacular chapters in the Book of Mormon. This chapter begins with Jesus Christ asking the Nephites to pray unto the Father that they might understand His words regarding the restoration of the House of Israel in the last days.

In 3 Nephi 17:4, Jesus Christ specifically states that He will momentarily return to the presence of the Father and then go out again to travel and administer to the Lost Ten Tribes. When the Nephites learned that Christ was about to leave them, they began to weep. Seeing their tears and the tenderness of their hearts, Christ knelt amongst them and prayed to the Father on their behalf. Upon hearing Christ's prayer to the Father on their behalf, the Nephites become overwhelmed. The Nephites described Christ's intercessory prayer for them in the following manner:

> The eye hath never seen, neither hath the ear heard, before, so great and marvelous things as we saw and heard Jesus speak unto the Father; and no tongue can speak, neither can there be written by any man, neither can the hearts of men conceive so great and marvelous things as we both saw and heard Jesus speak; and no one can conceive of the joy which filled our souls at the time **we heard Him pray for us** unto the Father. (3 Nephi 17:16-17)

Here, then, we have three examples of Christ uttering marvelous intercessory prayers on behalf of the three separate groups of the House of Israel to whom the Father sent Him to minister. We read of His intercessory prayer over His Jewish disciples in John 17. We learn of His intercessory prayer over His disciples from the tribe of Joseph in 3 Nephi 17. Finally, we learn from Enoch that Christ visited and interceded with the Father on behalf of the Holy Race and the lost tribes of Israel as well. Thus, we see that there is a pattern to the workings of the Lord.

Imagine how incredible it would be to hear the Son of God praying to His Father on your behalf. The Nephites could not describe the things Christ prayed for, nor did we learn what things were said over the Holy Race. However, we have part of the intercessory prayer that Christ prayed over His Jewish disciples. Given the pattern in Christ's actions, I suggest His words to the Jews are relevant to all of the House of Israel. Consider, therefore, these few extracts from that great intercessory prayer for which we do have an account.

I have manifested Thy name unto the men which thou gavest Me out of the world: Thine they were, and thou gavest them Me; and they have kept Thy word. Now they have known that all things whatsoever Thou hast given Me are of Thee. For I have given unto them the words which Thou gavest Me; and they have received *them,* and have known surely that I came out from Thee, and they have believed that Thou didst send Me.

I pray for them: I pray not for the world, but for them which Thou hast given Me; for they are Thine. And all Mine are Thine, and Thine are Mine; and I am glorified in them. And now I am no more in the world, but these are in the world, and I come to thee. Holy Father, keep through Thine own name those whom thou hast given Me, that they may be one, as We *are.*

While I was with them in the world, I kept them in Thy name: those that thou gavest Me I have kept, and none of them is lost, but the son of perdition; that the scripture might be fulfilled. And now come I to thee; and these things I speak in the world, that they might have My joy fulfilled in themselves.

I have given them thy word; and the world hath hated them, because they are not of the world, even as I am not of the world. I pray not that thou shouldest take them out of the world, but that thou shouldest keep them from the evil. They are not of the world, even as I am not of the world. Sanctify them through Thy truth: Thy word is truth.

As Thou hast sent me into the world, even so have I also sent them into the world. And for their sakes I sanctify Myself, that they also might be sanctified through the truth. Neither pray I for these alone, but for them also which shall believe on Me through their word; that they all may be one; as thou, Father, *art* in Me, and I in Thee, that they also may be one in Us: that the world may believe that Thou hast sent Me.

And the glory which thou gavest Me I have given them; that they may be one, even as We are one: I in them, and Thou in

Me, that they may be made <u>perfect</u> in one; and that the world may know that Thou hast sent Me, and hast <u>loved</u> them, as Thou hast loved Me.

Father, I will that they also, whom Thou hast given Me, be with Me where I am; that they may behold My glory, which Thou hast given Me: for Thou lovedst Me before the foundation of the world. O righteous Father, the world hath not <u>known</u> Thee: but I have known Thee, and these have known that Thou hast sent Me. And I have <u>declared</u> unto them Thy <u>name</u>, and will declare *it:* that the <u>love</u> where with Thou hast <u>loved</u> Me may be in them, and I in them. (John 17:6-26)

Christ's intercessory prayer for His Jewish disciples was about their salvation and exaltation. Christ prayed for them because they believed in Him and in the Father's message, which the Father had explicitly commanded Christ to share with them. Therefore, it is important to note that the Father also gave Christ a very explicit message to share with the Nephites and, in turn, with the Gentiles of the last days. This message is the foundation upon which all of my books have been built. It is the foundation of His message to the Nephites. Consider the following extracts from that message:

Ye are My <u>disciples</u>; and ye are a <u>light</u> unto this people, who are a remnant of the house of <u>Joseph</u>. And behold, this is the <u>land</u> of your inheritance; and the Father hath given it unto you. And not at any time hath the Father given Me commandment that I should <u>tell</u> it unto your brethren at Jerusalem. Neither at any time hath the Father given me commandment that I should tell unto them concerning the <u>other tribes</u> of the house of Israel, whom the Father hath led away out of the land.

This much did the Father <u>command</u> Me, that I should tell unto them: that other sheep I have which are not of this fold; them also I must bring, and they shall hear my voice; and there shall be one fold, and one <u>shepherd</u>. And now, because of <u>stiffneckedness</u> and <u>unbelief</u> they <u>understood</u> not my word; therefore I was commanded to say no more of the <u>Father</u> concerning this thing unto them. (3 Nephi 15:12-18)

And

I <u>perceive</u> that ye are weak, that ye cannot <u>understand</u> all My words which I am commanded of the Father to speak unto you at this time. Therefore, go ye unto your homes, and <u>ponder</u> upon the things which I have said, and ask of the Father, in My name, that ye may understand, and <u>prepare</u> your minds for the <u>morrow</u>, and I come unto you again. But now I <u>go</u> unto the Father, and also to <u>show</u> Myself unto the lost tribes of Israel, for they are not <u>lost</u> unto the Father, for He knoweth whither He hath taken them. (3 Nephi 17:2-3)

And

> Behold now I finish the commandment which the Father hath commanded Me concerning this people, who are a remnant of the house of Israel. Ye remember that I spake unto you, and said that when the <u>words</u> of <u>Isaiah</u> should be fulfilled—behold they are written, ye have them before you, therefore search them. (3 Nephi 20:10-11)

All of these passages clearly indicate that the message accompanying these passages was given to Jesus Christ by way of commandment directly from the Father to share with us. Parts of the Father's messages are the Isaiah chapters that are included in the Book of Mormon. I am always shocked and saddened at how little attention the Father's message receives. It is hardly ever spoken of, yet it must be among the most profound Divine messages ever shared in recorded history. Just as the Jews were unbelieving about these things, so are the majority of our generations today. They will not believe the Father's message, nor will they take time to study it, yet this message might serve as a Godsend unto them during the coming days of trial that will soon overtake the world.

Consider the following extract from the first Isaiah chapter that the Lord caused to be transcribed within the Book of Mormon:

> Hearken unto me, O Jacob [*Judah and Joseph*], and Israel [*the lost ten tribes*] My called, for I am He; I am the <u>first</u>, and I am also the last. Mine hand hath also <u>laid</u> the foundation of the earth, and My right hand hath spanned the heavens. I <u>call</u> unto them [*the inhabited worlds*] and they stand up together. All ye, assemble yourselves, and hear; who among them hath declared these things unto them? The Lord hath loved him; yea, and He will <u>fulfil</u> His word which

He hath declared by them; and He will do His pleasure on Babylon, and His arm shall come upon the Chaldeans.

Also, saith the Lord; I the Lord, yea, I have spoken; yea, I have called him to declare, I have brought him, and he shall make his way prosperous. Come ye near unto Me; I have not spoken in secret; from the beginning, from the time that it was declared have I spoken; and the Lord God, and His Spirit, hath sent Me. And thus saith the Lord, thy Redeemer, the Holy One of Israel; I have sent Him, the Lord thy God who teacheth thee to profit, who leadeth thee by the way thou shouldst go, hath done it.

O that thou hadst hearkened to My commandments—then had thy peace been as a river, and thy righteousness as the waves of the sea. (1 Nephi 20:12-18)

The passages above clearly have an embedded message from the Father to the righteous. The words of Isaiah contain a particular message from the Father to the Gentiles of the last days. If we hearken unto that message and believe it, it will bring us peace in the troubled days to come. Yet, most will not take the time and effort required to hear the Lord or study His words. Most will receive the word of the Lord in the same manner in which Laman and Lemuel received it. Laman and Lemuel received what others told them and a little more. Unto such, there is little hope of learning the deeper, healing doctrines of the Father. Yet, those who will dedicate the time and effort to understand the Father's message and then proclaim it to others, how beautiful their feet upon the mountains of Zion shall be! The Father hath loved such because of their diligence in receiving His word, even if they are despised by the world as a result. Unto all those who have paid the price to understand the Father's words and then tried to impart those words to others, you know what I am talking about.

For this reason, Christ prayed diligently in the presence of the Nephites for blessings that the Nephites themselves had never even thought to ask for. They were amazed at His generosity and thoughtfulness, particularly given the unfathomable gap between Christ and themselves. Hearing Christ pray on their behalf was a transformative experience for all those who witnessed it. And who were they that witnessed it? These were those who were cast out of their houses because they believed in the coming Son of God. These were those who were rounded up and threatened with death unless they denied Christ. These were those who survived the destructions that came upon the Americas because of the wickedness and unbelief of its inhabitants. In short, these were those who clung to the hope of Christ when the society in which they lived had turned against Him. Surely, you can see that there is a type and a shadow in this regarding the coming days.

These had endured great hardship and loss, but through that great loss and hardship, they had lived to see the bright and glorious day when the joy of their hope was manifest in the flesh before them. These did not understand all of the Father's words. Christ said as much admonished them to pray unto the Father for more strength and understanding in this regard, yet, despite their lack of understanding, they remained faithful to the Lord Jesus Christ despite all the lies, persecutions, and threats of their adversaries.

Yet, this experience did not end with the Savior's prayer; it was just beginning. After they heard the Lord pray marvelous things unto His Father on their behalf, the following experience occurred:

> And [Jesus] spake unto the multitude, and said unto them: Behold your little ones. And as they looked to behold they cast their eyes towards heaven, and they saw the heavens open, and they saw angels descending out of heaven as it were in the midst of fire; and they came down and encircled those little ones about, and they were encircled about with fire; and the angels did minister unto them. And the multitude did see and hear and bear record; and they know that their record is true for they all of them did see and hear, every man for himself; and they were in number about two thousand and five hundred souls; and they did consist of men, women, and children. (3 Nephi 17:23-25)

What a remarkable experience the Nephites had with Jesus Christ. Yet, according to the writings of Enoch, it does not seem that the experience of the Nephites was unique. Indeed, it would seem that something very similar happened amongst the lost tribes of Israel, possibly on the very same night when the Lord announced that He would return first to the Father, and then He would minister to them. It would seem that the only group of Israel that this kind of miraculous experience did not happen to was the Jews, and that was because of their unbelief.

Now, returning specifically to Enoch's account, reconsider the following:

> **39.3**. And in those days a whirlwind carried me off from the earth, and set me down at **the end of the heavens**.

Enoch traveled via whirlwind to the end of heaven, to the place where the Father had taken the lost tribes of Israel. The fact that Enoch saw these things in vision thousands of years before they occurred shows that all things stand before the Lord simultaneously, past, present, and future. It was as easy for God the Father to show Enoch a vision of His Son ministering to the lost tribes of Israel as it was for Him to show Nephi the birth and ministry of Jesus Christ among the Jews six hundred years before those things would occur. Yet, God was not showing these things to Enoch for Enoch's edification, nor did He show Nephi Christ's ministry for Nephi's edification. God showed these incredible visions to both of these incredible men so that the Gentile of the last days could read and study them and be better prepared for the coming days of trial as a result. Enoch expressly told us this himself in the open verses of his writings.

This is an incredible thought. We are the intended audience for these incredible revelations. The Lord revealed these things thousands of years ago, just as He said He would, "Behold, I have declared the former things from the beginning; and they went forth out of My mouth, and I showed them." (1 Nephi 20:3). Why? The Lord did this so that we would take hope in the moments of our greatest extremity that our God knows the end from the beginning. Because He knows the end from the beginning, He prepared the way for our deliverance from before the foundations of the Earth. If we will but have faith, the experiences of our extremity will be transformed into experiences of miraculous divine ministration and intercession. Just as it was for the Nephites in the extremity of their North American destruction, so it will be for us in the extremity of our days of trial. These visions were reserved for our generation because, like the Nephites, we are uniquely qualified to comprehend these things. Or at least we should be.

The parallels between Christ's visit to the Nephites and Enoch's vision of Christ's administration to the lost tribes of Israel will continue.

> **39.6**. And in that place mine eyes saw the Elect One of righteousness and of faith, and righteousness shall prevail in His days, and the righteous and elect shall be without number before Him for ever and ever.

In the above passage, Enoch witnesses that Jesus Christ, the Elect or Chosen One, was among the Holy Race ministering to them, just as He had done among the Nephites. According to our scriptures, Christ's personal ministry was limited to the House of Israel, meaning Christ did not go in the flesh to minister amongst the Gentiles. We must understand this in the context of the history of the post-Abrahamic world. God covenanted to Abraham that the world would receive the gospel through the ministration of his posterity. Thus, Christ did not minister to the Gentiles directly but left that ministration to the House of Israel to carry out. This does not mean that Christ has not personally ministered unto the inhabitants of other worlds who are not of the lineage of Abraham. He most certainly has, and He explained as much in D&C 88:46-62. We just do not have accounts of His ministrations upon those worlds. That does not mean that such accounts do not exist. Indeed, before this volume is through, we will learn some inquisitive things about Christ's ministrations to the inhabitants of other worlds. Consider the following passage:

> And the first man of all men have I called Adam, which is many. But only an account of this earth, and the inhabitants thereof, give I unto you. For behold, there are many worlds… innumerable are they unto man; but all things are numbered unto Me, for they are Mine and **I know them**. (Moses 1:34-35)

The English language, being of more modern origins, is less expressive than some of the world's more ancient tongues. In English, the phrase "I know" suggests merely knowledge of a fact. Yet in Latin-based languages, such as Spanish, the more insightful phrase "las conozco" is used instead. Conozco comes from the Spanish verb conocer, which means being acquainted with firsthand experiences. The Father and His Son have had firsthand experiences with all of their creations, and we would do well to remember this.

Yet, despite the Father's firsthand experiences with worlds without numbers, Christ clearly taught that the gospel would go forth to some by the administration of others rather than by His own lips, see 3 Nephi 15:22-23. Indeed, this is part of the Abrahamic covenant, not just the Abrahamic covenant, but the same covenant that Abraham saw had been made with his forefathers, including Enoch – see Abraham 1:2-3. This covenant of the patriarchs declares that all the nations of the earth will be blessed through the administrations of the children of this covenant.

To the righteous children of the covenant, the following promise is given:

> Let thy bowels also be full of charity towards all men, and to the household of faith, and let virtue garnish thy thoughts unceasingly; then shall thy confidence wax strong in the presence of God; and the doctrine of the priesthood shall distil upon thy soul as the dews from heaven. The Holy Ghost shall be thy constant companion, and thy scepter an unchanging scepter of righteousness and truth; and thy dominion shall be an everlasting dominion, and without

compulsory means it shall flow unto thee forever and ever.
(D&C 121:45-46)

This is an incredible promise. Let us now contrast the language of the above promise with the language of a recent passage in the Book of Enoch we have reviewed about Enoch's vision of the society that exists amongst the lost tribes of Israel at the time of his visitation.

> **39.5**. Here mine eyes saw their dwellings with His righteous angels, and their resting-places with the holy. And they petitioned and interceded and prayed for the children of men, and righteousness flowed before them as water, and mercy like dew upon the earth: thus it is amongst them for ever and ever.

We have failed to create a modern society such as this on this earth. This is due in no small part to the lack of modeling. We have only read of such societies; we have never experienced them. It is challenging to replicate heavenly concepts when those concepts are nebulously understood because, at present, we see through the glass darkly. The Church attempted to establish such communities in the past, but none of them succeeded due to our present natures. Still, as troubled as our history may be, such a Zion-like society is something that the pure in heart still long to establish. I believe those days will come sooner than most are prepared to accept. I believe that as troubled as the North American continent is now, Zion will be brought forth upon its hallowed shores within this decade. Zion will burst forth suddenly, in an instant. Its miraculous appearance will result from the restoration of our long-lost brethren and the purging of this continent. This purging will occur at the hands of a society that has lived after the manner of happiness for at least two thousand years, ever since Christ ministered to them in the flesh.

Yet, before Zion can be established, the land of the Lord's most choice vineyard must be unencumbered by the wild overgrowth that has choked and corrupted its lands. This wild overgrowth will be pruned and burned in a single day. Then, to the astonishment of all, the New Jerusalem will descend from the heavens as a bride adorned for her husband. This brilliantly beautiful city center will break forth as the dawning light illuminates the darkest night the world will have ever known.

The great coming darkness will have had a tremendous refining effect that will have been designed to be purposeful in its intensity. As a result, the saints that will emerge on that day will come forth from the refiner's fiery, pure, and radiant blaze as the golden wedge of Ophir.

Well spoke the prophet Isaiah of these things when he wrote the following:

> Who hath heard such a thing? Who hath seen such things? Shall the earth be made to bring forth in one day? *S*hall a nation be born at once? For as soon as Zion travailed, she brought forth her children.
>
> Lift up thine eyes round about, and behold: all these gather themselves together, *and* come to thee. *As* I live, saith the LORD, thou shalt surely clothe thee with them all, as with an ornament, and bind them *on thee,* as a bride *doeth.* For thy waste and thy desolate places, and the land of thy destruction, shall even now be too narrow by reason of the inhabitants, and they that swallowed thee up shall be far away.
>
> The children which thou shalt have, after thou hast lost the other, shall say again in thine ears, the place *is* too strait for me: give place to me that I may dwell. Then shalt thou say in thine heart, Who hath begotten me these, seeing I have lost my children, and am desolate, a captive, and removing to and fro? Who hath brought up these? Behold, I was left alone; these, where *had* they *been?* (Isaiah 66:8; 49:18-21)

According to Isaiah, the greatest of our days of trial will act as the birthing pains of Zion. As such, we will break forth from the womb of affliction as the butterfly from its chrysalis. America will be renewed overnight. From one day to the next, our lands of promise will be restored! The unrighteous will be destroyed at the hands of the Remnant of Jacob, and we will be engulfed within the righteous throngs of the Holy Race who will ride to our deliverance upon whirlwinds of fire. These will have returned to us from the ends of heaven.

On that day, our brothers will model for us righteous living on a societal scale we have never considered possible. This instantaneous immersion will transform our lands and our sufferings overnight. America will become a safe haven, a place of refuge in an otherwise turbulent storm of chaos and death that will be sweeping across the rest of the globe. Every man who would not take up his sword had to make it to Zion that day. The righteous will be gathered into Zion from the four corners of the globe by miraculous means. I believe we will see all these things occur within the present decade - buckle up!

Chapter 3: Those Who Sleep Not

In the prior chapter, we followed Enoch on an incredible journey. The journey began with him being lifted off the planet in a great whirlwind. He was then taken to the ends of heaven, to the dwelling place of the Holy Race – the Lost Ten Tribes of Israel. There, he witnessed the administration of Jesus Christ among them, in an experience that mirrored Christ's ministrations to the Nephites. Nephi promised that the day would come when we would have a full account of these things, for Joseph will have the record of Judah and the lost tribes, and the lost tribes will have the records of Judah and Joseph, and we will all rejoice in God's miraculous workings amongst us.

Before I begin analyzing the present chapter, I must confess myself as a blubbering fool before the Throne of the Almighty God of Heaven and Earth. As such, please do not believe anything I have written simply because I have written it. Throughout the next several chapters, you will read things of a most incredible nature. As such, I pray that the Spirit will guide you through the stepping stones of my ideas to the reality of things as they really are and not as I have postulated them to be.

Seek more to understand why I have written what I have written rather than accepting these words as truth. There is a reason that I am writing them, but they are first and foremost theories. We live in days when the truthfulness of all things is about to be restored upon the earth. May the Lord hasten that day. However, until that day arrives, I look through a darkened glass at things of an unfathomable scope and depth without the words to adequately describe what I see. My vision is surely distorted in ways I do not yet comprehend. Yet, with sure knowledge, I know that the day will soon come when the most mysterious of all things will be as clear as the noonday sun. May God hasten that day. However, until that day comes, know that the ideas and theories you are about to read come from the heart and mind of a deeply flawed disciple of Jesus Christ, who has no hope of standing before the Great God of Heaven but for the borrowed grace and light of His Only Begotten Son. May the God of Heaven forgive me for my shortcomings and any errors in the following writings, and may He help you see more clearly than I have seen. With this understanding, we descend into the rabbit hole of Enoch's writings.

This chapter begins with Enoch beholding the Household of God. This is not the first time Enoch has been in the presence of God, but the descriptions accompanying this experience shed light upon one of the greatest mysteries of all time–the true order of heaven. Consider the following:

39.7. And I saw His [Christ's] dwelling-place under the wings of the Lord of Spirits. And all the righteous and elect before Him shall be †strong† as fiery lights, and their mouth shall be full of blessing, and their lips extol the name of the Lord of Spirits, And righteousness before Him shall never fail, [And uprightness shall never fail before Him.]

39.8. There I wished to dwell, and my spirit longed for that dwelling-place: and there heretofore hath been my portion, for so has it been established concerning me before the Lord of Spirits.

Here, we learn some essential things. Enoch beheld the Celestial world - the dwelling place of God, and all those that are heirs to His kingdom, which he described as being strong fiery lights. In addition, Enoch added that this had been his former dwelling place. By this, we can understand that Enoch was raised there before the worlds were. By his pen, his soul longed to return to dwell with his heavenly family, but it was not his time to do so. He still had work to perform.

This passage also indicates that Enoch was still operating within the confines of the veil. We know this not because Enoch remembered being there but because God had told him he used to live there. This is an astounding confirmation of the concept of premortal life and an apparent confirmation of a similar experience held by another prophet of God. Consider the following:

> Then the word of the Lord came unto me, saying, before I formed thee in the belly I knew thee; and before thou camest forth out of the womb I sanctified thee, and I ordained thee a prophet unto the nations. (Jer 1:4-5)

This demonstrates once again that the knowledge held by the ancient world has been restored rather than originating with us. This aspect of Enoch's vision has just begun, so there is much more to come.

From Enoch's opening description above, we can say that it is clear that he longed to return to his premortal home. He also clearly knew that his visit with God would be of temporary duration. He longed for the day when he could enter into the presence of the Lord, to go no more out. This highlights the fact that Enoch valued the Father's presence above all else. To be in the actual presence of the Father is to be energized, magnified, and glorified by an incredible outpouring of love, energy, and joy for which we have no present equal. Nothing was more important to Enoch than being with his family forever in this environment. God's very presence is ennobling, enabling, empowering, and invigorating. One does not leave the presence of God unchanged, nor without longing to return as soon as possible. God makes everything better. There are no tears, troubles, sorrows, or fears in His presence.

Satan has produced a terrible counterfeit for those who live upon his prison planet. Millions of people with an addiction around the world spend their short lives chasing the feeling that comes from illicit drugs. Illicit drugs produce a chemical counterfeit sense of belonging, love, confidence, worthiness, and well-being. Satan's counterfeit is a pathetic imitation. Yet, for those who have felt such feelings, as counterfeit and fake as they are, the lasting pursuit of such a sense of well-being becomes overpowering.

The addicted slaves of Satan's chemical counterfeits are not edified by the practice; rather, they are consumed by it. In pursuing such things, all else is secondary: food, drink, shelter, hygiene, etc. They would rather let their teeth rot out of their skulls than never feel those things again, just one more time. They would rather jab their veins with dirty needles, spreading disease and cantankerous festering sores all over their bodies. Such live in filth and squaller, sleeping on the streets and under overpasses to chase Satan's fleeting counterfeit. So it is; Satan's power tears, decays, and destroys those who interact with it.

Conversely, God's pure love and enabling glory and grace lift and ennoble, making more of the experience than they had ever imagined possible. Nor is God's love fleeting, but it results in a fullness of everlasting and transformative joy. I believe that this is why all those who have experienced such things, like Enoch, describe them similarly. I believe that this is what the great historian and teacher Mormon was trying to say when he inserted the following scribal note into the narrative of the Book of Helaman:

> Thus we may see that the Lord is merciful unto all who will, in the sincerity of their hearts, call upon His holy name. Yea, thus we see that the gate of heaven is open unto all, even to those who will believe on the name of Jesus Christ, who is the Son of God. Yea, we see that whosoever will may lay hold upon the word of God, which is quick and powerful, which shall divide asunder all the cunning and the snares and the wiles of the devil, and lead the man of Christ in a strait and narrow course across that everlasting gulf of misery which is prepared to engulf the wicked— And land their souls, yea, their immortal souls, at the right hand of God in the kingdom of heaven, to sit down with Abraham, and Isaac, and with Jacob, and with all our holy fathers, to go no more out. (Helaman 3:27-30)

Mortals can't enter the full glorified presence of God and remain in the flesh. The glory of God exalts and lifts them to a higher state of being. Therefore, the glory that radiates from the Father's physical presence has a profoundly transformative effect on the physical bodies of those around Him. The glory of God goes forth from His presence to fill the immensity of space. We call this glory the Light of Christ, and we understand from the scriptures that it is this power whereby God does all that He does. Therefore, to live in the Father's presence and constantly absorb His unfiltered fullness is to obtain the highest joy the multiverse has to offer.

We do not, at present, comprehend what God's glory and light actually are comprised of. However, the fact that they are actually a substance and source of power is beyond doubt. Access to this incredible power was at the heart of the war in heaven. In that war, Lucifer and his angels were terrified at the prospect of being cut off from this source through the introduction of the veil and free agency. As such, they were willing to forgo their agency to guarantee that they could both obtain physical bodies and retain the power they had obtained in the premortal realms.

The ultimate consequence of Satan's actions was that he and his disciples would eventually be cast out into Outer Darkness. Outer Darkness is the only place in the multiverse where the glory of God is entirely absent. You would think this would be a welcome consequence to Lucifer's demonic hosts, but nothing could be further than the truth. The total absence of the glory of God is too terrible for even demons to contemplate. As such, when legions of demons were cast out by the Son of Man, they cried out in terror, "Art thou come hither to torment us before the time!"

Therefore, it is worth considering that the greatest punishment for both angels and demons that the multiverse has to offer is to be cut off from the glory and influence of God. In contrast, unbridled access to that same glory is its greatest reward. Outside of Outer Darkness, all other kingdoms of glory receive some portion of God's glory and light.

These are important things to consider as Enoch's vision continues:

> **39.9**. In those days I praised and extolled the name of the Lord of Spirits with blessings and praises, because He hath destined me for blessing and glory according to the good pleasure of the Lord of Spirits.

Enoch stated that in "those days," he rejoiced in the name of the Lord of Spirits. I believe that Enoch is referring to the days of his premortal childhood. Each of us experienced this for ourselves. God said as much to Job when He asked him the following probing question:

Gird up now thy loins like a man; for I will demand of thee, and answer thou Me. Where wast thou when I laid the foundations of the earth? declare, if thou hast understanding. When the morning stars sang together, and all the sons of God shouted for joy? (Job 38:3-4; 7)

This last phrase is curious, "the sons of God shouted for joy." Like the Book of Enoch, The Book of Job is one of the few ancient Biblical texts in ancient Aramaic, a language predating written Hebrew. It is therefore curious that the "Aramaic Bible in Plain English" translation of this verse does not use the phrase sons of God; instead, it uses the phrase "sons of the Angels shouted for joy." This is a very curious difference.

If taken at face value, the Book of Job is prediluvian. Job had the life span of the prediluvian fathers. As such, Job and Enoch both came from the same era in the earth's history. Therefore, it would be wise to consider these two references to the premortal realms as significant and representative of the understanding of the ancient world. This will become more meaningful after we read the next passage of Enoch's writings.

39.10. For a long time my eyes regarded that place, and I blessed Him and praised Him, saying: 'Blessed is He, and may He be blessed from the beginning and for evermore.

39.11. And before Him there is no ceasing. He knows before the world was created what is forever and what will be from generation unto generation.

39.12. Those who sleep not bless Thee: they stand before Thy glory and bless, praise, and extol, saying: "Holy, holy, holy, is the Lord of Spirits: He filleth the earth with spirits."'

39.13. And here my eyes saw all those who sleep not: they stand before Him and bless and say: 'Blessed be Thou, and blessed be the name of the Lord for ever and ever.'

39.14. And my face was changed; for I could no longer behold.

40.1. And after that I saw thousands of thousands and ten thousand times ten thousand, I saw a multitude beyond number and reckoning, who stood before the Lord of Spirits.

In the passages above, we learn of an innumerable host of beings Enoch describes as those who sleep not. This curious description will take on more meaning as the chapter unfolds. As Enoch was studying this host, a change came upon him, and he stated that he could no longer see. By this, we are to understand that the Lord withheld the true meaning behind the innumerable multitude that stood before the throne of God. Who were these people, and what does it mean they slept not? These are important questions that we should be considering.

Let us first begin by focusing on the numbers of this incredible host. Enoch describes this host as being beyond reckoning. This is astounding, given that Enoch once said that if you could number the particles of this earth and then millions of other earths like it, it would not be the beginning of the number of the Lord's creations. Therefore, Enoch was no stranger to large numbers. If this host was beyond reckoning for Enoch, it is incomprehensible. He specifically used the phrase thousands of thousands (000 and 000 or 000,000) and ten thousand times ten thousand (100,000,000+000,000 or 100,000,000,000,000). In other words, it's hundreds of trillions. Enoch was not the only one to see such a massive heavenly host before the throne of God. John the Revelator saw a similar host. Consider the following:

> And I beheld, and I heard the voice of many angels round about the throne and the beasts and the elders: and the **number of them was ten thousand times ten thousand, and thousands of thousands (100,000,000,000,000).**
>
> After this I beheld, and, lo, a great multitude, which no man could number, of all nations, and kindreds, and people, and tongues, stood before the throne, and before the Lamb, clothed with white robes, and palms in their hands;
>
> And cried with a loud voice, saying, Salvation to our God which sitteth upon the throne, and unto the Lamb. And all the angels stood round about the throne, and about the elders and the four beasts, and fell before the throne on their faces, and worshipped God, Saying, Amen: Blessing, and glory, and wisdom, and thanksgiving, and honour, and power, and might, be unto our God for ever and ever. Amen.
>
> And one of the elders answered, saying unto me, What are these which are arrayed in white robes? and whence came they? And I said unto him, Sir, thou knowest. And he said to me, these are they which came out of great tribulation, and

have washed their robes, and made them white in the blood
of the Lamb. (Rev 5:11; 7:9-14)

Both John and Enoch witness hundreds of trillions of glorified beings around the throne of God. John described them as being a host in white robes without a number. This host was of particular focus. They were identified as having overcome great tribulation and having washed themselves and their robes in the blood of the Lamb. What do we understand from this symbolism? Earlier in John's revelation, we learned about the nature and destiny of those who wore white robes and who overcame this world through the blood of the Lamb. Consider the following:

He that overcometh, the same shall be clothed in white
raiment; and I will not blot out his name out of the book of
life, but I will confess his name before my Father, and before
His angels… To him that overcometh will I grant to sit with
me in my throne, even as I also overcame, and am set down
with my Father in His throne. (Rev 3:5, 21)

Christ specifically states that He will confess these people's names before His Father's throne and before the angels, meaning they are not angels themselves. Christ then states that these will sit upon His throne, even as He will sit upon His Father's throne. By this, we are to understand that these are gods and are given kingdoms, thrones, powers, principalities, dominions, exaltations, and eternal lives, meaning an increase in their eternal posterity forever. If an innumerable host such as this is described as existing before the throne of God in Enoch's day, as we have learned, then this host of gods must have obtained their exaltation in a prior iteration of the great plan of happiness.

This appears to be the case since Enoch describes them as they who sleep not. When an individual dies, we say that they are sleeping with their fathers. In reality, they are with their fathers in the spirit world, continuing the second phase of their second estate, where they await the morning of the first resurrection. At that time, they will be judged according to their works and will be resurrected into a kingdom of glory. A resurrected and glorified being is quicked and sleeps not.

Furthermore, the spirit world is very different from the Celestial Kingdom. The Throne of God is in the Celestial Kingdom, not the spirit world. The fact that this innumerable host is before the throne of God night and day means they are the inhabitants of the Celestial world, not the spirit world. Therefore, we must conclude that the innumerable hosts of gods that Enoch saw are the graduates of prior iterations of the Father's plan of salvation. As gods, they need to have posterity, meaning spirit children. Who would the spiritual offspring of this innumerable host of heavenly parents be? Those offspring can be none other than the children of the gods who caused the heavens to ring with joy at their opportunity to participate in this iteration of the Father's plan of salvation. We are included amongst their offspring; these gods are our heavenly parents.

Some might think I am overstepping and that these are not gods but angels. You will note that both Enoch and John did see angels, but these were not described as such by either. Enoch described them as those who sleep not, and John described them as those who wear white robes and overcome the world through the grace and power of Christ and have obtained thrones. Some might not see a distinction between angels and beings such as these. However, through the restoration, we know that angels do not bear children; however, gods can and do. Consider the following passage that removes all doubt of this concept:

> For these angels did not abide my law; therefore, they cannot be enlarged, but remain separately and singly, without exaltation, in their saved condition, to all eternity; and from henceforth are not gods, but are angels of God forever and ever.

> [Abraham] abode in my law; as Isaac also and Jacob did none other things than that which they were commanded; and because they did none other things than that which they were commanded, they have entered into their exaltation, according to the promises, and sit upon thrones, and are not angels but are gods.

> … they [*those that overcome this world through Christ*] shall pass by the angels, and the gods, which are set there, to their exaltation and glory in all things, as hath been sealed upon their heads, which glory shall be a fulness and a continuation of the seeds forever and ever. Then shall they be gods, because they have no end; therefore shall they be from everlasting to everlasting, because they continue; then shall they be above all, because all things are subject unto them. Then shall they be gods, because they have all power, and the angels are subject unto them. (D&C 132: 17, 37, 19-20)

These passages from Modern Revelation are astounding. They speak of the difference between gods and angels. Angels are servants, and gods are above all and have an eternal increase in posterity. Indeed, heavenly offspring is what makes them gods in the first place. Therefore, when I consider Job's writings, wherein the Aramaic version has been translated as "the son of the Angels shouted for joy," it should probably read, "the sons of the gods shouted for joy."

This concept is problematic for the majority of the Christian world. The concept of multiple gods is blasphemy to them. This belief is born of the Nicene Creed, which in turn confirmed with the post-Babylonian rendering of the Jewish writings. After both the Kingdom of Judah and the Northern Kingdom of Israel had been destroyed for worshiping the apostate versions of the gods held by the surrounding nations, the scribes went to great lengths to edit polytheism from their writings.

However, the restored gospel of Jesus Christ has no issue with the heavens being filled with gods, as the passages above clearly indicate. The Book of Abraham includes a creation account where "the gods" command the elements, and the elements obey them. Who were the gods, if not those that have been discussed above? It all must reconcile together, particularly when every good Latter-day Saint aspires to join the ranks of the gods in the Celestial realms on high.

Therefore, when Enoch is describing an innumerable host of bright, fiery ones that sleep not, I believe we must understand such things in this light. It makes far more sense that the inhabitants of worlds without numbers would spring forth from the nuclear families of hundreds of trillions of different heavenly mansions rather than one singular household. After all, if worlds without numbers are required to house such a vast host, it would be impossible to have all that literally have been raised by God the Father. It would take hundreds of trillions of families to produce hundreds of trillions of heavenly children. It would take hundreds of trillions of households to provide the meaningful and personal relationships and development that the Father encourages and fosters. We do not raise children in mass faceless communal centers on earth; why would we suppose it is done that way in the heavens?

If we acknowledge the fact that it would have been impossible for all the children of Heaven to have been personally raised by God, it prepares us to receive the actual answer to this question. A passage in the Doctrine and Covenants speaks of these things. Most overlook it because the things it speaks of are strange, but they are only strange when they are not properly understood. The passage of which I am speaking teaches a profound truth about the order of heaven. The context of this passage is the relationship between men and women, their heavenly offspring, and the Father. Consider it closely:

> ...they [*meaning righteous exalted goddesses*] are given unto him [*meaning a righteous exalted god*] to multiply and replenish the earth [*worlds without number*], according to my commandment, and **to fulfil the promise which was given by My Father before the foundation of the world**, and FOR THEIR EXALTATION IN THE ETERNAL

WORLDS, that they [*the goddesses*] may bear the souls of men [*heavenly children in the eternal world*]; for herein is the work of my Father CONTINUED, that He may be glorified. (D&C 132:63)

The passage above is packed with information. The verse that talks of exalted men and women is clear. After all, this same section of the D&C differentiates between gods and angels in terms of their ability to have children. In the verse above, we are told that in the ETERNAL world, the goddesses will bear the sons of men, meaning the children of heaven, who will participate in the next iteration of the Father's plan of salvation. Furthermore, you will note that their ability to bear the sons of men for the next iteration of the Father's plan fulfills the Father's promise to the daughters of heaven. At the same time, they themselves were still spirits before the world was created. We are then explicitly told that this is how the work of the Father continues, wherein He is glorified. As such, we are to understand God is our Father, not because we are His literal offspring but because He is the Father of the process wherein such things happen.

Consider another passage about the preexistence and our relationship to God the Father. I think that you will find this passage to be very meaningful in light of the context of this chapter so far.

Blessed be the God and Father of our Lord Jesus Christ, who hath blessed us with all spiritual blessings in heavenly places in Christ: according as **He hath chosen us in Him before the foundation of the world**, that we should be holy and without blame before Him in love: having **predestinated us unto the adoption of children by Jesus Christ to Himself**, according to the good pleasure of His will, to the praise of the glory of His grace, wherein He hath made us accepted in the beloved. (Eph 1:3-6)

According to Paul, the greatest gospel scholar among Christ's apostles, God the Father chose us from among the many children of Heaven because of His Son. By this, we are to understand that we have distinguished ourselves from the other children of heaven because of our faith and good works based on the life and example of the Son of God. Paul then explicitly states that God will adopt us as His own children through the grace and power of Jesus Christ. This is not the only time that Paul spoke of such things.

For ye have not received the spirit of bondage again to fear; but ye have received the Spirit of adoption; whereby we cry, Abba, Father. (Romans 8:15)

In this passage, it is clear that Paul was teaching us that we call God the Father, Father, through the spirit of adoption. Each one of us has a father and mother in heaven. We were raised by them, just as they were raised by heavenly parents of their own. These heavenly parents are all part of this grand council of gods, all of which fall under the authority and jurisdiction of God the Father. There is much more that needs to be said, and I will say much more on this subject in the next chapter titled The Family Business; however, for now, we need to further discuss the mighty host of our heavenly parents, which both Enoch and John saw standing before the throne of God.

First, let us address the sheer scope of their numbers. This host of exalted beings existed as gods before the foundations of this earth were ever laid. As such, it should be obvious that their redemption and exaltation came forth from a prior iteration of the plan of salvation. Yet, they are still clearly subservient to God. He is the great King and undisputed Sovereign of the Multiverse. There is no question of that whatsoever. These are lowercase gods, and He is God with a CAPITAL G.

We are, therefore, left to ask ourselves a curious question: how long has this process been going on? The answer to this question is without the beginning of days. We are in the midst of a process with no beginning and no end. While this is totally mindboggling, it is the only explanation for the innumerable host of resurrected gods and goddesses Enoch witnessed before the throne of God.

While we are letting this soak in, let us pause for a moment and do what President Nelson has asked us to do by beginning with the end in mind. If we obtain that which we seek and become gods and goddesses ourselves, then we are merely following in the footsteps of those who have gone before us. There is nothing new under the sun. It has all been done before. Indeed, this is the message of the mirrors upon the walls of the sealing rooms in our temples. If we obtain godhood, those mirrors whisper that we are not the first generation to do so, nor will we be the last. We have the great privilege of becoming another link in an endless and eternal chain of heavenly parents within the cosmic household of God.

By examining the religions of the ancient world, one can see the fingerprints of this ancient truth everywhere. It is certainly not an isolated concept found only in the Book of Enoch or the writings of Job. Every ancient religion believed something very similar to this. The Sumerians, Egyptians, Assyrians, Babylonians, Canaanites, and Israelites all believed in a heavenly council of gods that was presided over by an all-powerful God. This God of gods was the All-Father. In every civilization and religion noted previously, in every instance, the Great All-Father had a beloved Son upon which the kingdom was conferred. We see this in Sumer with An and Enki, in Egypt with Ra and Osiris, in Assyria with Ashur and Nabu, in Babylon with Ea and Marduk, in Canaan with Elohim and Ba'al (the Lord), and in Israel with Elohim and Jehovah. This is not some bizarre coincidence. The religions of the ancient world all stem back to one great original religious tradition, which was given to Adam and Eve in the Garden of Eden, the Earth's first temple.

For those who are interested in learning more about such things, and I highly recommend that you do, I would point you towards a podcast by the name of The Ancient Tradition by Jack Logan. There is much that you can learn from such a study. These ancient traditions were then mimicked by the Greeks and Romans. However, the greater the time differential between the prediluvian world and the society, the more corrupt and apostate the world's religions became.

Today, we understand that the purpose of the plan of salvation is to provide us with an opportunity to become like our heavenly parents. As the following scripture explains, we do so through faith in Christ.

> But, behold, I say unto you that I, the Lord God, gave unto Adam and unto his seed (*curious God describes us as Adam's seed, and not his own children*), that they should not die as to the temporal death, until I, the Lord God, should send forth angels to declare unto them repentance and redemption, through faith on the name of Mine Only Begotten Son. (D&C 29:42)

The passage above intrigues me in light of what has been discussed up to this point. God does not refer to us as His children but as Adam's children. To highlight this distinction, He then references His Only Begotten Son. This title is used numerous times in the Bible, Book of Mormon, Pearl of Great Price, and in the Doctrine and Covenants. For those who have been brought up believing themselves to be literally the Sons of God rather than the gods, it is a curious title.

For this reason, sometimes we add the supplemental phrase, "according to the flesh," after the title Only Begotten Son. However, this qualification is inconsistent with the scriptures themselves. The scriptures never qualify this title; it is always used as a standalone title. Consider the following examples:

> By the power of the Spirit our eyes were opened and our understandings were enlightened, so as to see and understand the things of God— even those things which were from the beginning before the world was, which were ordained of the Father, through His ONLY BEGOTTEN SON, who was in the bosom of the Father, even from the beginning; of whom we bear record; and the record which

we bear is the fulness of the gospel of Jesus Christ, who is
THE Son, whom we saw and with whom we conversed in
the heavenly vision. (D&C 76:12-14)

In the passage above, Joseph describes Christ as being both THE SON and the Father's Only Begotten Son. Clearly, Christ is unique, but I worry that we downplay just how unique He is. The title, Only Begotten Son, is used twice as much in the Doctrine and Covenants as any other book of scripture. As such, we have the title directly from God and are not potentially mistranslated from an ancient document. The revelation above, which uses this title, was given a mere four years after the first edition of the Webster Dictionary, which was published on April 14, 1828. As such, the meaning of the English words used in this vision should most closely translate with understanding the language spoken when this first edition of Webster's dictionary was provided. The following is the original Webster's dictionary for the word ONLY:

> *This and no other. This is an only child. Singly, without more; as in only-begotten.*

Combine the meaning of this term with the fact that God the Father used it to describe Christ from before the foundations of the world, and in conjunction with the posterity of Adam, we have something to think about. If we are all the literal begotten children of God, then this title makes no sense. As noted previously, people try to make this title more reconcilable by qualifying it – Only Begotten according to the flesh. Yet God never uses this qualifier. Both ancient and modern prophecies seem to suggest that Jesus Christ is literally God's only Son. I realize that we have scratched the surface of this topic and that there are miles to go before it can be properly understood and conceptualized. Still, before we take this any further, we need the additional light and knowledge that Enoch's incredible vision provides.

Consider the following:

> **40.2**. And on the four sides of the Lord of Spirits [*God the Father*] I saw four presences, different from those that sleep not [*the gods*], and I learnt their names: for the angel that went with me made known to me their names, and showed me all the hidden things.
>
> **40.3**. And I heard the voices of those four presences as they uttered praises before the Lord of glory.
>
> **40.4**. The first voice blesses the Lord of Spirits for ever and ever.

40.5. And the second voice I heard blessing the Elect One
and the elect ones who hang upon the Lord of Spirits.

This particular scene was the inspiration for this volume's cover art. According to Enoch, God was not sitting alone in this particular vision in front of these innumerable congregations of gods. Instead, four other entities stood at the four corners of His majestic throne. Enoch could clearly discern that these entities differed from those that slept not, which is they differed from the congregation of gods before them. We will learn how they were different in a movement. However, before we do, we learn that these four entities had a specific message that they were engaged in delivering. Enoch sees each relay their specific message in turn. The first messenger blessed God the Father. The second blessed the Elect One, by which we are to understand the Chosen or Anointed One—the second also blessed the elect ones who hang upon the Lord of Spirits. By this, we are to understand the noble and great ones who supported the Father's plan of redemption, hanging their futures upon it. This is similar to John's description of those who did not love their lives unto death but fought and overthrew the Dragon and his angels from heaven for rebelling against the Father.

We will now learn about the messages of the other two entities:

40.6. And the third voice I heard pray and intercede for those
who dwell on the earth and supplicate in the name of the
Lord of Spirits.

40.7. And I heard the fourth voice fending off the Satans and
forbidding them to come before the Lord of Spirits to accuse
them who dwell on the earth.

The last two entities' prayers focused upon the noble and great ones, those that hang upon the Lord of Spirits or loved not their lives unto the death. These are in desperate need of prayers because they are being tested upon the Earth. Interestingly, the last of the entities prohibited the Satans from accusing those who dwelt upon the earth. By the term "Satans," we are to understand the third of the hosts of heaven who were banished to the Earth by the noble and great ones. One of the hallmarks of Lucifer's fallen angels is their accusatory nature. Recall the following passage that described their premortal behavior even before the war in heaven had begun.

And the great dragon was cast out, that old serpent, called
the Devil, and Satan, which deceiveth the whole world: he
was cast out into the earth, and his angels were cast out with
him. And I heard a loud voice saying in heaven, now is come
salvation, and strength, and the kingdom of our God, and the

power of his Christ: **for the accuser of our brethren is cast down, which accused them before our God day and night**. (Rev 12:9-10)

According to this passage, Satan and his minions accused the children of heaven both night and day before the throne of God. That is to say that they were constantly pointing out the failures and shortcomings of the children of the gods to the Almighty King of Heaven and Earth. Even now, the demonic hosts of Satan want nothing more than to shout our sins from the rooftops and to condemn us before both God and man.

The fact that the Satans are now prohibited from bringing our sins before the throne of God is encouraging. It tells me that God is not looking for reasons to condemn me. He knows that I will continue to struggle and fall and that I depend upon the continual atonement of His Only Begotten Son. Yet, while Satan would define me by my worst moments, God seems far more interested in magnifying the best that is within me.

We arrive at the point in Enoch's narrative where the difference between the four entities next to the Throne of God is identified.

> **40.8**. After that I asked the angel of peace who went with me, who showed me everything that is hidden: 'Who are these four presences which I have seen and whose words I have heard and written down?'

> **40.9**. And he said to me: 'This first is Michael, the merciful and long-suffering: and the second, who is set over all the diseases and all the wounds of the children of men, is Raphael: and the third, who is set over all the powers, is Gabriel: and the fourth, who is set over the repentance unto hope of those who inherit eternal life, is named Phanuel.' And these are the four angels of the Lord of Spirits and the four voices I heard in those days.

As we learned earlier, Enoch knew that these four individuals were different from the rest of the hosts of heaven before the throne of God; now we learn why. These four beings are identified as Michael, the great prince, Raphel, Gabriel, and Phanuel. Michael is Adam, Gabriel is Noah, and Raphael's identity is unknown, but we know he participated in the restoration – see D&C 128:21. This leaves only Phanuel. The name Phanuel literally means the face of God. The fact that Phanuel was also given power over both repentance and eternal life clearly indicates that Phanuel is another name for the premortal Son of Man, whose image was in the express image of His Father.

This is the only instance in which Phanuel is mentioned. Consider that Phanuel prohibited the satans from accusing us before the Throne of His Father. Said another way, Phanuel is the Gatekeeper to the throne of God, our advocate with the Father and none else.

We can now see why these four men were described as being different from the host of gods before them. The gods before them were described as they who sleep not. In other words, these once slept but have long since been quickened and now have glorified resurrected bodies. Christ, Michael, Raphael, and Gabriel were all spirits at the time of this revelation. These four were the leaders of the great and noble ones in the premortal realms. Given the prayers that were offered in connection with those who dwelt upon the earth, we can discern that this meeting was being held on behalf of the noble and great ones who were getting overwhelmed by Lucifer and his minions in mortality.

This reminds me of a prior message that the archangels had for God the Father, which was discussed in volume one of this series when those in Spirit Prison were praying for their posterity upon the earth and for the Lord of Spirits to intervene on their behalf. This is how the archangels address God the Father at that time:

> **9.4**. And they said to the Lord of the ages: 'Lord of lords, **God of gods**, King of kings, and God of the ages, the throne of Thy glory *standeth* unto all the generations of the ages, and Thy name holy and glorious and blessed unto all the ages!

Michael addressed the Father as the Lord of lords and the God of gods. In the present context, this makes all the sense in the world. God the Father is the God of all gods. Furthermore, it would seem that the entire purpose of this grand heavenly council of the gods is to advocate for the children of the gods dwelling upon Satan's prison planet. This advocation was not just for the prediluvian world but also for the generation that would live upon the earth in the last days, during the times of trial that would be brought to pass due to the return of the Watchers. If I jump ahead seven chapters in the Book of Enoch, we find this passage, which I am sure is to be understood in the present context of this grand council of gods advocating for their posterity upon the earth. Consider the following:

> **47.1**. And in those days shall have ascended the prayer of the righteous, and the blood of the righteous from the earth before the Lord of Spirits.

> **47.2**. In those days the holy ones who dwell above in the heavens shall unite with one voice and supplicate and pray

[and praise, and give thanks and bless the name of the Lord
of Spirits] on behalf of the blood of the righteous [*the Son of
Man - Phanuel*] which has been shed, and that the prayer of
the righteous may not be in vain before the Lord of Spirits,
that judgement may be done unto them, and that they may
not have to suffer forever.

From the context of the above passage, it is clear that this council of gods will meet again and plead for mercy for their posterity before the Throne of God. Every human being on the earth today is a child of the gods. Their heavenly parents love and care for them and want the best for them. The majority of the world has not gone after sin. Our heavenly parents know that this will have consequences. This sin will grow until their children will take up arms against each other, filling the earth with violence not seen since the days of Noah.

It is obvious from the passages that these heavenly parents know that their children, both the righteous and the unrighteous alike, will suffer. These are not petitioning the Lord that these things stop happening altogether to their posterity, for such is life upon Satan's prison planet. We knew what we were signing up for before we came. We loved not our lives unto the death. Our heavenly parents are advocating that those who were deceived upon this planet will not have to suffer forever and that there will be an end. Therefore, when the days of trial are upon us, and you look to the heavens with a broken heart and wonder if there will ever be an end to your suffering, know that the heavens are looking back. Mothers are weeping for their children. Fathers are petitioning the God of gods. The heavens are focused upon us, and the bounds of Satan's trials have already been laid. Strength and power and blessings will come. We will receive endowments of power and glory that will arm us with the power of God Himself. This will come, in no small part, because the heavens are shaking for our good. We are not lost to them, and our sufferings are not unknown. We must endure it well. It may not seem like it at the time, but these sufferings will be but for a small moment. If we endure it, we, too, will be received into the heavenly courts to be reunited with loved ones whom we have forgotten existed. But they do exist, and they are for us.

Now that we have identified who this miraculous group represents and why they have gathered before the Throne of God, we are prepared for a deeper analysis of this topic. The true order of heaven and the nature of the Family Business bring man's immortality and eternal life to pass. What is it actually like in heaven? Contrary to the popular belief of mainstream Christianity, gods do not sit around all day strumming harps and singing songs. Joseph Smith taught the following:

That same sociality which exists among us here will exist
among us there [*in the Celestial Kingdom*], only it will be

coupled with eternal glory, which glory we do not now enjoy.
(D&C 130:2)

Joseph Smith did not preach in Church every second of every day. Most of his time was spent either trying to earn a living, raising his family, or enjoying life with those he loved. Why would it be any different in heaven? If the same sociality exists here, then society will be similar. Yet, we should consider this statement in the context of this grand council of the gods, which Enoch described. This grand council of gods is not the norm; rather, it is the exception.

Consider that this grand host of gods was all praying over the inhabitants of this earth. Given that there were more gods present in this grand council than the entire population to have ever lived on this earth, most of these gods would not have direct posterity on this planet. Why then were they present? I believe they were present because God promised that His rulers would be selected from those who would spend mortality on this earth. As such, whether the posterity of the gods was present upon this earth or not, their posterity would most certainly be influenced by the noble and great ones that would rise to positions of power here to rule and reign in the House of Israel forever, as sovereign kings, queens, priests, and priestesses.

If you recall from volume one of this book, I suggested that the world's inhabitants have been administering to the cosmos since Enoch and his people were translated. In volume one, I shared Joseph's teachings regarding the beings translated from this earth. These beings minister the ordinances of the gospel to other worlds. Yet we also learned that no other worlds throughout the multiverse administer to the inhabitants of this world, only those that have or will belong to it.

I believe this is why all of the gods in heaven are gathered before the Throne of the Great God of gods. They are petitioning for their posterity as the events of this current iteration of the plan of salvation begin to draw to a close. As this heavenly cycle's last great culminating event transpires, the heavens will surely be abuzz with excitement and anticipation as billions of years in the making are now coming to a head in the most spectacular grand finale imaginable. As time goes by, all eyes will be on planet Earth.

The last thing that I will point out regarding this massive host of gods is their absolute deference to the supremacy of God. There is no doubt in Enoch's vision who is in control – it is God the Father, or as Enoch calls Him – the Lord of Spirits. It is God's work and His glory to exalt the spirits of this iteration of the plan of salvation. The gods are helping Him in that work. None of the gods are independent; all are subservient to Him. Furthermore, it is God's Only Begotten Son upon whom the salvation of the entire cosmic family hangs. Consider the following passage in the context of this chapter:

Let all the nations be gathered together, and let the people be assembled: who among them can declare this, and shew us former things? Let them bring forth their witnesses, that they may be justified: or let them hear, and say, It is truth. Ye are my witnesses, saith the Lord, and my servant whom I have chosen [*meaning the House of Israel*]: that ye may know and believe Me, and understand that I am He: before Me there was no God formed, neither shall there be after Me. I, even I, am the Lord; and beside Me there is no Savior. (Isaiah 43:9-11)

Some have postulated that God is not the God of the entire multiverse but just of the Milky Way Galaxy. There does not seem to be much wiggle room in the passage above. Jesus Christ is the Savior of all the worlds the Father has created. There are no other Saviors besides Him. How, then, does it work? We will address this question in the next one.

Chapter 4: The Family Business

In the prior chapter, Enoch introduced us to a host of gods beyond reckoning for the number that had been assembled before the Throne of God. These gods were petitioning the Father on behalf of their mortal posterity. The events transpiring upon Satan's prison planet impact the cosmos in ways we do not presently comprehend. Great concerns were expressed in that heavenly council regarding the catastrophic results of the Watchers mixing with Lucifer and his minions. The result was total corruption of the earth, save the followers of Enoch, who were removed from the earth and could administer to the cosmos' residents.

The results were disastrous. As such, it is easy to understand the concern regarding the future day when Satan and his minions would be released from their prison planet to wreak havoc across the multiverse. With unfettered access to the children of heaven, what chance did they have? Therefore, it seems to me that the gods of heaven met in council before the throne of God with an urgent petition for their children. They wanted assurances that the Father would prepare a way for their escape.

Such brings new meaning to the following passage from Isaiah's mighty writings:

> I, *am* He that comforteth you: who *art* thou, that thou shouldest be <u>afraid</u> …and <u>forgettest</u> the LORD thy maker, that hath stretched forth the heavens, and laid the foundations of the <u>earth</u>; and hast feared continually every day because of the fury of the oppressor, as if he were ready to destroy? and where *is* the fury of the oppressor? (Isaiah 51:12-13)

God the Father is the Lord of the hosts of heaven. All things are before Him. He was not surprised by the oppressor's fury, even if others were. He knew what would happen before it happened and prepared a way for our escape. The foreknowledge of God is as comforting to us as it is for the hosts of heaven, be they gods or men! We know of the corruption of the prediluvian world and how that corruption occurred. We know that it happened again in the land of Canaan in the post-diluvian world, and it was extinguished by the swords of the House of Israel. We know that the Earth will become corrupted once more in the last days and that the righteous will be liberated once again by the fiery weapons of the House of Israel. As such, there is little doubt that the hosts of heaven, who are our fathers and mothers, are praying for us. They are beseeching the Father on our behalf. After all, the multiverse's fate depends on the House of Israel, particularly its favorite Son.

In this chapter, we will further delve into the workings of heaven in an attempt to understand how it all works. This will bring us even further into the theoretical realms of our doctrine. As we begin this theoretical discussion, we must begin with the end in mind. The righteous everywhere hope for exaltation in the Celestial Kingdom. To obtain such exaltation is to become a heavenly father or mother endowed with the sacred power to raise spirit children of our own.

The process by which this is accomplished did not originate with us. This is the great promise of the patriarchs, which Abraham diligently sought to obtain for himself. The pursuit of this promise is what President Nelson referred to as the gospel of Abraham. Since Abraham's covenant, every righteous man or woman who has come to understand such things has desired to secure this same covenant for themselves. As such, we do not blaze new trails but follow in the footsteps of those who have gone before us. Thus, Elohim, the great All-father, is a God of gods and the sovereign King who reigns over all the hosts of heaven.

Yet, I believe there is a significant misunderstanding regarding what it means to become a god. Enoch's vision clearly demonstrated that the innumerable hosts of gods in heaven are subservient to the Almighty. Some have supposed that such would not be the case. Indeed, some have supposed that to become a god means that the day will come when they will call forth a Savior from their posterity whose mission will be to redeem their children. Such a belief presumes that the multiverse is filled with innumerable independent microcosms of salvation that are independent of the beings that comprise the current Godhead. I believe this idea is patently false and utterly inconsistent with every scripture that addresses this subject. Consider the following:

> I, *even* I, *am* the LORD; and beside me *there is* no savior. (Isaiah 43:11)

God is the God of all, and besides His Son, there is no Savior. All cosmic truth must reconcile with this basic gospel tenant, for God Himself said as much, and He does not lie. The righteous love and honor the God of heaven. They want His will to be done in their lives. There is no kinder, gentler, or more loving being in the multiverse than God the Father and His Son. Yet, God is the Head. He is the order in all things and the power whereby all things function.

Where does this confusion come from regarding the nature of godliness? I believe that the confusion regarding the nature of what comes next is based on a misunderstanding of Joseph Smith's teachings.   We are all familiar with Joseph's incredible doctrinal bombshell statement:

As man now is, God once was, and as God now is, man may become.

While this statement is true, it is prone to misunderstanding. I believe that the true meaning behind this teaching would best be understood by phrasing it as follows instead:

As man now is, Christ once was, and as Christ now is, man may become.

You may think the difference here is semantics, but the things of heaven are nuanced. By phrasing it this way, we frame this concept so that we can more readily relate. God the Father is something of an enigma to most. We know little of His history. However, His Only Begotten Son's history, life, and mission is less mysterious. For example, we clearly understand that Jesus Christ was born on this Earth and was subjected to the conditions of mortality. However, we also know that Christ was different from us. While His mother was like all of our mothers, meaning Mary was mortal, Christ's Father was literally the Almighty God– the King of the Universe! As such, Jesus Christ was not mortal; He was and is and will always be God's Only Begotten Son. As such, while in the flesh, Christ was half mortal, half God –a demigod. As a demigod, we understand that He could not be killed unless He voluntarily surrendered His life. Consider the following:

> When the chief priests therefore and officers saw Him, they cried out,   saying,   Crucify *Him*, crucify *Him*. Pilate saith unto them, Take ye Him, and crucify *Him*: for I find no fault in Him. The Jews answered him, We have a <u>law</u>, and by our law He ought to die, because He made Himself the <u>Son of God</u>.

> When Pilate therefore heard that saying, he was the more afraid; and went again into the judgment hall, and saith unto Jesus, Whence art thou? But Jesus gave him no <u>answer</u>. Then saith Pilate unto Him, Speakest thou not unto me? knowest thou not that I have power to crucify thee, and have power to release thee?

> Jesus answered, Thou couldest have no <u>power</u> *at all* against Me, except it were given thee from above: therefore he that

delivered me unto thee hath the greater <u>sin</u>. And from thenceforth Pilate sought to release Him. (John 19:6-12)

Christ allowed Himself to be ransomed for the sins of the world, for unto this end was He born. In this regard, there was an insurmountable difference between Him and us.

Yet, in other ways, He was very much like us. Like us, He was born with the veil. As such, He progressed just like us, grace for grace, line upon line, precept by precept. Therefore, when Joseph spoke of God once being as man now is, he meant it in the same sense that Christ was once like us. Yet there is an insurmountable difference between us and Jesus Christ, and always has been. He is the ONLY BEGOTTEN OF THE FATHER!

I believe that the following passages will help to further illustrate this point:

> the Jews persecute Jesus, and sought to slay Him, because He had [*healed a man*] on the sabbath day. But Jesus answered them, My Father worketh hitherto, and I work… Verily, verily, I say unto you, The Son can do nothing of Himself, but what He seeth the Father do: for what things soever He doeth, these also doeth the Son likewise. (John 5:16-17, 19)

In the passage above, Christ explained that He did nothing but that He saw His Father do it first. Does Christ mean this literally, or do you suppose that He is just trying to sound impressive to the Jews? Obviously, He means what He is saying literally! As such, without question, we know with absolute certainty that Jesus Christ witnessed His Father do the same things that He was then doing. That is to say, Christ witnessed the earthly ministry of His Father before Him. Given Christ is the Savior of this iteration of the cycle of salvation, His Father had to have been the Savior of the cycle before this. This concept is further supported by the following passage:

> When ye have lifted up the Son of man, then shall ye know that I am *He,* and *that* I do nothing of myself; but as My Father hath taught Me (John 8:28)

According to Christ, His Father taught Him everything He knew, including how to serve as a ransom for the sins of an entire celestial cycle. After all, Christ explicitly stated that the Jews would understand that He only did those things He was taught by the Father in conjunction with His crucifixion. In this regard, the Father and the Son are not only one in mind and purpose, but also they are one in experience.

A father who has served a mission can counsel his child who is also serving a mission. The father knows what his child is experiencing firsthand. In this way, the Father taught and counseled Jesus Christ. God the Father had literally walked the same path His Son was asked to walk in mortality. Let me be very clear about what I am suggesting. As Jesus Christ stated that He did nothing but saw His Father do it first, I believe that Jesus Christ witnessed His Father fulfill the role as the Savior for the previous iteration of the cycle of salvation.

Therefore, for this to be possible, Jesus Christ must be physically present to witness His Father's actions. I believe that this is precisely what is implied by God the Father in the following passage:

> Behold, My Beloved Son, which was my Beloved and Chosen **from the beginning**, said unto Me—Father, Thy will be done, and the glory be thine forever. (Moses 4:2)

The context of the above passage is the grand council of the noble and great ones, which occurred before the foundations of this world were laid. At this council, we already understood that Jesus Christ was the Father's Beloved Son from the beginning. Given this statement was made in the context of that council of the noble and great ones about to come to the earth to experience mortality, Christ was already much older than any of us. After all, if Christ was with the Father from the beginning, it stands to reason that this beginning long preceded that particular primordial council. Yet, we know that Jesus Christ was a spirit during that great council, just like us, but His Father was a glorified and resurrected being.

How long had Christ been a spirit before this meeting? Well, if He witnessed everything His Father did during His mortal ministry, then Christ had to have been a spirit for a minimum of the entire duration of the previous iteration of the cycle of salvation. How long, then, is a cycle of salvation?

Bruce R McConkie theorized about the length of these cycles of salvation. He believed that this cycle of salvation would last 7,000 years on this earth's surface. However, he believed that the greater cosmic cycle of salvation, of which this earth is a part, would take 7,000 years, according to the timing of the Lord, to complete. That is a very long time! If one day unto the Lord is as a thousand years unto man, then one year unto the Lord is the equivalent of 365,000 years to man. Therefore, if a whole cycle of salvation lasts 7,000 years according to the timing of God, one cycle of the plan of salvation lasts 2,555,000,000 (7,000 x 365,000) years according to man's timing.

Furthermore, Elder McConkie believed this earth was reserved to come forth at the end of the cosmic cycle of salvation. Therefore, Elder McConkie theorized that events were not just winding up for this earth but for the entire cycle of salvation. This might explain why all the hosts of heaven were gathering before the throne of the Almighty. They knew that things were winding up across the board, regardless of the world their specific offspring were in.

If this is true, what happens when this cycle concludes? We can postulate what happens from Christ's teaching regarding His witnessing His Father. Christ's Father is the God of this iteration of the cycle of Salvation. However, if I understand Christ correctly, His Father was the Savior of the previous iteration. Therefore, in the prior iteration of the cycle of salvation, Christ's Grandfather would have been the God of the cycle, His Father the Savior, and leaving Him in the position of the Holy Ghost to witness and attest to the truthfulness of all things.

This may seem strange to you, but it is exactly what Joseph Smith taught. Consider the following:

> Jesus Christ was the Son of God, and John discovered that God the Father of Jesus Christ had a Father (*see Rev 1:6*), you may suppose that He (*God*) had a Father also. Where was there ever a son without a father? And where was there ever a father without first being a son? Whenever did a tree or anything spring into existence without a progenitor? And everything comes in this way. Paul says that which is earthly is in the likeness of that which is heavenly, hence if Jesus had a Father, can we not believe that He had a Father also? I despise the idea of being scared to death at such a doctrine, for the Bible is full of it. (Teachings of the Prophet Joseph Smith page 373)

Thus, we see that the Godhead represents a royal lineage of Fathers and Sons. God the Father mentored His Son, Jesus Christ. He did this not from a theoretical perspective but because He had fulfilled that role before Christ did, in the prior iteration of the plan of salvation. His Father fulfilled it before Him, and so forth in an unbroken line of Gods.

This unbroken line of Gods makes our progression from spirits to mortals to gods possible. As such, those who become gods through adherents to the covenant path do not supplant the Gods that enabled their progression; rather, they assist them in their family business. How do we assist Them? By raising up offspring for the next iteration of the cycle of salvation. This is the meaning of the following passage reviewed in the prior chapter:

> ...they [*meaning righteous exalted goddesses*] are given unto him [*meaning a righteous exalted god*] to multiply and replenish the earth [*worlds without number*], according to my commandment, and **to fulfil the promise which was given by My Father before the foundation of the world**, and FOR THEIR EXALTATION IN THE ETERNAL WORLDS, that they [*the goddesses*] may bear the souls of men [*heavenly children in the eternal world*]; for herein is the work of my Father CONTINUED, that He may be glorified. (D&C 132:63)

The Father's work is continued through our heavenly offspring. We do not veer off into some independent microcosm of our design to save our future offspring. Enoch's vision clearly shows that there will be no reinventing of the wheel. Just as there is one faith, baptism, and Savior, there is one plan of salvation.

Therefore, as God's Only Begotten Son from the beginning, Christ witnessed the Father's life and ministry long before this world existed. As such, Christ would have also witnessed His Father's ascension to the throne, wherein His Father sat down upon the throne of His Father, just as we have been told Christ will one day do the same. Therefore, as Elder McConkie postulated, if each cycle of salvation lasts 2.6 billion years, then God the Father has been part of the Godhead for approximately eight billion years!

This is a staggering concept, but it makes much sense to me. If a cycle of salvation lasts 2.6 billion years, consider how many spirit children could be born to a vast host of heavenly parents, which themselves number in the hundreds of trillions! During the duration of the cycle, these children would have plenty of time to learn and grow to spiritual maturity. After all, they will have lived long enough to see entire solar systems come and go!

The entire plan of salvation is built upon the concept of eternal progression. If I am correct in what I have stated above, this progress is not limited to the mortals alone. After all, mortals are simply gods in embryo. Therefore, the Gods themselves progress. We have seen this progression in Christ's own life. While He was living amongst the Jews, He commanded them to be perfect like His Father in Heaven was perfect. However, when He came to the Nephites after His resurrection, He told them to be perfect even as He and His Father in Heaven were perfect. Christ had progressed via the resurrection.

Let us delve further into this concept of the progression of the Godhead itself, for in it, we can understand the order of heaven. The Godhead comprises three separate and distinct individuals: the Father, Son, and Holy Ghost. All three of these beings have separate and distinct roles. The Father stands in the supreme position of authority and leadership. He is the Steward over the entire cycle of salvation. He is the only member of the Godhead at the start of a new cycle of salvation to have a glorified, resurrected, and perfect Celestial physical body.

The Son is second to the Father and does the will of the Father in all things. This includes being born into mortality so that His life might be ransomed as an infinite and eternal sacrifice for the sins of all those participating in the present iteration of the cycle of salvation. Lastly, the Holy Ghost is a personage of spirit and the only member of the Godhead to remain a spirit for the entire duration of the cycle. As a Spirit, the Holy Ghost serves as a witness and testifier of the works of both the Father and the Son. This is a covenantal relationship between the Holy Ghost and the other members of the Godhead. Consider the following:

> The Holy Ghost, which witnesses of the Father and the Son,
> unto the fulfilling of the promise which He hath made. (2
> Nephi 31:18)

According to Nephi, the Holy Ghost covenanted with both the Father and the Son that He would bear witness to all the participants of the present iteration of the cycle regarding the truthfulness of all things. Before the cycle began, the Holy Ghost would have had to have made this covenant with both the Father and the Son. That is to say that this covenant had to be made from the very beginning. Therefore, when the Father states that Jesus Christ is His Only Begotten Son who has been with Him from the beginning, He means it in this context. Regarding the nature of the Godhead, the Father is in the role of the Father for the entire cycle.

In what capacity would Jesus Christ have witnessed His Father heal the sick, raise the dead, calm and reorganize the elements, atone for sin, suffer death, and rise triumphantly from the grave? In the context of the Godhead, Christ could have only witnessed these things if He served as the Holy Ghost, bearing witness to the actions of His Father and His Grandfather before Him. Again, as we have already seen, Joseph Smith taught that Christ's Father has and Father and so on in an unbroken line of Upper Case Gods.

It should be understood that the mantle of responsibility for managing the cycle of salvation shifted from Upper Case Gods to lower-case gods. The gods assist in continuing the Father's work, but there is never any doubt about whose work we are engaged in. This is the Father's work. Consider the following teaching of Joseph Smith:

> Here, then, is eternal life—to know the only wise and true
> God; and you have got to learn how to be gods yourselves,
> and to be kings and priests **to God**, the same as all gods have
> done before you—namely, by going from one small degree
> to another, and from a small capacity to a great one—from
> grace to grace, from exaltation to exaltation, until you attain
> to the resurrection of the dead, and are able to dwell in
> everlasting burnings and to sit in glory, as do those who sit
> enthroned in everlasting power. (Journal of Discourses 6:1)

In heaven, there are lowercase and Uppercase Gods. God the Father is the God of gods. He is Elohim. He rules supreme. His Only Begotten Son redeems all the sons and daughters of heaven, and there is no Savior besides Him. There is no qualification for the scope of the Savior's redemptive power; it applies to the entire cosmos. This concept is confirmed in the following passage:

> And now, after the many testimonies which have been given
> of him, this is the testimony, last of all, which we give of
> him: That He lives! For we saw Him, even on the right
> hand of God; and we heard the voice bearing record that He
> is the Only Begotten of the Father— that by Him, and
> through Him, and of Him, the worlds are and were created,
> and the inhabitants thereof are begotten sons and daughters
> unto God. (D&C 76:22-24)

If Christ is the Savior of the multiverse and the only means by which the inhabitants of worlds without number can become the begotten sons and daughters unto God, in that case, there are not multiple iterations of the cycle of salvation happening in tandem across the multiverse. There is One God, One Savior, and One Comforter. Everything else falls underneath them, be they gods or kingdoms.

Yet, the same pattern of progression within the Godhead itself that has always existed will continue to be going forward. Therefore, the Savior of the next iteration of the cycle of salvation is with us now, witnessing the truthfulness of all things to us. We know Him and have known Him from the beginning. At least, this is my theory on the subject.

Therefore, I conclude that God the Father was the subservient Son of the prior iteration of the plan of salvation. Jesus Christ witnessed all He did as a spiritual Being without a physical body, nor did He have one for the duration of that iteration of the plan of salvation. Our heavenly parents became exalted because they learned to listen to Him and heed His counsel. If it were not so, they would not have survived the horrors and trials of mortality. To this end, our prophet has warned us that we will not survive the coming day's trials and challenges without the Holy Ghost's constant guiding influence.

We pray to the Father and none else because He is the source of all power and glory within the multiverse. He is the Supreme authority and Patriarch of this iteration of the plan of Salvation. He, and His Fathers before Him, exalted our heavenly parents, and their parents before them, and their before them back into the far reaches of eternity. This is how hundreds of trillions of gods came to be. Yet all of these gods bow their knees in deference to the Supreme Ruler of the present iteration of the plan of salvation.

Therefore, the utterly ridiculous trend that has started to arise within LDS communities of praying to one's heavenly parents is both ignorant to the true workings of the heavens and an affront to the commandments of God. We revere our heavenly parents. They raised us, loved us, taught us, inspired us, and are unquestionably the primary reason we opted to participate in the Father's current iteration of the plan of salvation. However, we worship the Supreme Power of the Multiverse, not His servants. The Supreme power in the Multiverse is none other than God the Father. There can be no doubt about this.

With this understanding, let us now discuss the nature and role of Jesus Christ in more detail. We refer to Jesus Christ as both the Father and the Son, but why do we do so? We can gain insight into this practice through the angelic instruction that was given to King Benjamin; consider the following:

> And now, because of the covenant which ye have made ye shall be called the children of Christ, **HIS** sons, and **HIS** daughters; for behold, this day He hath spiritually begotten you; for ye say that your hearts are changed through faith on His name; therefore, **ye are born of Him** and have become His sons and His daughters. (Mosiah 5:7)

We are not born the sons and daughters of Jesus Christ, but we must become so if we are to inherit all that the Father has. We become the children of Christ by covenant. Through our covenants, we link ourselves to the royal lineage of heaven in no other way. Thus, while we are all the sons and daughters of gods through birthright, we become the sons and daughters of both God the Father and His Only Begotten Son by choice. This brings us back to Paul's mysterious teachings, which were touched upon in the prior chapter.

> For ye have not received the spirit of bondage again to fear; but ye have received the Spirit of adoption; whereby we cry, Abba, Father. (Romans 8:15)

And

> Blessed be the God and Father of our Lord Jesus Christ, who hath blessed us with all spiritual blessings in heavenly places in Christ: according as He hath chosen us in Him before the foundation of the world, that we should be holy and without blame before Him in love: having predestinated us unto the adoption of children by Jesus Christ to Himself, according to the good pleasure of His will, to the praise of the glory of His grace, wherein He hath made us accepted in the beloved. (Eph 1:3-6)

And

> For ye are all the children of God by faith in Christ Jesus. (Gal 3:26)

In three separate letters to three separate bodies of the Church, Paul taught that we become part of the Royal Household of God by adoption. By becoming the children of Christ, by being born again through His atonement, we become His children and the heirs of His Kingdom. There is no other way to become a rightful heir to the Kingdom of God. Thus, through the spirit of adoption and the atonement of Jesus Christ, all become God's Begotten Sons and Daughters. Yet there is so much more to it than this.

In the literal sense, parents are our parents because our bodies were created by their physical bodies coupled with the power of God. Jesus Christ is the ONLY BEGOTTEN SON because His physical body was literally derived from the Father's DNA. He was also resurrected through the power of the Father. In this, He was once again unique. Christ is the only graduate of this iteration of the plan of salvation resurrected by the Father's power. All others will be resurrected through His atonement. The Father was able to raise His Only Begotten Son because He wrought an infinite and eternal atonement.

Every mortal to have ever breached the matrix will be resurrected via the power of Christ. Thus, Christ will literally be the Father of their resurrected bodies. This can be thought of in no other way. This is how we become the sons and daughters of God through faith in Christ, as attested to in Galatians 3:26.

If we do not become the sons and daughters of God without the atonement, why are we taught that we are the children of God? There can be no doubt that this is a fundamental belief and core tenet of our faith. I will explain this now.

Our heavenly parents walked the same covenant path that we now walk. Through their obedience, faith, and covenants, they took upon them the name of their Savior and were born again in Him. When they were resurrected through the power of their Savior's atonement, they received their resurrected bodies directly from Him. As such, their Savior became the literal Father of their new physical body – an incorruptible, ageless body that will endure forever.

As such, our heavenly parents became the literal children of God the Father, who was their Savior. Everything that they have and are is because of Him. Because God is their Father, He is also the Father of our spirits. Thus, the Father is known as the Lord of Spirits. Our heavenly parents' physical bodies would not have been blessed with the powers of procreation if not for Him and the power of His resurrection.

As such, our heavenly parents raised us to look to Him as our Father, for our very existence is a product of His power, and our heavenly parents are copartners with Him in bringing to pass the immortality and eternal life of man. Therefore, heaven's nuclear families become intertwined with the direct lineage and power of the Godhead. God the Father is the literal grandfather of our spirit bodies, and His Only Begotten Son will become the literal Father of our resurrected bodies. So it is that the righteous become inextricably linked to the Household of God.

Yet, this is not the only means by which we are called the children of God. While we are the literal spiritual offspring of heavenly parents, the offspring of the gods are spirits and not physical. Therefore, the first mortal man and woman upon this earth would not have been the product of lowercase gods, for they required tangible bodies. Therefore, they would have either needed to have come to the earth from another planet or have been created by the all-powerful Father and Son Themselves. The temple account shows that man was not found on the earth before Adam and Eve. We also know from that account that the Father and Son literally created the physical bodies of Adam and Eve in their own image. As such, the Father was literally the father of Adam and Eve and the entire human race. This same process has taken place across the cosmos. As such, although the mortal children of the cosmos stem from innumerable heavenly households, through their respective Adams and Eves, everyone in this iteration of the Father's plan of salvation can literally trace their mortal ancestry back to God and are literally His Sons and Daughters. Yet, mortality is a transitory state. Therefore, if we are to become permanent members of the household of God, we must do so voluntarily through the election process.

With this in mind, let us return to Paul's previous teachings, wherein he instructed us regarding these things.

> For ye have not received the spirit of bondage again to fear; but ye have received the Spirit of adoption, whereby we cry, Abba, Father. The Spirit itself beareth witness with our spirit, that we are the children of God: And if children, then heirs; heirs of God, and joint-heirs with Christ; if so be that we suffer with Him, that we may be also glorified together. For I reckon that the sufferings of this present time are not worthy to be compared with the glory which shall be revealed in us. For the earnest expectation of the creature waiteth for the manifestation of the sons of God. (Romans 8:15-19)

Here, we learn that when Paul speaks of adoption, He is speaking of adoption into the literal household of God. As we have seen, God the Father is the grandfather of all of the Spirits of this iteration, and His Only Begotten Son will become the Father of our resurrected bodies. A detailed study of D&C 76 will demonstrate that only those who become the Children of Christ in mortality, by deliberate choice, will inherit the kingdom and household of God as joint heirs.

We do not find this path by accident. All who find it are led to it by the still, small voice of the Holy Ghost. As such, we learn to trust the Father and His Son because we have first learned to hear and trust the Holy Ghost. Thus, the Father, Son and Holy Ghost are one. They are one in purpose, they are one in capacity, and they are one in destiny. Therefore, the Godhead itself stands as a brilliant example for us to follow and testifies that the Father's plan of eternal progression applies equally to Gods and men. By adhering to its principles and strict obedience, men can become far more than most have ever supposed.

The question then becomes, what happens to the Father when the great plan of salvation moves forward, when the Son obtains His Father's throne and, via the resurrection of the dead, has become the Father of all this cycle's children? What then happens with the Father? We find the answer to this question where you might expect to find it, in the words of Isaiah. Consider the following passage:

How art thou fallen from heaven, O Lucifer, son of the morning! *How* art thou cut down to the ground, which didst weaken the nations!

For thou hast said in thine heart, I will ascend into heaven, I will exalt my throne above the stars of God: I will sit also upon the mount of the congregation, in the sides of the north: I will ascend above the heights of the clouds; I will be like the most High.

Yet thou shalt be brought down to hell, to the sides of the pit. (Isaiah 14:12-15)

What does this passage say concerning the aspirations of Satan? Lucifer aspired to exalt himself above the stars of heaven. In other words, Lucifer wanted to become more than a god; he wanted to become an Uppercase God, to whom all the gods of Heaven bend the knee. Specifically, Isaiah stated that Lucifer wanted a seat upon the Northern Slope of the Mount of the Congregation, and herein lies our answer. The inference here is that the Northern Slope of the Mount of the Congregation is reserved as the highest seat of honor in the heavens. The fact that Lucifer wanted to sit there "also" infers that others are already sitting there. Who are these others who occupy seats of honor above the Throne of God on the Mount of the Congregation? I believe these represent the unbroken line of Uppercase Gods, who each served upon heaven's golden throne themselves during their time as the culminating member of the Godhead. After their service, these transcendent beings of incomprehensible glory obtained their seats upon the north face of the Mount of the Congregation.

Lucifer thought that he could interject himself into the Godhead by usurping Christ's position. He believed that by so doing, through the passage of time and the completion of cycles, He would then become like the Most High Himself. He envisioned himself claiming a seat of honor alongside the Great transcendent Gods whose Thrones reside upon the northern face of the Mount of the Congregation. If Lucifer succeeded in his attempted coup, he would have become the equal of the most powerful beings in the multiverse, beyond which there is no greater power. Yet he failed, and rather than ascending to a golden Throne of honor upon the Mount of the Congregation, he will descend into the fiery pit of Outer Darkness, where he will rule over the eternally damned instead.

Yet, Lucifer is no fool. If his rebellion had no hope of success, he never would have attempted it. Lucifer has tremendous intelligence and capability; just look at what he has accomplished here on Earth. He has conquered the world numerous times, destroyed the church, and will overcome the saints of God. He knows what he is doing. Why, then, did he do what he did?

He did so because He knows the Golden Throne is centered on free agency. God the Father would never impose His will by force upon the children of heaven. Indeed, as we will see as this book progresses, the Father's plan was not mandatory. It was always presented as an option for those wishing to become like their heavenly parents and like their GrandFather, the great God of the multiverse.

Lucifer was numbered amongst the noble and great ones, the leaders of the children of heaven, those who stood with authority in the presence of God. Lucifer planned to turn the tide of opinion amongst the rising generation. He knew that he could do it. How many times has he demonstrated this ability here on Earth? Therefore, with all his might, he sought to turn the tide of heaven by turning the order of the ages upon its head.

We tend to think of Lucifer's rebellion as an event, but before the event, it was a carefully calculated process that spanned eons of time. Gently and tenderly, Lucifer turned the hearts of heaven. He has always been patient and methodical. We are eyewitnesses to the effectiveness of his plan here on this earth. Here, he has done the same incredible flipping of the narrative he skillfully performed in heaven. Through his cunning arts, many who initially rejected his schemes in heaven and even helped banish him to the earth have since been overcome by his deceptions – hook, line, and sinker.

Did Satan ever have a chance at winning? Define winning. If God rules the heavens with the consent of the governed, then the answer is clearly yes. This was never a contest of power; Lucifer could never win such a battle. It has always been a battle for the hearts and minds of heaven. Lucifer turned one-third of the noble and great ones from the Father, and he did so right under His nose. Here in mortality, he has corrupted the world numerous times, once to such a degree that a global reset was required. Since then, all three nations of Israel have fallen: the Northern Kingdom, the Kingdom of Judah, and the Nephite nation of Joseph. He is an absolute master of his craft. Those who can navigate Lucifer's labyrinth of lies and deceptions have always been the exception, not the rule.

Therefore, when Lucifer began his scheming in heaven, he did so with supreme confidence that, given the time, he would eventually have overturned the order of heaven. Given his track record on the earth, it is hard to deny this. Yet, while Lucifer was free to exercise his agency, he could not control how long God would permit him to continue unchecked. Satan prefers to act in the background, secretly whispering in our ears. For his plan to work, he must achieve a critical mass before the light of day shines upon his works. When the light of heaven illuminated Lucifer's secret machinations, a war in heaven ensued, and he was cast out through the strength of our testimonies in the Father's Only Begotten Son.

However, the war did not end; it merely had a venue change. The noble and great ones that defeated Satan primordially are now navigating a society wherein Satan is on the verge of flipping the script once more. As bad as it is now, his greatest deceptions lay ahead of us. Yet, many of the most valiant amongst us are going into this last great battle as ill-prepared as the most foolish of the ten virgins. May God have mercy upon us, and may He grant the prayers of our heavenly families that are praying on our behalf before His mighty throne both day and night as the events of this earth cycle near their epic concluding crescendo.

As I consider these things, I can't help but contemplate the majesty of the Father's plan, His incredible humility, generosity, mercy, and longsuffering compared to the breathtaking audacity and pride of Satan. Although the vast majority of heaven's hosts will succumb to Satan's lies and deceptions to one degree or another, the Father has prepared the way for our deliverance. He will not cause us to suffer in Hell forever. All our sufferings are for our good. The full consequences of those who believe Satan's lies will eventually transform all but the very few.

Even the vilest sinner, who will be relegated to the burning mountain ranges overlooking Satan's great pit of hellish fire, will eventually be transformed and perfected, receiving from the Father all that they are willing to receive. Ultimately, even these will inherit kingdoms of glory that are beyond description for their wonder and glory. As I contemplate the writings of Enoch and his insights into the mysteries of the multiverse, I am compelled to consider the very powers of heaven and the forces that govern all things. I speak of the Glory and Power that is held by the Almighty Gods. I will dedicate the next chapter to this subject.

Chapter 5: Glory and Power

Let me begin this chapter with a disclaimer. We do not know the true nature of Glory and, thereby, the powers upon which the heavens operate. As such, just as with the previous chapters, this chapter will still take us deeper into the quantum realms of gospel theory. Let us begin with the only resource provided by the Church regarding the study of this topic. Consider the following:

> In the scriptures, glory often refers to God's light and truth. It may also refer to praise or honor and to a certain condition of eternal life or to the glory of God. (Guide to the Scriptures - lds.org)

Per the statement above, it is clear that we do not understand what glory is. However, based on the many scriptures that speak of it, our best minds believe it may be correlated with praise and honor. What a curious concept! Could the glory or power of God really be derived from the praise and honor of those who worship Him? The very concept sounds crass and even blasphemous. Yet, Enoch and many others have often spoken of the innumerable host of heaven, praising God with both prayer and song. At its most fundamental level, worship is based on praise, honor, and veneration. As such, consider the following insights into the overt satanic activities of which the scriptures have made us aware:

> The devil taketh [Christ] up into an exceeding high mountain, and sheweth Him all the <u>kingdoms</u> of the world, and the glory of them; and saith unto Him, **All these things will I give Thee, if thou wilt fall down and worship me.** Then saith Jesus unto him, Get thee hence, <u>Satan</u>: for it is written, Thou shalt <u>worship</u> the Lord thy God, and Him only shalt thou serve. (Mat 4:8-9)

And

> <u>Satan</u> came <u>tempting</u> [Moses], saying: Moses, son of man, **worship me!** And it came to pass that Moses looked upon Satan and said: Who art thou? For behold, I am a <u>son</u> of God, in the similitude of his Only Begotten; and **where is thy <u>glory</u>, that I should worship thee?**

Behold, I could not look upon God, except His <u>glory</u> should come upon me, and I were transfigured before Him. But I <u>can</u> look upon thee in the natural man. Is it not so, surely?...

Now, when Moses had said these words, <u>Satan</u> cried with a loud voice, and ranted upon the earth, and commanded, saying: **I am the <u>Only Begotten</u>, worship me!**

And it came to pass that Moses began to <u>fear</u> exceedingly; and as he began to fear, he saw the bitterness of <u>Hell</u>. Nevertheless, <u>calling</u> upon God, he received <u>strength</u>, and he commanded, saying: **Depart from me, Satan, for this one God only will I worship, which is the God of <u>Glory</u>.** (Moses 1: 12-14; 19-20)

And

And they [the world] **worshipped the dragon** which gave power unto the <u>beast</u>: and **they <u>worshipped</u> the beast**, saying, Who is like unto the beast? Who is able to make war with him? And there was given unto him a <u>mouth</u> [the antichrist] speaking great things and <u>blasphemies</u>... And he opened his mouth in blasphemy against God, to blaspheme His <u>name</u>, and His tabernacle, and them that dwell in heaven.

And it was given unto him to make war with the saints, and to overcome them: and <u>power</u> was given him over all kindreds, and tongues, and nations. **And all that dwell upon the earth shall worship him**...

And he doeth great wonders, so that he maketh fire come down from heaven on the earth in the sight of men, and <u>deceiveth</u> them that dwell on the earth by the means of those <u>miracles</u> which he had power to do in the sight of the beast; saying to them that dwell on the earth, that they should make an image to the beast...

And he had power to give life unto the image of the beast, that the image of the beast should both speak, and **cause that as many as would not worship the image of the beast should be killed**. (Rev 13:4-8, 13-15)

In all three of these overt examples, Satan sought, first and foremost, to be worshiped. Both Christ and Moses rebuffed Satan, stating that they would only ever worship God. In those two examples, the power of Satan remained constrained. However, in the last example, Satan obtains his ultimate desire and is worshiped openly across the globe by this cycle's most noble and great ones. Therefore, are we to believe that it is merely a coincidence that the ubiquitous worship of Satan that will prevail upon this earth in the last days aligns with the days of the dragon's greatest power? Such an exhibition does indeed suggest that there is a direct correlation between glory/power, worship, praise, and honor.

For some peculiar reason, many in the LDS community believe that God would never allow Satan to obtain so much power upon the earth. Indeed, most of the saints do not believe there will be an antichrist. Such do not know the half of it. If they cannot accept that there will be an antichrist, they will in no way be prepared for the events and personalities that will be described in one of the last chapters of this book.

These have come to believe that rather than a few compelling individuals, there will instead be merely a state of generalized apostasy and forsaking of Christianity. These believe the powers at work, while pervasive, will remain hidden. Such will not be the case. These naive beliefs render them woefully unprepared for the day of Satan's greatest power. Many will justify their ignorance through the false belief that the prophets have never spoken of such things.

This is not the case; many simply choose to ignore prophets as soon as they die. By this reckoning, a dead prophet is no prophet at all. I hear things like, "nobody has talked about secret combinations since Ezra T. Benson, if it was important they would keep talking about it." President Nelson turns 100 this year. When he dies, will all his teachings become irrelevant? This line of thinking happens all the time, and is utter foolishness.

President John Taylor, another dead prophet, is credited with writing an urgent letter to the entire Church regarding issues they would face in the last days. The title of this letter was THE COMING CRISIS AND HOW TO MEET IT. His letter occupied the lead story in two back-to-back editions of the Millennial Star. The Millennial Star became the Ensign in 1970. Consider what it would mean today if two consecutive Ensigns ran the same lead story. This highlights the importance that the Church gave this letter at the time. Consider the following excerpts from this letter.

> A GREAT and awful crisis is at hand — such a crisis was never known before since the foundation of the world.

…Perhaps you will be disappointed, if I tell you that the time is coming, and now is, when, not only God, the Highest of all, shall be revealed in spirit and in mighty power, but the Devil or Satan also, will be revealed in signs and wonders, and in mighty deeds! This, reader, is the great key to all the marvelous events that are to transpire shortly upon the earth.

Now just stop right here, and pause, and mark emphatically this key. Then you and I will proceed to unlock the mysteries and to prepare ourselves to the battle. For there will be no neutrals in the approaching controversy, I say again, that God the Highest of all will make bare His arm in the eyes of all nations. And the heavens even will be rent, and the lighting down of His power will be felt by all nations. But this is not all. Satan also will be revealed. He has made some manifestations of his power in different periods of the world, but never before has there been such an array of numbers on his side, never before such a consolidation of armies and rulers, never before has there been such an imposing and overwhelming exhibition of miracles as Satan will shortly make manifest. Don't suppose for a moment, that I am uttering dark sayings or speaking unadvisedly upon speculation or the strength of mere human opinion.

Don't tell me about Popes and Prelates sitting in the Temple of God as God. One far greater than any Pope or Prelate is soon to be revealed, and he will claim to be worshipped as God. Now, remember, that it is no modern wicked man that is going to claim divine honors. No, it is that old Serpent, the Devil. He it is that will head the opposition against God and His Christ. And he, the son of perdition it is, that will be allowed a much longer chain than heretofore.

Such will be the greatness of his power, that it will seem to many that he is entirely loose. He will be so far unshackled and unchained that his power will deceive all nations, even the world. And the elect will barely escape the power of his sorceries, enchantments, and miracles! And even God, Himself, the true God, will contribute to put means and instruments in his way and at hand, for his use, so that he can have a full trial of his strength and cunning, with all deceivableness of unrighteousness in them that perish.

Now there is a greater destruction coming upon the wicked nations of the earth, than was even experienced by Pharaoh at the Red Sea. But before that destruction can be made manifest, men's hearts will be hardened, and wickedness will rise to a more over towering height than many bygone generations have been allowed to witness... And great shall be that scene. The Devil in the last stage of desperation, will take such a pre-eminent lead in literature, politics, philosophy, and religion; in wars, famines, pestilences, earthquakes, thunderings and lightnings, setting cities in conflagration, etc., that mighty kings and powerful nations will be constrained to fall down and worship him. And they will marvel at his great power, and wonder after him with great astonishment. For His signs and wonders will be among all nations.

Men will be raised for the express purpose of furthering the designs and marvelous works of the devil. Every description of curious and mysterious arts that penetrate beyond the common pale of human sagacity and wisdom, will be studied and practiced beyond what has been known by mere mortals. The great capabilities of the elements of fire, air, earth, and water, will be brought into requisition by cunning men under the superior cunning of the prince and the god of this world. And, inflated with the knowledge of these wonderful arts and powers, men will become boasters, heady, high-minded, proud, and despisers of that which is good. But the God who is above all, and over all, and who ruleth in the armies of heaven, and amongst the inhabitants of the earth, will not be a silent observer of such spiritual wickedness in high places, and among the rulers of the darkness of this world. For the master spirits of wickedness of all ages, and of worlds visible and invisible, will be arrayed in the rebellious ranks before the closing scene shall transpire...

Who shall be able to withstand? Do you think that your great sagacity and the compass of your profound, philosophical turn of mind will enable you to detect the error and delusion of these arts? Oh, man, this is a vain hope. Your mind will not be competent to detect the delusion. God Himself will allow Satan to ply your scrutinizing eye with powers and sophistications far beyond your capacity to detect. Do you say then, I will stand aloof from investigation, I will shun all acquaintance with these mysterious workings, in order that I may not be carried away with their delusive influence. Vain hope. Oh, man, you cannot be neutral. You must choose your side and put on your armor.

Those that come not up to the help of the Lord in the day of battle, will be sorely cursed. The captive Hebrew Daniel stood up boldly against all the governors and whole realm of Babylon with their monarch at their head. Daniel readily acknowledged that it was not from any wisdom in him, above other men, that he could surpass the astrologers and magicians. By holding intercourse with the God of heaven, he became endowed with supernatural comprehension that effectually shielded him against supernatural delusion. Thereby he escaped the snare that entwined around the great statesmen and governors of that immense empire of Babylon. Thereby those who take refuge in the name of the Lord and in immediate revelation from heaven, will be safe, and no others.

He that is not for God and the principle of immediate revelation, will inevitably be ensnared, overcome and destroyed. Because he that is not for Him must be against Him. No man in any age was ever for God, that did not hold intercourse with Him personally, and receive for himself the revelations of His will. The rock of revelation, by which Peter knew Jesus Christ, is the only basis upon which any man can escape the strong delusion which God will send among the nations through Satan and his mediums and coadjutors.

You cannot know God without present revelation. Did you ever think of this most solemn and essential truth before? You may have been accustomed to pray, all your life time, and as yet you, even you, do not know God. You may have heard many thousand sermons, with a sincere desire both to remember and practice them, and yet you do not know God. But it has been decided in the court of heaven, that no man can know the Father but the Son, and he to whom the Son

REVEALETH Him. Now, has Jesus Christ ever revealed God the Father to you, dear reader?

Be honest with yourself, and do not err in your answer to this most important question. However much the Son may have revealed the Father to Prophets, Patriarchs, and Apostles of old, the question still remains in full force — has He revealed the Father to YOU? A revelation to another man is by no means a revelation to YOU!

Don't say now, as some do, that revelation was anciently given in order to establish the truth, and being once established it is no longer necessary to be revealed to subsequent generations of people. Don't say this for your life, for revelation is just as necessary to establish truth now as it was then. You need the ministry of angels now, just as much as people did then. They in past ages could not know God, nor say for a certainty, from personal knowledge, that Jesus Christ was the Christ, only by the Holy Ghost — and **you are just as weak and dependent as they!** You most assuredly cannot call Jesus, Lord, only by the Holy Ghost.

Now, reader, you need present revelation from God to your own dear self, in order to help you out of this nasty, confused labyrinth, and to set your feet firmly upon the solid rock of revelation. Mere flesh and blood cannot help you now. It requires an Almighty arm to effect your deliverance. Therefore, put no more trust in man, for a curse rests upon him that will be guided by the precepts of man.

I do not ask you to be guided by what I say to you, unless the Lord from heaven shall reveal to you that I speak the truth, even as it is in Christ. Although I know that I am declaring heaven's truth to you, in all sobriety, yet, my knowing it, does not suffice for you. You also must know it for yourself, and not from another. This is your right and your privilege. For God has made this promise to you, and not to you, reader, only, but to all others whom He calls to repentance. Now, go and get revelation for yourself!

Reader, be resolute! This is a critical and trying moment with you…. if you are honestly, without prejudice, meditating upon what you now read, then God's Spirit is sweetly persuading you to believe what I say. The faint dawn of the Spirit is even now upon your mind. Now, reader, cherish this little dawn of light until the daylight of more truth shines more clearly upon your mind. Pray mightily for the Spirit of Revelation to rest upon you, that you may KNOW the things that are freely given to you of God… And you will not barely believe, and hope, and fear, but you will KNOW, from present and personal revelation, that the Lord is a God at hand, revealing Himself as freely as He ever did in Patriarchal days… You will then feel deep pity and sorrow for anyone that says he doesn't need present revelation! You will then discover the pride of such an one's heart, and mourn over him as one that is blinded by the god of this world. (Millennial Star, April 30, 1853 Vol 15, page 273)

According to John Taylor, the trial days will be challenging because Satan will obtain more power than the saints were prepared for him to obtain. His power and miracles will be omnipresent in the last days, and the only hope that men will have on that day of not being deceived will be the ability to receive the constant guiding influence of the Holy Ghost. Does this sound familiar? Clearly, President Taylor's admonishment and warnings strike a familiar tone with any who have diligently studied these events while seeking to be taught by the Lord.

We have been warned and forewarned! Yet, President Taylor is dead, unfortunately, for some, because he is now dead, so are his words of warning. Why would Christ command us to study the words of the prophets if they became obsolete upon their death? This idea is the epitome of foolishness. Such a belief is the primary reason that the Lord stated that the entire Church was and remained under condemnation for taking the things we have received lightly.

It is, therefore, up to us to act for ourselves or to be acted upon. All such fools believe they are different and stronger than every preceding generation. Recall that all the great kingdoms of the earth have ended in abrupt albeit spectacular failure because of their own stupidity and spiritual blindness. For the majority, our generation will be no different! The last days' events will soon be upon us, whether you believe in them or not or are prepared for them. May God have mercy upon those who have been apathetic in their approach to receiving personal revelation.

Now, with this sidebar concluded, we return to the subject at hand. I believe that evidence suggests that Satan will be empowered and glorified by the worship and honor that the world will freely give him. To understand the mechanics of how such a thing is possible, we must, as noted at the beginning of this chapter, turn to the theoretical realm. Within the appendices of my book – Delight In Plainness, I spoke at length regarding the Light of Christ. In conjunction with that analysis, I referenced the dual slit experiment. The Dual Slit experiment has been reproduced numerous times to the absolute astonishment of the scientific community. The takeaway of the Dual Slit experiment is that human consciousness changes the behavior of quantum particles, causing subatomic particles to act like either waves or particles depending upon whether they are being observed by human consciousness or not.

Therefore, there is scientific evidence that the Universe's physical and spiritual forces interact inexplicably in quantum realms. The Lord has stated that all things were created spiritually before they were created physically. Therefore, if there is a quantum realm in the physical world, there is also a quantum realm in the spiritual world. Indeed, it would seem that the quantum realm is where the physical and spiritual intersect.

I believe the same force of consciousness that impacts the physical nature of subatomic particles also impacts their spiritual counterparts. If so, glory must be a real and derivative force of nature that stems from this phenomenon. I suggest that just as human conscience has a real and physical impact upon the behavior of subatomic particles, so the act of worship has real, quantifiable impacts upon both the spiritual and physical realms at the quantum level. I further theorize that if the consciousness of one human observer can have a physical impact on subatomic particles in the quantum realm, then the concentrated and focused efforts of many practitioners can and will have a more pronounced impact on those same quantum forces. Thus, where one or two are gathered in the Lord's name, He has promised to be in their midst.

Therefore, consider now that the vast majority of the human family that chose to participate in the Father's great plan of happiness will eventually inherit a degree of Glory within the kingdoms of heaven, except for the sons of perdition, who will be few in number. We are told that throughout all these kingdoms, every knee will bend, and every tongue will confess that Jesus is the Christ. As has been discussed previously, at this time, I believe that Jesus Christ will become the Great Father and Architect of the next iteration of the Father's plan of happiness. However, until this happens, all the spiritual energy, worship, and devotion is centered not upon Jesus Christ but upon His Father. Not at any time has the Son asked to be worshiped in place of the Father. Indeed, in 3rd Nephi, Christ apologized for the ignorance of His disciples, who prayed to Him instead of the Father. Thus, the great plan of happiness concentrates this incredible and endless source of spiritual energy upon one being - God the Father.

Now, in addition to the worship and veneration by participants in the current iteration of the plan of salvation, consider the focused worship of all prior iterations of this plan. Then add to these the power and force of will of those mighty Patriarchs who sit enthroned upon the northern sides of the Mount of the Congregation. The consciousness of each God likely rivals the cumulative consciousness of all the beings in an entire iteration of the plan of salvation. These ascendent Gods are just as one with the Father as are the Son and Holy Ghost.

As such, if these things are true, then the power of God is the result of the most concentrated dose of praise, honor, worship, and veneration available in the multiverse. As such, with but a word, worlds are and cease to exist. With nothing more than Divine Utterance, galaxies form or are obliterated. It simply is not possible that a greater power than this could exist. This power and glory is concentrated upon a single Man. He's a Man who, throughout the process of time, has proved Himself to be the Unquestioned Peer of the kindest, Most Loving, and Merciful Beings in the multiverse. Indeed, it is only upon such a being as this that such power can or ought to be concentrated. This power source is as vast and endless as the multiverse itself.

Therefore, as if by design, the most powerful force in the multiverse can only be wielded by the most righteous of Men. That Man is the Almighty God of Heaven and Earth. Only a being as benevolent as this would voluntarily relinquish such power to be conferred upon another and then rise to take His place upon the Mount of the Congregation. It is not difficult to see the types and shadows of the divine order of heaven manifested in the Constitution of the United States of America, which constitution was authored by God Himself through the inspiration of inspired men to whom He raised up for the cause.

As such, Satan has, from the beginning, sought to establish himself as a king and a father over those who would venerate and honor him. Truly, it would seem that such incredible power such as this can only be obtained through the consent of the governed. However, once this power is obtained, it may be wielded according to the will of the endowed. As such, the elements themselves will obey. Thus, in the last days, Satan will exercise real and marvelous power, for which the world will have no answer. Yet, as astounding as the power of Satan will be, it will be absolutely nothing compared to the power and glory of God and upon those to whom He so chooses to endow. While this power cannot be self-imposed, God can most certainly confer it upon any with whom He will share it. This is the meaning behind priesthood power abiding upon a god and his posterity throughout all time and eternity. This is the precise meaning behind the following passage:

And no man taketh this <u>honor</u> (the honor of priesthood power) unto himself, but he that is <u>called</u> of God, as was <u>Aaron</u>. So also Christ glorified not Himself to be made an high priest; but He that said unto Him, Thou art my <u>Son</u>, today have I begotten thee.

As He saith also in another place, Thou art a <u>priest</u> <u>forever</u> after the order of <u>Melchisedec</u>. Who in the days of His flesh [*meaning during the days of Christ's mortality*], when He had offered up <u>prayers</u> and supplications with <u>strong crying</u> and tears unto Him that was able to save Him from death, and was heard <u>in that He feared</u> [*referring to when Christ prayed unto the Father and begged Him to take the bitter cup from Him*]; though He were a Son, yet He <u>learned</u> <u>obedience</u> by the things which He <u>suffered</u>; and being made <u>perfect</u>, He became the <u>author</u> of eternal <u>salvation</u> unto all them that obey Him; called of God an <u>high priest</u> after the order of Melchisedec.

Of whom we have many things to say, and <u>hard</u> to be <u>uttered</u>, seeing ye are dull of <u>hearing</u>. For when for the time ye ought to be teachers, ye have need that one teach you again which be the first principles of the oracles of God; and are become such as have need of <u>milk</u>, and not of strong meat. (Hebrews 5:4-12)

Paul taught that Christ was endowed with priesthood power through His Father and not of Himself. Indeed, Paul taught that no man can take up priesthood power of his own will, but rather, it must be conferred upon him by the condescension of the All-Powerful God. After all, God is the ultimate source of such endowments, given that He is the only Being in the multiverse that is endowed with such a miraculously unfathomable and relentlessly inexhaustible source of power and glory. Paul concludes his teaching with a backhanded slap to the heads of the Hebrews, for he felt that they should be the ones teaching such doctrines instead of needing to be taught them from him. Such goes back to the teaching of President Taylor regarding the need for constant and immediate revelation to be able to survive the coming deceptions.

We learn the following through modern revelation regarding this same power, which I mean power in the priesthood.

All they who receive this priesthood receive Me, saith the Lord; for he that receiveth My servants receiveth Me; and he

that receiveth me receiveth my Father; and he that receiveth
My Father receiveth My Father's kingdom; therefore all that
My Father hath shall be given unto him. (D&C 84:35-38)

Christ can speak of such incredible promises because He and His Father are one. His Father was one in Christ's position, and Christ will soon take upon Himself the role of the Father. As such, these promises are indisputable and as sure and reliable as the sun's setting. They are incredible to consider!

Chapter 6: The Epiphany of Nicodemus

In the prior chapters, we have been reviewing Enoch's vision regarding those who sleep not and worship before the throne of God. We learned of their intense interest in the noble and great ones who dwell upon the earth. I expressed my opinion of how I believe these represent the hundreds of trillions of heavenly parents who have obtained the Celestial kingdom and Household of God from prior iterations of the Plan of Salvation. We also learned of four different beings on each side of the throne of God: Michael, Gabriel, Raphael, and Phanuel. I postulated that these four men, who were the only spirits described as being present at that meeting, were there because they were essential leaders amongst the spirits participating in this iteration of the plan of salvation. I speak not of the noble and great ones on this planet but throughout the cosmos. I theorized that of the four of these, Phanuel was the greatest of all. Phanuel means the Face of God, referring to the fact that Christ was created in the express image of His Father. I believe that Phanuel was simply another premortal title for Jesus Christ. Phanuel, we learned, holds the keys to repentance and eternal life. He also rebuked the Satans, prohibiting them from accusing the children of heaven before His Father's throne.

As Enoch's vision continues in this chapter, he moves from the heavenly courts of the Father to a sweeping overview of the degrees of glory. As such, he will discuss the sun, moon, and stars. In describing these, it is important to note that he is doing so allegorically, as will become clear. He also provides further insight into another class of heavenly beings, which we have only hinted at in prior chapters.

Enoch's vision continues as follows:

> **41.1**. And after that I saw all the secrets of the heavens, and how the kingdom is divided, and how the actions of men are weighed in the balance.

According to the passage above, Enoch considers the things he saw taking place before the throne of God in the prior chapter to be the secrets of the heavens. If the meaning behind the things I have postulated in the prior chapter are true, they represent some of God's greatest mysteries. The Mysteries of God are hidden for a reason.

One of the primary reasons such things are hidden is that they require spiritual maturity and strength to properly conceptualize and internalize. In this manner, growing in the knowledge of God is like a chick hatching from the shell. The baby chick must expend the energy to crack its shell on its own. If the shell is cracked and peeled by another to help the chick see the wonder of its awaiting world, the chick often dies a victim of its own weakness. The struggle of birth was a prerequisite. This is the meaning behind the following passage:

> It is given unto many to know the mysteries of God; nevertheless they are laid under a strict command that they shall not impart only according to the portion of His word which He doth grant unto the children of men, according to the heed and diligence which they give unto Him.
>
> And therefore, he that will harden his heart, the same receiveth the lesser portion of the word; and he that will not harden his heart, to him is given the greater portion of the word, until it is given unto him to know the mysteries of God until he know them in full. And they that will harden their hearts, to them is given the lesser portion of the word until they know nothing concerning His mysteries (Alma 12:9-11)

To lay the kingdom's mysteries before those who are not diligently seeking them is the equivalent of cracking and peeling open the shell of a baby chick. It is a service that does more harm than good. One can persuade others to seek knowledge from the Lord, but if they will not seek it, the information cannot and should not be forced upon them. I am often asked why we do not hear more of these things in general conferences. The Lord does not want His prophets and leaders to crack and peel away our shells for us. That is not their job. Their job is to invite us and encourage us to do this for ourselves. How often have you heard invitations to come and hear the Lord for yourself? Consider one such admonition from President Nelson at the General Conference:

> I urge you to stretch beyond your current spiritual ability to receive personal revelation, for the Lord has promised that "if thou shalt seek, thou shalt receive revelation upon revelation, knowledge upon knowledge…" Oh, there is so much more that your Father in Heaven wants you to know.

This is a powerful and important invitation for us to rend the confinement of our shells by piercing the veil of our disbelief through faith in Jesus Christ. We must believe that He means the things that He says. Yet, our living prophets give us marvelous counsel about such things, and yet few have ears to hear it.

On the other hand, not all that is mysterious is true. I have offered many theories within this and other books I have written. Because I have made some true observations, it does not mean all of my observations are true. Consider the things I have shared, but you must ponder them yourself. You must take them to the Lord and learn for yourself. Too many people skip this important step. As such, they are deceived by false mysteries. To be taught of God's mysteries by men rather than God is inherently dangerous. It exposes you to deception and apostasy.

God is the keeper of truth, and by the power of the Holy Ghost, you may know the truth of all things. Truth exists independent of opinion and often eludes the human mind because of preconceived bias or erroneous understanding. Yet the truth is out there, and if we are to find it, we must bring ourselves to it, for rare are the times that it comes to us unsought for. With regards to these things, and particularly the postulated theories I have put forth, particularly in the present series on Enoch's writings, the Lord has said the following:

> God shall give unto you knowledge by His Holy Spirit, yea, by the unspeakable gift of the Holy Ghost, that has not been revealed since the world was until now; which our forefathers have awaited with anxious expectation to be revealed in the last times, which their minds were pointed to by the angels, as held in reserve for the fulness of their glory; a time to come in the which nothing shall be withheld, whether there be one God or many gods, they shall be manifest. (D&C 121:26-28)

Our forefathers saw that the mysteries of God would be revealed in the last days by the power of the Holy Ghost. Given the agency's vital role in the Plan of Salvation, the Holy Ghost reveals truths to those seeking them. God does not force truth upon anyone. Indeed, in the opening verse of this chapter, Enoch associated the mysteries of God with how the children of heaven would be judged and the kingdoms of glory divided. Do the mysteries of God really impact our salvation? Consider the following extracts that were taken from the Bible dictionary's definition of revelation:

> Divine revelation is one of the grandest concepts and principles of the gospel of Jesus Christ, **for without it, man could not know of the things of God and could not be saved with any degree of salvation in the eternities**…The principle of gaining knowledge by revelation is the principle of salvation.

Do the mysteries of God impact our salvation? ABSOLUTELY! This is a profound, albeit terrifying, concept. We are responsible for receiving the personal revelation that we must receive. Without revelation, we could not be saved with any degree of salvation in the eternities. Said another way, if all you or I know about the gospel of Jesus Christ is what others have taught us and not by the Lord Himself through personal revelation, our foundation is built upon the sand and will eventually be washed away. The concept of unlocking the mysteries of God is a constant theme of Enoch's writings. As such, we will revisit this topic continuously. Enoch's revelation continues:

> **41.2**. And there I saw the mansions of the elect and the mansions of the holy, and mine eyes saw there all the sinners being driven from thence which deny the name of the Lord of Spirits, and being dragged off: and they could not abide because of the punishment which proceeds from the Lord of Spirits.

Yikes! This reminds me of a scene from the movie Ghost, where the wicked are dragged to Hell, desperately scratching and clawing at anything in their reach in an attempt to escape. Conversely, the passage also references heavenly mansions that are located in the presence of the Lord of Spirits. The wicked have no place amongst these mansions and also in the presence of the Father. If the Book of Enoch is what it claims to be, then this reference to the Father's heavenly mansions is the oldest such reference in any Biblical text. It is an odd reference. One typically does not think of houses as heaven, much less mansions, yet throughout the scriptures, there are many confirmations that the heavenly mansions of Enoch's visions do exist. For example, consider how Enos, the Book of Mormon prophet, chose to conclude his record:

> And I soon go to the place of my rest, which is with my Redeemer; for I know that in Him I shall rest. And I rejoice in the day when my mortal shall put on immortality, and shall stand before Him; then shall I see His face with pleasure, and He will say unto me: Come unto Me, ye blessed, there is a place prepared for you in the mansions of My Father. Amen. (Enos 1:27)

Enos engraved these words upon plates of gold around the year 420 BC; as such, outside of the Book of Enoch, this is the second oldest known reference to the Father's heavenly mansions. Yet, Enos's usage of this concept was presented very matter-of-factly. The next person to use this phrase would be Jesus Christ. This suggests that the concept of heavenly mansions was familiar to people of antiquity by way of the Book of Enoch. As such, the Brass Plates must have included a copy of these writings.

> In my Father's house are many mansions: if it were not so, I would have told you. I go to prepare a place for you. (John 14:2)

Christ's used the same matter-of-fact approach to this concept as Enos. Indeed, Christ is effectively saying, guys, if Enoch's book was fake, I would have told you it was. Instead, Peter, John, and Jude quote it in their New Testament accounts. This should provide much food for thought, particularly when the Lord bluntly states that the Book of Enoch will be testified of in due time – see D&C 107:57.

As Enoch's vision continues, it becomes more allegorical, which is why this section of his writings has been called the Book of Parables. The mystery behind his allegory is the distinction between the righteous and the wicked and the separations of the kingdoms of God, as noted in the opening verses of this chapter. We will discuss these things in due course:

> **41.3**. And there mine eyes saw the secrets of the lightning and of the thunder, and the secrets of the winds, how they are divided to blow over the earth, and the secrets of the clouds and dew, and there I saw from whence they proceed in that place and from whence they saturate the dusty earth.

> **41.4**. And there I saw closed chambers out of which the winds are divided, the chamber of the hail and winds, the chamber of the mist, and of the clouds, and the cloud thereof hovers over the earth from the beginning of the world.

Enoch opens this next verse by saying, "**And there,**" referring to the same location where the mansions of the righteous would be located. We know that the righteous will inherit the New Jerusalem, and this Earth will become the Celestial Kingdom. We also know that these lands will be purged from all unrighteousness before the New Jerusalem is established. The wicked will literally be dragged away by the upcoming judgements of God. The flashes of lightning, thundering, winds, and rains are all associated with the coming storm that will purge the lands of their wickedness.

You will recall that the destruction upon the North American continent that preceded the Lord's first coming was initiated by a storm that had never been seen. Consider the following description of that event:

> And it came to pass in the thirty and fourth year, in the first month, on the fourth day of the month, there arose a great storm, such an one as never had been known in all the land. And there was also a great and terrible tempest; and there was terrible thunder, insomuch that it did shake the whole earth as if it was about to divide asunder. And there were

exceedingly sharp lightnings, such as never had been known
in all the land. (3 Nephi 8:5-7)

I believe this is the meaning of the lighting, thunder, winds, and rains that Enoch saw being held in heavenly chambers on high. The Lord is merciful and longsuffering. He has reserved these judgements until the Earth is fully ripened in iniquity; yet, just as the heavenly judgements of God were poured out upon the American continent in times past, these chambers will be emptied soon.

Enoch will expound upon some of these elements further in the narrative. When he does so, we will be reminded of the double-edged sword so often spoken of concerning the judgements of heaven. The sword of justice is double-edged because it cuts both ways. This storm brings unimaginable horrors to the wicked but to the blessings of righteousness. Just as the winds and lighting of a storm can destroy and burn, the rains can water and nourish.

This dual symbolism is found throughout the teachings of Jesus Christ. Earlier in this volume, I reviewed the title Son of Man and its origins from the Book of Enoch. I discussed how Jesus Christ used this term to describe Himself more than any other messianic phrase. I have found that when Christ uses the term, He typically expounds a doctrine that originates in the Book of Enoch, like the title Son of Man. I believe this is the case for the meaning of the wind, as portrayed in Enoch's allegory. Consider Christ's teachings in this regard:

> The wind bloweth where it listeth, and thou hearest the sound thereof, but canst not tell whence it cometh, and whither it goeth: so is every one that is born of the Spirit.
>
> Nicodemus answered and said unto him, How can these things be?
>
> Jesus answered and said unto him, Art thou a master of Israel, and knowest not these things? Verily, verily, I say unto thee, We speak that we do know, and testify that we have seen; and ye receive not our witness. If I have told you earthly things, and ye believe not, how shall ye believe, if I tell you of heavenly things?
>
> No man hath ascended up to heaven, but He that came down from heaven, even the Son of Man which is in heaven. And as Moses lifted up the serpent in the wilderness, even so must

the Son of Man be lifted up: That whosoever believeth in
Him should not perish, but have eternal life. (John 3:8-15)

In the above passages, Christ is teaching Nicodemus, a "master of Israel," regarding things he should have known but did not. This is not dissimilar to Paul's rebuke to the Hebrews about needing milk when they should be eating meat. Christ spoke of the wind as a metaphor. When the wind blows through a town, it blows upon everything within the town, but its impact on its residents varies. For example, the laundry out on the line will flap away in the wind, yet a person within the walls of their home may not even be aware that the wind is blowing. A person's acknowledgement of the wind has no bearing on its existence. However, those who acknowledge its presence can learn to engage the wind, using it to dry the laundry or pump water via a windmill.

The same is true for the spiritual winds in our lives. In this regard, Christ likened the wind to the Holy Ghost. You cannot see the wind itself, but you can feel its presence and observe how it impacts things. So, just as the wind is all around us, so is the Light of Christ, which is given to every man and is also all around us. Yet, not every man will acknowledge its presence nor engage with it. To be born of the Spirit is to open your heart to God's influence through the Holy Ghost in your life. The more you focus upon this Spirit, the more its presence is felt in your life and its utility harnessed.

Christ likened the knowledge born by the wind or Holy Ghost to the knowledge of the Son of Man, the mysterious figure from the Book of Enoch. To many, the Son of Man was nothing more than an obscure figure from a strange book of ancient scripture attributed to a little-known prediluvian character. However, to those who were paying attention to the proverbial winds in their lives, the mystery of the Son of Man became their saving grace.

Christ specifically likened the brazen serpent lifted up in the wilderness to heal the people as a type and shadow of Enoch's Son of Man. Those who sought to be taught by the Spirit of God could learn and understand these things. To such, the Spirit could whisper to both heart and mind. Yet, those who were otherwise engaged or had outsourced their spiritual education to others learned nothing from the passing winds. Nicodemus had ignored the winds for many years, yet now the winds had prompted him to seek a private audience with a true Master in Israel. While Nicodemus was also a master in Israel, his knowledge was largely based upon the teachings of men and not the Spirit.

When Nicodemus realized the shortcomings of his own ignorance, he was shocked. Before Christ opened his eyes, despite being a master in Israel, he had no idea of the true nature of the gospel that he had spent his whole life studying. Nicodemus's shocking experience has played out countless times. Everything changes when you seek to be taught by the Spirit of God.

The Spirit of God is typically the quietest voice in the room. On the other hand, the spirit of the evil one is loud and proud and rings with unsolicited noise in our heads. Satan's message is amplified and broadcast across every platform in the Whore of Babylon's arsenal. Many people believe that any thought or idea that comes into their mind is of God. Nothing could be further from the truth. Satan can put fully developed thoughts and ideas into our minds at will. He can use images and cravings to further his demonic ends. He can monitor our reaction to his impressions and refine his messaging accordingly. He is the Father of lies and a true master of his craft.

There are ardent believers of an innumerable number of different faith traditions. Each is just as convinced they have found the truth as the next. Yet, reason dictates that this cannot be. Believing in something does not make it true. Despite what the world teaches, the truth is not subjective. Something is true, or it is not. Real truth can be circumscribed into one great whole. Truth cleaves unto the truth; it reconciles and fits. Lies and falsehoods contradict the gospel and, as such, stick out like neon signs of falsehoods.

I am so saddened by how easily people are deceived by blatantly obvious lies. LGBTQIA2S+ is a terrifying example of this. The lie is easy to see. If the entire world practiced strict adherence to homosexual behavior, the human race would go extinct. If fifty men and fifty transgender "women" were stranded on an island together, they would go extinct. The universal truth is that the family is based upon a biological man and woman. Strict adherence to any other philosophy or ideal will result in personal extinction. Strict adherence to "truths" that inevitably will result in extinction-level events do not come from God.

Religious violence motivated by extremist beliefs is another example of blatant falsehoods. God's law is rooted in free agency, love, persuasion, and longsuffering. It is Satan's work that is based on force. Radical environmentalism is another example of lies masquerading as truth. Critical race theory, engineered civil unrest, and agenda-driven news media are additional examples of this. The world is literally being torn apart by lies that are at total odds with the restored gospel of Jesus Christ and, therefore, easily identifiable as falsehoods. Yet, the gospel is brought into question and not the lie. Without the constant guiding influence of the Holy Ghost, people will be deceived.

The Light of Christ has been given to all men and women in every country and culture of the world. However, many become hardened by sin to the point that they become past feelings. When this happens, the hearts of loved men turn cold, and death lies at the door.

For the Spirit of the Lord will not always strive with man. And when the Spirit ceaseth to strive with man then cometh speedy destruction, and this grieveth my soul. (2 Nephi 26:11)

When the Holy Spirit is denied to the point that society becomes ripened in iniquity, the Spirit's gentle breeze will cease striving with men. When this happens, woe unto the world, for extinction lays at the door. Look to the rubble heap of dust and stones of every major civilization that has turned its back upon the Lord. These heaps of rubble were once vibrant and beautiful kingdoms now whispering from the dust. Beware! When the gentle winds of the Spirit cease to blow, society will soon reap the whirlwind! Beware the bitter east wind!

Enoch's vision continues:

> **41.5**. And I saw the chambers of the sun and moon, whence they proceed and whither they come again, and their glorious return, and how one is superior to the other, and their stately orbit, and how they do not leave their orbit, and they add nothing to their orbit and they take nothing from it, and they keep faith with each other, in accordance with the oath by which they are bound together.

> **41.6**. And first the sun goes forth and traverses his path according to the commandment of the Lord of Spirits, and mighty is His name for ever and ever.

> **41.7**. And after that I saw the hidden and the visible path of the moon, and she accomplishes the course of her path in that place by day and by night--the one holding a position opposite to the other before the Lord of Spirits. And they give thanks and praise and rest not; For unto them is their thanksgiving rest.

> **41.8**. For the sun changes oft for a blessing or a curse, and the course of the path of the moon is light to the righteous and darkness to the sinners in the name of the Lord, who made a separation between the light and the darkness, and divided the spirits of men, and strengthened the spirits of the righteous, in the name of His righteousness.

In the passages above, Enoch likens the separation of the spirits of men to the fixed orbits of the sun and the moon. He described how these orbits are fixed by the Lord of Spirits. If God can control the orbits of the sun, moon, and stars, He can also control the orbits of our personal lives. He can and will place us where we need to be, when we need to be there, and with whom we need to be for us to be able to accomplish His will in our lives.

The orbit of the sun and moon is such that the moon receives and reflects the sun's light when it would otherwise be dark on Earth. The moon has no light of its own but reflects the light of a higher order. Earlier in this chapter, we learned about the mansions in the Father's kingdom. This concept of heavenly mansions, first put forth in the writings of Enoch, is to be understood in the context of the fixed orbits of the sun and moon. There are many mansions in the kingdoms of the Father, and each mansion receives its light and glory from the same source, God the Father; however, how these various kingdoms of God receive their light mirrors how their inhabitants obtained light while they lived upon the Earth.

Previously, in this chapter, we reviewed certain extracts from the Bible Dictionary that stated that without personal revelation, humankind could not be saved with any degree of salvation. Revelation is light and truth. The more revelation one receives, the more light and knowledge one acquires. Light cleaves to light, and truth cleaves to truth. The righteous progresses from light to light and from truth to truth. Those who seek to obtain light will obtain an inheritance in a kingdom of light. Consider this concept in the context of the following passage:

> [Men] shall be judged according to their works, and every man shall receive according to his own works, his own dominion, in the mansions which are prepared (D&C 76:111)

I will be judged according to the light and knowledge that I was willing to receive, and you will be judged for the light and knowledge that you were willing to receive. The light and knowledge we receive enable us to fulfill the individual measures of our respective creations. The scriptures teach us that Christ did not receive fullness at first but received grace for grace. Line upon line, the Lord learned through the Spirit what He had come to earth to do. He learned how to fulfill the measure of His creation. Consider the following passages that speak of this.

> Now is my soul troubled; and what shall I say? Father, save Me from this hour: but for this cause came I unto this hour. (John 12:27)

Father, if thou be willing, remove this cup from me: nevertheless not my will, but thine, be done. And there appeared an angel unto Him from heaven, strengthening Him. And being in an agony He prayed more earnestly: and His sweat was as it were great drops of blood falling down to the ground. (Luke 22:42-44)

Behold I have given unto you my gospel, and this is the gospel which I have given unto you—that I came into the world to do the will of my Father, because my Father sent me. And my Father sent me that I might be lifted up upon the cross; and after that I had been lifted up upon the cross, that I might draw all men unto me… therefore, according to the power of the Father I will draw all men unto me, that they may be judged according to their works. (3 Nephi 27:13-15)

I have finished the work which thou gavest me to do. And now, O Father, glorify thou Me with thine Own Self with the glory which I had with Thee before the world was. (John 12:27; John 17:4-5)

All of these scripture passages, to one degree or another, discuss Christ fulfilling the measure of His creation. He was given work to perform by the Father before the world was created. He completed that work through personal revelation. The personal revelation led Christ to subject His own will to the will of the Father. This is the law of the Celestial Kingdom, and Christ was the perfect model for its completion.

It is not required of us to fulfill the measure of Christ's creation. We are not called upon to take upon ourselves the sins of the world. That was Christ's mission. As Christ learned of His personal mission from His Father, so must we learn from the Father regarding our personal missions in life. This is the pattern we must follow if we would return and become joint heirs with Him amongst the mansions of His Father.

In this respect, those who seek constant guidance and revelation in their lives will inherit a kingdom of light that is likened to the sun -the Celestial kingdom. The sun is our solar system's original light source, just as God the Father is the original source of truth and light. Others who choose not to receive their light directly from God but opt to receive it from men instead will inherit kingdoms of reflected glory rather than of fullness. Such kingdoms are represented by the moon. The moon does not generate light; it merely reflects a portion of the light from the original source. This is the difference between the Celestial Kingdom and the Terrestrial Kingdoms. Those who inherit kingdoms of reflected light do not receive the fullness of the Father.

Those who inherit the Telestial Kingdom are likened to the stars. Stars do not reflect the light of the sun nor of the moon but are lights unto themselves. Starlight is nothing compared to the blinding brilliance of the sun, nor does it compare to the moon's reflected brilliance. In like manner, those that will inherit the Telestial Kingdom rejected the light of the Father, and as such, they did not utilize the atonement of His Only Begotten Son. Instead, these paid the price of their own sins. Men can never make of themselves what the Father and His glorious Son could have made of them. As such, there are far fewer lights, and they receive the portion they are willing to receive.

We now return to Enoch's parable:

> **41.9**. For no angel hinders and no power is able to hinder;
> for He appoints a judge for them all and He judges them all
> before Him.

At the end of the day, there is nothing mysterious about God's judgement; we will understand and know without a doubt. Did we fulfill the measure of our creations by tapping into the direct source of light and knowledge while upon the Earth? The Chinese man who knows nothing of Christianity can still fulfill the measure of his creation by honoring and following the Light of Christ within him; otherwise, to what end was he born? The Muslim man, who has been taught an alternate version of history, can still fulfill God's purposes in his life. All of us have been born where we were born for a reason. The Lord knew our life circumstances before He placed us on this Earth. The circumstances of our lives are not coincidental. God is in the details of our lives. The purpose and life missions He has given us are custom-tailored to those circumstances.

We of little understanding judge each other unjustly from the perspective of our own life circumstances. For this reason, the Righteous Judge has asked us to withhold judgement from one another. Instead, He has asked us to treat one another with mercy. We have been promised that He will judge us with whatever mercy we judge our fellow man. As such, we should bend over backwards to forgive one another.

Chapter 7: Lady Wisdom

In the prior chapters of this volume and the greater series, we have discussed heaven's order and its various societies. We have discussed the nature of the Godhead. We have discussed the innumerable hosts of the gods, who are anxiously engaged with the Father, petitioning Him on behalf of their posterity. We have discussed much about the Father's plan of salvation throughout the cosmos. We have discussed some of the leadership among this iteration of the children of heaven who opted to participate in the Father's plan. Among these leaders are Michael, Raphael, Gabriel, and Phanuel.

We have discussed much of Enoch's insight about the nature of the second estate. We have learned the vital importance of personal revelation and the dire need to discern between truth and error. We have discussed the need to attempt to reconcile the world's messaging with the greater gospel picture so that we might reject the evil and accept the good. Truth reconciles with the gospel, while lies conflict and contrast with it.

Without the groundwork of my prior theories, it would be challenging to understand the subject matter of the present chapter. Before we begin, we must disabuse ourselves of the notion that we know how the kingdoms of heaven are organized. We do not. We understand almost nothing of these things. What we do know is this: those who choose to participate in the Father's plan of salvation will inherit a mansion among the many mansions that the Father has prepared. These mansions span numerous kingdoms of glory: the Celestial Kingdom, the Terrestrial Kingdom, and the Telestial Kingdom. We also know of another kingdom that is devoid of glory called Outer Darkness.

We know that Outer Darkness and the Celestial Kingdom are polar opposites. Yet, of all the kingdoms, we know these are the only two where spirits and resurrected beings live together as full-time residents. The Terrestrial and Telestial Kingdoms appear to be kingdoms that are inhabited only by beings with resurrected bodies of equivalent degrees of glory. The resurrected beings of these two kingdoms are incapable of spiritual offspring, or can they enter the Celestial Kingdom and enjoy the full, unbridled radiance of God's glory. However, beyond this, we know next to nothing about these or any other kingdoms that may exist.

However, this chapter, like many other chapters within this series, will introduce us to aspects of Enoch's vision that will push the boundaries of our present understanding. From this chapter, we will learn that there are more kingdoms in the heavens than those described above. I started laying the groundwork for this chapter in Volume I, in the chapter titled The Lady. I discussed the Lady in Volume I because of the role that she has played in this earth's prior history. I demonstrated that she is active now and may have a very deceptive role to play in the near future events.

You will recall that the Lady has, throughout time, been known by many names. She has been called the Queen of Heaven, Asherah, Hathor, Ishtar, Ianna, Jesse, Our Lady, etc. Indeed, the ancient world had so many names for the Lady and her male counterpart, Ba'al, which they were sometimes referred to as Baalim and Asharoth. Baalim is the plural form of Ba'al, and Asharoth is the plural form of Asherah. The plural forms of these two names were meant to serve as the two umbrellas under which the false gods of the ancient world could be understood and worshiped. Consider the following passage:

> And the children of Israel did evil again in the sight of the
> Lord, and served Baalim, and Ashtaroth, the gods of Syria,
> and the gods of Zidon, and the gods of Moab, and the gods
> of the children of Ammon, and the gods of the Philistines,
> and forsook the Lord, and served not Him. (Judges 10:6 –
> see New King James Translation)

The fact that the gods of Syria, Zidon, Moab, Ammon, and the Philistines all centered on Ba'al and Asherah speaks of the Universality of this type of religious thought in antiquity. Modern society returns to these ancient religious beliefs like a dog to its vomit. In January of 2024, Scripture Central published a Come Follow Me YouTube video that linked the Tree of Life to the veneration of Asherah. They proclaimed Asherah to be our heavenly mother and depicted her standing next to God. Their presentation made me feel heartsick and caused me to mourn the pervasive ignorance in the Church today and how vulnerable this ignorance makes us to the deception that will occur as part of the coming events.

In the opening verses of the Book of Enoch, Enoch explained that his writings were meant to bless the elect that would live upon the earth in the days of trial when the wicked would be removed. Those days are upon us, and I fear that Asherah will play a major role in those events. As such, it should be no surprise that Enoch would speak of her and the role she has played in the past.

Enoch begins by using a new title for the Lady, one to which I have not yet introduced you but by which she was often referred to in antiquity – Lady Wisdom. Consider the following passage wherein Enoch introduces us to Lady Wisdom.

42.1. Wisdom found no place where she might dwell; then a dwelling-place was assigned her in the heavens.

Enoch tells us that Lady Wisdom found no place to dwell in heaven. By this, we understand that Lady Wisdom chose a different path. In a prior chapter, I discussed the importance of agency in the Father's plan. Because of the supreme and sacred nature and importance of agency to the King of the multiverse, God the Father would never have compelled any of His children to unwillingly participate in His plan of salvation. However, another kingdom of glory must have been provided for those who chose not to qualify for the Celestial, Terrestrial, or Telestial Kingdoms of Glory. It is to one of these kingdoms that Lady Wisdom was sent.

Before this earth, we lived in the Celestial Kingdom with our heavenly parents. However, children are not meant to live with their parents forever. The time eventually comes when they go out on their own and begin to choose for themselves what future they would like for themselves. All those living as mortal beings upon worlds without numbers made the same choice in the premortal worlds. We wanted the opportunity to become like their parents.

Even Lucifer and his minions wanted to be born into mortality; however, they wanted to do it on their own terms, not according to the Father's plan. Lucifer wanted to remove the risk from the equation and remove agency. The Father would not permit this to occur, and so Lucifer and his followers were assigned a separate dwelling place – Earth. We will learn more about Lady's Wisdom's world and how it differed from those that rebelled against God as Enoch's vision progresses. Consider the following:

42.2 Wisdom went forth to make her dwelling among the children of men, and found no dwelling-place: Wisdom returned to her place, and took her seat among the angels.

In **42.1,** Enoch saw that Lady Wisdom was assigned a separate location, apart from the Celestial Kingdom, where those who did not want to risk the perils of mortality could dwell. However, it seems from the passage above that the Lord did not confine Lady Wisdom to that location, and why would He? She was not being punished for not participating in the plan of salvation. Still, she was provided with a society wherein she would be among those of a similar disposition to her.

According to Enoch, however, at some point, Lady Wisdom left her kingdom and came to Earth to visit Lucifer's prison planet. Lady Wisdom had certain things in common with Lucifer and his minions; they were the same class of heavenly beings – the mature spiritual offspring of heavenly parents. Enoch does not specify how long Lady Wisdom's first field trip to Earth lasted. He only states that she found no place among Adam's posterity and left to return to the home kingdom the Lord had assigned to beings like her. Enoch described this as her returning to take her seat among the angels. When we think of angels, many people think of the celestial servants of God, like Michael, Raphael, Gabriel, and Phanuel. This is not the way that we should think about Lady Wisdom. In this sense, the term angel refers to a category of beings. Angels can be either resurrected or spiritual beings; both are referred to as angels because while they are the children of gods, they themselves are not gods in the literal sense of the word. Consider the following scripture that speaks of this difference:

> Therefore, when they [*the disobedient*] are out of the world they neither marry nor are given in <u>marriage</u>; but are appointed angels in <u>heaven</u>, which angels are ministering <u>servants</u>, to minister for those who are worthy of a far more, and an exceeding, and an eternal weight of glory. For these angels did not abide my law; therefore, they cannot be enlarged, but remain separately and singly, without exaltation, in their saved condition, to all eternity; and from henceforth are not gods, but are angels of God forever and ever. (D&C 132:16-17)

In the passage above, God is speaking concerning those who choose to participate in His plan of salvation. God explains that most of these will be exalted and better off than they would have been had they not chosen to participate in His plan of salvation. We are told that there are some for whom it has been said that it would have been better had they never been born. By this, we are to understand that they would have been better off had they opted not to be born into mortality, i.e., participate in the Father's plan of salvation. I believe it is fair to say that Lady Wisdom chose not to participate in the Father's plan because she knew enough about herself to know that she would be worse off if she did. Given what we know about her, I would have to agree with her assessment.

The fact that the Father created additional kingdoms for such spiritual beings is telling. It tells us just how little we know about the nature of the multiverse in which we live and the many different kinds of kingdoms within it.

> There are many kingdoms; for there is no space in the which there is no kingdom; and there is no kingdom in which there is no space, either a greater or a lesser kingdom. (D&C 88:37)

We know of only a handful of the many kingdoms that exist throughout the multiverse, and of those of which we do know something, what we know is a little more than nothing at all. We know that there are mortal kingdoms that can serve as rendezvous points for all kinds of beings. Earth, in its present state, is one of these kingdoms. God the Father has come to the Earth on numerous occasions. Lady Wisdom has come here, and probably others like her. Earth is home to Lucifer and his demonic host, and the Watchers have come here. Given the traffic that the earth has experienced, I have to imagine that other mortal worlds have had much greater visitations than these—worlds where gods, spirits, and men mingle in ways that we are unaccustomed to but that may be hinted at in the tales and narratives of the ancient world.

However, not all kingdoms are as open as the earth appears to be. It appears to me that the more glory with which the kingdom is endowed, the more restrictive the kingdom becomes to outsiders. Consider the following passage, which speaks of the nature of the Telestial Kingdom and its inhabitants:

> These all shall bow the knee, and every tongue shall <u>confess</u> to Him who sits upon the throne forever and ever; for they shall be judged according to their <u>works</u>, and every man shall receive according to his own <u>works</u>, his own <u>dominion</u>, in the <u>mansions</u> which are prepared; and they shall be <u>servants</u> of the Most High; but <u>where</u> God and Christ <u>dwell</u> they <u>cannot</u> come, <u>worlds</u> without end. (D&C 76:110-112)

While the passage above speaks specifically regarding the inhabitants of the Telestial Kingdom, it is clear that similar geographical restrictions apply to the inhabitants of the Terrestrial Kingdom, for neither telestial nor terrestrial beings can enter the Celestial Kingdom. However, Celestial beings can minister to those in the terrestrial Kingdom, and terrestrial beings can minister to those of the telestial kingdom. Thus, it would seem that beings are free to enter kingdoms of equal or lower orders of glory to their own but are not permitted to enter kingdoms of greater glory. As this applies to beings of a resurrected and glorified nature, it must also apply to beings of a spiritual nature as well. This, it would seem, is a general rule, for God can and will bring all beings, regardless of their order, to stand before His throne of Glory; however, they cannot come unbidden. You will recall that the satans would have loved to come before the throne of God to accuse the offspring of the gods, but they were prohibited.

This brings us to the mortal kingdoms of men. Such kingdoms must be of a low order indeed, for they appear to be open to all beings, men, angels, both good and evil, Watchers, and even the greatest being in the Multiverse – God the Father, have all come to and interacted with one another upon its surface. Therefore, while there are limitations to where most beings can travel of their own volition, the kingdoms of men appear wide open. The Multiverse is full of diversity, the extent of which we will not be able to fully contemplate until Enoch's visions conclude. I say this because Enoch will continue to add to our understanding of the nature of the reality around us line upon line as his visions progress.

Now, regarding the kingdoms of men specifically, we sometimes refer to the earth as a telestial sphere. Indeed, according to Enoch's conversation with God the Father, as recorded in the seventh chapter of Moses, the world upon which we now stand is the most wicked in the multiverse. As such, it is reasonable to believe that it is a mortal kingdom of the lowest order in its present state of being. Therefore, there must be mortal kingdoms of higher orders than ours found throughout the cosmos. Indeed, there are likely mortal planets of a terrestrial order and of a celestial order as well. I expect we would be shocked by what occurs in these mortal kingdoms, which exist on higher spiritual planes than our own.

As we have seen in prior chapters, there were times in this Earth's history when pockets of society transcended the telestial nature of the Earth itself. During such occasions, we have been taught that the visitations and interactions with Gods (the Father, Son, and Holy Ghost) and angelic beings increased to shocking degrees. For example, Christ appeared often amongst the early Christian disciples who had created communities patterned after the law of consecration, or the united order. The same was true in America after the initial coming of Christ. Both the Nephites and the Lamanites began living with all things in common, and their societies were frequented by Gods and angels - more than we know. As such, I am left to conclude that throughout the cosmos, there are kingdoms of mortal men of various orders higher than those known to us, wherein beings of all orders, Gods, gods, angels, spirits, and mortals comingle in ways that have only been contemplated in works of science fiction. Consider how fascinating and varied the civilizations throughout the cosmos must be!

I return now to the discussion of our home planet – Earth. We speak of our planet as being a telestial sphere. While this is true, it is a mortal telestial sphere. As I contemplate the cosmos, I cannot help but conclude that a telestial sphere of a mortal order is far inferior to an undying glorified telestial sphere, such as would be found within the Telestial Kingdom of glory. Joseph Smith taught that the glory of the Telestial Kingdom surpasses all understanding.

Therefore, I have come to believe that worlds themselves are like people in that they, too, have phases of progression. The world is in its mortal stage right now, and as such, the day will come, as with all mortal things, and it, too, will die. When that day comes, we are told that the Earth itself will be quickened. When this happens, it will cease to be part of the mortal kingdoms of men, but in a process that will mirror the resurrection;

the Earth itself will be glorified with a new body. It will become part of the Celestial Kingdom itself, where it will join other planets that have obtained that same high and holy order throughout the many iterations of the Father's plan of salvation.

When this day happens, the Earth will no longer be accessible to the hosts of heaven but only to those of a celestial order. Therefore, while the multiverse is clearly filled with kingdoms in all its parts, it is segregated. Some portions, like the Celestial Kingdom, are inaccessible to those of a lower order. Therefore, the multiverse, with all its many worlds and dimensions, is only truly accessible in all its parts to Celestial beings. These can visit any kingdom, anywhere, if they so choose. Therefore, only Celestial Beings will know what true freedom is.

Along this line of reasoning, Outer Darkness is the most constricted kingdom in the multiverse. Indeed, the beings that dwell there are so base that they are restricted in their movements to kingdoms as base as their own. Thus, their movement, influence, and experiences will be forever restricted or damned – worlds without end. If a being of a higher order was so inclined to visit Outer Darkness, I suspect nothing would prohibit them from doing so, but the kingdom's residents would never be able to leave it. Thus, the limitations and movements placed upon the beings of the various kingdoms of glory represent the self-imposed estoppel or damnation of their own creation. Again, the only beings that will know true freedom to move throughout the multiverse are those of the highest order of the Celestial kingdom, the gods.

Now, returning to the Lady and those of her order. Having opted out of the Father's plan of salvation, these received their kingdom of glory already. They are free to move about the cosmos, amongst the kingdoms that are equal or inferior to their own, and can exercise their agency as they go. We simply do not know what laws the Father has placed upon their kingdoms, but they can operate as agents of chaos.

Therefore, while Lucifer and his vast host of the demonic fallen have been confined to this earth, they are not the only agents of chaos to exist throughout the multiverse. It appears that there are kingdoms of spirits that are entirely populated by beings who believed that it would have been worse for them if they had chosen to be born into the Father's plan of salvation, and as such, they opted to remain in their premortal state. Given these beings' lack of confidence in their own ability to navigate mortality without imploding, we must conclude that such beings were well aware of their own mischievous natures before the foundations of this earth were ever laid.

As such, we must also conclude that their mischievous nature was no surprise to God. Therefore, the omnipotent God of the Multiverse created their kingdom with such things in mind. Indeed, Lady Wisdom and her kind can hardly be the first generation to have opted out of the Father's prior plan iterations; therefore, there must be an innumerable host of such beings and kingdoms throughout the multiverse. However, for reasons that I will explain as this chapter continues, I believe that Lady Wisdom is of our heavenly generation. She was one of us. We grew up together in the heavenly communities above. I envision her as the mischievous heartthrob of many, flirtatious, devious, and fun. As with all the children of heaven, she was no stranger to the court of God or the God of Heaven Himself.

Enoch was not the only person in antiquity to speak of Lady Wisdom by this name. She was known by this name amongst the Gnostics. King Solomon, who had the ten tribes of Israel stripped from him because he began to worship the Queen of Heaven, also knew her by the name of Lady Wisdom. It is, therefore, from the writings of King Solomon that we learn more of the role of Lady Wisdom in the premortal courts on high. This narrative makes me sad. It is the only passage in the scriptures I know that Lady Wisdom speaks to us in the first person. Consider the following:

> I Wisdom dwell with prudence, and find out knowledge of witty inventions. The LORD possessed me in the beginning of His way, before His works of old.
>
> I was set up from everlasting, from the beginning, or ever the earth was. When there were no depths, I was brought forth; when there were no fountains abounding with water. Before the mountains were settled, before the hills was I brought forth: while as yet He had not made the earth, nor the fields, nor the highest part of the dust of the world.
>
> When He prepared the heavens, I was there: when He set a compass upon the face of the depth: when He established the clouds above: when He strengthened the fountains of the deep: When He gave to the sea His decree, that the waters should not pass His commandment: when He appointed the foundations of the earth: then I was by Him, as one brought up with Him: and I was daily His delight, rejoicing always before Him; rejoicing in the habitable part of His earth; and my delights were with the sons of men. (Proverbs 8:12, 22-31)

I said that the narrative above saddens me because it speaks of Lady Wisdom's childhood. Childhood is a magical time in mortality and a magical time for us in heaven as well. God the Father, a grandfather to us all, loved and welcomed us all in His mighty presence, in which we most certainly took great delight. Lady Wisdom explains in her narrative above one such memory of hers. I do not doubt the authenticity of this memory, for I believe it is verily true. However, the way that it is presented is mischievous and deviant. It is presented in such a way as to create the illusion of her own greatness and sense of divinity. Wisdom describes herself as being brought into the presence of God. As such, she witnessed the creation of this Earth, literally being present as the Earth was made. While all this sounds very impressive, the same could be said for you. Wisdom is describing the circumstances of every child of heaven. These things were as commonplace for us as seeing the President of the United States in the news. We all knew God; He was a Father to us all. The difference between us and Lady Wisdom is that we were willing to risk anything to become just like Him. She was not.

Wisdom stated in her opening remarks: "I Wisdom dwell with prudence." Prudence implies a state of cautious deliberation in obtaining one's objectives. Lucifer was not prudent; he was reckless, and his attempt to dethrone God is the culminating pinnacle of his recklessness. In her prudence, Lady Wisdom did nothing of the sort but opted out of the Father's plan altogether. She knew her own nature, as did everyone else who knew her. She did not want to risk mortality, nor was she stupid enough to seek to overthrow God to obtain godhood by force of arms.

God loves all the children of heaven, and He wants them to be happy. However, based on Lady Wisdom's experience, it is clear that happiness does not look the same for all people. All those who opted to participate in the Father's plan of salvation did so because they loved the Lord and wanted to become as similar to Him as possible. All of these, save the sons of perdition, will obtain their desire to varying degrees. Yet Lady Wisdom will never receive such advancement.

This causes me to ponder upon the nature of such beings throughout the cosmos. Satan and his ilk will be restricted in their influence once the day of their final judgement comes. What is not clear to me is the fate of Lady Wisdom and those like her. Such beings chose to be what they were and received an inheritance in a kingdom specifically designed for them. They know who they are, and God knows who they are. They made this choice long ago and are now living their lives according to their choices. It would seem that, unlike Lucifer, such beings will continue to retain their influence among the kingdoms of men perpetually, for such was the desire of their hearts.

Lady Wisdom stated that although she grew up in the presence of God, her delights were with the sons of men. By this, I believe that we are to understand that because of her choices, she can no longer sojourn amongst the gods, although they could, if they desired, visit her kingdom. Lady Wisdom didn't want to be with the gods anyway. After all, she stated that she takes her delights amongst the kingdoms of men. Among mortal men, Lady Wisdom can be venerated as a goddess without requiring the substance of one. This is what she delights in. As we learned in Volume I of this series, she has been doing this for a long time and continues to do it even today. Indeed, since publishing Volume I, I have learned of another of the Lady's visits to a man named Fr. Oliveira, a Catholic priest from Rio Grande do Sul in southern Brazil.

On June 17, 2023, Fr. Oliveira claimed to receive a prophecy from the Lady, in which he was told that the trial times would begin in October of the same year. I first read Fr Oliveira's alleged revelation in September of 2023, the month before it was supposed to happen. The following is a translation of relevant portions of Fr. Oliveira's alleged revelation from Lady Wisdom.

> Beloved son, listen carefully: In October of this year, a period of great tribulation will begin, which I predicted when I was in France [La Salette 1846], Portugal [Fatima 1917] and Spain [Garabandal 1961-1965]. On these three occasions, I spoke about the cause of these tribulations.

> Be prepared, above all spiritually, because this period will not come with a bang, but will be gradual and will spread slowly throughout the world. The war that has started [*meaning the war in Ukraine*] will increase, as you have already seen. There will be droughts, great storms and earthquakes in many places of the world. But as my Divine Son said, when you hear these rumors, do not be afraid!

> Seek to remain in a state of grace, because the demons have set upon humanity with strong temptations, especially against priests. Pray for them and pray for yourself too, as you are a priest. Always remember who you are! Pray also for your bishop and for all bishops. Pray much for the Holy Father [the Pope]: make fasts and sacrifices for him. I, your Mother and Queen, will be with all those who entrust themselves to my care, and I will not leave any of my children helpless. As I have promised many times, this time is part of what I said in my third secret in Portugal (the beginning of Christian persecution).

> On October 13, I will give you a sign as you asked me to do. That is why I have shown you this date.

> I have received from God the mission to guard, together with the holy angels that the Lord has placed at my service, all

those who have entrusted their lives to me. There will be great devastation from Russia, instigated by the infernal Dragon. This will harm the whole world. But do not fear. This is the opportune time for holiness. Remember that the great saints rose up in times of great darkness. Times of tribulation, especially this one, should not be faced with fear and cowardice, but with love and courage. You see, my son, this is why I have called you in this hour, so that you would remember and proclaim that the opportune time for holiness is now, today — not tomorrow, but now.

Eucharistic adoration should be your anchor, and the Holy Rosary the chain of that anchor. Eucharistic adoration, acts of reparation and sacrifices, united with the Holy Rosary, can change all prophecies! Do not forget this: Adoration and the Holy Rosary. Do penance, offer sacrifices for the salvation of souls, for the conversion of sinners and the sanctification of the clergy. Remember that the Lord knows everything and is in command of everything. Soon there will come the Triumph of my Immaculate Heart! Remain faithful in this time of purification; trust in the help of your Guardian Angel. The time for the saints is now. Pray, dear son, pray and watch, as I have called you today — pray and watch.

In the passages above, the Lady stated that the times of trial, long since prophesied, would begin in October 2023. In retrospect, this seems to correlate with the largest single terrorist attack in Israel's modern history. On October 7, 2023, Hamas crossed the Gaza Strip into Israel and committed atrocious acts of violence and murder. Girls were raped; fathers and mothers were gleefully slaughtered before the eyes of their children and children before the eyes of their parents. Murdered infants were displayed as trophies in radicalized Islam's overflowing showcase of atrocious memorabilia.

The Lady specifically gave October 13, 2023, as a sign to attest to the truthfulness of her prophecy. Imagine the significance, therefore, when Palestinian leaders called for a global day of rage to be celebrated on this exact date. In cities around the world, large crowds gathered, chanting hateful slogans and vowing to finish what Hitler started. "Gas the Jews, Gas the Jews" and "Palestine will be free, from the river to the sea" rang out in communities around the world. Of course, alongside the antisemitic rhetoric were the anti-American death chants as well. "Death to America" has been a family favorite amongst the more hardened regions of the Islamic world for years. As noted above, America is the country of Joseph. While the world does not know this, demons most certainly do. Therefore, they rage not only against Israel but against the nation of Joseph. Israel and America; Judah and Joseph: two nations, two brothers. These represent the only two sons of Jacob on earth today that exist in sufficient numbers to constitute two separate nations.

Judah and Joseph have influenced the modern world more than any other nation. Judah influenced the modern world through his brilliant scientific mind and business acumen, and Joseph was the standard bearer of the nations. The following scripture comes to mind:

> And it shall come to pass in that day, *that* the Lord shall set His hand again the second time to recover the remnant of his people, which shall be left, from Assyria, and from Egypt, and from Pathros, and from Cush, and from Elam, and from Shinar, and from Hamath, and from the islands of the sea.
>
> And He shall set up an ensign for the nations, and shall assemble the outcasts of Israel, and gather together the dispersed of Judah from the four corners of the earth. The envy also of Ephraim shall depart, and the adversaries of Judah shall be cut off: Ephraim shall not envy Judah, and Judah shall not vex Ephraim. (Isaiah 11:11-13)

The Lord has now performed this portion of His work. Ephraim and Judah have been gathered from among the nations and are no longer enemies as they were in ancient times but allies. If it were not for his younger brother, Judah would not exist as a nation today. If it had not been for the brilliance of many Jewish scientists, Ephriam would not have risen to its status as the world's greatest superpower. Yet the other nations envy these brothers and want to see them both destroyed.

It is, therefore, no surprise that the Lady's sign, October 13, 2023, turned out to be a global day of rage against these two nations, whose founders dedicated both of them to the God of Israel. The lateness of the hour and the Lady's sign specifically, call to mind the following scripture:

> But behold, that great and abominable church, the whoreof all the earth, must tumble to the earth, and great must be the fall thereof. For the kingdom of the devil must shake, and they which belong to it must needs be stirred up unto repentance, or the Devil will grasp them with his everlasting chains, and they be stirred up to anger, and perish; for behold, at that day shall he rage in the hearts of the children

of men, and stir them up to anger against that which is good.
(2 Nephi 28:18-20)

Nephi prophesied that the kingdom of the Devil would fall, but before that day, he would rage in the hearts of men. Therefore, the rage of men is an appropriate sign of the times. The Lady indicated that this would be a sign that she was about to rise to power and that the victory of her immaculate heart would soon be at hand. Many prophets have likened the Whore of Babylon to the Kingdom of the Devil. This is not really true. Satan is certainly the inspiration behind the formation of the Whore of Babylon. It most definitely serves his purposes and agenda, but once it has accomplished the purpose he designed, it will be of no further use to him. His ultimate objective is not to empower and enrich sinful men. Rather, it is to use sinful men and their power and influence to empower himself. If the Lady is claiming that she is about to rise to power, then we are to assume that the Whore of Babylon is about ready to fall.

We now return to the Lady in the context of Enoch's teachings. As a spiritual being who opted not to participate in the Father's plan of salvation, she is not capable of reproduction or of maintaining relationships of physical intimacy that would result in her own family. However, it seems that she has always been more interested in the veneration and worship of men than in family.

It is a tenant of God that there must be opposition in all things. Opposition is an essential element of progression. For precisely this reason, God has placed the mortal kingdom under the influence of kingdoms inhabited by chaos-inducing beings such as Lady Wisdom. I liken this to the animal kingdoms. Piranhas, for example, attack and devour bleeding and wounded animals entering their kingdoms. It is simply what they do. It is their nature. In like manner, Lady Wisdom and those like her cause chaos and mischief among the mortal realms within their sphere of influence. It is what they do. It is in their nature. Mortal men do not seek to destroy piranhas for that which comes naturally to them within their own habitat. However, men currently do everything in their power to ensure that piranhas do not spread throughout the world freshwaters.

So I believe it is with God and such beings of power such as Lady Wisdom. I do not believe that God will compound the damnation under which such beings already operate, for He has already restricted them. In this regard, they are not so much infiltrating our kingdoms as our kingdoms are within their jurisdictions. Lucifer and his minions, who literally sought to overthrow God, will eventually be far more constrained than these, for they are destined for Outer Darkness, a kingdom far inferior to that to which Lady Wisdom belongs.

Because Lady Wisdom and her kind are operating within the constraints of their existing damnation, I still do not expect them to be punished further. If they were, it would be to constrain them beyond the reaches of their current kingdom. God has intentionally chosen to place the mortal kingdoms of men within the spheres of influence of such beings for a wise purpose. Therefore, in the coming days, I do not believe that the Lady will be further constrained; rather, I believe that the Earth itself will be relocated into the Kingdom of Glory, to which she has no access. This will require the physical relocation of the Earth, wherein it will move through the cosmos as the chased roe. Yet, Lady Wisdom and those like her will continue to remain where they are; the bounds of their habitation are set. That is to say, they are damned, and so are all such kingdoms of glory to one extent or another throughout the cosmos, except for those of the highest order of the Celestial realms. Only these will have unfettered access to the full scope and range of the infinite multiverse with its myriad of wonders, kingdoms, and glories, the breadth of which eternity itself is insufficient to explore. There will be no boredom in the worlds beyond!

With this understanding in place, we are now in a position to continue with Enoch's narrative, where he will continue to reveal many more wonders about the cosmos, line upon line, precept upon precept, just as he himself received them:

> **42.3** And unrighteousness went forth from her chambers:
> whom she sought not she found, and dwelt with them, as rain
> in a desert and dew on a thirsty land.

This passage is interesting. It confirms to us that unrighteousness went forth from Lady Wisdom's chambers. By this, we are to understand that the kingdom from which she hailed was a source of opposition and chaos in the cosmos. Curiously, Enoch stated that Lady Wisdom came across a group of people for whom she was seeking. This sounds very different from her travels to Earth, which were clearly premeditated.

Lady Wisdom does not operate within the veil. She has known all about the Earth from the very beginning. As we have previously read, she witnessed its creation. In addition, she would have witnessed the rebellion in heaven and the subsequent banishment of Lucifer and his followers to the earth. Given what we know of Lady Wisdom, she most certainly had many friends among this fallen host. She likely tried to convince many of them not to rebel but rather to remain with her and her kind. Obviously, they made their choices, and she made hers. However, such friendships did not end simply because they were banished to the prison planet of Earth. As we have seen, Earth is within her sphere of influence, so she visits with them, just as friends visit their friends in jail.

However, Lady Wisdom was not seeking this encounter; it just happened. How is such a thing possible? Let us consider this in light of the greater aspects of Enoch's writings. Enoch's writings are, first and foremost, about the Watchers. I believe that the Watchers were mortal beings that were capable of transversing the immensity of space. As such,

I believe they are simple mortal men who arrived on Earth from another mortal realm somewhere else. Presumably, their realm was of a higher order than our own, for they were described in Enoch's writings as leaving their holy habitations to come to Earth. As such, their world could have been a terrestrial or even a celestial planet, according to the kingdoms of men, and not after the manner of the Kingdoms of undying glory that is associated with resurrected beings.

Enoch stated that the Watchers would return to the Earth in the last days. For those who are curious enough to look, it is evident that the Earth is now being visited by a trans-medium craft capable of transversing the vacuum of space, the challenges of a planetary atmosphere, and the crushing pressure of our deepest oceans. As such, it is a natural presumption that the Watchers descended from the heavens to the peak of Mount Hermon in a craft such as those now being witnessed on an exponentially increasing basis.

As such, it is far easier for me to envision a chance encounter with a craft exploring the vast cosmic sea that surrounds us than for this encounter to have occurred upon a world. After all, if you seek the kingdoms of men, you look for them on planets. Therefore, in my opinion, for Lady Wisdom to have had a chance encounter with intelligent beings for whom she was not looking, a chance encounter with her and a crew of beings exploring the cosmos makes sense to me, particularly in light of the narrative of this book.

In my mind's eye, I see a magnificent starship exploring the immensity of space on a voyage of discovery. By random chance, I envision this starship crossing Lady Wisdom's path. In her curiosity, I envision Lady Wisdom appearing to the ship's occupants, to their shock and delight.

You will recall that Enoch stated that when Lady Wisdom first traveled to Earth, she found a place among the children of men and returned home. That is to say that the posterity of Adam and Eve was not buying what she was selling. They were too close to the Spirit to be deceived. However, Enoch stated that when this chance meeting occurred, these beings embraced Lady Wisdom and her teachings.

In the chronology of Enoch's writings, Lady Wisdom's chance encounter with this star-traveling race took place after she had visited Earth. Enoch clearly stated that she had found no place to dwell amongst Adam and Eve and their posterity, and she had left. Why would Enoch bring this up if this knowledge would not somehow bless the righteous living on Earth in the last few days?

I do not think that he would. Therefore, the Lady's chance encounter with these beings must have played a role in the events of the earth's distant past. Is it possible that the

Lady's chance encounter was with a starship carrying the two hundred men that we now refer to as the Watchers? Could these beings arrive on Earth precisely because Lady Wisdom showed them where it was? This seems to be a very curious connection that Enoch's writing suggests did in fact, actually occur. We will explore this concept more fully in the next chapter.

Chapter 8: Starships and Rumors of Starships

In the prior chapter, we were introduced to Lady Wisdom, whom I believe is none other than Chris Bledsoe's Lady, which was discussed at length in Volume I. In the prior chapter, we learned that Lady Wisdom chose not to participate in the Father's plan. As such, she and others were assigned a separate kingdom of glory. Enoch spoke specifically of the Lady's ability to leave her kingdom and travel to other mortal worlds throughout the cosmos. The prior chapter concluded with the Lady encountering an advanced civilization by chance, which lapped up her deceitful dogmas like rain upon a dusty land. I postulated that this chance encounter was with the two hundred men that would later descend atop Mount Hermon in the days of Enoch's father, Jared.

Jared was born in the days when the posterity of Adam and Eve had begun to become exceedingly numerous, four hundred and sixty years after the fall of Adam. We learned that before this time, Lady Wisdom had made a trip to the Earth but was rebuffed, finding no foothold among the sons of men. With her corruption of the Watchers, things would be very different upon her second visit. When the Watchers arrived with their incredible starship, advanced knowledge, technology, and witty inventions, Adam's posterity went crazy.

Therefore, when the Watchers themselves proselyted to the posterity of Adam regarding Lady Ishtar - the Queen of Heaven, the sons of Adam and daughters of Eve bought into the narrative hook, line, and sinker. The Watchers became known as the Anunnaki, and from that point onwards, they became the de facto leaders of the ancient world. The Anunnaki founded the world's first modern city – Sumer. From the ancient clay tablets discovered in Sumer, we learn of the high regard in which the Anunnaki held Lady Ishtar. She was worshiped alongside El, or Elohim, and His Son, Enlil, whom the Anunnaki called the Great Creator of Heaven and Earth. Curiously, among these ancient writings, we also learn of another mysterious group of beings, the servants of the Anunnaki. These servants were described as accompanying the Anunnaki on their heavenly journey and were called the Igigi.

Who the Igigi were is something of a mystery. Many different theories have been put forth by many different people, but the most interesting to me was not presented as a theory but as a statement of fact. The man making the statement was Colonel Phillip J. Corso. Colonel Corso headed up the Pentagon's R&D program during the Roswell, NM incident. Before his death, Colonel Corso wrote a book titled "The Day After Roswell" about his incredible experiences. He also gave an unprecedented interview with George

Knapp. Colonel Corso told George Knapp point blank that he was there in Roswell at the time of the infamous UFO crash.

Colonel Corso stated that the crash was real and that his team at the Pentagon was tasked with reverse engineering artifacts recovered from that crash. He stated that his team was comprised of German scientists the government had recruited as part of Project Paperclip. His team worked on reverse engineering numerous artifacts. In his interview and book, Corso stated that the crashed disks contained the bodies of both living and deceased gray alien beings. In his interview with George Knapp, he stated that the ancient Sumerians referred to the gray aliens as the Igigi.

Therefore, a credible source links the grays to the Igigi servant class of the Anunnaki. He further went on to describe that based on the autopsy reports, the Igigi, or grays, were, in fact, clones, a type of hyper-advanced biological android, and were sentient. He also told George Knapp that the skin of the greys looked to be made of little scales, like those belonging to a reptile. These are curious things to consider, yet why am I talking about them? I demonstrate the link between the Watchers of antiquity, the Igigi, or grays, and the Lady.

If my hypothesis is correct, the Lady's chance encounter, spoken of by Enoch, introduced her to two classes of beings, the Watchers and the Igigi. The Watchers' worship of the Lady is evident from the archeological record. Chris Bledsoe's description of the Lady always being accompanied by creatures matching the description of the Igigi is further evidence of this fact. Chris did not describe the Igigi by this name but as black aliens with glowing red eyes in the shape and size of the classic gray alien. The Lady's ability to command these strange beings and the orbs that are so often associated with them has been orchestrated into prior acts of deception. The Miracle of the Sun in Fatima, Portugal, is among the most famous of these orchestrated deceptions.

As we contemplate the Lady's influence throughout the cosmos, I want to share another curious data point that has come to my attention. The reader will recall that in volume one of this series, I shared an incredible interview with Brigadier General Haim Eshed from Israel. Mr. Eshed astounded the world in that interview by discussing his knowledge of the grays and the Galactic Federation group.

I believe Mr. Eshed to be an honest man with legitimate access to astounding information. To this end, I wish to share with you another fascinating interview of the most incredible nature. As with all interviews of such a spectacular nature, I do not expect the reader to believe it. Rather, this information should be cautiously considered alongside other spectacular claims. As we do so, we must realize that true facts must be fished out from an otherwise turbulent sea of lies and disinformation.

I am about to share the interview with General Thomas Jeremiah Davis, who claimed to have been offered by the US Government to the Galactic Federation as an emissary. He eventually obtained the command of the Federation's largest local ship, called the Alliance. He described the Alliance as being several miles wide and over twice as long.

One of the reasons that I have chosen to share this account is because of who General Jeremiah said the Galactic Federation is. It is not anything like most stories of this nature. In addition, others have corroborated General Jeremiah's story, including a group of ranchers from Utah. Of particular note is a series of experiences that allegedly occurred at Blind Frog Ranch. Duane Ollinger, the ranch's owner, claimed that General Jeremiah scanned his property from space to show him the precise location of all the valuable minerals on his property. Duane also stated that he personally met General Jeremiah and saw several of his spacecraft. He further mentioned that General Jeremiah sent several doctors from the Galactic Federation to cure his daughter, who was dying from an otherwise incurable illness.

The particular interview I will share occurred when General Jeremiah called the radio program Evident Footprints, hosted by Don Nicoloff, on May 29, 2009. Don Nicoloff was a guest host for a scientist named Jim Murry, who specialized in electrical power management and mechanics. Jim Murry is the founder of Convergent Power, Inc.

The following is a transcription of that interview:

> **Don**: Jim, we have another caller here. Would you like to take another call?
>
> **Jim**: Sure, why not?
>
> **Don**: Ok, we have General Jeremiah on the phone; welcome to Evident Footprints; how are you this evening?
>
> **General Jeremiah (GJ)**: Hello Don, how are you today? Can you hear me?
>
> **Don**: Yes, I can, very well; where are you calling from?
>
> **GJ**: I'm calling from a spacecraft rotating around this planet right now. I am the commanding officer of a spacecraft called the Alliance, which is part of the United Galactic Federation. We are monitoring your planet, and this is not a joke; your listeners probably think this is a joke, but it is not. We want you to know that we have often listened to your

show. We wanted to let Jim know that he is one of the scientists we plan to contact soon about some projects we are working on.

Don: Now, this is not a spoof, right?

GJ: This is not a spoof. No. This is real.

Don: Jim, what is your response to what you have heard so far?

Jim: I am flattered and excited, but it is hard to accept. I don't often participate in phone calls from outer space, but I am glad you called in.

GJ: Thank you. We have been planning to contact you for some time now. We feel that the time is right for the people of this continent and planet to understand what is happening here. We have been monitoring the progress of this nation, not only this nation but all the planet's nations. We have been listening to your conversations with Don for the past year or so. We realize you are a scientist worthy of our attention and would like to honor you. Hopefully, we will contact you very soon and pull you into some of the projects we are working on.

Jim: Well, I would certainly be happy to participate, and I am grateful for your singling me out for whatever reason you did so. Is it okay to ask you a question?

GJ: Sure, go ahead.

Jim: I have always pondered this issue. Of course, I do not know exactly what I base it on, perhaps the common sense associated with normal evolution, but is there such a thing as a Prime Directive that limits your interference with another planet? If there is, do you interpret your intervention as a violation of that Prime Directive?

GJ: Yes, there is a Prime Directive; I will answer that question. The alliance is made up of several different people on many different planets. We have 26,000 people aboard the spaceship Alliance. We are in orbit in your solar system and have been here for thirty-two years, watching the progress of this nation and this continent. But we do not interfere with the affairs of humankind. We do assist in some situations on occasion. We are not an interfering agency. Our federation is made up of 574 planets throughout and from this galaxy. We have become religiously involved with each other. We have the same goals and the same outlook on things. Our alliance was formed many centuries ago when the Person you call Jesus Christ visited your planet and the federation's planets, too. Many of these planets have accepted Him as our Savior and our Lord, and we have allied to that aspect. We are a non-warring federation. We do not have wars amongst our continents or among our planets. We have formed a very wonderful relationship amongst these 574 planets. We are gradually adding more planets to it. Earth is supposedly one of those planets we have picked out, but unfortunately, I do not think you are quite ready for it now.

Jim: That would have been my next question anyway. General, what changes must we make to become worthy of entering that federation?

GJ: We are looking for continents that are willing to lay down their warmongering ways and their nuclear weapons and exist peacefully with not only the other nations of their world but with the other planets of the federation. I know that you know, and I know that Don knows, that thousands of other planets are currently monitoring the situation on this globe. We are just one faction of those. There seems to be a mass invasion now; thousands and thousands of other spacecraft are coming from other parts of the galaxy to observe what is taking place. We hope there will be no conflicts and this will be a peaceful situation; however, that remains to be seen.

Don: I'd like to ask a question. You say you have been listening to this program for about a year. Actually, I have been on BBS radio since 2007, but on the air, next month it will be two years. What is your opinion of the information you heard on this show? Obviously, we are doing our best to bring the truth to light and tell people what is happening.

GJ: Don, you are so on track that it is almost to the point of being unbelievable. Our intelligence network is probably the greatest in this galaxy. We monitor the events on this planet in every nation. We know what is happening inside of governments, as well as what is happening inside of private organizations. You have opened the door to many of these things with your research and knowledge. We have saluted you many times and would like you to be part of our intelligence network. It seems like you have an outstanding knack for finding these things. Our people are very astute at finding these things, too, but you fall right into that category.

Don: I am happy to hear that we are on the right track. Obviously, we do not have the assets to go deeper into some of these things than we otherwise could. Doing these investigations costs a lot of money, so we must use our discernment. I know this about Jim as well. We honor the gifts of the spirit to make up for the lack of funding and support. Do you see us continuing on the right track?

GJ: Don, you will miss the boat if you go in any other direction. The things you have discovered and brought up on this radio program are incredible and almost unbelievable that you could have discovered them. Our scientists are monitoring the situation with technology and equipment of the most advanced nature, and you have often discovered things before they have. We thank you for that. You are on the right track; please keep it up.

Don: I will take that to heart. Can I ask another question? I have some chat messages popping up, and I cannot keep up with them as fast as they are coming through here. Some of the listeners are asking if there is some way of verifying your presence without the interference of these evil and corrupt governments that don't want the masses to know. If we had a way for you to make your presence known in a non-threatening way, would the federation be willing to make its presence known? If they could do so without risking their safety, I imagine it would be dangerous for them. Are you considering ways to do this?

GJ: Yes, we are, Don. Our presence has been seen all across this planet. We have thousands of spacecraft coming to and from this planet daily. Our biggest concern is the safety of our personnel. I won't say we have been attacked numerous times, but I'll say thousands of times by other spacecraft from other plants that want to hinder our progress. They know that we want to help Earth move forward in its progress, and they want to hinder us in this aspect. They have their objective of taking over this planet. As such, we cannot just liberally give ourselves to the public for this reason. I was observing and watching a friend of yours recently, and we were about to descend to meet with him; as we were preparing to do so, we were attacked by twelve spacecraft from what you would call the grays. We had to defend ourselves from that. That is one example of many thousands of different examples. So, that is why we do not always make ourselves completely visible.

Don: Well, a thought going through my head as you speak is how clear this call is. It is much clearer than a call that we get on a landline. So, I would have to say that this call is not coming in from a wire but is not a cell phone.

GJ: Our communication equipment is so sophisticated that I cannot describe it to you; however, we do hit one relay over this continent from where we are at, which is, I believe, over Texas right now.

Don: Suppose I can ask a technical question. BBS does its best to estimate the number of listeners we have worldwide, and I get messages from people worldwide. There was a time when we could track where most people were listening from. At one point, one of the Alexis services suggested that 10% of the listeners at the time were from Paraguay, which I found to be very interesting. This was just after I had released the information about the secret compound that the Bush had bought. The 98,000 acres spread over one of

109

eastern Paraguay's largest aquifers. But it is tough for me to pull accurate numbers. Are you able to track the audience listening to this show around the world?

GJ: Yes, we are. I have not looked at the numbers tonight. We have seen you have had as many as twenty million listeners simultaneously. I do not know if that is the case at this present time, but you are tracking a huge audience, not only from this planet but also from other solar systems.

Don: My goodness! That is humbling. Jim, do you have any thoughts on that?

Jim: I am humbled into silence.

GJ: Jim, on one occasion, two of our doctors visited you in the hospital one night when you had some ailments. We did not want to make ourselves known because we did not want to attract attention. Do you remember that occasion?

Jim: I remember it very clearly, and I will say that my lungs are doing well right now. Whoever those technicians or doctors were, I would extend my thanks.

GJ: I will pass the word onto them; they are very good men.

Don: General, we have another question regarding crystal skulls. Are our scientists currently working on advanced crystal storage going to make any breakthroughs regarding those skulls or other energy devices?

GJ: There are three scientists on your planet, one in Australia, one in the United States, and one in Great Britain, who have already made breakthroughs in that area. They will be stifled by their governments, but that technology will be known to some within months to you and to this station. Those skulls were left by a civilization in a very distant and remote solar system within this galaxy. They are really wonderful people. They had brilliant crews that were working on this planet at that time. Our federation was not part of what I know of.

Don: This is somewhat of a rhetorical question that might be answered specifically. In terms of the federation, I don't know if it's bylaws or agreements they have with each other from each of these 574 planets you have described. We are obviously talking about different races. People who look different have different roles and are guiding us. What do we need to do to assist them with this work? We talk about the dumbed-down masses and the propaganda. I am not belittling these people. It is obvious to those of us who know what is happening that most people are oblivious to what is happening. What must we do to ascend to a higher level of consciousness and become part of the federation?

GJ: What brings us all together is our belief in the Man whom you call the Messiah, whom we also call the Messiah, who is Jesus Christ. He is the One who came to each of these planets and preached the gospel. He is the One who presented the truth. He presented His laws and doctrines of peace, love, and care for everyone. Most of these planets accepted His teachings. However, when He came to this planet, you crucified Him and killed Him. I am not saying you, Don, but the planet did. When this planet becomes reconciled to Him, and to His laws and teachings, and the basic tenets of what you call Christianity, that will be the deciding factor for when this planet will be included in the federation. There will be many other stipulations, of course. We are ruled by a council of twenty-four elders. These are some of the wisest men in the galaxy. These gentlemen have life spans of five hundred-plus years and have been in situations of government control and leadership. These men have been chosen and made the rulers of this righteous federation. They are benevolent. They have love for all humankind. They have been looking at this planet. I have entertained three of those elders this week on our Alliance spacecraft. As I have said before, we are orbiting in your solar system. They know about planet Earth. They are very concerned for the stability of each nation. They are concerned about the warfare that is going on and the unnecessary lives that are being wasted. When they see evidence of change, a council of other types of men, such as themselves, will be formed. Hopefully, then, the transition can be made.

I have been selected because of some connections that I have. I am from this planet. (General Jeremiah was recruited from the CIA to work with the Federation as part of his military career) Over the years, I have been trained and become part of this Federation and made part of the leadership of it. As I have said before, we have 26,000 people assigned to the Alliance spacecraft, and thousands of smaller craft come and go from our craft each day. We constantly contact this planet and what is happening within each nation. You have seen our craft; other people have seen them. We are willing and able to serve when we can.

Don: I am glad that you mentioned the craft. There was a sighting of a craft over the capital mall on the day of the Presidential Inauguration on January 20, 2009. A media site posted some videos and pictures of one of your craft. I sensed that there were four craft there and that they were there for benevolent reasons. When it hit the media, people started to say it was a bird or a bug on the camera lens. When I posted a message on this blog site stating that those four craft were from the Galactic Federation of Hendon, was I telling the truth?

GJ: You told the exact truth. You caught us on camera. That was a slip-up on our part. One of our craft became uncloaked on that day. We were watching the inauguration.

Don: I have seen those crafts before and recognized them from the photograph. I was invited to a blog site and posted a paragraph about who that was. So now, thanks to you, we have that verified. So, to all those who wanted to say it was a bird, a bug, or swamp gas, it was the Galactic Federation.

GJ: At least thirty of our huge craft were present that day. According to your measurements, we have large crafts that are about a thousand feet in diameter. We have several craft that are a hundred feet in diameters and sixty feet or thereabouts. There are multiple designs because we come from different planets.

I want to mention one thing, Don: we are all human. If you went to any of these 574 planets, you would think you were on Earth. There is a slight difference in skin color and eye shape, but we are all humans.

Don: I would not have any reason to doubt that. Many other species' stories may be accurate, but they are stressed and focused upon to create fear. Those are the monsters that we see in movies, for example. People must wake up to the fact that there are trillions of planets and stars in our vicinity. This is in no way talking about the entirety of the universe. I have heard it described as comprising seven grand universes. It is incomprehensible how large God's creation is. We are tiny yet important despite the fact that we are mere specks, even smaller than bacteria.

GJ: I will not comment on the extent of God's creation. There is no way to describe it. We, as part of the Federation, can travel beyond this galaxy. However, when we do, we find that there are hostile races, so we have limited our travels inside this galaxy. There are so many planets within this galaxy that you would never be able to visit them even if you had a million years. That is how big this galaxy is. There is life on many millions of those planets.

Don: Can we expect to experience this in a grander sense, in terms of personal experience? I am not talking about just seeing crafts in the sky; I am talking about interacting with the federation personally within our lifetime.

GJ: That is what our plans are. Hopefully, some contacts will be made within this fiscal year, and you and Jim will be at the top of my list.

Don: Well, that has already occurred on this show tonight.

GJ: I would not have made myself know if that had not been the case.

Don: I would venture to say that this is the first time this has happened on any show, be it AM or FM, broadband, shortwave, or internet.

GJ: I am sure that is probably true. I will tell you a short story. I know that your time is limited. There is a race of people that you call reptilians. They are very bizarre-looking people. They are very hostile to our federation, but we have tried to be at least able to communicate with them and talk with them on occasion. I recently informed my staff that I would like to meet one of these people and interview them to develop an understanding of their thinking. Because you know, and I know, that this planet has been invaded by them for centuries.

We had an occasion where we stumbled upon a craft in a desert in New Mexico. Apparently, his craft was having issues, and he was forced to land and wait for assistance. Fortunately, our craft arrived at the right time, and we captured this individual. We did not harm him. He was a high-ranking general in his military, too. I went to rendezvous with this ship and talked to this person. We had five of our elders there with me. He informed us that people within this galaxy and on this planet want to cooperate with them. He said that they have found it necessary to take over governments of nations. He was accommodating in what he told us. He was a very astute and intelligent individual. He spoke perfect English, was about seven feet tall, and dressed elegantly in a battle garment.

He then began to tell us about the prophetic realm. He knew as much about scripture and prophecy as anyone I have ever known. He began to tell us about the prophets from his culture. Their prophets spoke of the time when Earth would be brought to the knowledge of Jesus Christ as the Lord and Savior. He said that his people feared that because they did not believe it. They do not want this acceptance of Christ to happen. However, he said Universal acceptance of Christ will probably happen within the next thirty years despite their efforts. I hope that he is right. We kept him for three days, then returned him to his spacecraft and contacted his people.

Don: Did he leave a calling card so we could contact him for an interview at this show?

GJ: He did not (laughing). His name is hard for me to pronounce, and I speak many languages. I believe it is pronounced General Gail-kah-tray.

Don: Okay, if he listens to the show, that invitation is open.

GJ: He might take you up on it.

Don: Okay (laughing), Jim, do you have a question? I am sure you probably have a million of them.

Jim: I am trying very hard to suppress the urge to ask technical questions.

GJ: Feel free; I will try to answer as much as possible.

Jim: The problem is that I will not be satisfied once we go down that track. I think that the things we have been talking about take priority. Don and I feel very strongly that humanity needs to take the reigns and control its own destiny if we do not want to succumb to the agenda of these individuals who want to rule this planet. That is where we have had to focus for the last six months. My work has revolved around that of Nicola Tesla, energy, and things of that sort. I am sure that you are aware of this. Even though these are my passions, I am trying to set these things aside and focus on the expansion of conscience, which we believe is an essential ingredient in accelerating the evolution of people to the point that they realize the kind of power that they really have, to be able to assist those of us on this planet that really want change. So that is where we have been concentrating.

GJ: That is very good; that is the right place, Jim. The human mind is so unlimited. We, as humans, use minimal percentages of our capabilities. The expansion of our consciousness and our minds is necessary before we can delve in to the realms that are before us. This has not happened in the scientific world because we have limited ourselves to the laws we have felt were appropriate. However, some laws are beyond that, even. I could give you examples of this, but it would be hard to describe it in English so you can understand it. Yet, I give you a vague description. Our spacecraft travel through space with antimatter generators and antigravity devices when we come close to other planets. Antimatter generators are the basic fundamental component of our propulsion systems. We probably have the most sophisticated and advanced propulsion systems of all the planets in the galaxy. We will let you look at one very soon, and you will understand what I am saying then.

Jim: That would be a great experience.

Don: Yes, it would be great if we could take a photograph as a memento to show people.

GJ: We will probably allow that.

Don: If it can be done where you are not compromising your safety. We are as aware of anyone else on the planet who is in danger of being here.

GJ: (Laughing) Uhhh – Yes!

Don: You must know that most people's hearts are not in the same place as those that rule the planet and the governments. There may be some exceptions, but what is being done in this world is leading this planet to destruction, leading this group of humans upon it to their destruction. Those who are hanging on to power seem desperate to do anything to retain that power. They will destroy it and bring everything down with it. So, if you could convey to the people of the federation, we intend to help elevate the conscience of full awareness of who we really are. Our purpose is to be alive here at this time and in this location, with the understanding of the gifts that the creator gave us. And with that understanding will come the understanding of the insanity of war and of murder and all that comes with it. Once we come to that collective understanding, and I think it will only take five percent for that shift to occur, we will be ready to meet our brothers and sisters in space.

GJ: Yes, Yes. Definitely. We are drawing very close to that time now. I know that you know that this nation has various black project technologies that are so advanced that you would not believe it. I have heard you mention it before Dawn. There are colonies on Mars already, and many, many, many projects are on the moon right now, also on Saturn. I won't say much more because I do not want to get all of your government people mad at me. I am sure all of the agencies are monitoring us right now if you could only see the number of people who are already living on planet Mars from this planet.

Don: Well, I have; that is my problem. I have. I know the derision that one faces when they state something so far out in left field. It is so diverse from the norm, yet others also know this. I may not know everything, but I do know many things. I give the glory and the credit to the God that I serve. That is where I stand. I don't mean the watered-down version of the truth or the propagandized version. I am in direct communication with the Creator. I don't always hear Him, but I know He hears me. I am working on my hearing in that respect.

GJ: (Laughing) Right. The basic message of Christianity, the gospel of Jesus, in the limited amount that you have it, is accurate. It is perfect to know that word, as we call it. So study it, and know what He said and did. If you do, you will be much closer to the truth.

Don: Okay, well, we are honored, and we know you must have more pressing things to do.

GJ: Well, I announced to the Alliance last night that I would make this phone call and that those who wanted to listen could do so. I imagine ten thousand people from the Alliance are listening to our conversation tonight. So you have fans from many places.

Don: Well, we send our greetings for successful and safe missions. I can speak for Jim, but I will let him speak for himself. But I look forward to the day when we all meet.

GJ: I hope that will be very soon, and I plan to work on that aspect myself. I have a crew that I am flying here tonight. They are my normal crew, and they also extend their greetings to you.

Don: Well, we reciprocate. Jim, do you have any closing comments?

Jim: Well, my closing comment is that I am most stunned by your extended offer to meet with us. If you know me and my psyche, this is something that I have wanted and thought extensively about since I was a young lad. So, if this comes to pass, I will be honored and ecstatic.
I look forward to the event with great anticipation.

GJ: Well, I am too, and the people I will bring with me are so wise that you will feel blessed just by being in their presence. They are very good people, humble, yet very intelligent. They will be glad to share their knowledge with you.

Jim: Well, that will be wonderful, thank you so much.

GJ: Well, I had better sign off. We have counted fourteen reptilian or gray alien spacecraft orbiting around us while we are sitting here. Fortunately, we have about twenty crafts of our own in the area, so we are okay.

Don: Well, give them a shout-out for us, too.

GJ: Okay, I shall.

Don: Okay, it has been a pleasure. I am sure that some people are just frozen to their seats listening to this show tonight, and the archive is going to go off the charts, I am sure. Thank you so much for calling us and sharing all this wonderful information with us. You are invited to call this show anytime.

GJ: I will be back; I will call you again. God bless you and thank you as well. My prayers are with you.

The above exchange is incredible, to say the least. According to General Jeremiah, the Galactic Federation comprises hundreds of planets to which Jesus Christ has personally ministered. I have already shared in this series how the Doctrine and Covenants 88 describes Christ's ministration to other worlds precisely as General Jeremiah suggested it happened. General Jeremiah spoke of most beings being totally human in appearance, with variations in skin tone, eye shape, etc. In addition, General Jeremiah claimed he captured and spoke with a seven-foot-tall humanoid being, who he described as reptilian. I understand this is strange, and I do not want to engage in the doctrinal ramifications of such things, but I promise to revisit this before the end of the present volume.

General Jeremiah said that this large beast's name was General Gailkahtray. General Gailkahtray was elegantly dressed, spoke perfect English, and was as familiar with the prophecies of the earth as anyone he had ever met. According to General Jeremiah, this experience took place around 2009. At that time, the creature and the society he represented believed that the world would experience wholesale conversion to Jesus Christ within the next thirty years or by the year 2039.

My real curiosity about this story centers upon the spiritual ramifications of General Jeremiah's encounter with Gailkahtray more than anything else. Gailkahtray and his people wanted to stop the Christianization of Earth because of the things the prophets had told them of their planet. If this account is true, then clearly, the Gailkahtray's people have been exposed to satanic influences despite being many light years from Earth. If Lucifer and his minions are quarantined upon this planet, in that case, what satanic influence could have breached the void to bring his people the false prophets and prophecies motivating their current behavior?

Given Enoch's description of Lady Wisdom's cosmic wonderings, I think we have found our prime suspect. The Lady is a deviant cosmic being with the access, knowledge, motivation, and capability to pull off a cosmic deception of this magnitude.

Thanks to Enoch, we know that she is capable of interstellar travel, unlike Lucifer and his imprisoned minions. Again, I do not share this account for you to believe it. I have heard many claims that ring false to me. I share this experience more than anything because of the implications it suggests: cosmic forces of opposition that exist beyond Satan's influence and the possibility of off-world beings receiving prophecies on the events that will transpire upon this world. Cosmic civilizations organize themselves for good or evil because of what is about to transpire upon this world. I believed things of this nature must have happened throughout the cosmos long before I knew this interview existed.

As of the publication of this book, General Jeremiah's interview occurred over fifteen years ago. If it is to be believed, GailKahtray's people now believe that the Second Coming of Christ will occur within the next fifteen years. I, too, have come to believe in a very similar time frame through completely independent means. Indeed, I fear something terrible will happen very soon - the events of Ezra's Eagle. These events, as I understand them, must occur by January 2025. Couple this with the fact that Chris Bledsoe's Lady has hinted that a global paradigm-shifting event will occur around Easter of 2026, and one begins to feel the walls closing in. If this 2026 Easter event correlates with the arrival of the latter-day antichrist and his approximate seven-year reign of terror, then the Second Coming of Jesus Christ would occur around the year 2034, which is well within the timeline put forward by General Gailkahtray. What do the Lady, the Antichrist, and the Beast-like creatures have in common? I believe the answer to this question is a mutual disdain for the Father's Beloved Son – Our Lord and Savior, Jesus Christ. I will have more to say about this topic before this volume is finished.

Chapter 9: Lightning Among the Stars

In the prior chapters, we reviewed many things. We began a theoretical discussion about the natures of multitudinous kingdoms that comprise the multiverse. We discussed the apparent limitations upon beings to travel in realms superior to their own and the freedom to explore those of equal or lesser glory. Enoch spoke of Wisdom's choice not to participate in the Father's plan of salvation and that she inherited a kingdom of glory suitable to those of her nature and disposition. Enoch also spoke of her ability to travel freely between her spiritual realm and the kingdoms of mortal men, in which she took great delight. We also contrasted her apparent freedom of movement to that of Lucifer and the others who are presently imprisoned here on this Earth. The prior chapter concluded with an indication that Lady Wisdom was on the move. Things are about to get very interesting. I believe that the gods of the ancient world are about to return to the shock and befuddlement of all humankind.

In this chapter, Enoch moves from the Lady to those who can withstand the deceptions of the last days through the gift and blessing of instant revelation through the Holy Ghost. You will recall that Enoch witnessed a storm that was gathering, with lightning, thunder, and powerful winds. I pointed out that these forces of nature can bless and destroy equally. So it will be with the burning fire of the last few days. While this fire will destroy the wicked, it will liberate and save the righteous. From this perspective, we should consider Enoch's words as he now describes the flip side of the lightnings and the forces of evil that pervade the multiverse.

> **43.1**. And I saw other lightnings and the stars of heaven, and I saw how He called them all by their names and they hearkened unto Him.

> **43.2**. And I saw how they are weighed in a righteous balance according to their proportions of light: I saw the width of their spaces and the day of their appearing, and how their revolution produces lightning: and I saw their revolution according to the number of the angels, and how they keep faith with each other.

> **43.3**. And I asked the angel who went with me who showed me what was hidden: 'What are these?'

43.4. And he said to me: 'The Lord of Spirits hath showed thee their parabolic meaning: these are the names of the holy who dwell on the earth and believe in the name of the Lord of Spirits for ever and ever.'

44.1. Also another phenomenon I saw in regard to the lightnings: how some of the stars arise and become lightnings and cannot part with their new form.

According to the passages above, the lightnings and the stars of heaven represent the righteous that would be blessed to live upon the Earth in the presence of the Lord forever and ever. These are those who will overcome the opposition and lies that are the common lot of the moral condition throughout the multiverse. I am both astounded and comforted by the fact that the Lord knows the names of all of these. He knows their stories, their hardships, and their triumphs. He called to them, and they harkened unto His voice.

How often has our prophet asked us to do the spiritual work necessary to HEAR our Father's voice? God is no respecter of persons. He loves the righteous, wherever they are, throughout the cosmos. The righteous are the lighting amongst the stars. Upon worlds without number they reside, but the Celestial Kingdom, which will be founded upon this Earth, will come forth from all the worlds His hands have made. While our life experiences will have been very different, we will all have in common our dependency and obedience to the promptings of the Holy Spirit.

Lamen and Lemuel had become hardened to the point they were past feeling. It was not that they could not feel the Holy Ghost in their lives at one point; rather, they chose to listen to science, reasoning, or the philosophies of men rather than to God. It would be wrong to assume that all other mortal worlds exist in various degrees of utopian societies. While Lucifer and his demonic legions are unparalleled in their intensity, as the Lady has demonstrated, opposition exists throughout the multiverse.

Regardless of where they spend their mortality, the children of heaven must overcome this opposition by learning how to act upon the Spirit's promptings, even if we do not understand why or what it all means. Many would call this weakness or foolishness, but God calls it being wise. A family friend once told me a story that illustrates the process of exercising these spiritual muscles. She and her family used to live and work in Japan. While grocery shopping, one day, she was prompted to buy bananas. This was odd because her family did not eat bananas. However, recognizing both the prompting and who was giving the prompting, she purchased the bananas without knowing why.

Later that day, she encountered a distraught woman with a crying child. The woman had only recently moved to Japan and could only speak English. Her husband was not at home, and she was waiting for her moving container to arrive, which had all of the family's supplies. As such, she had nothing but an empty house and a starving child. Her child, it turned out, had severe food allergies and, as such, had a minimal diet. When my friend asked her what her child could eat, to her surprise, the woman said bananas. Imagine the comfort and tender healing that this young mother experienced. After moving to a foreign country and feeling utterly alone, she discovered that the Lord had inspired a stranger to buy her bananas.

When we learn to hear the voice of the Lord and how to act upon it, we can truly become the Lord's hands in His children's lives. Conversely, a person whose spiritual choices have rendered them deaf, dumb, and blind to the promptings of the Father is no different than Lamen and Lemuel. Lamen and Lemuel lived life for themselves, while true disciples live to serve the Lord by serving His children.

Returning to Enoch's parabolic teachings of cosmic lighting, lightning does not rip forth from a clear blue sky. It is born of opposition and adverse conditions. Similarly, it is only under such conditions, which are common to mortals throughout the multiverse, that we can be proven. Lighting energizes the air around it. It lights up the night sky, dissipating darkness. Similarly, those who have learned to hear the voice of the Father are like lightning bolts illuminating the darkness of mortality's storms. Therefore, the Lord called two of His apostles, the Sons of Thunder, for they were brilliant examples of light in the gathering storms of darkness that otherwise engulfed the Jewish nation.

Enoch beheld that there was a correlation between the lightning and the cosmic revolutions. Due to the conservation of angular momentum, all heavenly bodies rotate, be it a moon, planet, sun, solar system, or galaxy. As such, rotations have come to denote the passage of time. Therefore, when Enoch speaks of the correlation between lightning and cosmic revolutions, he is speaking of the process of eternal progression. For men, this plan of progression is based upon men's ability, over time, to remain as faithful to God as the planets and stars are to their orbits and rotations. However, the primary difference here is that men must choose to remain in the orbit and influence of God, and planets and stars have no say in the matter. Just as the Lord did not force Lady Wisdom to participate in His plan of redemption, He does not force us to remain in His orbit.

Specifically, Enoch stated, "I saw their revolution according to the number of the angels and how they keep faith with each other." In this respect, the term angel is simply a child of heaven rather than a specific order of being. In this regard, the Lady is an angel in the same way that Lucifer and his demonic host are described as being angels. The heavens are filled with mortal worlds; upon each of these worlds, some sons and daughters are exercising their agency and gravitating to the orbits of their own design. The orbits they choose will follow them into the next world. Those with Celestial orbits will inherit the Celestial Kingdom. Those with baser orbital trajectories will inherit baser kingdoms of glory.

However, I believe that there is also more to be understood from the concept of angels keeping faith with one another. What are we to understand by this? To keep the faith with one another implies that there have been promises or covenants made between individuals that can and should be kept. I have alluded to this as fulfilling the measure of one's creation. Christ covenanted with us that He would come to Earth and atone for our sins, that we might be enabled to become heirs to the kingdom of God. We, too, have made covenants with each other.

David O McKay was the ninth president of the Church of Jesus Christ. He wrote an article titled The *Angles of God Were Among Us*. In that article, he shared the following story:

> According to a class member some sharp criticism of the Church and its leaders was being indulged in for permitting any company of converts to venture across the plains with no more supplies or protection than a handcart caravan afforded.
>
> An old man in the corner sat silent and listened as long as he could stand it, then he arose and said things that no person who heard him will ever forget. His face was white with emotion, yet he spoke calmly, deliberately, but with great earnestness and sincerity. In substance he said:
>
> I ask you to stop this criticism. You are discussing a matter you know nothing about. Cold historic facts mean nothing here, for they give no proper interpretation of the questions involved. Mistake to send the Handcart Company out so late in the season? Yes. But I was in that company and my wife was in it and Sister Nellie Unthank whom you have cited was there, too.
>
> We suffered beyond anything you can imagine and many died of exposure and starvation, but did you ever hear a

survivor of that company utter a word of criticism? Not one of that company ever apostatized or left the Church, because everyone of us came through with the absolute knowledge that God lives for we became acquainted with him in our extremities.

I have pulled my handcart when I was so weak and weary from illness and lack of food that I could hardly put one foot ahead of the other. I have looked ahead and seen a patch of sand or a hill slope and I have said, I can go only that far and there I must give up, for I cannot pull the load through it. I have gone on to that sand and when I reached it, the cart began pushing me. I looked back many times to see who was pushing my cart, but my eyes saw no one. I knew then that the angels of God were there.

Was I sorry that I chose to come by handcart? No. Neither then nor any minute of my life since. The price we paid to become acquainted with God was a privilege to pay, and I am thankful that I was privileged to come in the Martin Handcart Company.

In this story, an older man bore testimony that he and his company were aided in times of utmost need by angels from beyond. In similar ways, the Lord has not left us comfortless. I know this is true because I have felt the same forces at work in my own life. Things were so difficult a few times that I thought I could make it go no further. In these times, I felt strength and power beyond my own, enabling me to do what I could not do for myself. The angels of God are among us, and they minister to us. Indeed, we are told that the Aaronic Priesthood holds the keys to the ministering of angels. I wonder if priesthood holders exercise these keys as often as they should. Consider the following scripture:

And now Jesus knew that John was cast into prison, and He sent angels, and, behold, they came and ministered unto him. (JST Matt 4:11)

How was it that Christ was able to send angels to minister to John? It started with His asking for it to happen. Have you asked the Lord to send ministering angels to aid your loved ones? Do you remember in volume I of this series how we learned that God only intervened on behalf of the Watchers when He was petitioned to do so by the deceased family members in the Spirit World? Early in this book, we learned of the vested interest of those who sleep not in our success. They petition the Father night and day for our deliverance. Are we adding our petitions to theirs? Our God exercises His power when we exercise our agency. Ask, and ye shall receive. Parents should pray for angels to minister to their children and those in need. This is real, and it happens every day. We are all in this together. Let us keep faith with one another. We will need this power more and more with each passing day. Angels are among us.

Lastly, Enoch associated lighting with the bodies of the righteous. "I saw in regard to the lightnings: how some of the stars arise and become lightnings and cannot part with their new form." I am immediately reminded of Joseph Smith's account of the visage of the resurrected Moroni. Consider Joseph's description:

> I often felt condemned for my weakness and imperfections; when, on the evening of the above-mentioned twenty-first of September, after I had retired to my bed for the night, I betook myself to prayer and supplication to Almighty God for forgiveness of all my sins and follies, and also for a manifestation to me, that I might know of my state and standing before him; for I had full confidence in obtaining a divine manifestation, as I previously had one.
>
> While I was thus in the act of calling upon God, I discovered alight appearing in my room, which continued to increase until the room was lighter than at noonday, when immediately a person age appeared at my bedside, standing in the air, for his feet did not touch the floor. He had on a loose robe of most exquisite whiteness. It was a whiteness beyond anything earthly I had ever seen; nor do I believe that any earthly thing could be made to appear so exceedingly white and brilliant.
>
> His hands were naked, and his arms also, a little above the wrist; so, also, were his feet naked, as were his legs, a little above the ankles. His head and neck were also bare. I could discover that he had no other clothing on but this robe, as it was open, so that I could see into his bosom.
>
> Not only was his robe exceedingly white, but his whole person was glorious beyond description, and his countenance truly like lightning…He called me by name,

and said unto me that he was a messenger sent from the presence of God to me, and… that God had a work for me to do (JSH 1:29-33).

In the above passage, not only is Moroni's resurrected body described as having a countenance like lightning, but he calls Joseph by name, telling him that God had a work for him to do. All three of these elements correlate with Enoch's message to us in the last days. Enoch saw that God knew the inhabitants of the stars and that He called them by name. He saw that God had a work for us to do and that we should keep faith with those to whom we have covenanted. Lastly, Enoch saw the righteous inherited bodies of lightning, from which no power of darkness could separate them.

Enoch clearly uses lightning to refer to the glorified state of the physical bodies of the righteous, just as Joseph did about Moroni's resurrected body. It is hard for us to truly comprehend this because we know so little of the resurrection. How many of us have seen a resurrected being?

However, what has been revealed suggests that the differences between resurrected bodies themselves are profound. Consider what Paul taught concerning the resurrection:

> God giveth it a body as it hath pleased Him… All flesh is not the same flesh: but there is one kind of flesh of men, another flesh of beasts, another of fishes, and another of birds. There are also celestial bodies, and bodies terrestrial: but the glory of the celestial is one, and the glory of the terrestrial is another. There is one glory of the sun, and another glory of the moon, and another glory of the stars: for one star differeth from another star in glory. So also is the resurrection of the dead. (1 Cor. 15:38-42)

From the passage above, we understand that just as there are pronounced physical differences between the bodies of men, animals, birds, and fish, there are profound differences between the physical characteristics of resurrected bodies. It is important to understand the differences that Paul was referring to. However, to understand this more fully, we must first understand the differences between men, beasts, fish, and birds. A dog can smell as much as 100,000 times better than a human. A mantis shrimp can discern ten times the colors that human eyes can and can see in ultraviolet, infrared, and even polarized light. Humans are blind to such wavelengths. A human can respond to sounds between 20 and 20,000 Hz; anything outside of this range is not perceptible to the human ear. Bats, on the other hand, respond to sounds between 9 to 200,000 Hz.

Clearly, there are many differences between the different classifications of flesh. Yet, in all the animal kingdoms, nothing compares to the mind and genius of humankind.

Furthermore, the animal kingdom clearly demonstrates that there are more than five senses. For example, Humans are oblivious to magnetic fields. However, many creatures have highly adapted senses that enable them to feel and orient themselves via such forces. This additional sense enables many in the animal kingdom to circumnavigate the globe with astonishing accuracy. Indeed, some fish migrate from the depths of the sea back to the exact location in a river where they were born. Sharks have a different sensory organ in their nose, enabling them to sense the electric fields as small as a beating heart from miles away. Other creatures are capable of using echolocation with astonishing accuracy.

If such astonishing abilities exist between various creatures of mortality, what enhanced abilities must exist amongst the various degrees of resurrected beings? The possibilities are truly astounding. Do we have any ideas about what some of these abilities might be? Curiously, we do. Earlier in this chapter, we reviewed Joseph Smith's first encounter with Moroni. This was not his only encounter with him. The following account was published in the Deseret News on November 27, 1878, under "Report of Elders Pratt and Joseph F. Smith." The article is based on an interview with Joseph F Smith and David Whitmer. Consider the following curious encounter with Moroni and its implications for Celestial beings.

> David Whitmer (DW): When I was returning to Fayette with Joseph and Oliver all of us riding in the wagon, Oliver and I on an old fashioned wooden spring seat and Joseph behind us, while traveling along in a clear open place, a very pleasant, nice-looking old man suddenly appeared by the side of our wagon who saluted us with, "good morning, it is very warm," at the same time wiping his face or forehead with his hand. We returned the salutation, and by a sign from Joseph I invited him to ride if he was going our way. But he said very pleasantly, "No, I am going to Cumorah." This name was something new to me, I did not know what Cumorah meant. We all gazed at him and at each other, and as I looked round enquiringly of Joseph the old man instantly disappeared, so that I did not see him again.
>
> Joseph F. Smith (JFS): Did you notice his appearance?
>
> (DW) – I should think I did, he was, I should think, about 5 feet 8 or 9inches tall and heavy set, about such a man as

James Vancleave there, but heavier, his face was as large, he was dressed in a suit of brown woolen clothes, his hair and beard were white like Brother Pratt's, but his beard was not so heavy. I also remember that he had on his back a sort of knapsack with something in, shaped like a book. It was the messenger who had the plates, who had taken them from Joseph just prior to our starting from Harmony.

Soon after our arrival home, I saw something which led me to the belief that the plates were placed or concealed in my father's barn. I frankly asked Joseph if my supposition was right, and he told me it was. Sometime after this, my mother was going to milk the cows, when she was met out near the yard by the same old man (judging by her description of him) who said to her, "You have been very faithful and diligent in your labors, but you are tried because of the increase of your toil, it is proper therefore that you should receive a witness that your faith may be strengthened." Thereupon he showed her the plates.

My father and mother had a large family of their own, the addition to it therefore of Joseph, his wife Emma and Oliver very greatly increased the toil and anxiety of my mother. And although she had never complained she had sometimes felt that her labor was too much, or at least she was perhaps beginning to feel so. This circumstance, however, completely removed all such feelings, and nerved her up for her increased responsibilities.

We learned that Moroni was the older man in the above account. As such, Moroni was clearly able to alter his appearance. When he appeared to various members of the Whitmer family, his countenance was not like lightning. Rather, he looked like a shorter older man. This is not the only resurrected being that we know of who was able to alter his appearance at will. Christ, too, was able to alter His appearance. He did so on the road to Emaus so His disciples did not recognize Him. Then, when it suited Him, He changed back to a recognizable state in an instant right before the eyes of His amazed disciples.

After Christ's disciples recognized Him, Christ vanished before their eyes, just as Moroni had vanished. Therefore, not only were these two Celestial beings able to alter their physical appearance at will, they seem capable of bending space-time at will. We have another example of Christ appearing miraculously inside a locked room and Moroni moving through the roof of Joseph's cabin.

Christ once asked His followers an interesting question, "Which of you by taking thought can add one cubit to his stature?"- Matt 6:27. The obvious answer was none of them. In asking this question, Christ was highlighting the limitations of mortality. It would appear, however, that resurrected celestial beings can do precisely this. Indeed, it would seem that with nothing more than a thought, not only can one's physical stature be changed in an instant, but one entire body can be changed instantaneously.

Should we be surprised by this ability? That's probably not. After all, what do we really look like? Based upon the many near-death experiences that have been recorded, people who are permitted to pass into the spirit world and return often see and recognize their loved ones on the other side. Sometimes, they appear to be in the prime of life, while others appear to be older or younger. It would seem then that spirits can assume the physical characteristics of any point along the timeline their physical bodies experienced in mortality.

This is very interesting to consider, particularly given that our physical bodies depend on our mortal ancestors' DNA. Our spirits, however, were not born of our same earthly parents. It, therefore, stands to reason that our spiritual DNA is dependent upon the DNA of our heavenly parents. While we cannot remember our heavenly parents, we know they have glorious, perfected bodies of flesh and bone. As such, our spiritual forms would be beautiful without the imperfections that plague our physical bodies. I suspect that the beauty of our spirits far surpasses that of any physical body we have seen in mortality.

This being said, the spirit is both flexible and impressionable. It would appear that by undergoing the process of mortality, our spirits took on the appearance of our mortal genetics. While we no longer appear as we once did, that spiritual identity is not lost to us; it simply lies beyond the veil of forgetfulness. That veil of forgetfulness accompanying us in mortality stays with us throughout our second estate, including the spirit world. Indeed, I suspect this veil of forgetfulness has something to do with our appearance. Why do I say this?

In mortality, only one set of parents could permanently pierce the veil of forgetfulness: Adam and Eve. They did so by eating the fruit of the Tree of Knowledge. As such, they could remember their premortal existence. It is therefore interesting that when Enoch sees Adam in the spirit world, as he has many times throughout the Book of Enoch, he is never recognized by Enoch as Adam but always as Michael, the great prince. Why?

Enoch was familiar with Adam, and they knew each other regarding mortality. Adam lived in mortality with Enoch and his people for hundreds of years together. However, when Enoch sees Michael, Adam's pre-mortal form, he never associates the one with the other. The reason, I believe, is because, in the Spirit world, Adam was not bound by the veil and reverted back to his premortal form. This is my working theory on the matter anyway.

Furthermore, we understand that every adult spirit can morph itself to such a degree that it can comfortably take the form of a newborn infant. If this were not the case, children would be born soulless, which is certainly not true. I believe that our mortal and spiritual appearance will forever remain part of who we are. It would seem natural to me that, as resurrected beings, we could move at will along the continuum of these two appearances since they are both us.

If you were to study the various recorded appearances of "The Lady", it would become apparent that she does not always appear the same. Sometimes, she appears as an adult woman, and sometimes as a girl, and at other times, she appears as an adolescent young woman. I believe she is limited in her ability to appear as she once was. She has matured from a spiritual child to an adult spirit woman. As such, it seems to me that each of these forms is readily available to her.

Similarly, Moroni first appears to Joseph Smith as a glorious god-like being. Later, he appeared as an older man. These were all likely forms that Moroni was already familiar with.

In addition, Satan has presented himself to be an angel of light. I believe this is because he once was an angel of light, and this form is, therefore, still available to him. Satan is also described as being very handsome. Beauty is the default state of a spirit because our spirits are the offspring of perfected, glorious heavenly parents who are incapable of producing anything other than a perfected spiritual body.

What, then, will our resurrected body appear after being born again by the power of Jesus Christ? The Lord has said that the righteous will receive a new name in the resurrection; why not a new appearance, remade not in the image of our heavenly parents or our earthly parents, but in the image of Christ, the Father of our resurrected body? As it were, this new and third form will be comprised of the radiance of lightning. As such, throughout our existence, we will have had three separate and distinct physical forms, all patterned after the form of God.

The first was created by our heavenly parents, the second by our earthly parents, and the third by our Lord and Savior - Jesus Christ, who becomes our literal Father. Thus, we will all have three fathers in the heavens, just as the Godhead comprises three separate and distinct men. Each of these three sets of parents will have contributed to our unique physical appearance in their own way. I would, therefore, theorize that because each of these three appearances uniquely belongs to us, we will, at a minimum, be able to move freely between these forms at will. If this is possible, what else might be possible? Paul taught that "some have entertained angels unawares." This might be the reason that this is possible. – Hebrews 13:2.

We do not know if such miraculous abilities are inherent in all classes of resurrected beings, but they are certainly held by Celestial beings, and they have been exhibited by both the Lady and Lucifer. Yet these last two will never have glorified physical bodies. They will forever remain as spirits, which I suppose will also limit their abilities in some manner, to which we are presently ignorant.

Therefore, while Enoch saw in his vision that some glorified beings with a countenance like lightning would not be parted from their new forms, it certainly does not mean they cannot do so if they choose. I believe that throughout the multiverse, the gods likely visit the worlds of mortals regularly and interact with us in ways we may be surprised. After all, it seems to me that it is as easy for a celestial being to rearrange the molecules of their own bodies as it was for Christ to transform water into wine.

Chapter 10: The Righteous Will Inherit the Earth

In the prior chapter, we learned of the incredible nature of the resurrection, which Enoch saw as the stars of heaven being clothed with lighting. I also reviewed some accounts about resurrected beings that suggest inherent abilities far beyond what we currently possess. I briefly wrote regarding our physical and spiritual ancestry. I speculated that resurrected beings may be able to take upon themselves any physical form they have had during their existence. I suggest both our spiritual and physical bodies have been the product of our parents, our spirit bodies derived from our heavenly parents, and our physical bodies from our mortal parents. I then discussed how, through the resurrection, we are all born again in Christ unto everlasting life, in a new immortal body of either a Celestial, Terrestrial, or Telestial nature, with very few sons of perdition receiving resurrected bodies that are without the glory of any kind.

As the Book of Enoch continues, Enoch shifts from the physical bodies of the righteous to their eternal dwelling places. You will recall from the prior chapter that the righteous were identified as those who chose to hang upon the name of the Lord of Spirits during Mortality. Said another way, these denied themselves, placing the will of the Father above their own. Consider the following in this context:

> **45.1**. And this is the Second Parable concerning those who deny the name of the dwelling of the holy ones and the Lord of Spirits.

> **45.2**. And into the heaven they shall not ascend, and on the earth they shall not come: such shall be the lot of the sinners who have denied the name of the Lord of Spirits, who are thus preserved for the day of suffering and tribulation.

In the passages above, Enoch is taught that those who denied the will of the Father, in place of the will of the natural man, will not only be cut off from His heavenly courts above but from being able to set foot upon the Earth. This goes back to the limitations that are placed upon beings of lower orders to travel the fullness of the multiverse. Beings of lower orders will be damned or prohibited from traveling beyond the realms of glory to which they have obtained.

Let us review Enoch's prior conversation with the Lord, which is relevant to the present topic. In that conversation, Enoch perceived the Earth as not an inanimate object but a living sentient entity that mourned the wickedness upon its surface. The scriptures teach us that a soul is the product of spirit and flesh combined – see D&C 88:15. God explained to Enoch that before He created things physically, He first created them spiritually, see Moses 3:4-5. What is spirit? Spirit, according to D&C 84:45, is synonymous with truth and light. Furthermore, D&C 93:29 describes intelligence as being light and truth; therefore, intelligence and spirit are the same. Joseph Smith taught that spiritual matter, like physical matter, cannot be created or destroyed.

However, as with physical matter, it can be organized and modified. The ultimate potential of spiritual matter cannot be realized until it is inseparably joined with physical matter. The one quickens the other in a synergistic relationship that makes more of the two than by itself. Those who have ever been to a funeral know that once the spirit has left a body, the body immediately reverts to unquickened matter. There is something very different about it.

On the other hand, there have been many accounts of near-death experiences wherein people claim to have seen flora and fauna in the next world shine with internal light and speak of a wonderful form of sentience in plant life. Some have described the ability to communicate on a spiritual level with such creations. If the Lord created all things spiritually before they were created physically, then all things must be fundamentally spiritual. This includes the Earth itself.

Enoch had an experience where he witnessed the spirit of the Earth morning for the wickedness that existed upon its face and observed it pleading to the Lord for relief. The experience was very moving for Enoch, who advocated for the Father on Earth's behalf. Consider the following as it is particularly relevant to understanding the subject matter at hand:

> And it came to pass that Enoch looked upon the earth; and he heard a voice from the bowels thereof, saying: Wo, wo is me, the mother of men; I am pained, I am weary, because of the wickedness of my children. When shall I rest, and be cleansed from the filthiness which is gone forth out of me? When will my Creator sanctify me, that I may rest, and righteousness for a season abide upon my face?

> And when Enoch heard the Earth mourn, he wept, and cried unto the Lord, saying: O Lord, wilt thou not have compassion upon the earth?

> The Lord said unto Enoch: Behold these thy brethren; they are the workmanship of mine own hands, and I gave unto them their knowledge, in the day I created them; and in the

Garden of Eden, gave I unto man his agency; and unto thy brethren have I said, and also given commandment, that they should love one another, and that they should choose me, their Father; but behold, they are without affection, and they hate their own blood… I can stretch forth mine hands and hold all the creations which I have made; and mine eye can pierce them also, and among all the workmanship of mine hands there has not been so great wickedness as among thy brethren. (Moses 7:47-49, 32-33, 36)

In the above passages, the mourning of the Earth is placed in context. The Father explains to Enoch that there is no other planet in the multiverse with such wickedness upon its surface as the Earth. This is astounding. It, therefore, stands to reason that Earth has suffered more than any other planet in the multiverse due to this wickedness. Therefore, it can be said that the Earth's experience has caused it to descend below all things. Therefore, it cannot be a coincidence that the Earth will rise above all things and become a Celestialized Kingdom of Glory upon which the God of Heaven Himself will reside forever. Christ described Himself as descending below all things and that He can rise above all things as well. We, too, have been sent to this planet to learn how to overcome Lucifer's prison rather than being overcome by it.

Furthermore, when the Lord has seen fit to remove large hosts of people from this planet in times past, why has He also removed large portions of Earth for them to dwell upon in the cosmos? Why not relocate them to another world rather than bringing portions of this one with them? It seems that the Lord has linked our destiny with this planet itself. As the Earth noted above, our physical bodies are formed from the elements of the Earth. Therefore, we are literally her children. She is part of us, and we are part of her. We are bonded, conjoined in common destiny.

Therefore, I must conclude that one reason the Earth wept at the wickedness upon her surface was her knowledge that these would be parted from her. As our mother, is it impossible that the Earth has a kinship with those who have gone forth from her? Might the Lord remove portions of her surface to accompany her children's cosmic adventures so that she might not be parted from them but rather be restored herself when they are restored?

Consider this interaction between Joseph Fielding, who asks questions, and Parley P. Pratt, who answers them:

> *Quest*. 7th.--How can the stars fall from heaven to earth, when they (as far as we know) are much larger than the earth?

Ans.--We are nowhere given to understand that all the stars will fall or even many of them: but only "as a fig tree casteth her UNTIMELY figs when she is shaken with a mighty wind." the stars which will fall to the earth are fragments, which have been broken off from the earth from time to time, in the mighty convulsions of nature. Some in the days of Enoch, some perhaps in the days of Peleg, some with the ten tribes, and some at the crucifixion of the Messiah.

These all must be restored again at the "times of restitution of ALL THINGS." This will restore the ten tribes of Israel; and also bring again Zion, even Enoch's city. It will bring back the tree of life which is in the midst of the paradise of God; that you and I may partake of it. When these fragments, (some of which are vastly larger than the present earth) are brought back and joined to this earth, it will cause a convulsion of all nature; the graves of the Saints will be opened, and they rise from the dead; while the mountains will flow down, the valleys rise, the sea retire to its own place; the islands and continents will be removed, and earth be rolled together as a scroll. The earth will be many times larger than it is now. -- "If I have told you of earthly things and ye believe not; what would you think if you were to be told of heavenly things?" *Millennial Star* volume 1 no. 10 (10 February 1841):257-59

According to Elder Pratt, portions of the Earth have been removed to accompany the children of Earth on their cosmic journeys. These fragments and their inhabitants will be restored in the coming days. This restoration will be part of the restoration of all things. According to Elder Pratt, when this happens, the Earth's surface area will be many times larger than it is now. This will enable the earth to hold many more inhabitants than it can hold now.

Elder Pratt taught that these fragments were removed as part of miraculous separation events, during which large bodies of the righteous were conveyed away. We have almost no record of what the inhabitants of such fragments have been doing. According to Enoch, however, we learn that the people of his fragment have been ministering to the cosmos, see Moses 7:31.

Elder Pratt is not the only one who speaks of such things. Eliza R Snow wrote a song about them based on teachings she had heard from the prophet Joseph Smith. This song was included in the first seven hymnals of the church and was titled, "Thou, Earth, was once a glorious sphere." The lyrics of the hymn are shown below:

Thou, Earth, wast once a glorious sphere
Of noble magnitude,
And didst with majesty appear
Among the worlds of God.

But thy dimension have been torn
Asunder piece by piece,
And each dismembered fragment borne
Abroad to distant space.

When Enoch could no longer stay
Amid corruption here,
Part of thyself was borne away
To form another sphere.

That portion where his city stood
He gained by right approved;
And nearer to the throne of God
His planet upward moved

And when the Lord saw fit to hide
The ten lost tribes away,
Thou, Earth, was severed to provide
The orb on which they stay.

An thus, from time to time, thy size
Has been diminished, till
Thou seem'st the law of sacrifice
Created to fulfill.

There can be no doubt that Eliza and Elder Pratt agreed regarding this alternate history of the Earth. Both of these would have learned these things from the same source – Joseph Smith.

Earlier, Enoch asked the Lord a pertinent question, "when will be Earth rest?" This is how the Lord answered this question.

And it came to pass that Enoch cried unto the Lord, saying: When the Son of Man cometh in the flesh, shall the earth rest? I pray thee, show me these things.

And the Lord said unto Enoch: Look, and he looked and beheld the Son of Man lifted up on the cross, after the manner of men; and he heard a loud voice; and the heavens were veiled; and all the creations of God mourned; and the Earth groaned; and the rocks were rent; and the saints arose, and were crowned at the right hand of the Son of Man, with crowns of glory; and as many of the spirits as were in prison came forth, and stood on the right hand of God; and the remainder were reserved in chains of darkness until the judgment of the great day.

And again Enoch wept and cried unto the Lord, saying: When shall the earth rest?

And Enoch beheld the Son of Man ascend up unto the Father; and he called unto the Lord, saying: Wilt thou not come again upon the earth? Forasmuch as thou art God, and I know thee, and thou hast sworn unto me, and commanded me that I should ask in the name of thine Only Begotten; thou hast made me, and given unto me a right to thy throne, and not of myself, but through thine own grace; wherefore, I ask thee if thou wilt not come again on the earth.

And the Lord said unto Enoch: As I live, even so will I come in the last days, in the days of wickedness and vengeance, to fulfil the oath which I have made unto you concerning the children of Noah; and the day shall come that the Earth shall rest, but before that day the heavens shall be darkened, and a veil of darkness shall cover the earth; and the heavens shall shake, and also the earth; and great tribulations shall be among the children of men, but my people will I preserve...
(Moses 7:54-61)

Enoch was told that the Earth would not rest until after the days of great tribulation. In the opening verses of Enoch's writings, he said he was writing his book to bless the righteous who would live during these days of trial. According to the Lady, those days of tribulation started in October 2023 and will progressively get worse going forward. Personally, I do not believe the days of trial will truly begin until the Lady herself manifests to the world at large, confronting it with her strong delusion. According to the Lady, she will save us with the "victory of her immaculate heart." This is, of course, nonsense. Both she and the antichrist will sift the world so that there are no more fence-sitters. All will be either for or against the God of Israel, and then the great purging of the wicked will come. Only then will the Earth be able to rest.

> Wherefore, let us go to and labor with our might this last time, for behold the end draweth nigh, and this is for the last time that I shall prune my vineyard. Graft in the branches; begin at the last that they may be first, and that the first may be last, and dig about the trees, both old and young, the first and the last; and the last and the first, that all may be nourished once again for the last time.
>
> And as they begin to grow ye shall clear away the branches which bring forth bitter fruit, according to the strength of the good and the size thereof; and **ye shall not clear away the bad thereof all at once**, lest the roots thereof should be too strong for the graft, and the graft thereof shall perish, and I lose the trees of my vineyard. **For it grieveth me that I should lose the trees of my vineyard**; wherefore ye shall clear away the bad according as the good shall grow, that the root and the top may be equal in strength, until the good shall overcome the bad, and the bad be hewn down and cast into the fire, that they cumber not the ground of my vineyard; and thus will I sweep away the bad out of my vineyard. (Jacob 5:63-66)

According to the passages above, the wicked will not be removed from the Earth all at once but gradually. This process will begin in the reverse order of the grafting of the House of Israel. As Joseph was the last to be scattered, he would be the first to be regrafted and purged. The stated purpose of purging the vineyard in the way the Father described above is to preserve as much fruit as possible. In other words, the Lord is not anxious to destroy us. He wants us to turn to Him. As such, He will start with the most wicked amongst us so that those who have eyes to see might repent and humble themselves before the Lord.

The sign we have been given that these things are about to take place is the regrafting of the original branches, Joseph and Judah. As has already been discussed, Joseph and Judah have been gathered, and two great nations have arisen from among them, The United States of America and Israel. Now that this has occurred, the process whereby the wicked will gradually be destroyed will accelerate. The main destructive event will not occur in America until the sinners here have come to the full. I believe that this will occur once they have moved to overtly seize control of the government through the events of Ezra's Eagle.

As such, peace is soon to be taken from the earth. In the last several years, we have seen the total destruction of ISIS's Islamic Caliphate. Next, we have seen neighbors take up the sword against neighbors in the war between Russia and Ukraine. The stories of corruption within both of these two countries are legendary. Now, we are witnessing the rise and fall of Hamas. Israel has vowed to purge its own vineyard from those who would continue committing horrific atrocities against innocent women and children. The Lord has given the Middle East to Israel; no mortal man or nation can invalidate the covenants and promises of the Lord, no matter how politically incorrect they broadcast them to be. Just look to the Canaanites or the corrupted Jaredite and Nephite nations who were all swept off of lands of promise because they turned their backs to the God of Israel.

Such purging events have always served as a call to arms. The world's nations will rise up in indignation, aligning themselves with one side or the other. There will be no refuge in strength of arms, for the battle is the Lord's, and His alone. As such, wars and bloodshed will continue, and as they do, the more wicked parts of the world's population will be removed and cast into the fire. The purging of the Lord's vineyard will gain momentum and awaken the wicked to the stark and terrifying realization that the Lord will not always permit them to take joy in their sins.

The day will soon come when, shortly after the antichrist arrives on the world stage, the Whore of Babylon will be purged. After she is cast into the fire, the wicked of America will be purged, and many of her fair cities will be rendered desolate. Yet, once the wicked branches of America have been lopped off and cast into the fire, a new host of Israel will be grafted in their place, and the desolate heritages that were forsaken by their former inhabitants will be reoccupied. The great purge will culminate in the Battle of Armageddon, wherein the antichrist lays siege against Jerusalem for three and a half years. He will be accompanied by all of the wicked nations of the Earth.

If you have eyes to see, you will realize that the polarizing events that are taking place right now in Israel are galvanizing the hearts of many against the Jews. In hate and rage, they even now cry out for the Jewish state to be eliminated. There are still holdouts as of yet, but even these will melt away in the heat of the coming hatred that is about to encircle the Earth. Eventually, all the Gentile nations will take up the sword against Israel. When that happens, the Lord will raise up two prophets in Israel. Through Priesthood power, these two will spare the country of Israel from total destruction. For three and a half years, these two will preserve Israel; however, in the end, the Lord will permit them to be killed as well. There have been apocryphal writings suggesting that these two witnesses will be Enoch and Elijah, who have been translated. Time will tell the truth of these things.

Regardless of the identities of these two men, The Lord Himself will come down and put a full end to war. Any remaining wicked across the entire globe will be eliminated in an instant. It will be the single largest day of destruction since the great flood. It is only after this event that the Earth will begin to rest.

The wicked will have no part of that rest. Indeed, they will be cut off and will never again be permitted to reside upon the Earth from that time forward. After the wicked have been removed and the Earth has been restored to its former size, the globe will enter a state of global rest and prosperity never before imagined. The wicked will be nowhere to be seen.

The narrative of Enoch continues:

> **45.3**. On that day Mine Elect One shall sit on the throne of glory and shall try their works, and their places of rest shall be innumerable. And their souls shall grow strong within them when they see Mine Elect Ones, and those who have called upon My glorious name:

> **45.4**. Then will I cause Mine Elect One to dwell among them. And I will transform the heaven and make it an eternal blessing and light

> **45.5**. And I will transform the earth and make it a blessing: And I will cause Mine elect ones to dwell upon it: but the sinners and evil-doers shall not set foot thereon.

> **45.6**. For I have provided and satisfied with peace My righteous ones and have caused them to dwell before Me: but for the sinners there is judgement impending with Me, so that I shall destroy them from the face of the earth.

According to the passages above, the Earth will ultimately become the new home for God the Father and His heavenly courts on high. We have seen that the size of the heavenly courts is innumerable, in the hundreds of trillions. As such, we must not believe that the Earth will be the sole Celestial sphere in the cosmos. After all, innumerable cycles of salvation have preceded us, and future cycles will continue onward forever and ever - without the beginning of days or the end of years. Therefore, not only will the Earth be Celestialized, but it will also be relocated in the cosmos to the Celestial realm of glory, where every world within that glorious kingdom will represent the glorious culminating prize of righteousness for the cycle of salvation with which their respective worlds were a part.

We have learned that when the Earth is glorified, it will be much larger than it is now. The entire sphere will be a place of habitation. Therefore, it can accommodate the righteous from throughout the cosmos. This will be partly because few will have qualified themselves by walking down the straight and narrow way their Father laid before them. Broad will be the path that leads to the lower kingdoms of glory, and many there will be that find those.

As has been discussed, this may be one of the reasons that the New Jerusalem will be so large, to accommodate the righteous millions. According to John, the New Jerusalem will be a cube that extends 1,400 miles above the present surface of the Earth. Might this suggest that the radius of the Earth might increase by 1,400 miles? The current radius of the Earth is approximately 4,000 miles. If this is true, then the Earth's surface area would be approximately two and a half times larger than it is now. Furthermore, John the Revelator had this to say about the new Earth:

> And I saw a new heaven and a new earth: for the first heaven and the first earth were passed away; and there was no more sea. And I John saw the holy city, New Jerusalem, coming down from God out of heaven, prepared as a bride adorned for her husband. And I heard a great voice out of heaven saying, Behold, the tabernacle of God is with men, and He will dwell with them, and they shall be His people, and God Himself shall be with them, and be their God. And God shall wipe away all tears from their eyes; and there shall be no more death, neither sorrow, nor crying, neither shall there be any more pain: for the former things are passed away. And He that sat upon the throne said, Behold, I make all things new. And He said unto me, Write: for these words are true and faithful. (Rev 21:1-5)

According to the passage above, there will no longer be a sea on the surface of the Earth. The oceans will be removed so that the entire surface area will be available for the Father's heavenly mansions. Where will the oceans go? Surely, there will still be oceans within the Celestial worlds. However, distance will no longer be a factor, for the immensity of space will be nothing for a Celestial being, who can bend space-time with nothing more than a thought. Therefore, even if oceans reside on other worlds, they will seem much closer than our oceans today.

I do not have all of the answers about these things; I have theories. What I do know is this. The Lord lives. The Earth is very special. Those fortunate enough to inherit the Earth will also inherit the Celestial Kingdom and join the community of the multiverse's most glorified residents. The righteous of this cycle will eventually be joined by God the Father and His Son, Jesus Christ, upon this globe. All Celestial worlds will be connected, as will all generations of time. Therefore, the Celestial Kingdom will be all about families and the types of relationships that bring true and everlasting joy. On that day, there will be no real estate more desirable for the participants of this iteration of the Father Plan than that of Earth. In those days, the earth's inhabitants will come forth from all the creations of the Father, and we will dwell together. There can be no greater joy or pleasure than residence here. For the future habitants of the earth, the multiverse will be well and truly open in all its kingdoms, glories, and wondrous mysteries and to none else. All others will be confined to the realms of equivalent or lesser glory to that of their resurrected bodies.

Chapter 11: The Hidden Son

In the prior chapter, we learned about the Earth's future status. The Earth will be created anew and become the righteous's inheritance. The wicked will be swept off, and the Earth will rest for a thousand years. The end will come, and the Earth will become celestialized and relocate to the Celestial kingdom within the cosmos. When that happens, God Himself will call the Earth home.

Enoch sees the greatest of all mysteries in the scriptures unfold before his eyes in this chapter. He sees the Son of Man. Before this point in Enoch's writings, there have been hints and foreshadowings of a Messianic figure, but nothing like what is about to take place in the present chapter. If the Book of Enoch is what it claims to be, then this chapter represents the oldest clear and unambiguous teachings that we have regarding the Son of God, the Savior of the World. Consider the following:

> **46.1**. And there I saw One who had a head of days, and His head was white like wool, and with Him was another being whose countenance had the appearance of a man, And his face was full of graciousness, like one of the holy angels.

The passage above introduces us to a new character, the Head of Days, while the head of days is another righteous man. In Richard Lawerence's translation of the Book of Enoch, he translated Head of Days as Ancient of Days. As such, the passage above closely aligns with a mysterious vision that was seen by the prophet Daniel. Consider Daniel's vision of these same two beings.

> I saw in the night visions, and, behold, *One* like the Son of Man came with the clouds of heaven, and came to the Ancient of days, and they brought him (the Ancient of days) near before Him (the Son of Man). And there was given Him (the Son of Man) dominion, and glory, and a kingdom, that all people, nations, and languages, should serve Him: His dominion *is* an everlasting dominion, which shall not pass away, and His kingdom *that* which shall not be destroyed. (Daniel 7:13-14)

In Daniel's writing, Christ comes to the Earth and receives the throne from the Ancient of Days. Perhaps CH Charles's translation of Head of Days is more accurate in this context. Head means beginning. Adam was the first man and is the Head of Days on Earth. This is confirmed by Doctrine and Covenants section one-sixteen.

> Spring Hill is named by the Lord Adam-ondi-Ahman, because, said He, it is the place where Adam shall come to visit his people, or the Ancient of Days shall sit, as spoken of by Daniel the prophet.

According to the passage above, the Ancient of Days is Adam, or Michael, the great prince. However, context is crucial, particularly with this title. Given that this title means "The First," it could also be applied to both the Father and the Son, both of which have also been referred to as the Beginning and the End, the First and the Last, which is similar to the Head of Days. As the first man, Adam is clearly the source of mortality upon Earth and, therefore, the Head of Days. However, God the Father created Adam, and as such is also the Head of Days. In addition, Jesus Christ is the Only Begotten of the Father. He was with Adam and Eve in the Garden when they were created and provided the means to overcome the fall by being born again through the power and grace of Christ's atonement, which they foreshadowed with their sacrifices. As such, the title 'Head of Days' applies equally to all three of these incredible individuals, for all three of them are the great fathers of humanity in their own rights.

As such, there are times in the scriptures where the title Lord refers to God the Father and other times when it refers to Jehovah, so there are times in the Book of Enoch when the title Head of Days refers to God the Father, who Enoch typically called Lord of Spirits. Therefore, context is important to discern to whom this title is being applied. When the titles Head of Days and Lord of Spirits are used together, they describe Michael and God the Father. There are other occasions when the title Head of Days and Michael are used together, and in this context, the title Head of Days is being used in the context of God the Father, the creator of Adam, the first man.

In the context of this chapter, the title Head of Days is used in the opening verse, and the title Lord of Spirits is used in verse three; as such, given the context, in this particular instance, the title Head of Days is clearly referring to Michael, the righteous man with the Head of Days is Jehovah. The Lord of Spirits is God the Father. As such, Enoch sees three familiar beings together in council: Michael, Jehovah, and Elohim. The vision continues:

> **46.2**. And I asked the angel who went with me and showed me all the hidden things, concerning that **Son of Man**, who He was, and whence He was, (and) why He went with the **Head of Days**? And he answered and said unto me:

46.3. This is the Son of Man who hath righteousness, with whom dwelleth righteousness, and who revealeth all the treasures of that which is hidden, because the Lord of Spirits hath chosen Him, and whose lot hath the pre-eminence before the **Lord of Spirits** in uprightness forever.

Again, Michael, Jehovah, and Elohim are referenced in these passages together. However, the Spirit of the Lord is moving upon Enoch to learn more about the Son of Man. Enoch learned that the Son of Man personifies righteousness. In addition to this, the Son of Man is also described as the gatekeeper of all hidden knowledge. This is very interesting to me because the identity of Jesus Christ as the Son of God was one of the greatest mysteries of the ancient world. This was by design. Only those who were seeking Him were able to find Him. Only those who sought Him learned of the Father's true nature and, therefore, the Godhead itself. Consider the following passage, which was recorded one hundred years before the birth of Christ.

> For it is I that taketh upon me the sins of the world; for it is I that hath created them; and it is I that granteth unto him that believeth unto the end a place at My right hand. For behold, in My name are they called; and if they know Me they shall come forth, and shall have a place eternally at My right hand.
>
> And it shall come to pass that when the second trump shall sound then shall they that never knew Me come forth and shall stand before Me. And then shall they know that I am the Lord their God, that I am their Redeemer; but they would not be redeemed. Therefore I say unto you, that he that will not hear my voice, the same shall ye not receive into my church, for him I will not receive at the last day. (Mosiah 26:23-26, 28)

When Christ spoke these words to Mosiah, His identity was a mystery to most of the planet. Yet, Christ clearly stated that for men to be saved, they must know Him! Not much has changed since then. Yes, the world professes to know the name of Jesus Christ, but they do not know Him. Knowledge of His true nature as a separate physical entity apart from both the physical nature of the Father and the spiritual entity of the Holy Ghost is so different to the modern Christian world that we are labeled as non-Christians. Our Christ is not their Christ, they say. They are right, for they know not the being they claim to worship. He is a mysterious enigma to them. He is nowhere and everywhere at the same time. Yet, the scriptures teach that Christ was resurrected in the express image of His Father. He asked Mary not to touch Him until He ascended into heaven to present Himself to His Father, which clearly indicates that He and His

Father are separate beings. Yet, modern Christianity is built upon foolish doctrines of the Nicene Creed, which compel Christianity to embrace a false notion of God in order to join the club. Such do not know the true nature of the Hidden Son nor the God they worship.

It is the modern version of the Arian controversy all over again. Yet many humble Christians know Christ through the Spirit and not through the dogma of their blind guides. So it is that all humankind must put off the teaching of the deaf, dumb, and blind, who claim to be authorities on the nature of God because of diplomas hanging upon their office walls. The spiritual equivalent of this has been happening since the world began. For the true nature of the Godhead is hidden and always has been. The true nature of the Godhead is only known by those who humble themselves before Them. Such will consider the wisdom of men to be foolish and seek instead to be taught by the Spirit of the Almighty.

Thus, the identity of the Son of Man has always been a mystery that comparatively few people have penetrated. Jesus Christ is mentioned often in the Book of Mormon, which gives the impression that knowledge of Him was universal among the Nephite nation. However, this was not true. Upon closer inspection of the narrative, the true believers of Jesus Christ are in the perpetual and persecuted minority. It was the believers who were forced to flee for their lives in the middle of the night. It was the believers who were rounded upon and told that they would be killed on the morrow unless they denied their faith. It was the believing mothers and their children who were rounded up and cast into the fires - burned alive for not denying their knowledge of Jesus Christ. It was the believers who buried their weapons of war and laid down in front of their enemies to be killed rather than offending the God that they had come to know.

Where did their knowledge of the Son of God come from? A few had dreams and visions of Him. Others were taught about Him through angelic visitation. Yet, the majority who believe in His name did so based solely upon the whispering of the Holy Ghost. The scriptural evidence that the Nephites themselves had was just as obtuse on the subject as our Old Testament and for the same reasons. Knowing the Father's hidden Son has always been the primary test of mortality. Remember that while the Book of Mormon is filled with references to Christ, the people of the Book of Mormon did not have this book. They had the writings contained within the Brass Plates. Consider the following pieces of evidence of Christ that the masters of the law put forward in an attempt to convince the Zoramites of the reality of Christ.

> We have beheld that the great question which is in your minds is whether the word be in the Son of God, or whether there shall be no Christ.

Ye also beheld that my brother has proved unto you, in many instances, that the word is in Christ unto salvation. My brother has called upon the words of Zenos, that redemption cometh through the Son of God, and also upon the words of Zenock; and also he has appealed unto Moses, to prove that these things are true. (Alma 34:5-7)

In the passages above, Amulek called to the people's minds three prophecies Alma shared to prove that Jesus Christ was the Son of God. What were these three smoking gun prophecies that Alma hoped would convince the Zoramites of the reality of Jesus Christ? Let's look at each of these in turn. As we do, you must ask yourself if these examples would have convinced you. We will begin with Alma's usage of the words of Zenos, the same prophet who gave us the allegory of the olive tree. Consider the following:

Do ye remember to have read what Zenos, the prophet of old, has said concerning prayer or worship? For he said: Thou art merciful, O God, for thou hast heard my prayer, even when I was in the wilderness; yea, thou wast merciful when I prayed concerning those who were mine enemies, and thou didst turn them to me. Yea, O God, and thou wast merciful unto me when I did cry unto thee in my field; when I did cry unto thee in my prayer, and thou didst hear me.

And again, O God, when I did turn to my house thou didst hear me in my prayer. And when I did turn unto my closet, O Lord, and prayed unto thee, thou didst hear me. Yea, thou art merciful unto thy children when they cry unto thee, to be heard of thee and not of men, and thou wilt hear them. Yea, O God, thou hast been merciful unto me, and heard my cries in the midst of thy congregations.

Yea, and thou hast also heard me when I have been cast out and have been despised by mine enemies; yea, thou didst hear my cries, and wast angry with mine enemies, and thou didst visit them in thine anger with speedy destruction. And thou didst hear me because of mine afflictions and my sincerity; and it is because of thy Son that thou hast been thus merciful unto me, therefore I will cry unto thee in all mine afflictions, for in thee is my joy; for thou hast turned thy judgments away from me, because of thy Son. (Alma 33:3-11)

In this passage of scripture, taken from the writings of Zenos, there is a cryptic passage that speaks of God hearing and answering Zenos's prayers because of His Son. This example was used by Alma because, in Alma's mind, it was obvious who Zenos was talking about. However, this was only obvious because the Father had already revealed the Son to him. Alma was not convinced by this scripture that Christ was the Son of God. He was convinced because of his personal experiences with God. As a result of the Spirit's prior workings upon his soul, when he read these passages, they resonated with mighty force in his heart that the prior things that the Father had already revealed to Him were true.

However, for the unbelieving among the Zormanites, these passages were not clear and convincing evidence that Jesus Christ was the Savior of the world. This is because, by design, the doctrine of the Son of Man has been hidden from the masses. Only those with eyes to see and hearts to feel can see it. To such, the nature of the Son of Man is as clear as day. All the prophetic passages above would produce an eye roll for those who do not. Let us now consider the next passage of scripture regarding the doctrine of Christ that Alma drew upon to convince the unbelieving Zoramites. Remember, the Zoramites zealously professed to believe in God. They claimed to know and worship Him. They built sanctuaries unto Him and prayed aloud to Him in those sanctuaries. Yet, while they drew near Him with their lips, their hearts were far from Him. Theirs was a religion of pomp and circumstance, not of humility and spiritual instruction. Therefore, consider the following example in this light:

> For it is not written that Zenos alone spake of these things, but Zenock also spake of these things—For behold, he said: Thou art angry, O Lord, with this people, because they will not understand thy mercies which thou hast bestowed upon them because of thy Son.
>
> And now, my brethren, ye see that a second prophet of old has testified of the Son of God, and because the people would not understand his words they stoned him to death. (Alma 33:15-17)

Zenock was stoned to death for proclaiming to the House of Israel that they could obtain mercy but through the Son of God. Obviously, the House of Israel did not have ears to hear. Because of the spirit of God within Alma, the words of Zenos and Zenock were smoking guns that God the Father would send His Son to atone for the world's sins.

Yet, while it was clear that both Zenos and Zenock were speaking of God's Son, Christ remained shrouded in mystery, not unlike the many mysteries we come across in the scriptures today. Today, when we read of mysteries in the scriptures, such as giants and the miraculous restoration of the House of Israel, we shrug them off. As such, we are guilty of the same behavior.

Most of us have inherited our faith in the true nature of the Son of God because of the faith and sacrifice of our ancestors. Too few of us have paid the price to be able to know these things for ourselves. As such, while many profess Christ with our lips, we have been warned that even the very elect, according to the covenant, will be deceived in the coming day. This could not happen if our faith were sure and unmovable. Yet, the faith of many is based solely upon the teachings of others. As such, in the coming days, when the world is flooded once more by great lies and strong delusions, will the houses of our faith be able to weather the coming storms?

We are surrounded by demons and their demonic narratives. We live within the resonating echo chamber of their lies and doctrines. As such, without God, it will be just as easy for us to shrug off the Father's hidden Son as it has been for every generation that has come before us. Reader, beware, you must come to know the Father's Hidden Son for yourself; otherwise, your faith will not withstand the coming days.

"Stick to the basics," many often cry, "Do not delve into the mysteries of God." Yet Jesus Christ has been, and continues to be, the greatest mystery in the scriptures. If you do not know Christ, who He really is, how can you worship the Father for who He truly is? No man knows the Father, except Christ reveals Him. No man knows the Son, except the Father reveals Him. No man knows anything unless they humble themselves and seek to be taught by God, not by men. This is easier said than done.

My wife once had a close friend with a remarkable spiritual gift. The Lord told this woman in a dream that there was another book of scripture besides the Bible. Following an impression, my wife gave her a copy of the Book of Mormon, and her friend began to read it. She was astonished by the book and told my wife of the dream the Lord had given her years before about the Book of Mormon. She would come over to our house and read the Book of Mormon with my wife, and the two would weep together because of joy. She then told my wife of another dream that she had. In this dream, she was in a strange building with long hallways and tightly woven carpet on the floors and walls. The halls were lined with classrooms, and people were being sealed with angelic stamps in the classrooms. She received a stamp, but her family would not enter the building or receive their own stamps.

My wife then arranged for her friend to have a tour of the church, guided by the missionaries. The church building matched her dream. She went and shared with her family what she had been learning. They mocked her. She spoke with her church leader, who convinced her it was wrong. Ultimately, she stopped studying with my wife to have peace in her family. We have since moved away, and I do not know what has become of her. I pray that she will have the strength to trust in the Lord above the teachings of men. This is not the first experience of this nature we have known; it will not be the last. While many will hear the voice of God, few will have the strength to act upon it, and when doing so, it will bring down upon them the wrath and scorn of man.

Let us consider Alma's last example of the Son of God.

> Behold, He was spoken of by Moses; yea, and behold a type was raised up in the wilderness, that who soever would look upon it might live. And many did look and live. But few understood the meaning of those things, and this because of the hardness of their hearts. But there were many who were so hardened that they would not look, therefore they perished. Now the reason they would not look is because they did not believe that it would heal them.
>
> O my brethren, if ye could be healed by merely casting about your eyes that ye might be healed, would ye not behold quickly, or would ye rather harden your hearts in unbelief, and be slothful, that ye would not cast about your eyes, that ye might perish?
>
> If so, wo shall come upon you; but if not so, then cast about your eyes and begin to believe in the Son of God, that He will come to redeem His people, and that He shall suffer and die to atone for their sins; and that He shall rise again from the dead, which shall bring to pass the resurrection, that all men shall stand before Him, to be judged at the last and judgment day, according to their works. (Alma 33:19-22)

This third example was well known by every Israelite, yet still, the symbolism is not uncontroversial. Wasn't Lucifer symbolized by a serpent? Didn't the Lord command Israel to not worship brazen images? Wasn't a serpent on staff the symbol of Ningishzida, one of the ancient Sumerian Watchers? The fact remains that while there was obvious recognizable truth behind all three of these passages, each of these examples could be easily rationalized away by "learned" men. Therefore, it is not from men that we should seek answers. Yet, men are loud and forceful. They communicate their ideas with forceful passion and make it easy to discard the truth for error. Let us consider men's reasoning in the Book of Mormon, which caused many to reject Jesus Christ.

> And they began to reason and to contend among themselves, saying: It is not reasonable that such a being as a Christ shall come; if so, and He be the Son of God, the Father of heaven and of earth, as it has been spoken, why will He not show Himself unto us as well as unto them who shall be at Jerusalem? Yea, why will He not show Himself in this land as well as in the land of Jerusalem?
>
> But behold, we know that this is a wicked tradition, which has been handed down unto us by our fathers, to cause us that we should believe in some great and marvelous thing which should come to pass, but not among us, but in a land which is far distant, a land which we know not; therefore they can keep us in ignorance, for we cannot witness with our own eyes that they are true. And they will, by the cunning and the mysterious arts of the evil one, work some great mystery which we cannot understand, which will keep us down to be servants to their words, and also servants unto them, for we depend upon them to teach us the word; and thus will they keep us in ignorance if we will yield ourselves unto them, all the days of our lives. (Hel 16:17-21)

The passage above represents a twisted and dangerous logic that is the tell-tale pattern of Satan. He projects his own depravity upon the accused. In the passage above, Satan accused the Prophets of setting themselves up as the gatekeepers to some great mystery and knowledge that they wanted to leverage to obtain power over their hearts and minds. Yet, in reality, the prophets have always attempted to teach the people that they must come to God and learn from Him directly. We must learn to hear Him. If we can learn how to discern truth for ourselves, we become dangerous to Satan and his kingdom. We can see through his lies.

It has always been Satan who has sought to control the flow of knowledge to obtain power and control over men. He did so with our first parents in the Garden of Eden. He convinced them to partake of the fruit of the Tree of Knowledge. His purpose was to get them to disobey God so they would be removed from the garden. He would then seek to use that punishment to make them angry at God. When Eve began to remember who Satan was and how he rebelled against God, he did not deny the fact but rather sought to reframe the narrative. He was not particularly successful at doing so at first. Adam and Eve humbled themselves before the Lord, repented of their sins, and looked to God to redeem them. Yes, Satan was able to prevail over Cain, but everyone else could readily see through his lies. Even when Lady Wisdom arrived the first time, her ideas found no purchase in the minds of men. It would not be until the arrival of the Watchers that Satan would be able to finally flip the narrative.

Ever since his first success, he has been honing and refining his craft. He wants to be the source of men's inspiration. He knows that if men learn to turn to God and seek to learn from the source, his power will be greatly diminished. Therefore, he has crafted many alluring ways to make accepting his ideas easy and the knowledge of God shameful. Those who teach his lies receive the honor, praise, and accolades of men.

Throughout history, Satan has ingeniously devised ministries of truth to reinforce his lies and cause the truth and those who believe it to appear ridiculous. In modern times, he has inspired the flow of disinformation and then coopted the term "fake news" to shout down any who oppose him. He hides the truth and seeks to undermine the credibility of those who would reveal it. He does so by calling them crazy conspiracy theorists or intolerant bigots. He then uses the full force of his mighty apparatus to crush them and does so under the guise and protection of a fabricated sense of moral supremacy. It is under such thinly veiled disguises that fascism has always risen to positions of great power. Under the cloak of truth and social justice with which they shroud themselves, these seek to control the narrative and thus decide what truth is acceptable in light of the greater good. As such, they censor and suppress conflicting ideas. They engineer social divisiveness and inequality throughout society. Yet, the upholders of the new mortality are themselves embroiled in scandal, intrigue, and wickedness in high places. From such gatekeepers of truth turn away!

All truth can be circumscribed into one great whole. Satan's lies will not reconcile with the restored gospel of Christ. As such, it is easy to discern between truth and error; however, it is not popular. However, following after the truth has never been popular.

Today, Jesus Christ is a character of historical fact. Yet, the same shroud of lies and misinformation that shrouds the philosophies of men now shrouds the doctrine of Christ. As such, while billions profess to know His name, few truly know Him. Their twisted concept of the Godhead is fed to them by the same demonic forces behind all lies. So much so that the true nature of the Godhead has become so radical that to believe it is to be branded as a heretic. It will result in being ostracized from the Christian faith by its self-appointed gatekeepers. Thus, in many ways, Jesus Christ is as mysterious to the world today as He ever has been.

As such, I fear that the world is as ill-prepared for the events of the Second Coming as the Jews were for His first. Too few understand the challenges that lie ahead. Too few are prepared for the trials of faith that are about to reign down fire upon the Earth. It is not that these things cannot be understood; it is that too few are interested in understanding them. As such, the world is about to undergo the greatest test of its temporal existence, blindfolded with both arms tied behind its back.

> These things have I written, which are a part of the things which He taught the people; and I have written them to the intent that they may be brought again unto this people, from the Gentiles, according to the words which Jesus hath spoken. And when they shall have received this, which is expedient that they should have first, to try their faith, and if it shall so be that they shall believe these things then shall the greater things be made manifest unto them.
>
> And if it so be that they will not believe these things, then shall the greater things be withheld from them, unto their condemnation. Behold, I was about to write them, all which were engraven upon the plates of Nephi, but the Lord forbade it, saying: I will try the faith of my people. (3 Nephi 26:8-11)

It is not enough to accept the scriptures as the word of God. The Pharisees and Sadducees claimed to accept the words of the prophets, but while they so proclaimed, they were blind to their meaning. Therefore, the scriptures are filled with references to the blind leading the blind.

The Book of Mormon is a wonderful tool. Indeed, a godsend is meant to bless us and prepare us for the last days' events. It contains Christ's unparalleled discourse within the third Nephi regarding the events that will transpire in the last days. The Book of Mormon contains many Isaiah chapters hand-selected by a prophet of God who saw our day and knew what would happen to us. His Isaiah selections are meant to prepare us for these things. Combine these things with Mormon and Moroni's commentary of the history of this continent, and not a single Latter-day Saint should be deceived by what is about to happen. Yet, despite all this and more, we are practically as blind as the rest of the world. This is so because we have taken lightly the Father's gifts. As such, the whole church was placed under condemnation and remains so today– see D&C 84:54-58.

As a Church, we have the Book of Mormon, yet we do not understand what it is that we have. Rather than studying the hand-selected prophecies within its pages, we strive to power through them as quickly as possible. Christ commanded us to study the worlds of Isaiah. Do you suppose it is enough to listen to another man's words about the words of Isaiah rather than seeking counsel from the God of Israel, who gave them to Isaiah in the first place?

Those who diligently seek to be taught by God will be taught by Him. Such will find the marvelous symmetry that exists within His gospel. Those who seek to be taught by men will receive the teachings of men. The philosophies of men often contradict one another, as well as the restored gospel of Christ. The teachings of men bring confusion and darkness, while the teachings of God bring light and truth.

There have been a great many who have pierced the veil of unbelief and have come to see things as they really are. The pattern for so doing has always been the same. Nephi, the first author of the Book of Mormon, taught us how to do this. He is an incredible example in this regard. His understanding of these things has changed my life, and I hope it has also changed yours. Consider his words:

> For he that diligently seeketh shall find; and the mysteries of God shall be unfolded unto them, by the power of the Holy Ghost, as well in these times as in times of old, and as well in times of old as in times to come; wherefore, the course of the Lord is one eternal round. For He is the same yesterday, today, and forever; and the way is prepared for all men from the foundation of the world, if it so be that they repent and come unto Him. And the Holy Ghost giveth authority that I should speak these things, and deny them not. (1 Nephi 10:18, 19, 22)

Nephi gives a powerful admonition of how we are to obtain truth. His record demonstrates that he practiced what he preached. However, too few of us do the things that he did. We are hearers of his words only. He lived them, and his writings are filled with the fruit by which we can judge the truthfulness of his words. I have taken Nephi's teachings to heart. I know that he was telling the truth. I have not learned them in the same way as he did. By this, I mean that I did not see them in vision upon an exceedingly high mountain. Yet, through the power of the Holy Ghost, I have seen them and know they are true. The Spirit has taught me about these things, and what I have been taught fits beautifully with every other teaching the Lord has ever revealed to His prophets. Nephi's teachings are not dangerous doctrines that lay at the periphery of the gospel; they are the mainstay foundational tenants whereby God the Father reveals His hidden Son to the inhabitants of the multiverse.

In the last few days, there have been many with itchy ears that go away after all kinds of strange doctrines, doctrines that are both bizarre and untrue. History has plainly shown that both angels and demons impart doctrines to the children of men. Not every idea and concept that pops into your mind will be of divine origin. Indeed, Satan is the loudest voice in most people's heads. He speaks clearly and regularly. Therefore, we MUST understand that there are guardrails to personal revelation.

The doctrines of the restored gospel of Jesus Christ are the guardrails. If you "received" ideas or promptings from God, they should easily reconcile within the greater whole of gospel knowledge. While on the other hand, the doctrine of demons will not reconcile with the restored gospel of Jesus Christ. Such doctrines will contradict the council and teachings of God. The philosophies of men will require you to discard the Proclamation to the Family, traditional teachings of morality, and other basic tenants of the gospel. The philosophies of men will cause you to see the Lord's prophets as the out-of-touch relics of a bygone age. You cannot believe such things without first stepping over the gospel's guardrails.

If you step over the guardrails of the gospel, you will be deceived. The scary thing is that the real deceptions have not even arrived yet. According to the covenant, Christ prophesied that even the very elect will wilt under the coming deceptions. To survive those days, we need to learn how to be taught by God directly and constantly. This is what the scriptures speak of as understanding the true mysteries of God. The knowledge of such things enabled many of the ancients to build upon a sure foundation many years before Christ was born. Consider Alma's teachings concerning these things:

> Yea, and the voice of the Lord, by the mouth of angels, doth declare it unto all nations; yea, doth declare it, that they may have glad tidings of great joy; yea, and He doth sound these glad tidings among all His people, yea, even to them that are scattered abroad upon the face of the earth; wherefore they have come unto us.

> And they are made known unto us in plain terms, that we may understand, that we cannot err; and this because of our being wanderers in a strange land; therefore, we are thus highly favored, for we have these glad tidings declared unto us in all parts of our vineyard.

For behold, angels are declaring it unto many at this time in our land; and this is for the purpose of preparing the hearts of the children of men to receive His word at the time of His coming in His glory. And now we only wait to hear the joyful news declared unto us by the mouth of angels, of His coming; for the time cometh, we know not how soon. Would to God that it might be in my day; but let it be sooner or later, in it I will rejoice.

And it shall be made known unto just and holy men, by the mouth of angels, at the time of his coming, that the words of our fathers may be fulfilled, according to that which they have spoken concerning Him, which was according to the spirit of prophecy which was in them. (Alma 13:22-26)

Alma said the Lord sent angels to proclaim the gospel to many in antiquity. King Benjamin was taught by an angel of God, and so were Abinadi, Alma, Ammon, Aaron, Omni, Himni, King Lamoni, Abish's father, Amulek, Nephi, Jacob, and Lehi. Yet, what do we understand by this? Did all of these men have to see a visible manifestation of an angelic being to be taught by an angel? This is not what Nephi taught. Nephi taught that the teachings of angels and the teachings of the Holy Ghost are the same:

Do ye not remember that I said unto you that after ye had received the Holy Ghost ye could speak with the tongue of angels? And now, how could ye speak with the tongue of angels save it were by the Holy Ghost? Angels speak by the power of the Holy Ghost (2 Nephi 32:2-3)

What difference does it make if you are taught by the Holy Ghost or if you are taught by an angel of light? Angels speak by the power of the Holy Ghost. The only difference between an angelic message and a message from the Still Small Voice is the faith required to believe it. Laman and Lemuel were past feeling and had to see an angel to be instructed. Yet, the Lord has said that more blessings are for those who do not require such manifestations to believe. Regardless of hearing the truth spoken from the lips of an angel that causes the earth to shake and tremble or hearing the Holy Ghost's gentle promptings within the recesses of your heart while pondering and praying in the solitude of your closet, it is the same. Truth is truth. It is by learning to be instructed by such promptings that the righteous throughout all the ages of the Earth have had the Son revealed to them by the Father and the Father by the Son.

Thus, we see that if one truly comes to know God, the Eternal Father, and His Son, Jesus Christ, they will do so through the administration of the Holy Ghost. Through the administration of the Holy Ghost, the mysteries of God are unfolded unto the children of men. Thus, in a genuine sense, men cannot teach the mysteries of God. Just try teaching these doctrines to those who are unwilling to pay the price to understand them, and you will know what I am talking about. Such incredible doctrines can only be taught and received by the Holy Ghost.

> Behold, I would exhort you that when ye shall read these things, if it be wisdom in God that ye should read them, that ye would remember how merciful the Lord hath been unto the children of men, from the creation of Adam even down until the time that ye shall receive these things, and ponder it in your hearts. And when ye shall receive these things, I would exhort you that ye would ask God, the Eternal Father, in the name of Christ, if these things are not true; and if ye shall ask with a sincere heart, with real intent, having faith in Christ, He will manifest the truth of it unto you, by the power of the Holy Ghost.

> And ye may know that He is, by the power of the Holy Ghost; wherefore I would exhort you that ye deny not the power of God; for he worketh by power, according to the faith of the children of men, the same today and tomorrow, and forever. And again, I exhort you, my brethren, that ye deny not the gifts of God, for they are many; and they come from the same God. And there are different ways that these gifts are administered; but it is the same God who worketh all in all; and they are given by the manifestations of the Spirit of God unto men, to profit them.

> For behold, to one is given by the Spirit of God, that he may teach the word of wisdom; and to another, that he may teach the word of knowledge by the same Spirit; and to another, exceedingly great faith; and to another, the gifts of healing by the same Spirit; and again, to another, that he may work mighty miracles; and again, to another, that he may prophesy concerning all things; and again, to another, the beholding of angels and ministering spirits; and again, to another, all kinds of tongues; and again, to another, the interpretation of languages and of divers kinds of tongues. And all these gifts come by the Spirit of Christ; and they come unto every man severally, according as He will. (Moroni 10:4-5, 7-17)

The gifts and knowledge of God are administered by the Holy Ghost. By the power of the Holy Ghost, you may know the truth of all things. By the power of the Holy Ghost, otherwise, normal men and women can be magnified to be able to do mighty works, impart the mysteries of God, heal the sick, raise the dead, be able to move mountains, command the trees, and even the waves of the sea. All these things are possible for all humankind, according to the will and pleasure of God. This being said, God's house is a house of order. You or I will not receive revelation regarding the ministration and governance of the Church. Only the Lord's key holders will receive revelations on the ordinances and administrations of the Kingdom of God. However, too many erroneously outsource their own spiritual education to the hands of others.

If you are to enter the covenant path by being baptized by one having authority, if you are to receive the gift of the Holy Ghost by the laying on of hands, these things can only be performed by keyholders. Regarding keyholder authority, no revelation can bridge the authority gap. As such, if you will receive the saving ordinances of the temple, you must enter by the gate. So, all the saving ordinances can be performed for both the living and the dead. These ordinances of the gospel can only be received from those having the authority to administer them.

However, all of the ordinances of the gospel represent the gateway of the covenant path and not the destination. If you are to progress down this covenant path to the highest degree of exaltation, you must fulfill the measure of your creation. Keyholder ordinances are not enough. Personal revelation is absolutely critical for you to fulfill your mission in life. This can be obtained in no other way. If your spiritual education consists of nothing more than the words of the prophets and apostles and all the other general authorities of the Church, then your education is incomplete.

> If all you or I know about Jesus Christ and His restored gospel is what other people teach or tell us, then the foundation of our testimony of Him and His glorious latter-day work is built upon sand. (Elder Bednar -Prepare to Obtain Every Needful Thing)

Jesus Christ, the Son of Man, is the gatekeeper to salvation. To obtain salvation, we must seek to be taught at His hand. This can happen in no other way besides personal revelation through faith, diligence, and effort. We must seek to be taught by the Lord Himself.

> And everyone that harkeneth to the voice of the Spirit cometh unto God, even the Father. And the Father teacheth Him of the covenant which He has renewed and confirmed upon you. (D&C 84:47-48)

159

Too many fall short in their spiritual progress because they see Jesus Christ only as the means to obtain a remission of their sins. He is so much more than this. Jesus Christ is The Way, The Truth, and The Life. He is the Living Water, the Bread of Life. He is our Exemplar, and He is our Teacher. We obtain salvation not by repenting of our sins alone but by FOLLOWING HIM. We obtain salvation by doing the things that He did. The most important example He provided for us was seeking to understand His Father's will and then fulfilling that will with exactness. This is what it means to be valiant in your testimony of Him.

> Not every one that saith unto me, Lord, Lord, shall enter into
> the kingdom of heaven; but he that doeth the will of my
> Father which is in heaven. (Mathew 7:21)

How did Jesus Christ learn the will of His Father? He prayed, meditated, and went into the mountains early and often. He spent time in the temple, His Father's house. He sought time to be alone with His Father, to be instructed by Him. Christ diligently learned His Father's will in His life, and then He did it. This is His greatest example to us. How can we claim to truly be His disciples if we do not follow His example by doing the same thing ourselves?

It is not by calling upon His name with our lips alone that we obtain the kingdom. It is by becoming like Him. We become like Him; if we become like Him, we do the will of the Father. The will of the Father in your life is one of the most important mysteries of God that you can know. As Enoch saw so many thousands of years ago, Jesus Christ, the Son of Man, is the gatekeeper to the Father's greatest mysteries. The greatest and most important mystery for you will be how to fulfill your mission and purpose in life.

When Jesus taught the people, He most often did so using parables. This masked the true meaning of His words. His disciples were confused by this practice and questioned Him about it. Consider His response as keeper of the mysteries of the Kingdom of God.

> Jesus' disciples came and said to Him, "Why do you use
> parables when you speak to the crowds?"
>
> Jesus replied, "Because they haven't received the secrets of
> the kingdom of heaven, but you have. For those who have
> will receive more and they will have more than enough. But
> as for those who don't have, even the little they have will be
> taken away from them. This is why I speak to the crowds in
> parables (Matt 13:10-13 Common English Translation)

As has been discussed, the very existence of the Son of Man was an impenetrable mystery to the Jews. There have been comparatively few people in the history of the world who have truly come to know the Son of Man.

To this end, I have discovered a very curious pattern in my study of the scriptures. I have discovered that whenever the phrase Son of Man is used by Jesus Christ, it is done in the context of the mysteries of God. In other words, the title Son of Man is a red flag that a bombshell doctrine is being revealed. This makes perfect sense given the context of the Book of Enoch, wherein the Son of Man was described as being the keeper of Heaven's mysteries. I will strive to include examples of this as the book's narrative continues.

Lastly, in the passages of the Book of Enoch that we have been discussing, Enoch learned that the Son of Man was given pre-eminence before the Lord of Spirits in uprightness forever. In another way, Enoch saw that the Son of Man sat on the Father's right hand and was second only to Him in the kingdom of God. This is an astounding doctrine for any age of the Earth, but particularly so given that this knowledge was held by the prediluvian world.

Many have come to know the mysteries of the kingdom of God, which are vital for us to fulfill the full measure of our creations. Nobody can do these things for us. Lehi and Nephi both tried on many occasions to teach Laman and Lemuel the mysteries of God, but they would not receive them. So it is with the vast majority of the human family.

Most will only receive what they can passively absorb from others as they are carried to and fro in life's swift, relentless currents. Only those who swim against the powerful currents of this world seeking to be taught by the Almighty directly will be able to know God's will in their lives. The mysteries of God are intended for kings and poppers alike. I challenge you to search the scriptures for yourself to find an example of a single person who has obtained exaltation without seeking to be instructed in the mysteries of the Kingdom of God. It has never happened, and it never will! The principle of personal revelation is the principle of salvation, and according to the Book of Enoch, the Son of Man is the keyholder to all such mysteries.

Chapter 12: Judge of Nations

In the prior chapter, we were introduced to the world's first usage of the term - Son of Man. We learned that the Son of Man was the personification of righteousness. We also learned that He is the keyholder of the mysteries of Heaven. I discussed how knowledge of the true nature and character of Jesus Christ is one of the greatest mysteries the world has ever known. Even today, when so many claim to know Him, they do not. Indeed, the reality of the true nature of Christ and His Father as two separate resurrected men is so revolutionary that the world believes that it disqualifies those who would hold such views from being Christians. Therefore, for the vast majority of the Earth's inhabitants, the true nature of the Godhead remains as mysterious as it ever has been. You cannot know the Father without knowing the Son, and you can only learn of them through the power of and administration of the Holy Ghost.

The prevailing concept of the Godhead as three entities in one intangible formless being that permeates the multiverse as a nebulous power without body, parts, or passions is at odds with the scriptures. Christ walked the earth with a body of flesh and blood. When He was baptized by John in the river Jordan, His Father spoke from the heavens saying, "This is my beloved Son, in whom I am well pleased." The Holy Ghost also descended upon the people in the symbolic form of a Dove. Furthermore, Christ repeatedly stated that He did nothing without witnessing His Father do it first. How, then, are they not three individual beings? Why would we believe that they are such a radical and damnably heresy?

Jesus Christ did not resurrect from the grave as an intangible, unknowable force. He rose from the grave on the third day with a resurrected body of flesh and bone. He showed His tangible body to many who witnessed this firsthand. The first of all of His disciples to see him was Mary of Magdala. When she recognized Him, she rushed to embrace Him, but He stopped her, saying, "Touch me not, for I have not yet ascended unto my Father." If Jesus Christ and the Father were physically the same, why would He need to ascend into the heavens to physically present Himself to Himself? It makes no sense. Again, the scriptures witness that while the Father and the Son are one in purpose, they are certainly not the same being. Yet, while men will continue to teach such nonsensical doctrines, only those seeking to be instructed by the Father can come to truly know Him.

> Whom say ye that I am? Simon Peter answered and said,
> Thou art the Christ, the Son of the living God. And Jesus
> answered and said unto him, Blessed art thou, Simon Bar-

jona: for flesh and blood hath not revealed *it* unto thee, but my Father which is in heaven. (Mathew 16:15-17)

So it is, and so it always has been. If we are to learn the mysteries of God, we must seek for them. If we do so with full purpose of heart and in humility and sincerity, God will make the truth of all things known to us—even the true nature of Himself.

We now return to Enoch's incredible vision when Enoch continues to be instructed regarding the mystery of the Son of Man.

> **46.4.** And this Son of Man whom thou hast seen shall †raise up† the kings and the mighty from their seats, [And the strong from their thrones] and shall loosen the reins of the strong, and break the teeth of the sinners.

> **46.5.** [And He shall put down the kings from their thrones and kingdoms] Because they do not extol and praise Him, nor humbly acknowledge whence the kingdom was bestowed upon thcm.

> **46.6.** And He shall put down the countenance of the strong, and shall fill them with shame. And darkness shall be their dwelling, and worms shall be their bed, and they shall have no hope of rising from their beds, because they do not extol the name of the Lord of Spirits.

> **46.7.** And these are they who †judge† the stars of heaven, [And raise their hands against the Most High],†And tread upon the earth and dwell upon it†. And all their deeds manifest unrighteousness, and their power rests upon their riches, and their faith is in the †gods† which they have made with their hands, and they deny the name of the Lord of Spirits,

> **46.8.** And they persecute the houses of His congregations, and the faithful who hang upon thc name of the Lord of Spirits.

Enoch's vision continues by describing the blind, unenlightened actions of the worldly wise. These judge the stars of heaven. In this context, the stars in heaven are the righteous who have risen above the blindness that is so prevalent upon the Earth. The leaders of men judge and persecute these men and women who have chosen to be taught by God instead of by them. As such, the men of earth rail against them. As such, the kings of the earth heap upon these crosses of shame. As the inhabitants of the great and spacious buildings of the world, they mock, scorn, and deride. Therefore, the kings of the earth force the true disciples of the King of kings to bear the world's crosses, just as they would cause the Son of Man to carry His cross and die upon it.

Enoch saw that the Son of Man would not sit idly by forever. God the Father has given the world's judgment to His Son. As such, vengeance is the Lord's, and He shall repay when the world has ripened in iniquity. When the Great and Terrible Day of the Lord arrives, Enoch foresaw that the Son of Man would break the teeth of the sinners and deliver the captive from the mighty. In the presence of the coming Son of Man, the wicked will shrink and seek to hide themselves in the holes of the rocks. The wisdom of the world will fail those who trust in it. The ancient gods in whom they have placed their faith and trust will abandon them, leaving them to crumble and fall just as every civilization who worshiped them before. No demonic force can resist the righteous judgement of the Son of Man.

The ancient psalmist drew upon the imagery of the Book of Enoch in the following psalm, which speaks of the unrighteous judgement of the sons of men:

> Do ye indeed speak righteousness, O congregation? Do ye judge uprightly, O ye sons of men? Yea, in heart ye work wickedness; ye weigh the violence of your hands in the earth. The wicked are estranged from the womb; they go astray as soon as they be born, speaking lies.
>
> Their poison is like the poison of a serpent; they are like the deaf adder that stoppeth her ear; which will not hearken to the voice of charmers, charming never so wisely.
>
> Break their teeth, O God, in their mouth; break out the great teeth of the young lions, O Lord. (Psalms 58:1-6)

The wicked attack the righteous, biting and gnashing their teeth upon them. Teeth have always symbolized power and the ability to enforce one's rule through destruction. Yet the Lord will break the teeth of the sinners, leaving them as powerless as ash under the soles of men.

The day will come when every knee will bow, and every tongue will confess that the Son of Man is the Christ, the very Son of God. On that great day, the wicked will confess that they could have known these things, but they chose the doctrines of demons instead. The Light of Christ has been given to every man, woman, and child. All the sons and daughters of God know how to choose between good and evil, right and wrong, light and darkness. Thus, the man in China who has never heard the name Jesus Christ can still follow the will of the Father by following the light of truth that he has received. In this way, all men everywhere throughout the multiverse can still fulfill the measure of their creations by acting upon the promptings they receive.

Abraham sought and obtained God's covenants because he knew there was more. He knew that such covenants could propel his progression like a rocket engine, and so it is - if we will utilize it. Many have been given the booster rockets of the restored gospel of Jesus Christ. Yet, while many have received these engines, few ever turn them on. Indeed, rather than soaring into the cosmos, these carry their engines upon their backs like dead weight and resent the incredible gifts they have received, looking at them as burdens rather than tools for the most epic cosmic journey ever told. Blinded by the world, many saints who have been geared up for interstellar travel trade their incredible engines to slither like serpents in the dust. Still, through the gift and power of the Holy Ghost, some will engage their engines and pierce the veils of the heavens on cosmic voyages to discover the likes the world is unworthy to hear. Have you engaged your engine, or have you traded it for the dust of the earth?

The Spirit can teach us how to engage our engines. However, the process must be deliberate. There is no standing still about spiritual things. When we do not seek the Spirit, our senses become dull, leading us away from spiritual clarity. Laman and Lemuel became past feeling. In their state of mindless spiritual stupor, they sought to kill their brothers and taught their children to do the same.

In the coming day, those who have rendered themselves past feelings will acknowledge that they did so of their own volition. Slowly, step by step, these lowered their heavenly gaze and licked up the earth's dust in its place. These become governed by urges rather than spiritual promptings. Urges masquerade as enticing freedoms, all silk and scarlet, yet they end in slavery and heavy chains. Thus, through the adversary's deceptions, many willingly trade the freedom of the cosmos for cages of darkness, where instead of wonder and glory, there is weeping, wailing, and gnashing of teeth.

No one on this Earth obtains the kingdom of God by some happy accident. The Kingdom of God is only available to those who seek it with all their hearts, minds, and souls. To these, the mysteries of God are unfolded before them, not because obtaining them was easy, but because they were diligent in their seeking. To these, the mysteries of God are the fuel that powers their journey through mortality, having a greater impact on their lives than any worldly force. The word of God flows through them as pure energy, revitalizing them and lifting them above the cares of this world to the great beyond. In the energy and power of the Word of God, the fiery darts of the adversary have no power over them. The lies and deceptions of man fall from their eyes as scales, and they begin to see things as they truly are.

You are not a fool if you are seeking the mysteries of God; you are a fool if you are not! You cannot obtain His Kingdom without them. As I have written many times before, the greatest mystery in the Kingdom of God is that Jesus is the Christ, the Son of the Living God. He is the Light and the Way. No man cometh to the Father but by Him. Therefore, Know Him! Not as the world knows Him, but as God would reveal Him unto you.

The vision of Enoch continues:

> **47.1**. And in those days shall have ascended the prayer of the righteous, and the blood of the righteous from the earth before the Lord of Spirits.

> **47.2**. In those days the holy ones who dwell above in the heavens shall unite with one voice and supplicate and pray [and praise, and give thanks and bless the name of the Lord of Spirits] on behalf of the blood of the righteous which has been shed, and that the prayer of the righteous may not be in vain before the Lord of Spirits, that judgement may be done unto them, and that they may not have to suffer forever.

In the passages above, once again, we learn of the righteous families in the heavenly courts of God, praying for their children who are in the chaotic throws of their second estate. These righteous parents are praying for their children, the wicked and righteous alike. They have hope for their wicked children because the Son of Man atoned for the sins of all humankind. Therefore, these heavenly families are praying that the judgements of God will transform their children, enabling them to become the most they can be.

As we learned from earlier portions of Enoch's writings covered in volume one, the punishments of God are not given out of vengeance but out of the desire to exalt and glorify. In volume one, we learned of trillions of the hosts of heaven that would rebel against God and be confined to the edge of the cosmos in the flaming mountain range that overlooks Outer Darkness. There, upon that terrible precious, they will observe the horrors of Outer Darkness and the miserable state of Lucifer – the great deceiver and all his minions. All Satan's lies and deceptions will be stripped away, and they will see things as they really are. In the light of a burning fire, they will be able to choose for themselves whom they will serve. Through the process of time, within that fiery mountain range at the edge of all things, the vast majority of these will have their evil tendencies consumed as dross. Those burning flames will refine them as silver and gold, and in the process of thousands of years, they will become the precious gemstones of God. It is for this transformation that their heavenly parents pray. They cannot bear the thought of their own children suffering forever.

Yet, the scriptures are unambiguous that those who fight against Zion and the House of Israel will perish and will not inherit the earth. Yet, Enoch has shown that in the due timing of the Lord, these will inherit kingdoms of glory. Lehi and Sariah mourned mightily for Lamen and Lemuel and their grandchildren. They feared the worst because they knew their children were hard-hearted and rebellious. They knew and understood that their children's choices would result in their physical separation from the presence of God. That is to say, Lehi and Sariah knew that where God and His Christ resided, their children and grandchildren would not be able to come, worlds without end. This is a sad reality, and it crushed their tender hearts and drove them to an early grave. However, I believe there is a tender flip side to this that we do not often speak of.

Celestial beings are not bound to the Celestial Kingdom. Indeed, the multiverse is truly an open book for those with celestial bodies. Such are the only ones that can travel it in its entirety unconstrained. Case in point, Christ did, in reality, travel to Hell and back. Furthermore, He did nothing but that He saw His Father do it first. Therefore, while there are certain limitations placed upon those with physical bodies of lesser glory, which most certainly restrict their ability to enter into Kingdoms of higher glory to that inherent within their being, I know of nothing that prohibits the inverse of this from happening. As such, there can still be reunions, adventures, and experiences upon open worlds of common glory wherein all can be together.

This fact does not eliminate the consequences of Laman and Lemuel's choices. Choices have real and lasting consequences, shaping our daily lives throughout the eternities to come. However, if children are sealed to righteous parents, in that case, no matter where those children reside in the multiverse, their Celestial parents will be able to be reunited with them in places of common ground, within realms of equal or lessor glory to those to which their children obtained. In its present state, the Earth is a perfect example of this. It is a beautiful place that glorious Celestial beings and disembodied spirits such as Lady Wisdom can visit.

Yet, post-mortal life will be just as busy then and there as it is here and now, if not more so. Given the cares and responsibilities of life, we do not have time for family reunions every day. Nevertheless, rest assured that the rising generations in heaven will have meaningful family relations with all their extended family. We will know, love, and interact with our heavenly families from before the world was created. Our heavenly children will be just as familiar with them. They will also be extremely familiar with our mortal families. We will all continue to interact in glorious and meaningful ways.

Our heavenly children will know their aunts, uncles, cousins, and grandparents for innumerable generations. They will laugh and play and have an eternity of loving memories with them, regardless of the choices that they have made and the kingdoms they call home.

Therefore, let your souls be at rest regarding your wayward family members who are walking paths you would not have them walk. They are the captains of their ships. Nevertheless, their agency will not negate the fact that God is good and is for His children, not against them. All creation will rejoice in His gifts and mercy, regardless of the paths that they have trodden. At the same time, it is an absolute truth that the Lord will bless His most faithful children with an exceeding and eternal weight of glory beyond comprehension and others with only those portions of glory they were willing to receive; all His blessings will bring joy, not sorrow. Remember, it is a great plan for happiness!

We return now to Enoch's vision:

> **47.3**. In those days I saw the Head of Days when he seated himself upon the throne of his glory, and the books of the living were opened before him: and all his host which is in heaven above and his counselors stood before him,

> **47.4** And the hearts of the holy were filled with joy; because the number of the righteous had been offered, and the prayer of the righteous had been heard, and the blood of the righteous been required before the Lord of Spirits.

In the verses above, we have the Head of Days sitting on his throne, with the books of the living opened before him. Accounting for the spilt blood of the righteous is now taking place, which reckoning has been required by the Lord of Spirits. Because both the Head of Days and the Lord of Spirits are being discussed above in connection to this event, I believe that the title Head of Days refers to Michael, the great prince. Specifically, it refers to him in his capacity as the father of humanity upon the earth and the prince of the host of noble and great ones that dwelt upon it. Indeed, another Old Testament prophecy mirrors this one, consider that prophecy:

> I considered the horns, and, behold, there came up among them another little horn, before whom there were three of the first horns plucked up by the roots: and, behold, in this horn were eyes like the eyes of man, and a mouth speaking great things. I beheld till the thrones were cast down, and the Ancient of days *[Head of Days]* did sit, whose garment was

white as snow, and the hair of his head like the pure wool: his throne was like the fiery flame, and his wheels as burning fire. A fiery stream issued and came forth from before him: thousand thousands ministered unto him, and ten thousand times ten thousand stood before him: the judgment was set, and the books were opened.

I beheld then because of the voice of the great words which the horn spake: I beheld even till the beast was slain, and his body destroyed, and given to the burning flame. As concerning the rest of the beasts, they had their dominion taken away: yet their lives were prolonged for a season and time.

I saw in the night visions, and, behold, one like the Son of Man came with the clouds of heaven, and came to the Ancient of days, and they brought Him [the Son of Man] near before him [*the Ancient of Days*]. And there was given Him [*the Son of Man*] dominion, and glory, and a kingdom, that all people, nations, and languages, should serve Him: His dominion is an everlasting dominion, which shall not pass away, and his kingdom that which shall not be destroyed.

And at that time shall Michael [*the Ancient of Days*] stand up, the great prince which standeth for the children of thy people: and there shall be a time of trouble, such as never was since there was a nation even to that same time: and at that time thy people shall be delivered, every one that shall be found written in the book.

And many of them that sleep in the dust of the earth shall awake, some to everlasting life, and some to shame and everlasting contempt. And they that be wise shall shine as the brightness of the firmament; and they that turn many to righteousness as the stars for ever and ever. But thou, O Daniel, shut up the words, and seal the book, even to the time of the end: many shall run to and fro, and knowledge shall be increased.

Then I Daniel looked, and, behold, there stood other two, the one on this side of the bank of the river, and the other on that side of the bank of the river. And one said to the man clothed in linen, which was upon the waters of the river, How long shall it be to the end of these wonders?

And I heard the man clothed in linen, which was upon the waters of the river, when he held up his right hand and his left hand unto heaven, and sware by him that liveth for ever that it shall be for a time, times, and an half; and when he shall have accomplished to scatter the power of the holy people, all these things shall be finished.

And I heard, but I understood not: then said I, O my Lord, what shall be the end of these things? And he said, Go thy way, Daniel: for the words are closed up and sealed till the time of the end. Many shall be purified, and made white, and tried; but the wicked shall do wickedly: and none of the wicked shall understand; but the wise shall understand.

And from the time that the daily sacrifice shall be taken away, and the abomination that maketh desolate set up, there shall be a thousand two hundred and ninety days. Blessed is he that waiteth, and cometh to the thousand three hundred and five and thirty days. But go thou thy way till the end be: for thou shalt rest, and stand in thy lot at the end of the days. (Daniel 7:8-15; 12:1-13)

This is a stunning prophecy that the students of my prior books know well. This prophecy speaks of the last days and the timing of the coming events. Particularly, this prophecy speaks to the liberation of America from the latter-day antichrist after he has plucked up the three heads of Ezra's Eagle by their roots. He then obtains the kingdom for himself through flatteries, destroys the Whore of Babylon, wages war against the saints of God, and overcomes them. He then enters into the House of God, proclaiming that he is god. The world will worship him in place of the true and living God. I associate this event with the removal of the Daily Sacrifice.

He is ejected from America by fiery wheels reigning destruction upon the earth. Elsewhere, Daniel 11:30, these wheels are called the ships of Chittim. These incredible crafts resulted in the deliverance of the American continent and the establishment of the American Zion. This represents the restoration of the House of Israel and the return of the Lost Ten Tribes. Their epic return will rival the Exodus of Egypt in wonder and might and result in the reclamation and restoration of the Lord's choicest vineyard. According to Ezekiel 39:2, the Remnant of Jacob's wheels will have decimated the antichrist's armies, destroying five out of every six men. He and his survivors will flee to the north seeking refuge.

The antichrist will be filled with rage at his stunning defeat and will realize that he had his head handed to him by the House of Israel. As such, he seeks intelligence from those who have knowledge of the covenant and have forsaken it. Based upon this ill-gotten knowledge, the antichrist will wage a war of extermination upon the portion of the House of Israel he believes to be within his grasp – the Jews. In his bloodlust, a great purge will occur in Europe and spread worldwide. This great purge will be worse than ever since there was a nation. This means the world will never have seen anything of this magnitude. There will be an insurrection upon those who love and fear the Lord. They will be driven from their homes, hunted down like dogs, and killed. Many will die. During this time, the Lord's hunters, the 144,000, will be sent forth throughout all the nations of the earth to gather the righteous into Zion.

This miraculous gathering is what the Christian community refers to as the rapture. On that day, two women will work in the mill; one will be taken to the New Jerusalem in America, and the other will be left. Two men will work in the field; one will be taken to the New Jerusalem in America, and the other will be left. Two people will be sleeping in a bed; one will be taken to the New Jerusalem in America, and the other will be left.

Not all of the righteous will be spared, and as Enoch foresaw, God will require an accounting for every drop of righteous blood that was shed. While these atrocities will condemn the wicked, they will sanctify the righteous. Just as the tokens of the cross have been engraved upon the hands of the Son of Man, so will God's sanctifying power and glory shine forth from the countenances of all those who suffered in the name of the Son of Man.

There have been many who have suffered in His name. Our forefathers were driven from city to city until they were forced to seek refuge in the Salt Lake Valley. The saints of the original Church were all too familiar with such sacrifices as well. Consider Paul's words to the Hebrews in this regard.

> And others had trial of *cruel* mockings and scourgings, yea, moreover of bonds and imprisonment: they were stoned, they were sawn asunder, were tempted, were slain with the sword: they wandered about in sheepskins and goatskins; being destitute, afflicted, tormented; of whom the world was not worthy: they wandered in deserts, and *in* mountains, and *in* dens and caves of the earth. (Hebrews 11:36-39)

All these bore great sufferings in Christ's name, yet their suffering was only small compared to the endless glory before them. So it shall be again in the coming days. Consider John's teaching on this matter:

> And I saw thrones, and they sat upon them, and judgment was given unto them: and *I saw* the souls of them that were beheaded for the witness of Jesus, and for the word of God, and which had not worshipped the beast, neither his image, neither had received *his* mark upon their foreheads, or in their hands; and they lived and reigned with Christ a thousand years. (Revelation 20:4)

According to John, many saints will lose their heads in the coming days because they are unwilling to worship the Beast. Who or what is the Beast that is so often associated with the latter-day antichrist? Let me just say that this is a far stranger topic of study than I have ever dared to adequately discuss. As such, I have never before given adequate attention to the nature and identity of the Beast in any of my prior books. This rabbit hole of EPIC proportions will take us off-topic if analyzed presently. As such, for now, I will place a pin on the topic of the Beast. However, given the peculiar nature of this series, the topic of the Beast will be revisited and discussed in detail before the conclusion of this volume. Enoch will also cover this subject in volume three of this series.

For now, we will return to the topic of persecution and martyrdom in the name of the Lord. If the time comes for us to lay down our lives in the name of Jesus Christ, we must remember that we are not alone in such sacrifices. He did it for us, and we can do it for Him if need be. We now return to Enoch's vision where the Head of Days and the Son of Man have been joined by the Lord of Spirits in honoring those that have endured such sufferings:

> **48.1**. And in that place I saw the fountain of righteousness which was inexhaustible: and around it were many fountains of wisdom; and all the thirsty drank of them, and were filled with wisdom, and their dwellings were with the righteous and holy and elect.

> **48.2**. And at that hour that Son of Man was named in the presence of the Lord of Spirits, and His name before the Head of Days.

48.3. Yea, before the sun and the signs were created, before the stars of the heaven were made, His name was named before the Lord of Spirits.

The three verses above describe the preeminence of Jesus Christ from the very beginning. As has been discussed previously, Christ was with the Father from the very start. By this, we are to understand that He witnessed His Father's mortal life and mission, wherein His Father showed Him from His own experience how to atone for the sins of the entire human family. Therefore, the preeminence of the Son of Man precedes our existence, spanning into the mortal probations of our own heavenly parents. All of these predate the creation of our solar system.

Enoch's writings are also in perfect harmony with the revolutionary doctrines discussed within the Book of Abraham. Apostates have shouted down the Book of Abraham in spital-riddled tirades of energetic fury. They condemn Joseph as a fraud, claiming his source materials were common funerary documents. Yet, the Book of Abraham speaks of the preeminence of the Son of Man in uniquely shocking ways that mirror the Book of Enoch, which was unknown in the Americas when the Book of Abraham was published. The fact that the Book of Abraham is in lockstep with the Book of Enoch is a testament to the veracity of both books.

Joseph Smith's translation of the Book of Abraham occurred in 1835. Richard Laurence's American publication of the Book of Enoch did not occur until 1838. Therefore, by the time the first Book of Enoch arrived in America, the entire Pearl of Great Price had already been written. As such, fools may mock Joseph's writings and seek to mar his reputation by claiming him to be a fraud and a fool. Yet, how on Earth could an uneducated farm boy from a backwater town such as Palmyra have written what he did in a manner that was perfectly harmonious with a previously unknown ancient record?

Are we to assume that when the most learned men in Germany could not obtain a copy of the Book of Enoch due to the book's scarcity, a young, uneducated country bumpkin from rural New York did? The idea is preposterous. Indeed, the doctrines in the Book of Enoch remarkably validate Joseph's seership. As a young boy, Joseph's personal experiences demonstrated that the Nicene Creed was false, for he saw both God the Father and His Son. We now learn from the passages above that Enoch taught that the Son of Man was a separate and distinct person from the Lord of Spirits; that is to say, God the Father and the Son of Man are two separate individuals.

Furthermore, Joseph's revelations state that the Book of Enoch would be testified of in due time. Little did we understand that the Book of Enoch would prove the truthfulness of the restoration of the gospel as well! While the Christian community struggles with the possibility of preexisting, both the Book of Enoch and the Restoration attest that God the Father, Jesus Christ, and Michael – the great prince worked together before the foundations of the solar system we now reside in were formed. This is not only astonishing, but it is also a loud and clear clarion call to the antagonists of the restoration. Open your eyes! Stop kicking against the pricks! Repent and return while it is still called today!

We now return to Enoch's vision, where Christ's critical role in the plan of salvation is expounded upon.

> **48.4**. He [*the Son of Man*] shall be a staff to the righteous whereon to stay themselves and not fall, and He shall be the light of the Gentiles, and the hope of those who are troubled of heart.

> **48.5**. All who dwell on earth shall fall down and worship before Him, and will praise and bless and celebrate with song the Lord of Spirits.

> **48.6**. And for this reason hath He [*the Son of Man*] been chosen and hidden before Him [*the Father*], before the creation of the world and for evermore.

Astounding doctrine for an ancient document known to have existed hundreds of years before Christ's birth! With such an unambiguous Messianic prophecy as this, it is no wonder that the Jews continue to decry the Book of Parables as somehow have been a post-Christian construct hellbent on deceiving the Jewish community. As we learned in the opening chapter of this book, Dr. John Strugnell, the chief editor of the Dead Sea Scrolls project, testified before heaven and earth that he both held in his hands and viewed detailed microfiche images of ancient Aramaic copy of the entire Book of Enoch, parables and all. Furthermore, he claimed that his was not the only such copy to exist. This proves the antiquity of the Book of Enoch as we now have it.

The Book of Enoch boldly and unapologetically declares that the Son of Man, Christ's preferred title for Himself, was, in fact, the Savior of the world, even before the world was made. However, Enoch also clearly states that the Son of Man's true character and identity have been masked from the world from the beginning of time. That is to say, the world would not know Him. The only ones who would know the Son would be those to whom the Father has revealed Him.

Many in the church tend to assume that if the Son is to be revealed to the world, it will happen through missionary work, such failure to consider that the Father can perform

His own work, see 2 Nephi 27:19-20. For those with eyes to see the Father's hands among the nations, it is evident that He is doing just that. While our sons and daughters sacrifice their own wills for that of the Father, becoming the fishers of men, their works are nothing compared to the labor of the Almighty Himself. Nowhere is His hand more visible than in the nations where His authorized servants are not permitted to go.

Al Jazeera, an Arabic language news company, hosted an interview between Maher Abdullah, the host of Sharia and Life, and Sheikh Ahmed Alqatani. The topic of the interview was the conversion of Muslims to Christianity. The interview was astounding. There are over two billion Muslims in the world today. However, according to Sheikh Ahmed, approximately six million Muslim men and women convert to Christianity every year. Some of these conversions occur under miraculous circumstances.

The following story was shared by Darren Carlson on May 31, 2018, in an article titled "When Muslims Dream of Jesus."

Consider the following:

> A Persian (Iranian) migrant arrived at a refugee center at 6 a.m., visibly upset. He told his story to a Persian (Iranian) pastor: During the night he saw someone dressed in white raise his hand and say, "Stand up and follow me." The Persian man said, "Who are you?" The man in white replied, "I am the Alpha and the Omega. I am the way to heaven. No one can go to the Father, except through Me."
>
> He began to ask the Persian pastor: "Who is He? What am I going to do? Why did he ask me to follow Him? How shall I go? Tell me."
>
> In response, the pastor held out his Bible and asked, "Have you seen this before?"
>
> "No," he replied.
>
> "Do you know what it is?"
>
> "No."
>
> The pastor then opened to the Book of Revelation: "I am Alpha and Omega, the beginning and the end." The man

started crying and said, "How can I accept Him? How can I follow Him?" So the pastor led him in prayer and peace came over him. The pastor then gave the man a Bible and told him to hide it, since the Muslims in the camps would cause him trouble.

But the man replied, "The Jesus that I met is more powerful than the Muslims in the camp." He left and an hour later returned with ten more Persians and told the pastor, "These people want a Bible."

Another very peculiar example of this is told by Ali Siadatan, an Iranian young man who converted to Christianity after moving to Canada. After converting, Ali studied the Bible voraciously. In his studies of the scriptures, his beliefs began to differ from those of his Christian friends. For example, while his friends believed in God the Father and His Son Jesus Christ, they believed they were literally the same beings, without body parts or passions. This did not resonate with Ali. He believed that they must have bodies of flesh and bone. He pointed to Christ appearing to His disciples after His resurrection with a tangible physical body. Christ showed His body to them and ascended into heaven to present it to His Father as well. Another way his beliefs began to differ from those of his other Christian friends was that he began to believe that Earth could not be alone in the Universe. He felt that the Holy Spirit was telling him that the events discussed in the sixth chapter of Genesis had something to do with the modern-day UFO phenomenon.

He felt God wanted him to return to Iran and share his understanding with his family there. He did so. Not only did he explain to them that the Bible was the word of God, he told them about his thoughts about the UFO phenomenon. The next day, while driving through the countryside, he and his family saw a massive UFO covered in thousands of green lights. His family estimated the craft to be as wide as a city block and about forty feet tall. The craft descended slowly from the sky until it was within five hundred feet of their car. Ali's family took this as a sign from God that the things their son was telling them were true. Ali's family and many of their friends and neighbors converted to Christianity as a result of this experience. Ali shared his experience on the episode "199 UFOs, Angles and Gods" of the Blurry Creatures Podcast, based in Franklin, TN.

Furthermore, Daryl Ireland, a professor at the Boston University's School of Theology, estimates that Christianity is growing faster in China than in any other nation in the world. According to his research, Christianity has grown from around one million Christians in China to over one hundred million over the last forty years.

According to the Council on Foreign Relations (CFR), Christians in China will double by 2033, causing China to become the largest Christian population in the world! Shockingly, the growth of Christianity in China has come despite the government's attempts to suppress it with strong anti-missionary laws. Pastors in China are commonly arrested under charges of "inciting subversion," a penalty that comes with a fifteen-year jail sentence. The following account was written by the leader of one such congregation. The Spirit told him that he was about to be arrested, and so he wrote this letter, which he gave to another to be published within forty-eight hours of his incarceration. It is a shocking and powerful testament to the faithfulness of the Chinese Christian community. Here is Wang Yi's letter, which he titled "Faithful Disobedience."

On the basis of the teachings of the Bible and the mission of the gospel, I respect the authorities God has established in China. For God deposes kings and raises up kings. This is why I submit to the historical and institutional arrangements of God in China.

As a pastor of a Christian church, I have my own understanding and views, based on the Bible, about what righteous order and good government is. At the same time, I am filled with anger and disgust at the persecution of the church by this Communist regime, and the wickedness of their depriving people of the freedoms of religion and of conscience. But changing social and political institutions is not the mission I have been called to, and it is not the goal for which God has given His people the gospel.

For all hideous realities, unrighteous politics, and arbitrary laws manifest the cross of Jesus Christ, the only means by which every Chinese person must be saved. They also manifest the fact that true hope and a perfect society will never be found in the transformation of any earthly institution or culture but only in our sins being freely forgiven by Christ and in the hope of eternal life.

As a pastor, my firm belief in the gospel, my teaching, and my rebuking of all evil proceeds from Christ's command in the gospel and from the unfathomable love of that glorious King. Every man's life is extremely short, and God fervently commands the church to lead and call any man to repentance who is willing to repent. Christ is eager and willing to forgive all who turn from their sins. This is the goal of all the efforts of the church in China—to testify to the world about our Christ, to testify to the Middle Kingdom about the Kingdom of Heaven, to testify to earthly, momentary lives about heavenly, eternal life. This is also the pastoral calling that I have received.

For this reason, I accept and respect the fact that this Communist regime has been allowed by God to rule temporarily. As the Lord's servant John Calvin said, wicked rulers are the judgment of God on a wicked people, the goal being to urge God's people to repent and turn again toward Him. For this reason, I am joyfully willing to submit myself to their enforcement of the law as though submitting to the discipline and training of the Lord.

At the same time, I believe that this Communist regime's persecution against the church is a greatly wicked, unlawful action. As a pastor of a Christian church, I must denounce this wickedness openly and severely. The calling that I have received requires me to use non-violent methods to disobey those human laws that disobey the Bible and God. My Savior Christ also requires me to joyfully bear all costs for disobeying wicked laws.

But this does not mean that my personal disobedience and the disobedience of the church is in any sense "fighting for rights" or political activism in the form of civil disobedience, because I do not have the intention of changing any institutions or laws of China. As a pastor, the only thing I care about is the disruption of man's sinful nature by this faithful disobedience and the testimony it bears for the cross of Christ.

As a pastor, my disobedience is one part of the gospel commission. Christ's great commission requires of us great disobedience. The goal of disobedience is not to change the world but to testify about another world.

For the mission of the church is only to be the church and not to become a part of any secular institution. From a negative perspective, the church must separate itself from the world and keep itself from being institutionalized by the world. From a positive perspective, all acts of the church are attempts to prove to the world the real existence of another world. The Bible teaches us that, in all matters relating to the gospel and human conscience, we must obey God and not men. For this reason, spiritual disobedience and bodily suffering are both ways we testify to another eternal world and to another glorious King.

This is why I am not interested in changing any political or legal institutions in China. I'm not even interested in the question of when the Communist regime's policies persecuting the church will change. Regardless of which regime I live under now or in the future, as long as the secular government continues to persecute the church, violating human consciences that belong to God alone, I will continue my faithful disobedience. For the entire commission God has given me is to let more Chinese people know through my actions that the hope of humanity and society is only in the redemption of Christ, in the supernatural, gracious sovereignty of God.

If God decides to use the persecution of this Communist regime against the church to help more Chinese people to despair of their futures, to lead them through a wilderness of spiritual disillusionment and through this to make them know Jesus, if through this He continues disciplining and building up His church, then I am joyfully willing to submit to God's plans, for His plans are always benevolent and good.

Precisely because none of my words and actions are directed toward seeking and hoping for societal and political transformation, I have no fear of any social or political power. For the Bible teaches us that God establishes governmental authorities in order to terrorize evildoers, not to terrorize doers of good. If believers in Jesus do no wrong then they should not be afraid of dark powers. Even though I am often weak, I firmly believe this is the promise of the gospel. It is what I've devoted all of my energy to. It is the good news that I am spreading throughout Chinese society.

I also understand that this happens to be the very reason why the Communist regime is filled with fear at a church that is no longer afraid of it.

If I am imprisoned for a long or short period of time, if I can help reduce the authorities' fear of my faith and of my Savior, I am very joyfully willing to help them in this way. But I know that only when I renounce all the wickedness of this persecution against the church and use peaceful means to disobey, will I truly be able to help the souls of the authorities and law enforcement. I hope God uses me, by means of first losing my personal freedom, to tell those who have deprived me of my personal freedom that there is an authority higher than their authority, and that there is a freedom that they cannot restrain, a freedom that fills the church of the crucified and risen Jesus Christ.

Regardless of what crime the government charges me with, whatever filth they fling at me, as long as this charge is related to my faith, my writings, my comments, and my teachings, it is merely a lie and temptation of demons. I categorically deny it. I will serve my sentence, but I will not serve the law. I will be executed, but I will not plead guilty.

Moreover, I must point out that persecution against the Lord's church and against all Chinese people who believe in Jesus Christ is the most wicked and the most horrendous evil of Chinese society. This is not only a sin against Christians. It is also a sin against all non-Christians. For the government is brutally and ruthlessly threatening them and hindering them from coming to Jesus. There is no greater wickedness in the world than this.

If this regime is one day overthrown by God, it will be for no other reason than God's righteous punishment and revenge for this evil. For on earth, there has only ever been a thousand-year church. There has never been a thousand-year government. There is only eternal faith. There is no eternal power.

Those who lock me up will one day be locked up by angels. Those who interrogate me will finally be questioned and judged by Christ. When I think of this, the Lord fills me with a natural compassion and grief toward those who are attempting to and actively imprisoning me. Pray that the Lord would use me, that he would grant me patience and wisdom, that I might take the gospel to them.

Separate me from my wife and children, ruin my reputation, destroy my life and my family – the authorities are capable of doing all of these things. However, no one in this world can force me to renounce my faith; no one can make me change my life; and no one can raise me from the dead.

And so, respectable officers, stop committing evil. This is not for my benefit but rather for yours and your children's. I plead earnestly with you to stay your hands, for why should you be willing to pay the price of eternal damnation in hell for the sake of a lowly sinner such as I?

Jesus is the Christ, son of the eternal, living God. He died for sinners and rose to life for us. He is my king and the king of the whole earth yesterday, today, and forever. I am His servant, and I am imprisoned because of this. I will resist in meekness those who resist God, and I will joyfully violate all laws that violate God's laws.

I am both astounded and humbled by this man's faith and millions more like him. At the same time, I am terrified by the Lord's writing on the wall. Truly, He can raise up from stones seed unto Abraham. All around us in the world today, Christians are turning to hedonistic practices like a dog to its vomit. Those who once professed His name are turning away. The Lord will have a righteous people. If we were those people, then we would be happy! However, if we turn to the world, fashioning Ba'als of our design and creation to worship, as surely as the sun rises and sets, we will be swept off from the face of this land, and others will inherit our defunct and desolate heritages. There is no doubt in my mind that the millions of our Chinese brothers and sisters will be entering the millennial reign of Christ before the children of Abraham, among whom there will be weeping and wailing and gnashing of teeth.

The missionary program of the Church of Jesus Christ of Latter-day Saints produces hundreds of thousands of converts each year. To some, this may be remarkable.

However, compared to the work that the Lord is doing, it is painfully clear that we are unprofitable servants in comparison. The Lord's mighty hand is gathering millions of souls from among the Muslim and heathen nations every year. Yes, surely the Lord can do His work!

Wang Yi lamented the wicked governments that suppress their subjects. He claimed his firm belief that the Chinese Communist Party would only serve as long as the Lord permitted it. Therefore, before leaving this subject, I must share the story of the Hidden Character Stone, for it, too, shows the Lord's hand at work among the nations.

In June 2002, a massive bolder was discovered that had fallen from a nearby Cliffside. The fallen boulder was split into two pieces, exposing six Chinese characters mysteriously written inside the stone. Because of the spectacular nature of the find, many studies were made of the stone, all of which concluded that the charters were not artificial. These six characters represent an ancient form of Chinese and are obviously read as follows: *The Chinese Communist Party Will Parish*.

The stone is displayed in the Zhangbu River Valley Scenic Area and attracts many visitors yearly. The following image shows a parking ticket to see the stone. An image of the characters is shown on the ticket's face. Many people have abandoned the Communist Party after witnessing the stone's message firsthand. I invite you to do your own research on this most curious occurrence.

Truly, the Lord moves in mysterious ways. There will always be those who will resist the Lord, no matter what happens. Enoch's vision continues by addressing those leaders of men who resist the King of kings and Lord of lords.

Enoch's vision continues along these lines:

48.7. And the wisdom of the Lord of Spirits hath revealed Him to the holy and righteous; for He hath preserved the lot of the righteous, because they have hated and despised this world of unrighteousness, and have hated all its works and ways in the name of the Lord of Spirits: for in His name they are saved, and according to His good pleasure hath it been in regard to their life.

48.8. In these days downcast in countenance shall the kings of the earth have become, and the strong who possess the land because of the works of their hands; for on the day of their anguish and affliction they shall not (be able to) save themselves.

48.9. And I will give them over into the hands of Mine elect: as straw in the fire so shall they burn before the face of the holy: as lead in the water shall they sink before the face of the righteous, and no trace of them shall any more be found.

48.10. And on the day of their affliction there shall be rest on the earth, and before them they shall fall and not rise again: and there shall be no one to take them with his hands and raise them: for they have denied the Lord of Spirits AND His Anointed (*Christ means – The Anointed of God*). The name of the Lord of Spirits be blessed.

Those who resist the Lord and suppress His people will fall and will not rise again, just as the mysterious Chinese Hidden Character Stone attests. In the Great and Terrible Day of the Lord, the wicked will be consumed as stubble, and those they suppress will live to inherit the earth they so gluttonously coveted for themselves. When the wicked are destroyed, all oppression will finally cease, and at long last, the Earth will rest. Such is the tone of Enoch's continued vision:

49.1. For wisdom is poured out like water, and glory faileth not before Him for evermore.

49.2. For He is mighty in all the secrets of righteousness, and unrighteousness shall disappear as a shadow, and have no continuance; because the Elect One standeth before the Lord of Spirits, and His glory is for ever and ever, and His might unto all generations.

49.3. And in Him dwells the spirit of wisdom, and the spirit which gives insight, and the spirit of understanding and of might, and the spirit of those who have fallen asleep in righteousness.

49.4. And He shall judge the secret things, and none shall be able to utter a lying word before Him; for He is the Elect One before the Lord of Spirits according to His good pleasure.

The Father is good, and so is His Beloved Anointed Son. Hastened to be the day of His coming, the captives might be liberated and the teeth of the sinners broken so they cannot cause harm again – worlds without end. Therefore, let us pray for our enemies, for those who persecute us and despitefully use us. Let us pray that their hearts might be softened, that they too can see God's marvelous works and wonders from the perspective of salvation rather than destruction and despair.

Chapter 13: A Strange Dream

Enoch revealed incredible things about the Anointed One, the Son of Man, in the prior chapter. We learned from Enoch that the Father has given all judgement unto His Son. We discussed how Enoch's teachings, although written long before the birth of Christ, testified to the reality of His life and mission and His hidden identity. By this, we are to understand that the knowledge and identity of the Son is held by the Father, and He reveals the Son unto whomsoever He will. I also shared numerous examples of the Father performing His own work amongst the nations.

Along these lines, before we proceed further with Enoch's writings, I want to share the peculiar experience of an unusual man named Brandon. I do not typically reference the dreams and visions of others. It is impossible to decipher dreams and visions without divine guidance. For this reason, I have typically chosen to rely on the written word that the Father has caused to be revealed. Nevertheless, the Lord has stated the following:

> I will <u>pour out</u> My <u>spirit</u> upon all flesh; and your sons and your daughters shall <u>prophesy</u>, your <u>old</u>men shall <u>dream</u> dreams, your young men shall see <u>visions</u>: And also upon the servants and upon the handmaids in those days will I pour out my spirit. (Joel 2:28-29)

The Lord has promised that He will not only pour out His spirit upon His servants and handmaids but upon all those who fear His name. As such, I will present the following experience of a humble janitor of little consequence in the eyes of the world. This man's name is Brandon, and he was the janitor of a local evangelical congregation at the time of this experience. According to Brandon, this strange experience occurred on the night of July 6, 2014. Very little of what this man claims to have seen can be readily understood by the larger Christian community, which gives this experience more credibility in my mind. Brandon does not seem to have intentionally shaped it to conform to the preconceived dogmas of the evangelical community he belongs to.

According to Brandon, when he first began to share his experience with members of his congregation, they did not know what to make of it. As such, he sat on it for nine years. However, he said that the Lord had put it on his heart to make his experience known beyond his own community, which had no box for it. As such, on June 29, 2023, he posted a YouTube video about his experience which he titled, "Jesus Took Me to the Tribulation". He has titled his YouTube channel "Last Days" and uses the posting name

"Bible Brandon." I have not watched any other YouTube videos he posted, so I cannot speak to any of them.

I transcribed the first portion of Brandon's experience from the YouTube video. In sharing this, I do not intend for you to believe his experience is out of hand. I share it simply for your consideration as another data point. In Brandon's own words, this is what happened to him on the night of July 6, 2014.

> I went to sleep and in the middle of my sleep all of the sudden I was, I don't know if I was in my body or out of my body, I don't know how it happened, I don't know, all I know is that all of the sudden I was standing with Jesus. He was on my right hand the whole time during this experience. He grabbed a hold of my hand and I'll go from there. The first, I will call it a scene perse, of what I saw, was Jesus standing on my right hand and He had a hold of my hand and we were in a town.
>
> I don't know what town we were in. I know that there was a big white building over to the side, and I was looking up at this big white building and I was looking up at the sky. The sky was alive. It was like it was moving. It was full of lightning. It was very spooky looking. I looked out over the horizon, and there was this lady running towards me and she started screaming. They were all screaming in terror. They were all freaking out. It was incredible.
>
> They were saying "They're gone! They're gone!" And I said, "Ma'am who's gone?" She said, "Did you not see?" I said, "Ma'am, did I not see what? What are you talking about?" Now this woman could see me. Not everybody in this experience was able to see me, but in this instance she was. She could not see Jesus, but she could see me. She said, "The aliens, the aliens came and got the Christians!" I said, "The aliens?" She said, "Yes!, They all disappeared. They went up!" And at that moment she just ran off. She was frantic. She was screaming in terror.
>
> I looked out over the horizon of this city from the top of a hill, and I could see everything on fire. Everything was on fire, the cars, the houses, the buildings. It was like chaos

beyond anything that you could ever comprehend. You could smell the smoke…

Jesus didn't say anything. I could perceive His thoughts when He was touching my hand. I knew what He was thinking, but He never said anything out of His mouth. He could understand what I was thinking too. I was just looking across the city saying, "Oh my gosh! What is going on?" All of the sudden we translated. I mean we left. We left that spot and went to another spot. He grabbed my hand and its like we went poof, we just disappeared, and we came to another scene.

In this time frame now, I'm looking over Europe. It was like watching a movie. It was very strange. I was looking out over Europe, and I saw this man, he was in Berlin. All the world leaders were behind this table. It was a round table in Berlin. It was big like an office. There were chairs all around it. All of these big leaders, world leaders, were all behind this big table and this man. I did not know who he was at the time. All the people were asking him for help. They were asking him for solutions for all the rioting and all the craziness that was going on. He was instructing them on what to do. He had all the wisdom. He was very very powerful in his demeanor. He was wearing a gray suit, and he looked like he was a middle eastern man.

All of a sudden, that scene was over, but the Lord at that time spoke to me about a scripture showing me about how everybody would give over their kingdoms to him within one hour. I'm not a Bible Scholar, I'm not a theology major. I'm just a guy that loves Jesus, and seeks Him with all my heart, and I had this experience.

The next scene I saw, I saw this man come on TV. He is on CNN, FOX, every channel. He is on TV, and he is telling all the people of the world what happened to the people that were taken (*by the aliens*). He was explaining to the people on TV that they were rebellious, and that they were taken away and that they were being punished. It was all the

Christians, and he said that they were being punished and taken out (by the aliens) because of this.

This is not Brandon's whole account; however, before continuing, I want to make some observations regarding key details. First, nine years passed between when Brandon had his dream and when he recorded his YouTube account. It takes a very long time to remember specific details. As such, it is natural to start filling in those details' blanks as the original memory fades. Projections and embellishments for the sake of flow and storytelling naturally creep into accounts such as this in repeated telling and based upon the reactions of others. That being said, I suspect the more central the detail is to the scene, the more likely it is to have actually happened as he claimed it did. Ancillary details are more subjective to change and embellishment.

As such, what are the main events of Brandon's vision so far? Brandon discussed two separate scenes in two separate locations. This is a major detail and is probably accurate to what he saw. We were told the second scene was definitely in Europe, and Berlin was mentioned specifically. Therefore, we are left to assume that since Brandon is from America, this is the general location of the first scene. This assumption is supported by his not describing it as being foreign and the fact that people spoke English.

The key details of the first scene are the sky, the righteous being taken by "aliens," and everything is consumed by fire, which presumably is the result of the same aliens that were seen taking the Christians. The second scene's key details are the European nations joining forces with a powerful man, who he later describes as the antichrist. The second key point is that this man fabricates a false narrative to rationalize the incredible disappearance of the Christians from among the people, which we are to assume took place in Europe as well.

It is clear to me, from the context of Brandon's commentary, that he is associating the aliens taking the Christians as a rapture event. Generally speaking, the larger Christian community believes that the righteous will be removed from the earth and will avoid the trials and turmoil of the last days. At the same time, everyone else is left to go to hell in a handbasket. In reality, what these people believe as the rapture is the miraculous gathering of the saints into the City of Refuge, the New Jerusalem. Since the conclusion of WWII, the United States has been the de facto leader of the free world. Another important detail is that Brandon did not describe any destruction when he looked out over Europe. Presumably, we are left to presume that the destruction he witnessed was limited to the United States of America.

Brandon then saw many European leaders placing their power behind a man he identified as the coming antichrist. These leaders turn to the antichrist out of fear that what happened in America could happen in Europe if not for the interventions of this man. Brandon did not describe why these leaders believed that the antichrist would be able to help them.

It should be noted here that the things that Brandon claimed to have seen are inconsistent with mainstream thought. However, those familiar with my writings will know that I believe these things can be readily reconciled with the last days' prophecies. For the sake of brevity, I will not share Brandon's entire account but the portions that I find to be most relevant. As such, consider the following:

> So okay, so then it goes off of him (the antichrist) and I see Christians that were left behind. Now, this is the part that gets hard and there's going to be probably a lot of you that will disagree with this. Some will get angry about this, but I have to tell you what I saw. And so, this is what it is.

> A lot of the grace messages that people preach enable people to live compromising lifestyles. Many Christians live like the world and those that did got left. They did. There were literally thousands of Christians that were here that thought they were born again, they thought that they were living right. They thought that they did everything right, but they didn't. They were living like the world and had the appearance of a godliness but their hearts were so far from the Lord. But they thought they were with Him. They were the ones that the Bible talks about, in my name, depart from me I never knew you. You know? And that's what happened. They were everywhere. There were literally Christians everywhere.

> There were pastors that I saw that preached that watered - down grace message. These were left here in punishment because of the fact that they were preaching a lukewarm gospel. So they were left here with those that followed them. And those people that followed them were mad as you know what. Man, it was terrible. They went after those false preachers, and they said –YOU LIED TO US!. You didn't tell us the truth!

> I was standing with Jesus the whole time and He said to me, "look at this. Watch this. Remember this." He didn't say it

with His lips, but I heard his thoughts. And I was gazing upon this this area, I know I'm back in time, I knew after it all this happened, I was back in time, back before all the antichrist was taking over stuff this. This happened back in the beginning, right after (the aliens take the Christians), okay?

So the people are mad. They are very angry that they are still around. And the pastors and these leaders, I saw some of them, and I'll never mention their names because the Lord told me not to. I saw people that were on TV, that were teaching the gospel on TBN (Trinity Broadcasting Network) and stuff like that. Those Christian channels. I'm not ever gonna say who they were, but I'm gonna tell you that they were still here.

There were some folks here that were so very, very, very angry that they were ready to kill them. It was awful! I saw one lady, and I know very well who she is. I worked at a church for with her for 13 years. She was one of the members there at the church where I was at. I was looking up and she looked up at the heavens and she flipped the Lord off. She gave the Lord the middle finger and she said some expletives. It was very, very bad.

I was watching them all just turn on God. Turn. and they were angry, turning on people. But there were some groups of them that were building colonies. They started saying, we've gotta get prepared. It's fixing to get really bad. We've gotta get our stuff around. We know what's about to happen. We know what's coming. A lot of them said this. They said that they needed to go to the mountains. They said that they needed places of refuge. They said, "We've gotta go now, because we're running out of time. This is fixing to get bad really fast."

And so I saw these people try to have a camaraderie. There were families that were left. And this is another thing, everybody below the age of 15 was gone. All the little children were gone. All of the younger teenagers and preteens, all those, were gone. They all got (taken by the aliens). But anybody that was age of accountability and older were left if you didn't know Jesus Christ and have a relationship with Him. And so I watched these younger people go with their families. And so during the tribulation I saw kids being birthed, kids being born. And so, this is a part that's really hard. I… I watched how the Christians all got together. Okay, Holy Spirit help me here… okay, so okay, so they all go to these mountain areas and they dig holes in the side of the mountains, these massive holes. They were trying to keep warm because you couldn't, You couldn't stay in your house. You couldn't go into town and buy groceries because of the Mark of the Beast.

I'm fixing to tell you about it. I saw how it happens. I saw how the Mark of the Beast changes you. I saw how they put it in your forehead. And so I'll get to that, okay? I don't want to skip around too much. And I don't want to make this too long. I respect people's time here. So Okay, so the Christians try to move at night. I am standing with Jesus and He takes me to this field and I don't know where I'm at. All I know is that it is dark outside and the Christians are moving from place to place at night, because they can't move in the day or they will be spotted. They are trying to get to places of safety. And so the farmers had guns. They had like .22s and rifles and stuff. So there were still firearms. There were still ways of protection for farmers. But I didn't see a lot of people have guns.

Like the Christians didn't have guns. I don't know why. I don't, nothing was really said about that. But I know that the farmers did and I remember seeing in this one place where these Christians were trying to go out through this guy's pasture, and there's dogs barking and they were alerting the farmer inside the house and he flipped the light on and he had a .22 in his hand. I know it was a .22. He fired it, and he called the authorities to tell them that there were Christians coming. You know, people moving at night.

He didn't know if they were Christians or not, he never said, but I knew they were Christians. But they were moving at night. So then, I see these men in these black Hummer trucks, there's like blue lights, and it was weird because they were blue lights, like infrared looking lights inside these Hummer trucks. They were all black with blacked out windows and they were armored trucks. They were driving over to the Christians, who would try to put like cement blocks and stuff in the road to slow them down so they would have enough time to get away.

They were running as fast as they could to try to get away. These men had black face mask on, kind of like COVID mask, but they were they were black. And they had black hoods on and they would jump out of their hummers, with black outfits on, with these vests on. They would jump out of these black cars and they had these guns. But this is what's weird, I've never seen these guns before. I've tried to find them online and I can't. There guns shot a pulse, it wasn't a bullet. It was a electric. It was like electric magnetic, like a magnetic pulse that just stunned you, like a wave of energy. It knocked you senseless for a couple of seconds. So they didn't have to reload it, they just pointed it and they went boom and people just fell out on the ground. The people that were running, they would pass out. Just boop. After a bit, they would get up, but it was too late. They were held, they were captive. Then those men in black would give them an ultimatum. I… I saw a woman, and she had these two children, it was a boy and a girl, that were born during the tribulation. They were probably three years old, four years old, maybe more…The men in black said, we're going to give the children the chip first. and if you don't deny your Jesus, we're going to cut your kids heads off. Or you can take the chip. They gave them this ultimatum. And so the dad said, no, we're not taking the mark.

The mother said, No! You can't cut my baby's heads off. Because the man had this huge sickle, this huge sword in his hand. And he was getting ready to cut off the baby's head. He was getting ready to just go and slice that kid's head off right there. There was no mercy. There was no conscience about it. It was just the way it was. And the dad cried out and said, no, you must not take the mark. And when he, said that, they cut his head off right there. And I'm talking, it fell and rolled at my feet and I could smell his blood. That's how bad it was. It was that awful. Jesus stood there with me the whole time. He never made a comment about it. He just told me to look. So I looked, and I watched the woman and she said I'll take the mark. I'll take it I'll take that. I'll take the chip. Don't take their heads.

This is what was so incredible. It was absolutely amazing. They take this chip. Those children were crying because they just saw their dad die right in front of them. And the mom is crying and she's bawling her eyes out because she saw her husband die right in front of her. And the moment she takes the chip, the baby, the two children and her, they instantaneously lose emotion. They don't have any emotion on their face. They totally lose the crying. It's, it's like went into a trance right there in front of me. Their minds and everything had a peace again. It's like the chip sent a peace to their brain somehow. I don't know how. All I know is the chip did something to them and it gave it made them calm. It put off some kind of endorphin in them and they just went like cold in their face and it was like they're not there. It's like hello, you're not there anymore. They were not crying anymore about their father and husband. It's like they didn't care anymore. I saw that. Then I then I saw a man trying to commit suicide. He already had the mark, he had the chip in his hand, and he was standing on a major bridge and all of a sudden the chip sent a signal to his brain and calmed him down and he did not kill himself.

I don't understand why, I don't understand how. All I know is that chip produced some kind of signal of some kind of endorphin somehow and calmed his mind down and instantaneously he became calm and he did not jump off that bridge. It knew. The chip knew. I don't know how, but it knew that he was fixing to do something like that. Then I would see people mowing their grass and I would walk by them but they couldn't see me. I would walk by them and they were mowing, but they were not there. It's like you could go say hello, but they were in another world like a zombie. It was weird, and they were just mowing their grass like robots, but the chip would bring some kind of something to their brain. I… I don't get it.

Another thing I thought was interesting is that Jesus took me to a place in like this town and there were these barricades all over these towns, massive gray barricades. Then there were these armed guards, with guns and everything all around. You would have to go through these barricades to get into these towns. You had to have your chip in your hand. Okay, and if you didn't have the chip you couldn't get in town. They would offer you the chip or you would die. They would kill you right there. No questions. If you didn't take it, they'd cut your head off. So, there was a woman, I remember her. I remember her face. She was a white woman. She had brown hair and she was standing in line. There were lots of people, and lots of people had a bruise on their head. It was like a burn sore. The body had a reaction to the chip and it caused sores on people's heads, or on their hands. Not everybody had this reaction though. So this woman was trying to fake it with makeup. She was trying to put that makeup on her hand to make it look like she had a burn sore.

She was standing in line waiting to enter the town, and when she got up to go in through the gate they saw that she was faking it. People were so desperate for food and for whatever resources they could get that they were willing to do whatever it took. She was a Christian who was trying to fake it and they cut her head off right there. There was no time for even repentance. They just took a sickle-like sword and they cut her head off like it was nothing. Her head went rolling and the people in line acted like it was nothing. There was no emotion, like I'm telling you, there was no emotion to these people. They were gone. It was weird…

And so, at this time, this last scene, I'm taken out of the earth. I'm sucked up out of the earth. And I go to the edge of heaven and earth. And I'm standing there and I can turn around and I can look and I see the gates of heaven, I see the holy city is beautiful all behind me and Jesus is standing right here this time on my left and He speaks to me this time and he says look at the earth. I want to show you something that's about to take place And I said, you know, I just wow, you know, I'm just excited I look over and I look at the earth and it's spinning. I can see it moving. You know it's moving and He said, do you see each one of those lights down there? And I said, yeah. He goes, those represent souls. He said there's a there's going to be a major revival about to happen throughout the earth a final push, a final harvest, a major harvest.

I don't want to add any words that He didn't say, but that's what He showed me…I look over at him, I'm looking over, and I look at His eyes and they're welled up with tears. He said, do you see China? And I said, yeah. He said, a lot of them died for my gospel. The gospel cost them something, Brandon. And I looked at Him and He was so filled with joy at the sacrifice that they gave for the gospel. They were like gold, gold streets, but they weren't because I knew each one of those lights represented a soul. And I said, Lord, what is that? He said, that's the underground churches in China. And He said, each one of those represent a soul. I was like, wow, wow, it's just amazing, you know, because I'm looking at the souls that get saved, and they're all, they spread all throughout Asia. You can see these gold veins that go up through North Korea a little, and South Korea, and go through Japan, and all of it.

Then I look over, and then I look at the Philippines, and there's lights in the Philippines. Then I look at Australia, and there's lights in Australia. And there's these crop circles. Like, that's all I can say. They're like a round circle. And they're in Europe. And they're all over Europe, France, and Germany. Each country had a circle and some circles were bigger than others and each one of them in those circles were lights. They were represented, like I would say they're like hotspots for revival, major places where people went for revival is the only way I can say it. He never, the Lord never said revival, but I'm assuming. But they were all round circles. And then I'm looking over to the Middle East, and there wasn't as many in the Middle East as what there was in Africa, and some of these places in Europe, and America, and Canada, and Mexico, and South America, and places like that. There was, like, in Pakistan, and Afghanistan, and Iraq, and Iran, and all those places, there was revival.

There were people getting saved and led to the Lord there. There was revival there. I'm not saying that there wasn't. There was, there was still, but it didn't seem as significant as what it was some of these other places that I saw. But it was amazing all over the place. But America, from coast to coast was lights everywhere, literally hundreds of thousands, if not millions of lights everywhere. And they went all up and down I -35 corridor from Texas to Oklahoma. There was major places of revival there, major places. Then I saw major revival on the West Coast and the East Coast. I mean it was everywhere. The revival was everywhere.

Then I went up and then I looked behind me and there was a wave coming out of heaven. On the edge of heaven there was like a wall and on this wall this massive golden brick wall around heaven like massive thick massive wall massive and there was a wave it was this wave was huge like a tsunami wave like the biggest wave you can comprehend it was massive like a tsunami like a 50 -foot huge thick wall of wet water. The Lord told me, this is the last outpouring. There is an outpouring coming upon the earth. And behind the wave were these angels. And they were like soldiers on these chariots of fire. There's these chariots and they were golden looking fire. It was the glory all over these chariots. They were angels, and they all looked similar. They had armor on, and they all looked very similar to each other.

They had these gifts, they were boxes, and they were wrapped perfectly, like with bows on them - presents. Each chariot had a box on there. I asked the Lord, what are those boxes? What are those presents? He said, those are end time giftings, end time mantles that have never been on the earth before. They never have been seen by anybody on the earth. Creative miracles, things that you have never experienced on the earth. Like when Jesus said, and greater works will you do, greater works. These gifts are the greater works. Greater works than even Jesus did. Things that the people, whenever Jesus was walking the earth, did not see. I don't, I can't

196

comprehend it. I'm just saying these were massive, massive, massive outpourings of something that is fixing to happen.

Then I look over to my left again, and I see these angels but these angels were different. They had longer hair and they were massive. They're strong looking. They had these big baskets, baskets of golden stuff, like gold, or it looked like money. It looked like something like that. They were taking it out of silos, these massive barn looking silos. They had money… I don't know if it was money or not, I believe it was. And they were pouring it out on the earth. They were pouring this out on the earth. And then there were people that were in these silos and there were bicycles and things like that that people in foreign countries needed.

Now how that comes from heaven like that to the earth, I don't know. I don't know if it was a type and shadow, if it was a representation of something, of what people are believing for, asking the Lord for in their prayers, or what. I didn't ask. I wish I would have asked more questions. I was too in awe of Him, of being in front of the King of Kings and the Lord of Lords. I was too in awe to even think. In that moment I could have asked a billion million things, you know? And now that it is over, you go, why didn't I? It was too holy. I don't know, I can't I can't tell you, but I but I see all this going on in heaven and Jesus looked at me and He said you need to tell my people I'm coming.

I kind of I looked at Him like, wow! He was urgent in His eyes. Tell my people I'm coming. And folks, this was in 2014. This is in 2014. Now we're in 2021. I saw things, when I was on the earth, some things that He told me I couldn't talk about, that I really would love to share, but I'm in obedience to Him, so I can't. Timeframes, things like that. And all I can tell you now is that we really are there. We really, really, really, really are. And I hope I'm coming across strong about this because Jesus is coming and it's serious.

This was an incredible experience for Brandon. I believe that Brandon is an honest person in that he is sincere in sharing what he remembers of his dream, even if, for seven years, the details may have blurred or morphed a little here and a little there to conform with his beliefs as to what they mean.

When interpreting dreams, such as the one Brandon saw, I have come to focus on the meaning of things rather than the literal depictions of the events themselves. For example, I do not believe that millions of flaming chariots are loaded up with heavenly gifts like Santa's sleigh, nor do I believe buff angels will literally pour money on the heads of the saints. What is important is the underlying meaning behind these actions. The events that Brandon saw indicate the type of spiritual outpouring prophesied in 1 Nephi 14:14.

I believe applying the same concept to everything Brandon saw would be wise. Remember, while Lehi saw a great and spacious building, a rod of iron, and a river of filthy waters, none of these things actually existed. However, all those things correlated with genuine phenomena that would confront all humankind, although they would be experienced differently.

As such, I am not excessively concerned about Brandon's description of mind-numbing microchips and barricaded cities, nor with his visions of foxholes and menacing drone swarms. However, I am laser-focused on the underlying meaning behind such things. These different scenarios resulted in pressure to force people to deny Jesus Christ. This, I absolutely believe, will occur. Whether it will happen in the manner that Brandon suggested doesn't matter. In the coming days, we must decide whom we will serve - the gods of this world or the Son of God. It may very well be that our choices will have real consequences. There is clearly a correlation between what Brandon saw in his dream and the following scripture from the Book of Revelation:

> I saw thrones, and they sat upon them, and <u>judgment</u> was given unto them: and *I saw* the souls of them that were beheaded for the witness of Jesus, and for the word of God, and which had not worshipped the beast, neither his image, neither had received *his* mark upon their foreheads, or in their hands; and they lived and <u>reigned</u> with Christ a <u>thousand</u> years. (Rev 20:4)

Brandon saw a mother of two young children faced with a terrible choice. She made her choice out of fear, not faith. What would you have done? Fear is a powerful tool in Satan's arsenal. He wielded it with such tremendous effect that one-third of the host of heaven followed after him, rebelling against God. Perhaps this is why the Bible Dictionary states that fear is unworthy of a child of God and is something that love and faith can overcome. Consider for a moment if you would be happier to deny Christ and survive living among the kinds of people that would force such decisions in the first place. Or would you rather return to the presence of the Almighty Creator of Heaven and Earth and leave the demons to their domain?

Another curious aspect of Brandon's dream was the alien theme. Brandon heard people screaming in terror, claiming to have witnessed aliens abducting Christians. He heard the antichrist explain that the aliens were abducting the rebellious to punish them. He also spoke of seeing glowing points of light representing the individual souls of the righteous around the world. He also claimed to see crop circles that designated their locations. Brandon only saw these crop circles outside of the United States and also noted that the United States was filled with the righteous, from coast to coast. What does it all mean?

To the average Christian, this might sound like nonsense, however, to those familiar with the prophecies of the restoration of the House of Israel, not so much. The arrival of the ships of Chittim and the lifting up of the Christians actually sounds about right. Brandon's description of burning American cities correlates perfectly with Christ's prophecy about the returning Remnant of Jacob, who will destroy the wicked by fire and render the cities of the wicked desolate. The lights around the globe being collected and concentrated in America are consistent with the 144,000 who gather the righteous into the city of refuge from the four corners of the globe. For those who understand such things, Brandon's dream is astounding.

Chapter 14: The End and the Beginning

In the prior chapter, we reviewed a peculiar dream about the last few days events. Before that, Enoch described the preeminence of the Son of Man and how judgement would be given into His hand. We learned in a prior chapter that Christ also prohibits the Satans from accusing us before His Father's throne. As such, He is the ultimate Gatekeeper before the throne of grace. He freely forgives the sins of the humble and penitent. It is for this express purpose that He gave unto men their weaknesses. His grace is sufficient to transform those weaknesses into strengths. Those who will utilize Christ's atonement and follow His example will be made mighty, not through their own power but through the grace and mercy of God.

On the other hand, those who reject the Messiah or turn away from Him out of fear, shame, or rebellion will never be able to make of themselves what Christ could have made of them had they been so disposed. Yet, the billions that fall into this last category will not be cast off forever. Christ came not into the world to condemn the world but to save it. Therefore, while many of these will be relegated to spirit prison, their experiences there will be designed to transform them. As Enoch's visions continue, he will repeatedly testify to this fact.

50.1. And in those days a change shall take place for the holy and elect, and the light of days shall abide upon them, and glory and honor shall turn to the holy,

50.2. On the day of affliction on which evil shall have been treasured up against the sinners. And the righteous shall be victorious in the name of the Lord of Spirits: and He will cause the others to witness (this) that they may repent and forgo the works of their hands.

50.3. They shall have no honor through the name of the Lord of Spirits, yet through His name shall they be saved, and the Lord of Spirits will have compassion on them, for His compassion is great.

50.4. And He is righteous also in His judgement, and in the presence of His glory unrighteousness also shall not maintain itself: at His judgement the unrepentant shall perish before Him.

50.5. And from henceforth I will have no mercy on them, saith the Lord of Spirits.

51.1. And in those days shall the earth also give back that which has been entrusted to it, and Sheol also shall give back that which it has received, and hell shall give back that which it owes.

51.2. For in those days the Elect One shall arise, and He shall choose the righteous and holy from among them: for the day has drawn nigh that they should be saved.

The passages above are astounding and fly in the face of traditional Christianity. Given Enoch wrote these words thousands of years before the birth of Christ, they are a testament that the doctrines of the Church of Jesus Christ are not new but restorations of doctrines formally known and understood thousands of years before Christ's birth to one extent or another. Enoch speaks of six distinct groups regarding the final judgement that will occur at the end of this iteration of the Father's great plan of salvation.

1. The holy and elect
2. Sinners who treasured evil
3. Repentant witnesses
4. Those on the Earth
5. Those in Sheol
6. Those in Hell

We will discuss each of these groups in turn.

1) The holy and elect

The first of these groups, the holy and elect, are mentioned as being transformed into a glorified state of being. This group took upon themselves the form of lighting, that is to say, glorious Celestial resurrected bodies. These are those who would be adopted into the household of God as the Children of Christ, of which has been spoken. These now join their heavenly parents, graduating from mortality with high honors, just as their parents before them. These overcame the world through faith in Jesus Christ and by making and keeping sacred covenants with Him. These fulfilled the full measure of their creation by following Christ's example and putting the will of their Father first in their lives. As such, all of these are made perfect in the grace and atoning power of the Son of Man.

2) The Sinners who treasured evil

The second group consists of those who treasured evil unto themselves. By this, we must understand that we are referring to a group of entities that relish in wickedness. These do not sin out of weakness but out of rebellion. These are the opposites of the first group – the holy and elect ones. These embrace the darkness, preferring it to the light. The vast majority of these hosts of sinful entities are Lucifer and his fallen minions. These are those who will be cast into that great and dreadful pit at the edge of the universe that we have come to call Outer Darkness. These will have no forgiveness, for they want none. These hate God the Father and His Christ. There will be very few beings amongst this group with physical bodies, but unfortunately, there will be some. These are known as the sons of perdition. They will be resurrected with immortal bodies void of godly glory. The Kingdom of Outer Darkness is the lowest in the known multiverse; as such, these are confined forever to this realm, for there is no place lower for them to travel. As these have been restricted to Earth, their eternal destiny will be restricted to the fiery pits of Outer Darkness for all eternity. The resurrected beings in this sorry group are the only ones in the Father's iteration for whom it could be said, "It would have been better had they never been born." Meaning it would have been better for them if they had joined with Lady Wisdom and opted out of the second estate altogether rather than have damned themselves to Outer Darkness forever.

3) Repentant Witnesses

The third group mentioned stands on the knife's edge of the burning mountain range at the world's end. These have front-row seats to the hellish state of those confined eternally to Outer Darkness. These have been there to be witnesses of their sufferings "that they might repent and forego the works of their hands." The Elect One has not given up hope for these. You will recall from volume one of this series that the Lord of Spirits banishes the hosts of heaven that will rebel against Him in the last great battle on the other side of the millennium.

According to Enoch, these will remain imprisoned there for ten thousand years. At the end of ten these thousand years, the dross of mortality will have been consumed away, and those who were once hateful and vile will have been transformed into the priceless gemstones Enoch saw that comprised the exotic landscape at the edge of all things.

In verse **50.3** above, Enoch foresaw that while these would be saved through the name of the Lord of Spirits, they would not be magnified with the honor of His presence ever again. The presence of God in its full glory is only found in the Celestial Kingdom.

These will not be worthy of such glory, but they will inherit kingdoms of glory and be servants of the Most High. According to D&C 76:109, the Telestial, or lowest kingdom of glory, will be by far the most populous. As a reminder, the inhabitants of this kingdom are distinguished by the fact that they did not utilize the atonement of Jesus Christ during their second estate but paid the price of their own sins. Enoch means this when the Lord of Spirits will have no mercy upon them. Their sins will be covered by their own atonements and not the atonement of His Only Begotten Son. Without the atonement, the process of atoning for one's sins is described as taking 10,000 years upon the burning mountains at the edge of all things. In time, these may be able to continue to progress, but according to D&C 76:112, they will never make it to the Celestial Kingdom – worlds without end.

4) Those on the Earth

The fourth group comprises those living on the Earth during the last days of the trial who are not consumed by the great and dreadful day of the Lord.

5) Those in Sheol

The fifth group is described as those in Shoel. Shoel is the Hebrew word for the Spirit World. As we know, the Spirit World is comprised of Spirit Prison and Paradise. Spirit Prison is another word for Hell. As Hell is specifically called out as a separate location from Sheol, we can assume Enoch refers to the righteous in the Spirit world or those in Paradise. This, again, is another incredible piece of evidence that the original gospel of Jesus Christ has been restored, as this knowledge was clearly known to the ancients.

6) Those in Hell

The sixth group represents those who are in Hell. Hell, or Spirit Prison, is a place of transformation. It is similar to the burning mountain ridge that overlooks Outer Darkness. As such, contrary to popular Christian belief, Hell is not a place of permanent residence. It is a temporary holding place. It is a place of decision. The entire purpose of Hell is to enable people to change. It is the last stop before the terrible pit of Outer Darkness from whence there is no return. God is merciful. Again, contrary to popular Christian belief, He does not want to condemn His children to an endless state of pain and misery.

Nevertheless, He will allow them to choose for themselves. However, He has designed Hell so that if they reject Him, they can do so with full knowledge of what that entails. As such, the lake of fire and endless torment, often called Hell, refers to Outer Darkness, the terrible burn pit of fire and brimstone designed exclusively for those who delight in such things.

With these six different groups of people defined, we are now prepared to elaborate upon Enoch's teachings. According to **51.2**, the Son of Man, the Father's Anointed One, will go among these groups and call out the righteous from among them. As such, Christ will go to the Spirit World and gather the righteous. Christ will go to Hell and gather in the repentant righteous who have been transformed by their experiences. Christ will also go among the witnesses of the horrors of the great pit, Outer Darkness. All those that will follow Him will be liberated. The only location from whence no condemned traveler ever returns is Outer Darkness. It is, and ever will be, the multiverse's great Alcatraz—a true pit of despair.

This is an astounding doctrine and speaks to the magnanimous nature of God. When those who are relegated to the burning mountains at the edge of all things become witnesses to Outer Darkness, it will fill them with absolute terror. Then, they will finally see through Satan's lies and illusions. They will want nothing to do with him or his final resting place. As such, these will repent and turn to the Lord. When His Son calls for them, they will answer and rejoice in His mercy and deliverance.

Yet, I suspect others may look into that great void and be drawn to it. To these, the darkness will resonate with them. As such, when the Lord calls, they will turn away and find their home in the terrible pit. While these will go into the pit, they will go with resurrected bodies; as such, they will be in positions of power and dominion. Because of their bodies, they will rule Satan and all the disembodied spirits with him.

We now return to Enoch's vision:

> **51.3**. And the Elect One shall in those days sit on My throne,
> and His mouth shall **pour** forth all the secrets of wisdom and
> counsel: for the Lord of Spirits hath given them to Him and
> hath glorified Him.

Here, at the end of all things, the Father ascends into the Mount of the Congregation, upon the sides of the North, and gives His throne to His Son. For God the Father, this incredible event of transcendence will have been eons in the making. It will be a time of tremendous joy, song, and thanksgiving, as is attested to in the continuation of Enoch's vision.

> **51.4**. And in those days shall the mountains leap like rams,
> and the hills also shall skip like lambs satisfied with milk,
> and the faces of [all] the angels in heaven shall be lighted up
> with joy.

51.5 And the earth shall rejoice, and the righteous shall dwell upon it, and the elect shall walk thereon.

The imagery of the mountains leaping like rams and the hills skipping like lambs with bellies full of warm milk is a joyful image indeed. This is what is meant by a fullness of joy. We can ponder such things, but we must experience this event to comprehend it truly. Events of this magnitude are so epic that they are forever imprinted into the fabric of the multiverse itself. The powers of the Universe can be molded and shaped through the majestic power of beings of such magnitude and might. Because of beings, such as those that inhabit the mount of the congregation, the elements willingly subject themselves to the commands of the righteous.

On that Day, the mantle of supreme Godship will be passed from Father to Son, and the Son will become the Father, and the Father will become transcendent. We can try to imagine what this day will be like, but doing so is impossible. Eye has not seen, nor ear heard, nor has entered into the heart of man the things that the Father has prepared for those that love Him.

I suspect that one of the most glorious things about all of it will be that we will have not lost the Father but gained another. We will be part of the Father's eternal story, and He will be part of ours. His Son, who will be the Father of our resurrected bodies, will now assume the role of the great Father of the multiverse and the great Overseer and Patriarch of the next iteration of His great plan of happiness. The incomprehensible gratitude we will surely feel towards the Father, Son, and Holy Ghost will be beyond description. We will imprint our heavenly children with our love for the Father, just as our heavenly parents did for us. So, the cycle will begin again, and the wheel of heaven will keep turning.

The progression of Gods and men is what the plan of salvation is all about. I admit that when I think of the Father standing up and giving up His throne to His Son, Jesus Christ, I feel a tinge of sorrow amongst the joy. Yet I understand this sorrow to be the same sorrow that is felt by a child who realizes he is a child no more. This will represent the end of an age. I love the Father with my whole soul. I do not want to see this age end because I do not want to be parted from Him. Yet He will not be gone at all. He will still be there, and we will be able to see Him and interact with Him all the time because we, too, will be Celestial beings, to come and go no more out!

Chapter 15: His Arm is Outstretched Still

In the prior chapter, we reviewed a portion of the Book of Enoch that pertained to God's final judgement. Enoch saw that the arm of the Lord was outstretched even to those who rejected Him. He allowed them to observe the chosen fates of the inhabitants of Outer Darkness so that they might determine if that is truly what they wished for themselves. For those who turn from their sinful ways, in time, we learned that the Son of God will come and reclaim them into kingdoms of glory. There, they will become His grateful servants and heirs to salvation, according to the salvation they were willing to receive.

In this chapter, Enoch continues expounding upon the many mysteries of God. He does so by reminding us how this vision began. Consider the following:

> **52.1**. And after those days in that place where I had seen all
> the visions of that which is hidden--for I had been carried off
> in a whirlwind and they had borne me towards the west

We are reminded that Enoch's miraculous vision began when the Remnant of Jacob, the Holy Race, descended from the heavens and mingled among the seed of men. You will recall that Enoch retraced their steps by being carried away from the Earth aboard the same miraculous whirlwinds that restored our long-lost brethren as described in Ezekiel chapters one and ten.

You will recall that there, Enoch witnessed the ministration of Christ to the Lost Tribes of Israel in a manner that mirrored His ministration to the Nephite Nation in the meridian of time. We are reminded that unlike the eastern arrival of the Watchers upon Mount Hermon, the Lost Tribes of Israel will arrive in the West. Their western arrival is confirmed in D&C 133:30-32, and the Hopi prophecy was discussed at length previously. As Enoch's whirlwind now restores him to the West, we understand that the things he discusses next will be centered upon the North American continent, the place of the Remnant's first appearance.

The vision continues:

> **52.2**. There mine eyes saw all the secret things of heaven that
> shall be, a mountain of iron, and a mountain of copper, and
> a mountain of silver, and a mountain of gold, and a mountain
> of soft metal, and a mountain of lead.

In the west, Enoch saw six mountains of various metals: iron, copper, silver, gold, soft metals, and lead. The number of mountains is significant here. From volume one of this series, you will recall Enoch observed seven gemstone mountains of burning fire at the edge of the universe overlooking Outer Darkness. The number seven is symbolic of completeness. The number six, on the other hand, is representative of man. The man was created on the sixth day. The number of the beast, 666, is also described as being the number of a man. While six is the symbol of men, the number three is a symbol of transformation through adversity. America transitions from wickedness to a continent of righteousness after three days of darkness. Jonah transitioned from a rebellious and disobedient man to a humble and willing servant after three days in the belly of the whale. Christ was killed and rose from the dead after three days in the tomb.

By reiterating the number six three times, as in the number 666, we are to understand that this represents the ultimate climax of man's power. Therefore, I believe these six mountains indicate the earthly power men will have obtained in the last days at the height of their power. These six particular metals, iron, copper, silver, gold, soft metal, and lead, are the backbone of modern technology. I will speak to these seven metals in turn.

Iron
Iron represents power. You will recall that the fourth kingdom of King Nebuchadnezzar's dream was symbolized by the statue's legs of iron. The kingdom's iron legs meant it would be mightier than all the kingdoms before it. In addition, you will also recall from volume one of this series that Sisera's nine hundred iron chariots plagued the Lord's covenant people and resulted in their enslavement. They were not liberated until the Lord called the kings of the stars to come to Israel's aid. Today, we have built iron chariots of our own. Indeed, as Isaiah prophesied, there is no end to the number of our chariots. Iron has also enabled us to build towering buildings that scratch the sky.

Copper
The second metal mountain represents modern man's ability to harness the power of electricity by channeling the mystical flow of electrons. Our copper wires literally circle the Earth. Copper is the circulatory system that moves the lifeblood of the modern industry.

Silver and Gold
These two precious metals are symbols of man's power and wealth and our mastery of advanced micro circuitry and technologies. These superconducting metals enable the creation of microchips of astounding capacity and design.

Soft Metals and Lead

Soft metals, also called rare earth metals and lead, are vital to man's ability to store power in the form of batteries. Additionally, the discovery of soft metals enabled the development of nuclear weapons capable of destroying worlds. Such devices' explosions cause the elements to melt together in fervent heat.

This is the meaning behind these six metal mountains seen by Enoch upon the West in the last days. They were seen in the West because the Industrial Revolution would begin in the West, modernizing the world in a concise period. Because we live in the last days, the mysteries of these types of metals are common knowledge, but the symbolic meaning of these metals has been hidden from the rest of the world until modern times. Enoch did not understand such things, so he sought clarification as to their meaning. Consider the following:

> **52.3**. And I asked the angel who went with me, saying, 'What
> things are these which I have seen in secret?'

> **52.4**. And he said unto me: 'All these things which thou hast
> seen shall serve the dominion of His Anointed that He may
> be potent and mighty on the earth.'

The angel told Enoch that these metals would be used to make the Lord mighty on the Earth. The Lord founded the United States of America. Only by divine providence could a rag-tag band of half-starved patriots could defeat the greatest military power on Earth. The Lord did this for His own purposes. This country would be the first to master the six metals, which would cause it to be the greatest force for good the world has ever known.

With a land-based upon religious freedom, America served as a fertile vineyard for transplanting Joseph and spreading the restored gospel to the world's four corners. The purposes of the Lord have been accomplished to no small degree because of the industry, wealth, and power that are personified by the United States' mastery of these metals. Beyond promoting and safeguarding the free agency of humankind, the Lord has absolutely no need for any technology Himself.

Because of our familiarity with the modern age, we are a little ahead of Enoch and his understanding of the relevance of these metals. However, Enoch is a quick study and will be brought up to speed as the vision progresses. We continue, therefore, with his instruction.

> **52.5**. And that angel of peace answered, saying unto me:
> 'Wait a little, and there shall be revealed unto thee all the
> secret things which surround the Lord of Spirits.

52.6. And these mountains which thine eyes have seen, the mountain of iron, and the mountain of copper, and the mountain of silver, and the mountain of gold, and the mountain of soft metal, and the mountain of lead, all these shall be in the presence of the Elect One as wax: before the fire, and like the water which streams down from above [upon those mountains], and they shall become powerless before His feet.

52.7. And it shall come to pass in those days that none shall be saved, either by gold or by silver, and none be able to escape.

52.8 And there shall be no iron for war, nor shall one clothe oneself with a breastplate. Bronze shall be of no service, and tin [shall be of no service and] shall not be esteemed, and lead shall not be desired.

52.9 And all these things shall be[denied and]destroyed from the surface of the earth, when the Elect One shall appear before the face of the Lord of Spirits.'

When the Lord comes again, the power of men, as represented by their mastery of these metals, will be brought low. The might and power of the United States of America will be shattered, just as the iron legs of King Nebuchadnezzar's great statue were shattered. This shattering event will be brought to pass because of corruption from within. The antichrist will also rise to great power in America before the Lord comes. However, the antichrist will also be brought low, despite the incredible devices that he will use to forecast against the nations.

The purification process of purging the Lord's vineyard will begin first at the Lord's house. It will culminate with the arrival of the miraculous ships of Chittim, which will sow destruction like a whirlwind from the Almighty. As foreseen by Enoch and foretold in the Hopi prophecy, these incredible whirlwinds will purge the West after arriving from the ends of heaven. When these ships come, the wicked in this country will be consumed as stubble before the flame. No weapon that is formed by man will prosper against them. The mighty cities of this country will be left desolate. Hulking iron skeletons will remain the only husks of their former glory. The wealth and power of men will be cast aside on that day. Our gold and silver will neither save us nor our copper or the power of our soft metals.

On that day, the Holy Race will descend from the heavens and inherit the desolate heritages of the drunkards of Ephraim. Tyranny and oppression will not be found in the land any longer. A new and glorious society will rise like a phoenix from the ashes of destruction. This society will not be fashioned after the manner of men nor the cities of men. The old corruptible ways will be done, and the new will be ushered in, beginning with the New Jerusalem.

The vision continues:

> **53.1.** There mine eyes saw a deep valley with open mouths, and all who dwell on the earth and sea and islands shall bring to him gifts and presents and tokens of homage, but that deep valley shall not become full.

The rest of the world will be cut off from America, for the waters of the great deep surrounding this blessed land will be cursed by the Lord's servant, John. On that day, only upright in heart can cross them – see D&C 61:14-19. Then, the work of gathering the righteous souls from all the world's nations will commence. Therefore, to the wicked, the oceans will become a deep and treacherous valley that is likened to the terrible gaping mouth that will devour the wicked who attempt to cross it. Desperate people seeking to flee to the city of refuge across the great divide will seek to secure safe passage across the waters, but these will find that righteousness is the new currency of the realm. Their gold and silver will account for nothing. Meanwhile, the righteous will continue to disappear from amongst their ranks. As we have seen from a prior chapter, the wicked will attribute their disappearance to alien abductions, for that is the only lie the wicked will have to tell.

Therefore, while the oceans will stand as impassable voids, millions of righteous shall be gathered unto the land of promise, and the desolate lands will be filled from coast to coast with safety and light. Those who come to the hallowed shore of the Father's choicest vineyard will fulfill the words of Isaiah:

> And it shall come to pass in the last days, *that* the mountain of the LORD's house shall be established in the top of the mountains, and shall be exalted above the hills; and all nations shall flow unto it. And many people shall go and say, Come ye, and let us go up to the mountain of the LORD, to the house of the God of Jacob; and He will teach us of His ways, and we will walk in His paths: for out of Zion shall go forth the law, and the word of the LORD from Jerusalem. (Isaiah 2:2-3)

At the mountain of the Lord's house, the righteous will fall at the feet of the children of Ephraim, the Lord's servants, and will be crowned with glory. Those will be days never to be forgotten, the bright and glorious dawn of a new age upon the Earth, and we shall see it. We shall live it. As the children of Ephraim and his fellows, we will be called upon to perform great work. It will truly be a marvelous work and wonder, of which, until now, we have only seen hints and shadows. Yet, it will be seen in its true light in the coming day. The foolishness and folly of men shall have been stripped away, and only that which is both true and eternal shall remain.

Yet, beyond the great oceans, the rest of the world will descend into chaos. War and bloodshed will erupt, the likes of which have never been seen since a nation was founded on Earth. Brother shall take up sword against brother. Fathers shall fight against sons, and the wicked shall kill the wicked. Thus, the wicked will reap the bitter fruits they have sown with their unrighteousness. These will be the day of recompense when the hirelings will receive the wages from the master's into whose service they have been employed.

Such are the circumstances as Enoch's vision continues:

> **53.2.** And their hands commit lawless deeds, and the sinners devour all whom they lawlessly oppress: yet the sinners shall be destroyed before the face of the Lord of Spirits, and they shall be banished from off the face of His earth, and they shall perish for ever and ever.

As foretold in ancient times, the meek and the righteous will inherit the Earth. As such, the wicked will be turned out, for they will not have a place amongst the righteous. Enoch states above that the wicked will perish forever. By this, we are not to understand that they will cease to exist, for the soul is eternal and cannot be destroyed. Yet, the wicked will be cut off from the Earth forever. They will never again set their foot upon it. For the Earth shall rest, and the meek will inherit it. Places of reform have been created for the wicked, which we have already read: Sheol, Hell, the seven burning mountains that stand as somber sentinels overlooking the firey gaping maw of Outer Darkness. These will become the temporary inheritances of the wicked, for despite their wickedness, they are still beloved of the Lord, and He will still seek to reclaim them. Therefore, the end will come. On that day, the Lord will hasten the work of destruction, just as He did in the old kingdoms. Enoch foresaw how that hastening would occur. Consider the following:

> **53.3.** For I saw all the angels of punishment abiding (there) and preparing all the instruments of Satan.

Enoch saw angels of punishment dwelling upon the Earth in the last days. You will recall that the Watchers of old were referred to by the ancients as angels, for they came to the earth from the heavens. You will also recall these Watchers taught men how to create the weapons of their own demise. History will repeat itself. Remember the following passages?

> **10.11**. And the Lord said unto Michael: 'Go, bind Semjâzâ and his associates who have united themselves with women so as to have defiled themselves with them in all their uncleanness.

> **10.12**. And when their sons have slain one another, and they have seen the destruction of their beloved ones, bind them fast for seventy generations in the valleys of the earth, till the day of their judgement and of their consummation, till the judgement that is for ever and ever is consummated.

In antiquity, the sons of Adam obtained terrible weapons of destruction from the Watchers. These weapons of destruction increased the speed and efficiency with which they could kill one another. According to Enoch, the Watchers will return once more after seventy generations. When they do, they will give their terrible gifts to humankind once more, and humankind will use them to bring about their own demise.

Enoch's vision continues:

> **53.4**. And I asked the angel of peace who went with me: 'For whom are they [*the Watchers*] preparing these instruments?'

> **53.5**. And he said unto me: 'They prepare these for the kings and the mighty of this earth, that they may thereby be destroyed.

> **53.6**. And after this the Righteous and Elect One shall cause the house of His congregation to appear: henceforth they shall be no more hindered in the name of the Lord of Spirits.

In the passages above, the angle of peace gives Enoch the order of events that will transpire in the last days. The return of the Watchers will proceed with the restoration of the House of Israel and the liberation of America. The Watchers will give the kings of the earth the weapons with which they will rise to power. The kings of the earth will facilitate the reintegration of the Watchers into society. Then comes the great deception that will cause many to be deceived; according to the covenant, even some of the elect will be deceived.

Yet, the wicked will not reign for long, for the Lord will cause the house of His congregation to appear. By this, we are to understand that the Remnant of Jacob shall come and destroy the wicked so that the New Jerusalem might descend from the heavens upon the North American continent. Therefore, it is important to make these things known to the children of men. However, they may not accept or receive them. They will not be warned, for their ears are dull of hearing, and their eyes cannot see afar off. Therefore, in their stupor, they will be made to believe a strong delusion and swallow the Watcher's lies hook, line, and sinker.

Nephi tried to warn and forewarn us of this coming day, but we refused to search out his words. As a result, Nephi lamented our blindness, for we did not follow his example and seek to be taught by the Lord as he had been taught. Therefore, despite his giving us the key to knowledge in his writings, we remained blind, but not all of us.

We return to Enoch's writings:

> **53.7**. And these mountains shall not stand [*the modern technology of mankind will be worthless in these days*] as the earth before His righteousncss, but the hills shall be as a fountain of water, and the righteous shall have rest from the oppression of sinners.'

> **54.1** And I looked and turned to another part of the earth, and saw there a deep valley with burning fire.

> **54.2**. And they brought the kings and the mighty, and began to cast them into this deep valley.

> **54.3**. And there mine eyes saw how they made these their instruments, iron chains of immeasurable weight.

> **54.4**. And I asked the angel of peace who went with me, saying: 'For whom are these chains being prepared?'

> **54.5**. And he said unto me: 'These are being prepared for the hosts of Azâzêl, so that they may take them and cast them into the abyss of complete condemnation, and they shall cover their jaws with rough stones as the Lord of Spirits commanded.

Here, we get confirmation that the Watchers will indeed be present on Earth in the last days, as they are described as the hosts of Azazel. The Watchers of the last days will suffer the same end as the former Watchers. You will recall from volume one of this series that the Lord ascribed all the sins of the ancient world to the Watcher Azazel. He was then bound and cast into a desert prison, with jagged stones placed upon him. After which, the world would be free from the global influence of the Watchers for seventy generations. Yes, there was a brief and isolated return of the Watchers in the lands of Canaan, but the Lord dealt with them by way of the House of Israel, providing a type and shadow for the events of the last days. We will live to see the Watchers return in the might and strength they possessed in the prediluvian world. Then they were worshiped as gods, and so they will be again.

Before the Lord makes a full end of things, Satan will be loosed from this prison planet for a time. As such, he will join Lady Wisdom in corrupting the cosmos in one last-ditch effort to overthrow the God of the Universe by laying siege to the New Jerusalem. This, of course, is utter foolishness. In that last great battle, the Lord will dissolve the hosts of heaven, and they will be imprisoned in the fiery burning mountain range at the edge of Outer Darkness. There is no power in the multiverse that can threaten the Almighty.

> **54.6**. And Michael, and Gabriel, and Raphael, and Phanuel shall take hold of them [*the Watchers*] on that great day, and cast them on that day into the burning furnace, that the Lord of Spirits may take vengeance on them for their unrighteousness in becoming subject to Satan and leading astray those who dwell on the earth.'

Enoch now reminds us of what happened to the Earth the first time that it was corrupted by the Watcher. By this, we are to understand that the wickedness and destruction that occurred in the prediluvian world is but a type and a shadow of what will befall our generation. The divergence is that the postdiluvian world will be destroyed as it is baptized with fire, as noted above, and the prediluvian world was destroyed when it was baptized with water.

> **54.7**. And in those days [*the prediluvian days*] shall punishment come from the Lord of Spirits, and He will open all the chambers of waters which are above the heavens, and of the fountains which are beneath the earth.

> **54.8**. And all the waters shall be joined with the waters: that which is above the heavens is the masculine, and the water which is beneath the earth is the feminine.

54.9. And they shall destroy all who dwell on the earth and those who dwell under the ends of the heaven.

54.10. And when they have recognized their unrighteousness which they have wrought on the earth, then by these [*the floods*] shall they perish.

55.1. And after that the Head of Days repented and said: 'In vain have I destroyed all who dwell on the earth.'

55.2. And He sware by His great name: 'Henceforth I will not do so to all who dwell on the earth, and I will set a sign in the heaven: and this shall be a pledge of good faith between Me and them for ever, so long as heaven is above the earth. And this is in accordance with My command.'

In the passages above, the title Head of Days does not pertain to Adam but rather to the God that created Adam from the dust of the Earth- the Lord of Spirits. God the Father mourned the destruction of the wicked in the days of Noah. He promised Enoch and Noah that he would never again make a full end of the Earth as He did with the flood. He gave the rainbow as a token of this covenant. So it is that He has made a place of refuge for the righteous to be able to weather the coming firestorm. He laid the foundations of our deliverance in antiquity. This is also why such destructions are so long in coming. He will give His children every possible opportunity to repent.

We now return to Enoch:

55.3. When I have desired to take hold of them by the hand of the angels on the day of tribulation and pain, because of this, I will cause My chastisement and My wrath to abide upon them, saith God, the Lord of Spirits.

The translation of the passage above is confusing. The meaning of the passage is the merciful nature of God. God does not begin with wholesale destruction, even on the great and terrible days. He first sends forth a precursor to afflict and torment men for five months, hoping to turn them from sin. This is spoken of in the ninth chapter of the book of Revelation. Yet, most will turn to rage instead of turning men to repentance. Then will come the firestorm. Thus, because of the hard-heartedness of men, Sheol, Hell, and the burning mountains at the end of all things become the only remaining pathways to repentance still available to them. Yet even there, the Lord's Arm of Mercy is outstretched still.

Once again, the Lord will use the antichrist as the world's scapegoat, just as he did with Azazel. The Lord will ascribe the sins of the world to the antichrist, and he will be cast into the lake of fire and brimstone that is Outer Darkness. Even in our gross wickedness, our Father is for us. He is long-suffering and kind. He is not against us. If He can show mercy, He will be merciful. It is who He is. Yet, true and lasting change can only come when we feel the consequence of sins. And so it will be that the wicked will feel the grave consequences of their sins.

> **55.4**. Ye †mighty kings† who dwell on the earth, ye shall have to behold Mine Elect One, how He sits on the throne of glory and judges Azâzêl, and all his associates, and all his hosts in the name of the Lord of Spirits.'

> **56.1**. And I saw there the hosts of the angels of punishment going, and they held scourges and chains of iron and bronze.

> **56.2**. And I asked the angel of peace who went with me, saying: 'To whom are these who hold the scourges going?'

> **56.3**. And he said unto me: 'To their elect and beloved ones that they may be cast into the chasm of the abyss of the valley.

> **56.4**. And then that valley shall be filled with their elect and beloved, and the days of their lives shall be at an end, and the days of their leading astray shall not thenceforward be reckoned.

> **56.5**. And in those days the angels shall return and hurl themselves to the east upon the Parthians and Medes: They shall stir up the kings, so that a spirit of unrest shall come upon them, and they shall rouse them from their thrones, that they may break forth as lions from their lairs, and as hungry wolves among their flocks.

> **56.6**. And they shall go up and tread under foot the land of His elect ones,[and the land of His elect ones shall be before them a threshing-floor and a highway:]

Enoch foresaw that the day of judgement would come, and the Son of Man will sit upon His throne, and He would judge the Watchers far more harshly than He would judge those that followed them. The Watchers will be cast into Outer Darkness, where there will be weeping, wailing, and gnashing of teeth. However, their disciples are not cast into the pit but deep valleys. Presumable are those same valleys that pervade the burning landscape at the edge of all things.

Enoch foresaw that those who went into the pit of Outer Darkness never returned. However, he saw that those who were imprisoned within the burning landscape overlooking Outer Darkness could be redeemed. It was not easy, nor was it quick. The process whereby their dross would be consumed would take thousands of years. But their dross would be consumed. Once consumed, all that would remain would be the jewels of God. That is to say, the Lord will have mercy upon them and make of them all they would permit Him to make of them. Mercy is at the core of the Father's nature. He plans to exalt His children. These terrible valleys at the edge of all things will be beautiful unto those who were transformed there.

However, before this great day of judgement comes, Enoch foresaw that the Watchers would stir the people of the Earth up in rage and anger against the people of Israel. This will be the first battle of Gog from Magog, which is the battle of Armageddon. This war will happen on two fronts. It will begin against the saints of God in America. The watchers will wage a war against them, and to the shock of the saints, they will prevail against them for a season. The saints will be overcome and will be in desperate need of deliverance. The second front of this epic battle between the Sons of Light and the Sons of Darkness will culminate in Israel. Therefore, it is really a continuation of the same battle. Just as the Watchers will overcome the Saints for a brief season, they will also overcome Judah for a brief season. However, Jerusalem will always be a stumbling block for the wicked.

Consider this as Enoch's vision continues:

> **56.7** But the city of my righteous shall be a hindrance to their horses. And they shall begin to fight among themselves, and their right hand shall be strong against themselves, and a man shall not know his brother, nor a son his father or his mother, till there be no number of the corpses through their slaughter, and their punishment be not in vain.

> **56.8** In those days Sheol shall open its jaws, and they shall be swallowed up therein and their destruction shall be at an end; Sheol shall devour the sinners in the presence of the elect.'

As the Lord has done so many times in the past, He will use the fog of war to cause the armies of the antichrist to battle against each other. All those who fight against Zion and

Jerusalem will perish. The destruction will be monumental. The souls departing the world on that day will flood the spirit world, just as happened in the days of the great flood. Consider how similar the passage above is to the following passage in modern revelation regarding this same event:

> And it shall come to pass among the wicked, that every man that will not take his sword against his neighbor must needs flee unto Zion for safety. And there shall be gathered unto it out of every nation under heaven; and it shall be the only people that shall not be at war one with another. (D&C 45:66-67)

The consistency of the prophecies found within the Book of Enoch and the rest of the scriptures is incredible. Despite the book's high strangeness, it fits. Enoch's incredible vision continues:

> **57.1**. And it came to pass after this that I saw another host of wagons, and men riding thereon, and **coming on the winds** from the east, and from the west to the south.

> **57.2**. And the noise of their wagons was heard, and when this turmoil took place the holy ones from heaven remarked it, and the pillars of the earth were moved from their place, and the sound thereof was heard from the one end of heaven to the other, in one day.

> **57.3**. And they shall all fall down and worship the Lord of Spirits. And this is the end of the second Parable.

Enoch saw that men riding upon the winds in wagons came from both the East and West to liberate the righteous in America. This great liberation occurred in a single day. This aligns perfectly with the Hopi's prophecy. America's greatest population centers both on the East and West Coasts and the South. This is precisely where Enoch saw these wind-riding hosts travel. Apparently, on the day this great purification occurs, Enoch said that a mighty sound would be heard from one end of heaven to the other. This incredible noise will strike terror in the hearts of the earth's inhabitants, and they will fall down to the earth and worship the Lord. Enoch was not the only one to speak of such things. Given Peter quoted from the Book of Enoch, it is clear that he would have known of this event as well. Indeed, he speaks of it in the following passages:

> But the day of the Lord will come as a thief in the night; in the which **the heavens shall pass away with a great noise,**

and **the elements shall melt with fervent heat, the earth also and the works that are therein shall be burned up**.

Seeing then that all these things shall be dissolved, what manner of persons ought ye to be in all holy conversation and godliness, looking for and hasting unto the coming of the day of God, **wherein the heavens being on fire shall be dissolved, and the elements shall melt with fervent heat**?

Nevertheless we, according to His promise, look for new heavens and a new Earth, wherein dwelleth righteousness. Wherefore, beloved, seeing that ye look for such things, be diligent that ye may be found of Him in peace, without spot, and blameless. (2 Peter 3:10-14)

It is clear from Peter's teachings that he understood Enoch's prophecy. He urged the saints of his day to keep these things in remembrance. If these things were important for the saints in Peter's time to understand, how much more important are they for us since we will literally witness them come to pass?

Nephi, the great American prophet and inspiration for all of my writings, also witnessed these things. He had seen them in vision but was not permitted to speak openly of them. As such, he spoke of them in conjunction with his explanation of Isaiah's writings. Consider his explanation of this coming day.

But, behold, in the last days, or in the days of the Gentiles— yea, behold all the nations of the Gentiles and also the Jews, both those who shall come upon this land and those who shall be upon other lands, yea, even upon all the lands of the earth, behold, they will be drunken with iniquity and all manner of abominations— And when that day shall come they shall be visited of the Lord of Hosts, with thunder and with earthquake, **and with a great noise**, and with storm, and with tempest, **and with the flame of devouring fire**.

And all the nations that fight against Zion, and that distress her, shall be as a dream of a night vision, for behold, all ye that doeth iniquity, stay yourselves and wonder, for ye shall cry out, and cry; yea, ye shall be drunken but not with wine, ye shall stagger but not with strong drink. (2 Nephi 27:1-4)

Nephi is awesome. It is obvious to me that he knew exactly what he was talking about but was under certain constraints because of the blindness of men. The Lord only permitted him to say so much. His real message is in the Isaiah chapters he transcribed, which speak plainly of these things for those with eyes to see them.

Isaiah associated this great noise with a massive host coming to the earth from the ends of heaven to destroy the wicked. Consider his writings on the subject:

> Lift ye up a banner upon the high mountain, exalt the voice unto them, shake the hand, that they may go into the gates of the nobles. I have commanded my sanctified ones, I have also called my mighty ones, for mine anger is not upon them that rejoice in my highness. **The noise of the multitude in the mountains like as of a great people, a tumultuous noise of the kingdoms of nations gathered together**, the Lord of Hosts mustereth the hosts of the battle.
>
> They come from a far country, **from the end of heaven**, yea, the Lord, and the weapons of his indignation, to destroy the whole land. Howl ye, for the day of the Lord is at hand; it shall come as a destruction from the Almighty. Therefore shall all hands be faint, every man's heart shall melt; and they shall be afraid; pangs and sorrows shall take hold of them; **they shall be amazed one at another; their faces shall be as flames**.
>
> Behold, the day of the Lord cometh, cruel both with wrath and fierce anger, to lay the land desolate; and he shall destroy the sinners thereof out of it. (2 Nephi 23:2-9)

Surely, Isaiah saw the same thing in the vision that Nephi, Peter, and Enoch saw. Something miraculous is coming. It will astound the world, and the wicked will have great cause to fear it, for it is coming for them. Yet, the righteous need not fear this event. For us, it will be a day of redemption, a day of salvation, a day of deliverance. However, the wicked will look up to the sky in terror, seeing the sky filled with Enoch's flying wagons riding upon the winds from the East and the West.

On that day, all the wicked who can will flee to Europe. Yet, of the Watcher's forces, only one out of every six will survive. There, they will regroup. Yet the Lord will turn their own swords upon their own heads. Cities will be rendered desolate as the wicked slay the wicked while the righteous are whisked away to the city of refuge across the mighty sea. The lands of Europe will be strewn with corpses, from the frigid north to the sultry south. The great cities of Europe will be Sumer, Nineva, Babylon, and Rome.

The survivors of this chaos will follow in the footsteps of the Jaredites of old, rallying to one standard bearer or the other in an epic battle of extinction. As they march forward, cities will fall, one after another. The surging tide of this destructive host will also break upon the cities of Judah. This prompted the Lord to provide the following warning to the Jews of the last days:

> But when they persecute you in this city, flee ye into another:
> for verily I say unto you, ye shall not have gone over the cities
> of Israel, till the Son of Man be come. Matt 10:23.

This invading host will attack Israel from the north. Galilee of the nations will fall. Nazareth will be overrun. Haifa and Telavi will be rendered desolate. It will not be until this host arrives in the walled city that it will be halted. This halt in their momentum will come because of the two servants of the Lord. Yet, in the end, even they will fall, and the Jews will need to flee once more, but not for much longer. For before the last city of Judah falls, the Lord will come again. He will save the Jews, for His arm is outstretched still!

Chapter 16: The Third Parable

In the prior chapter, we learned once again that the Watchers will play an integral role in the last days' events. Their technology will be had by the wicked, and the wicked will be emboldened as a result, thinking that no nation would be able to wage war with them. For a brief period, they will be right. However, the wicked will soon learn that the Lord's ways are not theirs. They will be confronted by a host they did not look for. This host will arrive riding upon wagons flying in the winds from both the east and the west.

These chariots will be the mighty ships of Chittim and will be the fulfilment of the Hopi's incredible prophecy. Nothing can stop them. Their arrival will make a great noise that will terrify the wicked and be heard worldwide. Yet the wicked will not repent and will fight until the last man. Yet, the Lord will preserve Israel, and the righteous will inherit the Earth. This concluded Enoch's second parable.

In the present chapter, we will begin our analysis of Enoch's third parable. As with all of Enoch's writing, it is truly fascinating.

> **58.1**. And I began to speak the third Parable concerning the righteous and elect.
>
> **58.2**. Blessed are ye, ye righteous and elect, for glorious shall be your lot.
>
> **58.3**. And the righteous shall be in the light of the sun. And the elect in the light of eternal life: The days of their life shall be unending, and the days of the holy without number.

From Enoch's words, we are to understand that the righteous and elect will be magnified with the full weight of the Celestial Kingdom, as is represented by the sun's light. We have previously touched upon the differences between the degrees of glory, yet the fact remains that very little of the true nature of the Celestial kingdom has been revealed. We do not have the slightest idea of what glories the Lord has treasured for those who love Him.

Yet, one thing that we do know from both Enoch's writings and modern revelation is that only those in the Celestial Kingdom will inherit the full blessings of Abraham. Those who do are endowed with an "exceedingly great weight of eternal glory." These become gods and are the only ones counted worthy of raising the rising generation when the cycle repeats itself once more. Enoch's vision continues wherein he makes a crucial observation regarding a behavioral pattern that distinguishes those who will inherit such glory.

> **58.4**. And they shall seek the light and find righteousness with the Lord of Spirits: There shall be peace to the righteous in the name of the Eternal Lord.

> **58.5**. And after this it shall be said to the holy in heaven that they should seek out the secrets of righteousness, the heritage of faith: For it has become bright as the sun upon earth, and the darkness is past.

> **58.6**. And there shall be a light that never endeth, and to a limit of days they shall not come, for the darkness shall first have been destroyed, [And the light established before the Lord of Spirits] and the light of uprightness established for ever before the Lord of Spirits.

Enoch foresaw that God would admonish the hosts of heaven to follow the pattern of the righteous and seek out the mysteries they had obtained. This is their legacy of faith and the greatest gift they could bestow upon their posterity. Spiritual wisdom does not happen by accident. Abraham did not receive the covenants of the early patriarchs by happy chance. He followed the pattern of the righteous. Consider how this happened for Father Abraham:

> **I sought** for the blessings of the fathers, and the right whereunto I should be ordained to administer the same; having been myself a follower of righteousness, **desiring also to be one who possessed great knowledge**, and to be a greater follower of righteousness, and to possess a greater knowledge, and to be a father of many nations, a prince of peace, and **desiring to receive instructions**, and to keep the commandments of God, **I became a rightful heir**, a High Priest, holding the right belonging to the fathers.

> **I sought for mine appointment** unto the Priesthood according to the appointment of God unto the fathers concerning the seed. (Abraham 1:2 & 4)

It is clear from the passages above that Abraham obtained the covenants of the Fathers because he was diligently seeking them. How did he know about them? He obtained a copy of their writings and diligently searched them. He did not just read their words; he acted upon them. He saw them for what they were, a road map to the kingdom of God for those with eyes to see. It is unsurprising to me that Abraham obtained the promises to the fathers. What is surprising to me is that, throughout history, relatively few have sought to do the same.

> [*The Jews*] answered and said unto [*Jesus Christ*], Abraham is our father. Jesus saith unto them, If ye were <u>Abraham's children</u>, ye would do the <u>works</u> of Abraham. (John 8:39)

Christ told the Jews that spiritual effort and work were what was needed to become the children of Abraham - not genetics. In order words, the fact that Abraham sought and obtained the fathers' blessings has nothing to do with you unless you do what he did. Yet, too often, we take upon ourselves the attitude of the Jews and presume the blessings of Abraham without following the pattern or gospel of Abraham. This is like professing Christ with your lips but doing nothing to actually know Him. He has said that to such, He will say, "Depart from me, for you never knew me." It is, therefore, utterly foolishness for us to presume all the rights and blessings of Abraham without mirroring his works. That is to say, we must seek these things. We must make our own spiritual journey and find our own lands of promise by coming before the God of Abraham and working out our salvation with fear and trembling before Him.

Abraham began his journey to find the Lord and obtain his fathers' covenants as a young, unmarried man. He sought them for many years before he obtained them. This is what Abraham said after the Lord appeared to him many years later, at the age of sixty-two.

> Now, after the Lord had withdrawn from speaking to me, and withdrawn His face from me, **I said in my heart: Thy servant has sought thee earnestly; now I have found thee** (Abraham 2:12)

Abraham spent decades seeking the Lord; this was not the end of his journey either. He would spend the rest of mortality seeking and waiting upon the Lord. He would not see those covenants fulfilled in mortality, yet he now sits in heaven as a god, for even in death, the Father can make good on all He says; see D&C 132:37.

As members of the Church, we believe that humankind will not be punished for Adam's transgression; rather, we will be punished individually for our own sins. If we will not be punished for the works of others, why would we be rewarded for the works of others? Abraham was blessed because of his works; you will be blessed for yours. Those who will do Abraham's works will receive Abraham's blessings; those who do not will not.

If you do not seek Abraham's blessings, why would they be given to you? Ask, and ye shall receive; knock, and it shall be opened unto you. If you will reap, you must sow. It is the law of the harvest.

Consider the blessings and covenants of the temple. Many obtain these covenants as wide-eyed youth and do so without knowledge or understanding. Have they obtained the promises while they have gone through the motions of rights and rituals? No. The promises are of no effect unless they are sealed upon you by the Holy Spirit of Promise. In this manner, the blessings of Abraham are aligned and reserved for those who will do the works of Abraham. This will not happen by accident.

You will see it everywhere once you open your eyes to this fact. As such, there are really two gospels, the outer and the inner. The outer gospel is the parable, which is spoken for all to hear. The inner gospel is the parable's meaning, which is to be acted upon. The value comes not in the hearing but in the doing.

This pattern is perhaps most prevalent in The Book of Mormon. This is no ordinary book. It represents the life's work of several of the greatest men ever walking the planet. They are men like Nephi, Mormon, and Moroni. These men were not hearers of the Word only; they followed in the footsteps of Abraham. They worked diligently to understand the mysteries of God. Once they obtained them, they were dramatically different from their peers. Their covenants with God became their most prized possessions, and they mourned for the spiritually blind who seeing would not see.

These men desired to share what they had learned in its fullness, but they were constrained. God is the keeper of such things, and if men would know them, they must follow the pattern that Enoch observed above. They must seek them. They will find them within the guard rails of the gospel if they seek them. Therefore, the writings of these men are reflective of both the outer and the inner gospel.

The words they have written on the page are important and meaningful, as the parable is important and meaningful. However, the real value of their words is only revealed through deliberate study, pondering, and seeking of the Lord. If you do not understand what I am talking about, perhaps you can begin by studying the context of the scriptures that gave rise to the following passages: 1 Nephi 14:25-28, 1 Nephi 22:29, 2 Nephi 32:7, Alma 12:9, 3 Nephi 26:11, 3 Nephi 26:16-18, Ether 13:13, and Moroni 10:3-5.

Indeed, the very first verse of the Book of Mormon highlights the importance of understanding the mysteries of God. Yet, the phrase "mysteries of God" has become all but a hiss and a byword unto the Saints. Why is this the case? It is because the world is full of mysteries, and we have itching ears. Secret combinations are founded upon mysteries. Yet, as we have learned in the Book of Enoch, there are the mysteries of God, and there are worthless mysteries, such as those that were pursued by the Watchers. The worthless mysteries ALWAYS lay beyond the guardrails of the restored gospel of Jesus Christ. Guard rails are there to keep you from going off the cliff.

Many public examples have been of former saints jumping the guard rails and falling to their deaths. It is not that the roads within the guardrails are unsafe; the areas beyond the guardrails are treacherous. Leaving the safety of the guard rails of the gospel is the spiritual equivalent of taking candy from a stranger in a creepy van with blacked-out windows. It doesn't feel right, yet people ignore the warning signs and do it anyway. People who engage in such behaviors are those who are most likely to get kidnapped.

Because some people have been spiritually kidnapped by men in creepy vans, others take upon themselves the irrational fear of men, mustaches, snakes, goats, and sharp sticks. Adopting such an attitude will directly and profoundly impact the quality of your spiritual education. Many who profess to be the servants of God refuse to seek knowledge of the Father's mysteries for fear of spiritual kidnappers. This is as foolish as it is shortsighted. Yes, Satan is the Father of Lies, and he does hand out poison candy from creeper vans. However, do not suppose that you are safe by avoiding creeper vans.

We are living in Satan's prison plant. His power and influence extend to every aspect of the globe; he is not limited to creeper vans. He is preaching false doctrines everywhere: in our children's and grandchildren's elementary schools, on our college campuses, and on every social media platform under the sun. In short, his power and influence are everywhere. Therefore, creeper vans or not, our children are confronted with lies and deceit daily. The greatest antidote to Satan's power is the word of God. True doctrine has a more powerful impact on the hearts of man than the sword or any other force on earth. As such, we should seek to be instructed by the Lord more today than at any other time on Earth. God the Father knows how to give good gifts to His children, but we must be seeking them.

If there is anything true and worthy of knowing, it will, without exception, reconcile within the restored gospel of Jesus Christ. Satan's greatest lies are mingled with scripture. Please do not overlook the evil because of its packaging. A fountain produces either good or bad water; it cannot produce both. If something overthrows, deviates, turns to the side, undermines, or replaces the restored gospel of Jesus Christ in any way, cast it off.

If you disregard the gospel's guardrails, as surely as the sun sets in the West, you will believe in the philosophies of men cleverly mingled with scripture. In doing so, you climb into a creepy van and drive away from the covenant path to a place where there is weeping, wailing, and gnashing of teeth. If we hold beliefs that are inconsistent with the restored gospel of Jesus Christ, we must discard them, for why will we die? The light is as easily discernable for us as it was for our forefathers. The mysteries of God are as accessible to us as they were to Nephi. Therefore, seek for the good things of God. They are mysteries because the world does not know their value. Nevertheless, they are of great worth.

We now return to Enoch's vision:

> [**59.1**. In those days mine eyes saw the secrets of the lightnings, and of the lights, and the judgements they execute: and they lighten for a blessing or a curse as the Lord of Spirits willeth.]

> [**59.2**. And there I saw the secrets of the thunder, and how when it resounds above in the heaven, the sound thereof is heard, and he caused me to see the judgements executed on the earth, whether they be for well-being and blessing, or for a curse according to the word of the Lord of Spirits.]

> [**59.3**. And after that all the secrets of the lights and lightnings were shown to me, and they lighten for blessing and for satisfying.]

Enoch likened the mysteries of God and the judgements and consequences of those mysteries to a powerful thunderstorm. Thunderstorms are symbolic of the turbulence and adversity of life. Powerful systems such as the one Enoch talks about mask the sun's light, bringing darkness, destructive winds, and rain. Lightning strikes light up the otherwise darkened sky and provides brief glimpses of the world around us. Such lighting strikes instantaneously superheat the air around them, rapidly expanding and collapsing. The result is the apocalyptic sound of thunder.

The brilliant illumination from lightning against the darkened sky represents the importance of the knowledge of God. Such illuminations can highlight tornadoes and other immediate threats often accompanying powerful storm systems, as Enoch describes. My wife grew up in Kansas and recalls a particular storm system such as this that occurred at night. Each flash of lightning illuminated several tornadoes on the ground, moving throughout her town. Each strike would show their relative position to great danger. So it is with the mysteries of God.

In the coming days of trial, we will not survive unless we can observe and interpret coming dangers as illuminated by the flashes of the Spirit. Jesus Christ is perhaps the greatest mystery of all. He came into the world in a time of great turmoil, as depicted by Enoch's storm. In that tumultuous time, Christ was the Light of the World. By pronouncing Himself as the Son of Man, He illuminated the pending dangers in the world around the Jews, yet for the most part, the Jews comprehended Him not. As such, the whirlwinds came, and Judah was obliterated.

Yet some comprehended Christ's radiant light and could flee from before the whirlwinds and lived to tell the tale as with Enoch's thunderstorm. The lighting flashes illuminated all of Israel, but most did not have eyes to see it. Men will be judged according to their works and how they were able to navigate the storms and threats of life on Satan's prison planet.

We alone choose what voices we will listen to, for each of us is responsible for our own spiritual education. We alone choose whether to accept or reject the light as something that has no value. However loud the accompanying sounds of a storm may be, the roll of thunder is unique. So, too, the righteous can pick out the inspiration and mysteries of God from amongst a multitude of sounds.

Sadly, the fear of men has always played a great role in the decision-making of many. The jeers and mocking of the crowds within the great and spacious buildings of the world cause many to be ashamed, even as the lighting strikes and the thunder rolls. This phenomenon is not new; it has always been this way. Consider the following:

> And angels did appear unto men, wise men, and did declare unto them glad tidings of great joy; thus in this year the scriptures began to be fulfilled. Nevertheless, the people began to harden their hearts, all save it were the most believing part of them, both of the Nephites and also of the Lamanites, and began to depend upon their own strength and upon their own wisdom, saying: Some things they may have guessed right, among so many; but behold, we know that all these great and marvelous works cannot come to pass, of which has been spoken. And they began to reason and to contend among themselves, saying: It is not reasonable that such a being as a Christ shall come… (Hel 16:14-18)

What a perfect illustration of Enoch's concepts in this chapter. Helaman's day mirrored the same turbulent storm system that existed amongst the Jews. In America, as in Judah, some wise men could discern the signs of the times. These wise men and women came from all classes of society, amongst every race and tongue. These had eyes to see and ears to hear, even when those around them did not. Yet, when these sought to share the mysteries of God with the people around them, they were rejected. Their knowledge was discounted, considered to be unreasonable, fanciful, supernatural, and science fiction. Yet, their knowledge clearly fell within the guardrails of the gospel for anyone who cared to check. Yet, such validation requires spiritual effort, and the status quo is easy.

Yet, regardless of how unreasonable such things seemed to the greatest minds within the great and spacious building, the lightning flashed, the thunder crashed, the whirlwinds came, and they were carried away, along with their status quo. Smooth places were made rough. Valleys became mountains, and mountains became valleys. Many great and majestic cities were burned with fire, buried in the Earth, and drowned beneath the depths of the sea. What consolation was, "I told you so" to the surviving righteous in the wake of such destruction as this?

This concludes Enoch's Book of Parables.

Section Two – The Son of Man's Latter-day Survival Guide

Chapter 17: The Son of Man

The last chapter saw the epic conclusion of Enoch's book of parables. Within those parables, humankind was first introduced to the epic and hidden character, the Son of Man. The identity of the Son of Man is the most important of all the Father's mysteries. Surprisingly, the true nature of Jesus Christ is almost as hidden as it ever has been. Yes, many profess to know His name, but there is a world of difference between knowing His name and Him.

> Many will say to Me in that day, Lord, Lord, have we not prophesied in thy name? And in thy name have cast out devils? And in thy name done many wonderful works? Then will I say, ye never knew me: depart from me, ye that work iniquity.
>
> And it came to pass, when Jesus had ended these sayings, the people were astonished at His doctrine: for He taught them as one having authority, and not as the scribes. (Mat 7:22 & JSM 7:33 -see footnote Mat 7:23a- & Mat 7:28-29)

The Joseph Smith translation of the passages above clarifies that to truly follow Christ, you must know who He is. Knowing His name and professing it to others is not enough. Israel worshiped an altered form of God called Ba'al – translated as the Lord. Regardless of the sincerity with which Israel worshiped Ba'al, their worship of a twisted version of God was an abomination.

Similarly, when God the Father and Jesus Christ appeared to Joseph Smith, They told him that all the creeds of Christianity then practiced were abominations. This is because their creeds professed a twisted version of the Godhead. Every religious creed then extant professed the Godhead as an amorphous conglomeration of a single organism with multiple personalities, yet without body parts or passions existing everywhere and nowhere simultaneously. This is utterly false and represents the twisted demonic doctrine of Lucifer every bit as much as Ba'al ever did. Any man or woman subscribing to such beliefs cannot enter the kingdom of God, for it is impossible to be saved in ignorance.

To worship God, you must know Him, not a bizarre and twisted version of Him that has been created by demons and men. Yet, according to the Book of Enoch, Christ's true identity has been hidden from the world since before the laying of its foundations. As such, only those who will humble themselves before the Father, seeking to be taught by Him, will have the true nature of the Godhead revealed unto them. As such, to most, He will remain a mystery. As such, Christians everywhere claim that members of the Church of Jesus Christ worship a different God than they do. The fact of the matter is, this is absolutely true. They do not know the being they worship, for their god, is an unknowable amorphous entity that exists everywhere and nowhere simultaneously. This is a totally different god. God the Father is a perfect resurrected being. He is the perfect Man, and His Son is like unto Him, as my son is like me.

Therefore, it is clear that the true nature of God is as unknown to most of humankind today as at any other time in history. I believe this is precisely why Jesus Christ referred to Himself as the Son of Man, the Enochian man of mystery, more than any other title. Indeed, I have come to believe that anytime this title is used in scriptures, it is in conjunction with a fundamental doctrine that is a great mystery to most of the earth's population. As such, this peculiar title is like a marker for those who have eyes to see, just like the symbols of the fish or the anchor were in times past.

Therefore, as we begin this section of this volume, we must do so by considering the Son of God's teaching regarding Himself. Christ was the most common title people used to refer to Jesus in His day. However, Jesus hardly ever used this title Himself in antiquity. Instead, He often referred to Himself with the Enochian title, Son of Man. No other title comes remotely close in His direct usage of this name. Indeed, Christ used this title to refer to Himself over eight dozen times in the New Testament alone. Yet, His usage of this strange title is somewhat baffling to modern Christians.

Christ is obviously knowledgeable. Therefore, His usage of this title was both calculated and deliberate. As such, Bible scholars have needed to come up with an explanation for why He did it. The prevailing reason, such scholars put forward, is that Christ referred to Himself as the Son of Man to emphasize His mortality. On the other hand, many LDS scholars suggest that He used it to emphasize that He was the son of the perfect Man. While either of these conclusions is false, both fail to consider the original source of this title – the Book of Enoch. I find this to be astonishing. Why do we dismiss the origin of this title so flippantly as to cause most Christianity to be ignorant of this important fact?

Given that the Book of Enoch was one of the most common books recovered amongst the Dead Sea Scrolls, it is evident that the Jews were clearly familiar with it at the time of Christ. If the Book of Enoch is to be understood purely as an apocryphal work, we must ask ourselves, why Christ would associate Himself so closely with it?
He wouldn't!

When the most intelligent being to ever have spent mortality upon this planet associates Himself with the Book of Enoch, we must conclude that there is a reason for it. The reason for His actions is not beyond our reach. They require us to open our minds and ponder. Therefore, let us go through mental exercise.

Imagine you were a Jew living in Jerusalem at the time of Christ. Suppose you heard of a man who claimed to be the Son of Man. Not only did this man claim to be the Son of Man, but all of Israel was in an uproar over His incredible miracles. This self-proclaimed Son of Man was reported as healing the sick, raising the dead, walking on water, calming the sea, giving sight to the blind, and opening the ears of the deaf.

Such astounding things would or should have piqued your curiosity. Hopefully, they would have led you to ask questions about what the prophecies spoke of regarding the Son of Man and, more importantly, who He was meant to be. If you had followed up on these questions, you would inevitably have been pointed directly to the Book of Enoch. Within this book, you would have discovered the following passages describing who the Son of Man is. What would you have made of these passages?

46.2. And I asked the angel who went with me and showed me all the hidden things, concerning that **Son of Man**, who He was, and whence He was, and why He went with the Head of Days. And he answered and said unto me:

46.3. This is the Son of Man who hath righteousness, with whom dwelleth righteousness, and who revealeth all the treasures of that which is hidden, because the Lord of Spirits hath chosen Him, and whose lot hath the pre-eminence before the Lord of Spirits in uprightness forever.

46.4. And this Son of Man whom thou hast seen shall †raise up† the kings and the mighty from their seats, [And the strong from their thrones] and shall loosen the reins of the strong, and break the teeth of the sinners.

46.5. [And He shall put down the kings from their thrones and kingdoms] Because they do not extol and praise Him, nor humbly acknowledge whence the kingdom was bestowed upon them.

46.6. And He shall put down the countenance of the strong and shall fill them with shame. And darkness shall be their dwelling, and worms shall be their bed, and they shall have no hope of rising from their beds, because they do not extol the name of the Lord of Spirits.

47.1. And in those days shall have ascended the prayer of the righteous, and the blood of the righteous from the earth before the Lord of Spirits.

47.2. In those days the holy ones who dwell above in the heavens shall unite with one voice and supplicate and pray [and praise, and give thanks and bless the name of the Lord of Spirits] on behalf of the blood of the righteous [the Son of Man] which has been shed, and that the prayer of the righteous may not be in vain before the Lord of Spirits, that judgement may be done unto them, and that they may not have to suffer forever.

48.1. And in that place I saw the fountain of righteousness which was inexhaustible: and around it were many fountains of wisdom; and all the thirsty drank of them, and were filled with wisdom, and their dwellings were with the righteous and holy and elect.

48.2. And at that hour that Son of Man was named in the presence of the Lord of Spirits, and His name before the Head of Days.

48.3. Yea, before the sun and the signs were created, before the stars of the heaven were made, His name was named before the Lord of Spirits.

48.4. He [*the Son of Man*] shall be a staff to the righteous whereon to stay themselves and not fall, and He shall be the light of the Gentiles, and the hope of those who are troubled of heart.

48.5. All who dwell on earth shall fall down and worship before Him, and will praise and bless and celebrate with song the Lord of Spirits.

48.6. And for this reason hath He [*the Son of Man*] been chosen and hidden before Him [*the Father*], before the creation of the world and for evermore.

62.1. And thus the Lord commanded the kings and the mighty and the exalted, and those who dwell on the earth, and said: 'Open your eyes and lift up your horns if ye are able to recognize the Elect One.'

62.2. And the Lord of Spirits seated Him on the throne of His glory, and the spirit of righteousness was poured out upon Him, and the word of His mouth slays all the sinners, and all the unrighteous are destroyed from before His face.

62.5. And one portion of them shall look on the other, and they shall be terrified, and they shall be downcast of countenance, and pain shall seize them, when they see that Son of Man Sitting on the throne of His glory.

62.6. And the kings and the mighty and all who possess the earth shall bless and glorify and extol Him who rules over all, who was hidden.

62.7. For from the beginning the Son of Man was hidden, and the Most High preserved Him in the presence of His might, and revealed Him to the elect.

What would be your reaction at the end of reading these passages in context with the uproar throughout all of Israel? Would you doubt that He was who He said He was? Would you place the teachings of men before the hidden teachings of God? Do you suppose that you would have been taught these things in the synagogue if you had not gone seeking them yourself? Has the world fundamentally changed between now and then? This mental exercise perfectly explains why Christ proclaimed Himself as the Son of Man. This also explains why the writings of Christ's apostles demonstrated such a familiarity with the Book of Enoch.

Now, let us return to our mental exercise for a moment. However, this time, let us imagine that we are a member of the Sanhedrin – desperate to hold on to power. We, too, hear of a Galilean stranger proclaiming Himself to be the Son of Man. We hear many incredible stories of incredible miracles and impossible deeds. In our curiosity, we, too, are led to the Book of Enoch. We are mortified by learning that when this Man refers to Himself as the Son of Man, He is effectively proclaiming Himself to literally be the Son of God. In our righteous indignation, we seek to eliminate the blasphemer by any means necessary. As a member of Israel's most prominent and wealthy class, it has taken us years of study to obtain our positions of prominence. The coming of the Son of Man is a threat that cannot go unanswered. We now consider the passages within the Book of Enoch describing the nature of the Son of Man to be incendiary and a grave concern. After all, what would happen if this information were to become public knowledge? As such, steps are taken with our peers to discredit and debunk the Book of Enoch and then ban it altogether. This would explain why so many copies of the Book of Enoch were found hidden away in caves throughout Israel. Do you suppose that modern-day Orthodoxy in Israel will have changed their tune much regarding the Book of Enoch with time?

Knowledge is power; as such, those in positions of power seek to control the flow of knowledge. Yet, while men can ban and destroy books to the point that they become lost, men cannot stop God from performing His work. To the student of modern revelation, very little is new in the Book of Enoch, for the Lord has brought this knowledge to light by other means. Yet, the Book of Enoch is an incredible validation of the doctrines of the restoration.

Christ is an unchangeable being. He is the same yesterday, today, and forever. Therefore, when we look at modern revelation, we should see embedded within it the same layered meaning that has always accompanied such scripture. To borrow a phrase from Hillary Clinton, just as Christ's usage of the title Son of Man was a "dog whistle" to the seeking, the same is true today. Therefore, I hope you will seek to understand the passages of modern revelation that use this peculiar title to guide your study of the hidden things about the events of the last days.

Out of the one hundred and thirty-eight sections in the Doctrine and Covenants, twelve contain the Enochian title, Son of Man; these sections are 45, 49, 58, 61, 63, 64, 65, 68, 76, 109, 122, and 130. The rest of this section will be dedicated to analyzing these chapters in order. I think that you will be surprised by how much hidden information the Hidden Son has given us in these revelations.

Chapter 18: The Coming of the Son of Man – D&C 45

This is the first section of the Doctrine and Covenant that speaks about the Son of Man. Curiously, this revelation was received within days of Joseph Smith finishing the Book of Moses found within the Pearl of Great Price. The book of Moses is filled with Enochian references. As such, it should not be lost on the reader that within this present revelation that we are about to discuss, Christ not only refers to Himself as the Son of Man but also as the God of Enoch. It is my theory that such is an indicator that there is hidden knowledge within this chapter that is best understood in the context of the Book Enoch.

Given that the stated purpose of the Book of Enoch was to bless the lives of the righteous that would be called to live during the days of trial, it should come as no surprise that this chapter is intensely focused upon the events of the second coming. Because of the layered meaning of Christ's teachings, I believe that this section, and many others like it, can only truly be fully understood in the context of the subject matter of this book. With this in mind, we begin our present analysis.

> Hearken, O ye people of My church, to whom the kingdom
> has been given; hearken ye and give ear to Him who laid
> the foundation of the earth, who made the heavens and all
> the hosts thereof, and by whom all things were made which
> live, and move, and have a being. (D&C 45:1)

This is quite the opening verse! In it, Christ pronounces Himself as the Creator of the heavens and earth and all of the inhabitants living therein. This astounding doctrine goes hand in hand with the Book of Enoch. As noted above, this revelation was given on March 7, 1831, only days after the completion of the Book of Moses. In the book of Moses, both Moses and Enoch give accounts of innumerable inhabited earthlike planets. Therefore, we are to understand this opening verse's reference to the inhabitants of heaven from this context.

In this opening verse, Christ seeks to expand our understanding of His creations, including all things with a being. I suspect this passage will become much more meaningful in the coming days than we are prepared to understand. Indeed, by the conclusion of this book, we will be forced to confront some of these concepts that will challenge our perception of the nature of life within the cosmos. Enoch himself discusses various incredible classes of heavenly beings, which we will explore in Volume III of this series. For now, suffice it to say that the multiverse holds many more surprises in store than we can explore within the scope of this chapter.

We now return to the present revelation:

> And again I say, hearken unto my voice, lest death shall overtake you; in an hour when ye think not the summer shall be past, and the harvest ended, and your souls not saved. Listen to Him who is the advocate with the Father, who is pleading your cause before Him—Saying: Father, behold the sufferings and death of Him who did no sin, in whom thou wast well pleased; behold the blood of thy Son which was shed, the blood of Him whom thou gavest that thyself might be glorified; wherefore, Father, spare these My brethren that believe on My name, that they may come unto Me and have everlasting life. (D&C 45:2-5)

Here, we have another incredible passage! Christ proclaims Himself our Advocate before the Throne of God, which perfectly harmonizes with the Book of Enoch. You will recall that earlier in this work, Christ pled before the throne of God that the Satans should not permitted to come before His throne to testify against the noble and great ones. Instead, as the ultimate keyholder to the atonement, He will present their cases before the Throne of God. If Christ is our advocate and the Satans are not permitted to speak against us, we have great cause to hope.

However, Christ warns in the passage above that His saints risk dying in a manner that they look not for. We are to assume this death is associated with His Second coming by referencing the end of both the Summer and the harvest. The saints who would die in an hour and manner that they looked not for did so because they could not perceive the signs of the times. In the Book of Enoch context, these knew little about God's mysteries. As such, they were not prepared for the coming trials and the strong delusion that would sweep the earth in the last days. These perished because of their ignorance. As this epic revelation unfolds, the Lord will expound upon this meaning line upon line.

> Hearken, O ye people of my church, and ye elders listen together, and hear my voice while it is called today, and harden not your hearts; For verily I say unto you that I am <u>Alpha and Omega</u>, the beginning and the end, the light and the life of the world—a <u>light</u> that shineth in darkness and the darkness comprehendeth it not. I came unto Mine own, and Mine own <u>received me not</u>; but unto as many as received me gave I <u>power</u> to do many <u>miracles</u>, and to become the <u>sons</u> of God; and even unto them that <u>believed</u>

on my name gave I power to obtain eternal <u>life</u>. (D&C 45:6-8)

Christ emphasizes the words of the previous passage by explaining that He came unto the Jews, who were literally His people, and because of their ignorance, they received Him not. They were spiritually blind and ill-prepared for His coming. They rejected Him because of the bribes, schemes, and deceitful narratives of powerful men. Yet, despite being rejected by the majority, some men and women did have eyes to see. His righteous disciples were empowered by Christ and even performed miracles in His name. The parallels between antiquity and the coming days should not be overlooked. Because of their belief, these were adopted into the household of God, just as their fathers before them, as has been spoken of previously. These become the adopted children of Christ and thus become joint heirs with Him and are given all that the Father has to give.

So it will be in the last few days. Many who call themselves the Lord's people will not be prepared for His coming. Despite professing His name, they will be blinded by the deceptions and schemes of powerful men. If we are to survive the coming day, we must do the same things that the early saints did. We must have eyes to see through the lies and deceptions that will masquerade as the new truths of an enlightened day. We must learn to live by the power and discernment of the Holy Ghost. If not, as it was for the Jews, that's how it will be for the saints of the last days.

> And even so I have sent mine <u>everlasting</u> <u>covenant</u> into the world, to be a <u>light</u> to the world, and to be a <u>standard</u> for my people, and for the <u>Gentiles</u> to seek to it, and to be a <u>messenger</u> before my face to prepare the way before me. Wherefore, come ye unto it, and with him that cometh I will <u>reason</u> as with men in days of old, and I will show unto you my strong reasoning. Wherefore, hearken ye together and let me show unto you even my <u>wisdom</u>—the wisdom of Him whom ye say is the God of <u>Enoch</u>, and his brethren, who were <u>separated</u> from the earth, and were received unto myself—a <u>city</u> reserved until a <u>day</u> of righteousness shall come—a day which was sought for by all holy men, and they found it not because of wickedness and abominations; and confessed they were <u>strangers</u> and pilgrims on the earth; but obtained a <u>promise</u> that they should find it and see it in their flesh. (D&C 45:9-14)

Yet another astounding passage! God is showing us that He is unchangeable. He is the God of Enoch and his people, whom He promised would return to the earth while they were still in the flesh. He is also our God and is just as capable of doing incredible things in our days as He ever has been. Ours will be the generation that will live to see the City of Enoch restored to the Earth and many more wonderful prophecies, of which the world is almost entirely ignorant. The things that the Lord is speaking of are strange, yet He clearly states that the righteous from all generations have sought such things. Reading between the lines, the Lord says that "ALL HOLY MEN" sought these things because they had learned of them from the Lord. Yet, these things have been reserved to come forth in our day despite the righteousness of prior generations who longed to see them.

Many true and amazing things are difficult to believe. Consider the supernatural origins of the gospel. The only reason that many believe these things is because they have inherited such faith traditions from their fathers. Yet, their utter lack of spiritual curiosity demonstrates that they would have remained ignorant if such things had been left to them to obtain. Indeed, far too many are completely ignorant of the incredible magnitude of the Father's merciful plan of salvation despite having the scriptures in their hands!

In this revelation, Christ is speaking of knowledge that was held by men in antiquity but had since been lost. The scriptures of the revelation are one of the ways that the Lord restored some of this ancient knowledge. The Book of Moses is a great example of this. However, in November of the same year that this revelation was given, Christ would make a passing reference to the fact the truthfulness of the Book of Enoch would be attested to in due time. While the Lord revealed snippets of that book, the Church itself has done nothing with it. As such, as in antiquity, the Lord is leaving breadcrumbs for those with eyes to see them. Yet, most are as blind to these things today as in the days of the Book of Enoch's Bodleian obscurity.

In the passages above, Christ mentioned His strong reasoning. His ability to reason is unparalleled in the multiverse. As such, there is a reason for everything that He does and says, particularly for those things that will be written down for future generations to study. The wise will study His incredible words of reason, while the foolish will read them and move right on. It is one thing to accept that Christ is wise and something quite different to comprehend the evidence that attests to His wisdom.

Therefore, when Christ extends an invitation for us to reason with Him like He reasoned with men of old and then explicitly references the people of Enoch, we need to pay attention. Consider, therefore, how this prophecy continues.

Wherefore, hearken and I will reason with you, and I will speak unto you and prophesy, as unto men in days of old. And I will show it plainly as I showed it unto my disciples as I stood before them in the flesh, and spake unto them, saying: As ye have asked of me concerning the signs of my coming, in the day when I shall come in my glory in the clouds of heaven, to fulfil the promises that I have made unto your fathers, for as ye have looked upon the long absence of your spirits from your bodies to be a bondage, I will show unto you how the day of redemption shall come, and also the **restoration** of the scattered Israel. (D&C 45:15-17)

In the passages above, Christ states that He will reason with us as He reasoned with those men of antiquity. He then mentions reasonings with His disciples, but also amongst the dead, who considered their extended separation from their bodies to be a prison. As such, we should understand that Christ speaks of His teachings to the living and the dead. After all, Christ went to the spirits that were in prison from the prediluvian world and taught them. He also taught His living disciples about His teachings amongst the dead. This is how Peter came to know these things:

For Christ also hath once suffered for sins, the just for the unjust, that He might bring us to God, being put to death in the flesh, but quickened by the Spirit: by which also He went and preached unto the spirits in prison; which sometime were disobedient, when once the long suffering of God waited in the days of Noah, while the ark was a preparing, wherein few, that is, eight souls were saved by water.

For this cause was the gospel preached also to them that are dead, that they might be judged according to men in the flesh, but live according to God in the spirit. (1 Peter 3:18-20, 4:6)

This is the connection that the Lord intended us to make by our collaborative reasoning with Him. When we chase this doctrine down to its source, we are led back to the Book of Enoch, as discussed before in these volumes. Therefore, we are to connect the Lord's ministrations to those who sinned in the prediluvian world and our preparations for the last days' events. According to Christ, the events that led up to the imprisonment of these men in Spirit Prison also pertain to the events of the last days and the RESTORATION, as compared to the gathering of the House of Israel.

To the casual reader, there is no correlation between the Book of Enoch and the RESTORATION of the House of Israel. However, the correlation could not be more astounding to those who have studied this incredible ancient document. Therefore, it is crucial to study the words of Christ.

Do you remember when Christ told the Jews to search the scripture "for in them ye think ye have eternal life"? Why did the Lord phrase it this way? Every Christian denomination interprets the Bible differently, yet all their creeds are an abomination to God and Christ. This is why Christ stated this the way that He did. If you are taught the meaning of the scriptures by men, you will learn the philosophies of men mingled with scripture. If you want to learn the true meaning of the scriptures, you must be taught by God. Such things are powerful and fundamental, yet often overlooked.

Now Christ transitions from His teachings to the spirits in prison, to His disciples during the days of His mortality. Particularly, He references His discussion with them about the Mount of Olives.

> And now ye <u>behold</u> this temple which is in Jerusalem, which ye call the house of God, and your enemies say that this house shall never fall. But, verily I say unto you, that <u>desolation</u> shall come upon this generation as a thief in the night, and this people shall be destroyed and <u>scattered</u> among all nations. And this <u>temple</u> which ye now see shall be thrown down that there shall not be left one stone upon another.
>
> And it shall come to pass, that this <u>generation</u> of Jews shall not pass away until every desolation which I have told you concerning them shall come <u>to pass</u>. Ye say that ye know that the <u>end</u> of the world cometh; ye say also that ye know that the heavens and the earth shall pass away; and in this ye say truly, for so it is; but these things which I have told you shall not <u>pass away</u> until all shall be fulfilled.
>
> And this I have told you concerning Jerusalem; and when that day shall come, shall a remnant be <u>scattered</u> among all <u>nations</u>; but they shall be <u>gathered</u> again; but they shall remain until the times of the <u>Gentiles</u> be fulfilled. And in <u>that day</u> shall be heard of <u>wars</u> and rumors of wars, and the whole earth shall be in commotion, and men's hearts shall

fail them, and they shall say that Christ delayeth His coming until the end of the earth.

And the love of men shall wax cold, and iniquity shall abound. And when the times of the Gentiles is come in, a light shall break forth among them that sit in darkness, and it shall be the fulness of my gospel; but they receive it not; for they perceive not the light, and they turn their hearts from me because of the precepts of men. (D&C 45:18-29)

In the passages above, Christ mentions the time of the Gentile multiple times. The first time, He states that when the time of the Gentiles "**is fulfilled,**" the Jews will be restored to their homeland at a time of global commotion. The second time the Lord mentions the Gentiles, He stated, "When the time of the Gentiles **is come in,**" then the gospel will be restored among them. Therefore, we are to understand that the Gospel would be restored at the beginning of the Gentiles' rise to power and that when they have achieved global dominance, then the Jews would be restored to their homeland. The word Gentile means non-Jew. From the context of the restoration, the Gentiles of this prophecy are the House of Joseph.

The hidden nuance of Christ's teaching regarding those who sit in darkness receiving a great light is meant to cause the reader of this prophecy to reflect upon a specific prophecy within the writings of Isaiah. Indeed, it is one of the Isaiah chapters that Nephi transcribed into the Book of Mormon for our benefit. This prophecy is very relevant to the timeframe in question, namely that of the Gentiles rejecting the light of the restored gospel. Consider the following from the words of Isaiah:

> To the law and to the testimony: if they [*the northern Kingdom of Israel*] speak not according to this word, it is because there is no light in them. And they shall pass through it, hardly bestead [*distressed*] and hungry: and it shall come to pass, that when they shall be hungry, they shall fret themselves, and curse their king [*Hoseha – the Gadianton King of Northern Israel*] and their god [*Ba'al and Asherah*], and look upward [*toward the King of king of Kings and Lord of lord.*].
>
> And they shall look unto the earth [*in a future day after they have been removed from the planet*]; and behold trouble and darkness, dimness of anguish; and they [*the inhabitants of the Earth at the day when the Gentiles come to the full*] shall

be driven to darkness. Nevertheless the dimness shall not be such as was in her [*the Northern Kingdom of Israel's*] vexation, when at the first he [*the King of Assyria*] lightly afflicted the land of Zebulun and the land of Naphtali, and afterward did more grievously afflict her by the way of the sea, beyond Jordan, in Galilee of the nations [*that is to say the Northern Kingdom of Israel was completely destroyed by Assyria, but the kingdom of the Gentiles – the USA, which they observe when looking to the earth from the heavens wherein they now reside will not be destroyed like the Northern Kingdom of Israel was*].

The people that walked in darkness [*the former inhabitants of the Northern Kingdom of Israel*] have seen a great light: they that dwell in the land of the shadow of death [*the Northern Kingdom of Israel was in the shadow of the Assyrian Empire*], upon them hath the light shined [*the Remnant of Jacob received the gospel when it was restored to them*].

Thou [*God*] hast multiplied the nation [*the Remnant of Jacob has become very numerous*], and increased the joy: they joy before thee according to the joy in harvest, and as men rejoice when they divide the spoil. For thou hast broken the yoke of his burden [*the King of Assyria*], and the staff of his shoulder, the rod of his oppressor, as in the day of Midian. For every battle of the warrior is with confused noise, and garments rolled in blood; but this shall be with burning and fuel of fire [*meaning the wicked of the earth will be consume by fire when the Remnant of Jacob returns to liberate America*]. (2 Nephi 18:20-19:1-5)

In the passage above, Isaiah prophecies that the days would come when the King of Assyria would come and destroy the Northern Kingdom of Israel. That day, they would learn to curse the wickedness of their wicked kings and the gods that those kings caused them to serve. On that day, they would look to heaven and desire to make and keep sacred covenants with God. In time, the Lord would lead them out of Assyria on an epic journey north, where they would travel for a year and a half. A portion of that group would opt to remain behind while the main body continued onward, crossing the Arctic Ocean. Eventually, the main body of Israel would be removed from the Earth until the latter days.

In the last days, the remnant of Jacob, whose nation was destroyed by the Kingdom of Assyria, would look down upon the earth once more and would find that another "Assyrian" was oppressing the people of the United States of America. Isaiah prophesied that the people of the United States would be destroyed. He said that their destruction would not be like the destruction of the Northern Kingdom of Israel, wherein the country was left desolate and without inhabitants. This is because the Lord would send the Remnant of Jacob, a God-fearing people, to liberate the righteous from their oppressors on the last day. Christ's warning to the Gentiles is that when the light of the restored gospel comes among them, the people as a whole will not accept it, just like the Northern Kingdom of Israel did not accept their God. As such, the main body of the Gentiles will be destroyed in the last days, leaving only a righteous remnant behind, just as in the days of the Northern Kingdom of Israel. This is the meaning behind Christ's prophecy to the Nephites:

> And thus commandeth the Father that I should say unto you: At that day when the Gentiles shall sin against My gospel, and shall reject the fulness of My gospel, and shall be lifted up in the pride of their hearts above all nations, and above all the people of the whole earth, and shall be filled with all manner of lyings, and of deceits, and of mischiefs, and all manner of hypocrisy, and murders, and priestcrafts, and whoredoms, and of secret abominations; and if they shall do all those things, and shall reject the fulness of my gospel, behold, saith the Father, I will bring the fulness of my gospel from among them.

> And then will I remember My covenant which I have made unto my people, O house of Israel, and I will bring my gospel unto them [*the Remnant of Jacob will receive what the Gentile rejected at the hands of the Lord's servants, the children of Ephraim*]. And I will show unto thee, O house of Israel, that the Gentiles shall not have power over you; but I will remember My covenant unto you, O house of Israel, and ye shall come unto the knowledge of the fulness of my gospel.

> But if the Gentiles will repent and return unto me, saith the Father, behold they shall be numbered among My people, O house of Israel. And I will not suffer my people, who are

of the house of Israel, to go through among them, and tread them down, saith the Father.

But if they will not turn unto me, and hearken unto my voice, I will suffer them, yea, I will suffer My people, O house of Israel, that they shall go through among them, and shall tread them down, and they shall be as salt that hath lost its savor, which is thenceforth good for nothing but to be cast out, and to be trodden under foot of My people, O house of Israel.

And then the words of the prophet Isaiah shall be fulfilled, which say: Thy watchmen shall lift up the voice; with the voice together shall they sing, for they shall see eye [*Ephraim*] to eye [*the Remnant of Jacob*] when the Lord shall bring again Zion. (3 Nephi 16:10-18)

The Father asked Jesus Christ to share this prophecy with the Nephites because He knew it would get to us. It is a warning to us that we need to repent and seek knowledge from Him directly rather than from men. If we seek to be taught by the precepts of men, we will reject the truth that He has to offer us in the last days. So it will be that the Gentiles will receive the fullness of the gospel, but it will be esteemed a thing of little worth by them. In contrast, when the Remnant of Jacob returns, they will consider the blessings that the children of Ephriam have to offer them to be of great worth. These will fall down at the feet of the servants of the children of Ephraim and receive their crowning ordinances. This is the line of thinking the Lord intended for us to pursue as we contemplate these things.

Christ's teaching now gets more specific.

And in that generation [*meaning the generation when the Jews have been restored to their ancestral homelands aka 1948*] shall the <u>times</u> of the Gentiles be fulfilled. And there shall be men standing in that <u>generation</u> [*1948*], that shall not pass until they shall see an overflowing <u>scourge</u>; for a desolating <u>sickness</u> shall cover the land. But my disciples shall <u>stand</u> in holy places, and shall not be moved; but among the wicked, men shall lift up their voices and <u>curse</u> God and die. And there shall be <u>earthquakes</u> also in divers places, and many desolations; yet men will harden their hearts against me, and they will take up the <u>sword</u>, one against another, and they will kill one another.

And now, when I the Lord had spoken these words unto my disciples, they were troubled. And I said unto them: Be not <u>troubled</u>, for, when all these things shall come to pass, ye may know that the promises which have been made unto you shall be fulfilled. And when the <u>light</u> shall begin to break forth, it shall be with them like unto a parable which I will show you—

Ye look and behold the <u>fig trees</u>, and ye see them with your eyes, and ye say when they begin to shoot forth, and their leaves are yet tender, that summer is now nigh at hand; even so it shall be in that day when they shall see all these things, then shall they know that the hour is nigh.

And it shall come to pass that he that feareth Me shall be looking forth for the great day of the Lord to come, **even for the signs of the coming of the Son of Man**. (D&C 30-39)

This is an incredible prophecy! The Lord gave one of the most incredible and timely prophecies in all scripture, yet nobody talks about it. Why? Because we are not spending the kind of time with the Lord, we ought to be. Basically, the Lord is stating that there will be people who were living in 1948 who will be alive to witness the Coming of the Son of Man. People who were born in the year of Israel's restoration are now 76 years old. Some, if not many of these, will live to see the desolating curse that will destroy the wicked around the world.

Isaiah spoke of this curse, which clearly has to do with the end of the world:

> The earth also is defiled under the inhabitants thereof; because they have transgressed the laws, changed the ordinance, broken the everlasting covenant. Therefore, hath the curse devoured the earth, and they that dwell therein are desolate: therefore the inhabitants of the earth are burned, and few men left. (Isaiah 24:5-6)

Isaiah said the Lord would send this curse upon the earth's inhabitants because they changed the ordinance and broke the everlasting covenant. I believe that the ordinance that has been changed and the everlasting covenant that has been broken both refer to the Lord's institution of marriage. This ordinance has been changed to allow same-sex marriage. If all the world's inhabitants practiced strict same-sex relationships, the population of the earth would go to zero in a single generation.

The world has broken the everlasting covenant in many ways. Today, most people engage in premarital sex. Marriage rates have decreased dramatically, with 70% of the population below thirty-four years of age choosing to remain single. As such, global birthrates are collapsing. As a result, China's population is expected to contract by seven hundred million people by the end of this century. Those who do get married have fewer children, and divorce is far too common. We did not come to mortality to eat, drink, and be merry. Yet the focus of too many is on nothing more than pleasure and self-gratification.

According to Isaiah, the collapse of the family will precede a terrible sickness that will decimate global populations far faster than any declining birth rate ever could. Few people will remain between this coming sickness and the Remnant of Jacob's consuming fire. Given the Lord's timeline, these things are knocking at our door.

Christ now provides additional signs and details that will befall the world simultaneously. Consider the following:

> And they shall see signs and wonders, for they shall be shown forth in the **1) heavens above**, and **2) in the earth beneath**. And they shall **3) behold blood, and fire, and vapors of smoke**.
>
> And before the day of the Lord shall come, **4) the sun shall be darkened, and the moon be turned into blood, and the stars fall from heaven. 5) And the remnant shall be gathered unto this place**; and then they shall look for me, and, behold, I will come; and **6) they shall see me in the clouds of heaven, clothed with power and great glory; with all the holy angels**; and he that watches not for me shall be cut off.
>
> **7) But before the arm of the Lord shall fall, an angel shall sound his trump, and the saints that have slept shall come forth to meet me in the cloud.** Wherefore, if ye have slept in peace blessed are you; for as you now behold me and know that I am, even so shall ye come unto me and your souls shall

live, and your redemption shall be perfected; and the saints shall come forth from the four quarters of the earth.

8) Then shall the arm of the Lord fall upon the nations. And **9) then shall the Lord set his foot upon this mount, and it shall cleave in twain,** and **10) the earth shall tremble, and reel to and fro, and the heavens also shall shake**.

And the Lord shall utter his voice, and all the ends of the earth shall hear it; and the nations of the earth shall mourn, and they that have laughed shall see their folly. And calamity shall cover the mocker, and the scorner shall be consumed; and **11) they that have watched for iniquity shall be hewn down and cast into the fire.**

12) And then shall the Jews look upon me and say: What are these wounds in thine hands and in thy feet? Then shall they know that I am the Lord; for I will say unto them: These wounds are the wounds with which I was wounded in the house of my friends. I am He who was lifted up. I am Jesus that was crucified. I am the Son of God. And then shall they weep because of their iniquities; then shall they lament because they persecuted their king.

13 And then shall the heathen nations be redeemed, and they that knew no law shall have part in the first resurrection; and it shall be tolerable for them.

14) And Satan shall be bound, that he shall have no place in the hearts of the children of men.

15) And at that day, when I shall come in my glory, shall the parable be fulfilled which I spake concerning the ten virgins. For they that are wise and have received the truth, and have taken the Holy Spirit for their guide, and have not been deceived—verily I say unto you, they shall not be hewn down and cast into the fire, but shall abide the day.

16) And the earth shall be given unto them for an inheritance; and they shall multiply and wax strong, and their children shall grow up without sin unto salvation.

17) For the Lord shall be in their midst, and His glory shall
be upon them, and He will be their king and their lawgiver.
(D&C 45:40-59)

In the passages above, Christ delineates eighteen signs and wonders that will occur in the last days, which He highlights as being particularly noteworthy. As such, I will discuss each of these in turn.

1) **Signs in heaven above**
    According to Christ, we will see signs and wonders in the heavens above us. Inherent within the Book of Enoch is the recurring theme that the heavens are not sterile and devoid of life. Rather, they are filled with kingdoms of different classes of beings. Some of these beings are spiritual, such as Lady Wisdom. By this, I mean that such beings are without bodies. There are also mortal worlds without numbers, who, if they are able, are free to transverse the cosmos. This has resulted in both good and evil propagation throughout the cosmos. When the Lord stated that we would see signs and wonders in the heavens above before His coming, I believe this is what is meant.

    The Book of Revelation states that upon opening the 7th seal, there would be silence in the heavens for about the space of half an hour. After this silence in heaven ends, chaos is experienced upon the earth in ways unknown to living memory. All of these things stem from the sky. A fiery burning mountain falls from the sky into the sea, killing a third of all sea life, destroying a third of all ships, turning one-third of the ocean to blood, and burning one-third of all green grass. Presumably, the smoke from these fires reduces the sunlight on the earth to a third of its former strength.

    This is followed by another wonder in heaven, described as a burning star-like object descending from the heavens as a lamp. We are told that the name of this object is wormwood and that it will poison one-third of the earth's waters. From the writings of Jeremiah, the name wormwood has typically been associated with false prophets. I believe that this latter event will represent the Watchers' formal return from heaven's end.

    If the half-hour mentioned above of silence corresponds with the Lord's time, wherein one day to the Lord is as a thousand years to man, about the space of half an hour would occur sometime shortly after the year 2020. As such, I find it fascinating to consider that since then, Congress has raised the alarm that unidentified transmedium craft are entering the earth's atmosphere from space and traveling in our most secure airspace with impunity. Is this just a curious coincidence?

In addition to these heavenly signs and wonders, we also know from the Book of Enoch that the holy race will return to the Earth and mingle among the seed of man in those days. I believe that this is speaking of the restoration of the lost tribes of Israel, along with all of the former fragments of the earth that have been removed in times past. I believe these could be the types of signs and wonders the Lord refers to.

2) Signs in the earth beneath

Note the specific verbiage of this phrase, "signs in the earth beneath." Contrast this with the following phrase, "Signs on the earth beneath." "In" versus "on" produces a very different connotation. Did Christ, the Most Intelligent Being to have ever lived on this planet, misspeak when He mentioned signs "in the earth"? I don't think Christ misspoke here, particularly when He said the same thing in D&C 29:14.

As such, I am left to wonder if there are things we do not understand about our planet that will surprise us in the coming days. Christ seems to suggest that this is true in another modern revelation. Consider the following:

> Yea, verily I say unto you, in that day when the Lord shall come, He shall reveal all things— Things which have passed, and hidden things which no man knew, things of the earth, by which it was made, and the purpose and the end thereof— Things most precious, things that are above, and things that are beneath, things that are in the earth, and upon the earth, and in heaven. (D&C 101:32-34)

In the passage above, Christ confirms that things we do not know are happening above the earth, upon its surface, and within it. He explained that these things are "most precious." In other words, the knowledge that He will share concerning these things will be precious to us and should profoundly impact our way of life ever after. I believe certain signs and wonders about this hidden knowledge will not be fully understood until it is made known to us soon. We will address this issue in more detail in a subsequent chapter.

3) Behold blood, fire, and vapors of smoke.

As I consider this revelation, I believe that the order in which Christ speaks of these signs is significant. He started by mentioning signs in heaven, then signs in the earth, and then blood, fire, and smoke follow. I believe that these are listed this way because the first two signs are a condition precedent for the last three signs mentioned. In other words, my mind returns to the Hopi prophecy I mentioned in Volume I of this series. Two purifiers will come, both from parts unknown. However, if we read between the lines, we might conclude that Christ indicates that one of these purifiers will come from the heavens and the other from within the earth. Time may prove this to be a silly interpretation, but it may not. It is known that "they that come shall burn them [*meaning the wicked*]" JSH 1:37.

4) The sun, moon, and stars.

Christ specifically notes that there will be signs in the sun, moon, and stars, as well as those discussed above. When taken together, the sun, moon, and stars are symbolic of both the judgement of humankind and the House of Israel. Remember that Joseph saw eleven stars, and the sun and moon bowed down to his star. Also, a woman, wearing a crown of 12 stars, clothed with the sun, and standing upon the moon, gave birth to the Son of God, who is to rule the earth, as is described in Revelation 12. As such, I believe that when these three signs are given, they will be in conjunction with both the judgement of the wicked and the restoration of the House of Israel.

5) The remnant shall be gathered at THIS place.

The next sign that the Lord provided was that the remnant would be gathered at THIS place. By "this" place, He clearly indicated the North American continent, which was the location from which this revelation was received. As such, I consider these first five signs and wonders to all be related to one another, and all pertain to the redemption of America through the restoration of the House of Israel. Christ's discourse to the Nephites, as recorded in 3 Nephi 15:10 – 3 Nephi 17:4, and then picking up again in 3 Nephi 20:10 to 3 Nephi 26:12, speaks of these things in great detail.

The first four of these signs pertain to the coming purifiers, the Lord's unstoppable army. This is the same group spoken of in the Lord's parable of the redemption of Zion spoken in D&C 101:43-58. In that parable, the Lord's choicest land is corrupted by conspiring men who break in and usurp its governance. The nation is then redeemed when the Lord sends forth His warriors, as verses 55 to 56 describe. Once His warriors have liberated His vineyard, the Lord will send for the rest of this mighty people. Then, the main body of this massive host will return, which return will rival the Exodus of Egypt and yet will mirror it in many respects. The Lord will cast up a highway out of the great deep, just as He did in the Red Sea. They will spoil their enemies, and they will enter into the lands of their inheritance. They will repopulate the desolate cities of the land's former inhabitants, just as Israel inhabited the desolate cities of the Canaanites.

Also inherent within this incredible gathering will be the miraculous global gathering of the righteous from out of every nation on earth. This will occur at the hands of the mighty 144,000 high priests spoken of in the book of Revelation. These were called and set apart in the sixth seal to perform this work. This will be one of the most spectacular seasons in the history of the North American continent. Yet, while this is happening, the rest of the world will remain in chaos, for the Lord will not destroy the wicked all at once, but in waves, that if it were possible, some might repent and be saved.

6) **The Lord will return.**
From the context of this revelation, it is clear that this sign refers to the Lord's return to Jerusalem. The Jerusalem return constitutes the main event of the Second Coming. However, nothing prohibits the Lord from visiting the North American continent before this time. Indeed, we know that He will be present at a great planning meeting in Missouri. Yet, He will not return to Jerusalem until after all the five signs previously discussed have been fulfilled to their utmost.

When the Lord does return to Jerusalem, He stated that He will return in glory with the hosts of heaven. This description is based upon the prophetic vision first described by Enoch as follows:

> And behold! He cometh with ten thousands of [His] [*saints*] to execute judgement upon all, And to destroy [all] the ungodly: And to convict all flesh Of all the works [of their ungodliness] which they have ungodly committed, And of all the hard things which ungodly sinners [have spoken] against Him. (BoE 1:9)

7) **The saint shall meet Him in the clouds.**
When Christ returns to Jerusalem, the righteous living and dead will rise to meet Him in the clouds. It is, therefore, highly likely that these will comprise the mighty hosts of saints that Enoch saw accompanying Him upon His triumphant return. Therefore, these will be numbered with the tens of thousands of saints joining Christ at His Second Coming to Jerusalem. This blessed scene was the inspiration for the cover of the first volume of the Book of Enoch.

8) **The Arm of the Lord shall fall on all nations.**

Once the Lord returns, He will immediately end all wickedness upon the earth in a single event. Before this event, according to the Father's instructions, the wicked would have been purged in a metered way. This metered approach aimed to maximize the amount of fruit that would be obtained from the vineyard. The Father will have as many of us repent even up until the very end. However, when Christ returns, the end will have arrived. His last great purge will instantaneously destroy every remaining wicked person on the planet. This event is spoken of in numerous places, including Isaiah 24:6, Zech 14:12, Rev 14:18-20, and Rev 19:15.

9) The Lord shall divide the Mount of Olives.

Before the Lord destroys the wicked, He will prepare a miraculous path of deliverance for the remaining Jews. These will have survived the antichrist's three-and-a-half-year siege of Jerusalem. The Lord will do this by dividing the Mount of Olives in half to provide another miraculous highway for their escape from their enemies. Christ will then fight their battles for them. Remember, Christ was born a Jew, and He will return as a Jew to save His people from destruction. This miraculous event is spoken of in Zechariah 14:4 and Revelation 19.

10) The heavens shall shake.

According to the context of this passage, the heavens will shake when the culminating main event of the Second Coming draws near. There are many sources for this heavenly shaking; three other examples are Joel 3:12-16, Moses 7:60-61, and Ether 4:7-10. In volume III of this series, we will go into much more detail concerning this event. For the time being, it is sufficient to say that the shaking of the heaven and earth together is the result of the restoration of the House of Israel and of the fragments of the earth that have been removed along with the bodies of the earth's inhabitants in times past. As part of the restoration of all things, the earth will be restored to its former size. This restoration will be violent and will cause the earth to sway and wobble like a drunken man. Large chunks of ice and rock will reign down from the heavens, many of which will weigh over seventy pounds or the weight of a talent. This will cause great fear amongst all humankind but will be a thing of wonder to the righteous.

11) The wicked will be burned.

The fact that the wicked will be burned as stubble and by whom they will be burned has been discussed at length throughout my writings. This is referring the destruction of the wicked by the remnant of Jacob.

12) Then shall the Jews look upon me.

As stated above, Jesus was born a Jew, He was raised as a Jew, He died the King of the Jews, and He will return as the Jewish Messiah. There can be no doubt about this. That being said, by and large, the Jews do not recognize Jesus Christ as their Savior. This will all change on the miraculous day of their deliverance. With horror, they will cry out, "WHAT ARE THOSE WOUNDS IN YOUR HANDS!" Then, the scales will fall from their eyes, and they will realize that it is all true. On that day, they will realize they have inherited lies from their Fathers. There will, of course, be some among the Jews that will have already come to this realization. Yet, in this last great day, all will know, for their Savior will be standing before their eyes. The prophet Zechariah spoke of these things as follows:

> And one shall say unto him, What are these wounds in thine hands? Then he shall answer, Those with which I was wounded in the house of my friends. (Zech 13:6)

> In that day shall the Lord defend the inhabitants of Jerusalem; and he that is feeble among them at that day shall be as David; and the house of David shall be as God, as the angel of the Lord before them.

> And it shall come to pass in that day, that I will seek to destroy all the nations that come against Jerusalem.

> And I will pour upon the house of David, and upon the inhabitants of Jerusalem, the spirit of grace and of supplications: and they shall look upon me whom they have pierced, and they shall mourn for Him, as one mourneth for his only son, and shall be in bitterness for Him, as one that is in bitterness for his firstborn. (Zech 12:8-10)

13) Then shall the heathen nations be redeemed.

Many dismiss the coming of the Lord because, in their minds, the gospel has not yet been preached to all nations. As such, they have presumed to tell the Lord that He cannot yet return. However, the passages above clearly suggest that the heathen nations will be redeemed after He comes. The word heathen means those who do not worship the God of Abraham. Many nations that claim to worship the God of Abraham do not realize that Jehovah is Jesus Christ.

While some forms of Christianity have already reached every corner of the globe, the restored gospel of Jesus Christ has not, nor will it until Christ returns. When

257

He does, He will blow open the doors of all nations, that the righteous nations that keepeth the truth may enter in (see Isaiah 26:2). The righteous nation that keeps the truth is clearly the United States of America, home to the restoration of the gospel of Jesus Christ. As such, a massive missionary effort will occur after the Lord returns. All those who are left living will be spared because of who they are. These did not accept the gospel earlier simply because they never had the opportunity to do so. They will receive that opportunity after Christ returns, and there will never be a field more ready to harvest than at that time. Then, on that day shall Isaiah's prophecy be fulfilled:

> And many people shall go and say, Come ye, and let us go up to the mountain of the Lord, to the house of the God of Jacob; and he will teach us of his ways, and we will walk in his paths: for out of Zion shall go forth the law, and the word of the Lord from Jerusalem. And he shall judge among the nations, and shall rebuke many people: and they shall beat their swords into plowshares, and their spears into pruninghooks: nation shall not lift up sword against nation, neither shall they learn war any more. (Isaiah 2:3-4)

14) Satan shall be bound.

During the millennium, because of the people's righteousness and the contrast that they will have seen between righteousness and wickedness, Satan will be bound. The earth will be as in the early days of its history when Lady Wisdom visited and found no place amongst the children of me. For a thousand years, the earth will rest. Yet, the time will come when Satan will be loosed from His prison, and he will return to the cosmos from which he had been banned. Then will come the last great battle for planet earth, when the heavens shall be set ablaze, and the hosts thereof shall be dissolved with fire, as was written of at length in volume I of this series.

15) The parable of the ten virgins

Christ specifically stated that at His Second Coming, the parable of the ten virgins will finally be understood and fulfilled. The events of the Second Coming will definitively demonstrate a fundamental divide within the Church between the foolish and the wise. The foolish will be spiritually unprepared for the coming events, and the wise will be prepared for the pending spiritual apocalypse about to be unleashed upon the planet. The difference between being prepared or not is largely based upon one's ability to hear and recognize the promptings of the Holy Ghost.

Half of the virgins in the parable depended upon other people's oil, whereas the other half had their independent supply. We must not be dependent upon other men to know of spiritual things. Rather, we should learn to tap into the source directly while there is still time. There is much that the Lord has commanded us to specifically study to prepare for the coming day. The foolish disregard the Lord's admonishments to study, assuming that if something were truly important, the general authorities would tell them what they needed to know.

While it is true that the Lord God does nothing without first revealing His plans to His servants, the prophets do not suppose that He will continue to repeat Himself over and over again. The Lord revealed many great and marvelous things to His prophets in times past and then commanded us to study them. Why would He command us to study these things unless He really intended us to do so? How many times have you heard the words of Isaiah expounded in General Conference?

In the coming day, we will understand why the Lord asked us to study the words of Isaiah and the prophets. Those who have made a study of Isaiah's words to the point of comprehension have learned to see the world as it really is rather than through the comfortable lens of Newtonian physics. Only the Lord Himself can prepare us spiritually for the coming day. Many will be swept away when the torrents of strong delusion and lies break forth upon the earth, for their testimonies have not yet found the solid bedrock below the sandy surface. For those who have relied upon others to teach them everything they know, and not the Lord, will come to understand that their foundations are built upon the sand. We know we will not survive the coming day without the Holy Ghost. If your plan is to be taught by the Holy Ghost in the coming day, you had better start learning from Him right now!

16) The righteous will inherit the earth.

Christ reiterated that the righteous would inherit the earth. The wicked have long ruled the world. Elitest and conspiring men have met secretly to plan, scheme, and devise the means to subject the masses to their authority. The meek and humble of the earth have been the fodder for the military-industrial complex that has greased its machinery of war for decades. Yet, the strong shall be brought down low, and the meek shall be exalted beyond measure. The earth will become the Celestial Kingdom; when that happens, the wicked will never reenter it.

17) I shall be in their midst.

During the millennium, Jesus Christ will personally reign on the Earth. In Jeremiah 31:31-34, God promised His people that He would make a new covenant with them in the coming day. Part of that covenant will be that He will teach them personally, and as a result, all men will know Him - from the greatest to the least. Because Christ will be with us, there will be no more darkness. Truth will illuminate the Earth and usher in a period of unimaginable enlightenment. The world will progress more in these thousand years than any other ever created world. It will transition from the most wicked mortal sphere in the cosmos to the most blessed. All the creations of the Father will flow unto it, and it will be marvelous beyond comprehension.

Many people interpret the signs and wonders above as separate, unrelated events. However, they are all interwoven and correlate with the main themes and events of the last days. These themes and events can be stated as follows: 1) the Whore of Babylon is real, and secret combinations have infiltrated our society at the highest levels to a staggering degree. 2) The Whore of Babylon will be destroyed and replaced by a much smaller organization led by a mighty false prophet that will unleash a deluge of lies mingled with historical facts. 3) The restoration of the House of Israel will occur in an awesome event that will result in the purging of America, the building of the New Jerusalem, and the gathering of the elect into it from the four corners of the globe in a miraculous fashion. 4) God is, first and foremost, a Supernatural Being, and the powers of the multiverse lay far beyond our comprehension of what is possible. The true laws of nature are quantum, not Newtonian. Those who have learned how to manipulate quantum forces will appear godlike as a result. As such, the last days' events will be both incredible and supernatural from the perspective of Newtonian physics. Unless you comprehend these fundamental concepts, you cannot be ready for what will occur on this earth.

This revelation continues:

> And now, behold, I say unto you, it shall not be given unto you to know any further concerning this chapter, until the New Testament be translated, and in it all these things shall be made known; wherefore I give unto you that ye may now translate it, that ye may be prepared for the things to come. For verily I say unto you, that great things await you… (D&C 45:60-62)

When the Lord says that great things await us, He refers to what I discussed in the preceding paragraph. These things will cause the mouths of Kings to shut in utter shock and disbelief. In those days, the incredible nature of the unfolding events will challenge our understanding of reality. The Lord told Joseph that the purpose of His translations was to enable us to prepare for these coming events. The Pearl of Great Price was given directly in conjunction with Joseph Smith's translation of the Bible. We have seen how that book includes numerous references to worlds without numbers. If these translations were given to us to facilitate our understanding of the last days, should we not expect that the things they discuss, such as life in other worlds, will be meant to prepare us for what is coming?

As part of Joseph's translation, he asked the Lord many questions he would not have asked. These questions are also of great benefit to us. An example is several question-and-answer sections within the Doctrine and Covenants. In one such section, Joseph asked about the four beasts with wings and eyes and the heads of men, lions, Ox, and eagles. Specifically, he asked the Lord if these beasts were symbolic or represented larger classes of animals. The Lord responded that they applied to those specific animals stated and were not symbolic of larger classes.

We have since learned that these four animals correlate with the four standards of the camps of Israel, which surrounded the Tabernacle of the congregation. When Joseph asked about the creatures' many eyes and wings, he was told that the wings represented their ability to move in ways a man could not and that their eyes represented intelligence that humankind does not now possess. Later, we learn that Joseph had obtained more information from the Lord regarding why these four creatures were selected as the standards for Israel. Consider the following extract from Church History:

> The four beasts were four of the most notable animals that had fulfilled the measure of their creation, and had been saved from other worlds, because they were perfect: they were like angels in their sphere. We are not told where they came from. (History of the Church 5:343-44)

The Lord told Joseph that these four creatures, the Ox, the Lion, the Eagle, and man, were chosen as symbols because none of them originated upon this earth but were brought to this world from elsewhere. This is a staggering revelation. Said another way, these four creatures are symbolic of extraterrestrial life. Concerning man, we know that he did not originate upon this planet. After all, the Father asked the Son, "Is man found upon the Earth?" The inherent meaning behind this statement is that man was found elsewhere in the cosmos and could arrive on the earth independently. Furthermore, consider that Adam and Eve were not created here on earth but were created elsewhere and then brought here. Consider the following:

> And I, the Lord God, had created all the children of men; and
> not yet a man to till the ground; for in heaven created I them;
> and there was not yet flesh upon the earth. (Moses 3:5)

Therefore, the symbolism of four off-world creatures used as the standards of the four camps of Israel is significant and should not be overlooked. The fact that Ezekiel describes all four of these in conjunction with flying wheels that come to the earth from the heavens becomes much more meaningful when understood from this context. To me, the meaning is clear. God is the God of the Universe, and He presides over the whole cosmos, and the creations of different worlds interact. It should, therefore, come as no surprise that portions of the House of Israel have been removed from the planet and will be restored to it in the last days for wise purposes known unto the King of the Multiverse. The scriptures contain these things that the Lord has commanded us to study, yet too few have done so.

The Lord now expands upon the things that will shortly come to pass during the days of Joseph Smith.

> Ye hear of <u>wars</u> in foreign lands; but, behold, I say unto you,
> they are nigh, even at your <u>doors</u>, and not many years hence
> ye shall hear of wars in your own lands. Wherefore I, the Lord,
> have said, gather ye out from the <u>eastern</u> lands, assemble ye
> yourselves together ye elders of my church; go ye forth into
> the western countries, call upon the inhabitants to repent, and
> inasmuch as they do repent, build up churches unto me. (D&C
> 45:63-64)

The passage above clearly speaks of the Civil War, which the Saints largely avoided by moving westward according to the Lord's instruction. This warning from the Lord came approximately thirty years before the start of the Civil War and approximately ten years before anyone began to threaten to succeed from the Union. As this prophecy has proven correct, we must believe that all other prophecies contained within this revelation will also prove to be correct. The Lord now expounds to the saints what it is that they will do in the West. Consider the following, which is both a commandment and a prophecy.

> And with one heart and with one mind, gather up your riches
> that ye may purchase an inheritance which shall **hereafter** be
> appointed unto you. And it shall be called the New Jerusalem,

> a land of peace, a city of <u>refuge</u>, a place of <u>safety</u> for the saints
> of the Most High God; and the <u>glory</u> of the Lord shall be there,
> and the <u>terror</u> of the Lord also shall be there, insomuch that
> the wicked will not come unto it, and it shall be called Zion.
> (D&C 45:65-67)

Here, the Lord commanded the saints to acquire land in what we now know to be Jackson County, Missouri. In their poverty, the saints acquired approximately 1,200 acres of the total 387,000 acres within the county – a fraction of a percent. They were told that hereafter, meaning a future day, this area would become an area of refuge for them, not just 1,200 acres but the entire area. I am taken by the similarities between this story and that of the History of the House of Israel. The Lord commanded Israel to enter the land of Canaan and take it for possession, which they did in the days of Joshua and Kaleb. However, the Israelites were driven from certain portions of their land because the Canaanites possessed nine hundred iron chariots. The Canaanites reoccupied their lands for two hundred years until the Lord called the kings of heaven to fight Israel's battles for them.

Similarly, the saints went into Jackson County and attempted to possess the land the Lord had promised to give them as their inheritance. Yet, the inhabitants of those lands drove them off. It has now been almost two hundred years since the Saints were driven from their lands, and the Lord has promised to restore those lands to them by calling the Remnant of Jacob from the ends of heaven. This book was published in 2024; seven years from now, it will have been two hundred years since this prophecy was given. I expect that within this period, the lands of Jackson County, Missouri, will be redeemed and returned to the saints by a heavenly force, just as occurred in the days of Deborah. These are fascinating times!

The revelation continues by explaining the future state of the world, particularly concerning Jackson County, MO, the future home of the New Jerusalem.

> And it shall come to pass among the wicked, that every man
> that will not take his sword against his <u>neighbor</u> must needs
> flee unto <u>Zion</u> for safety. And there shall be <u>gathered</u> unto it
> out of every <u>nation</u> under heaven; and it shall be the only
> people that shall not be at <u>war</u> one with another.
>
> And it shall be said among the wicked: Let us not go up to
> battle against Zion, for the inhabitants of Zion are <u>terrible</u>;
> wherefore we cannot stand. And it shall come to pass that the
> righteous shall be gathered out from among all nations, and

shall come to Zion, singing with <u>songs</u> of everlasting <u>joy</u>.
(D&C 45:68-71)

The passage above clearly refers to a future day when the security of the New Jerusalem is secured by the Remnant of Jacob. When Christ spoke of the New Jerusalem to the Nephites, He told them that the Remnant of Jacob would oversee the project and that the righteous Gentile could assist them if they wanted – (see 3 Nephi 21:23-24). Keep in mind that the city center of the New Jerusalem will descend to the earth from heaven, see Ether 13:3 and Revelation 21:2. With the New Jerusalem in place, the righteous will have a place of refuge to gather to, and the miraculous gathering of the saint will begin happening worldwide. Yet, with this prophecy, the Lord cautioned the saints in the following manner:

> And now I say unto you, keep these things from going abroad unto the world until it is expedient in me, that ye may accomplish this work in the eyes of the people, and in the eyes of your enemies, that they may not know your works until ye have accomplished the thing which I have commanded you, that when they shall know it, that they may consider these things.
>
> For when the Lord shall appear He shall be <u>terrible</u> unto them, that fear may seize upon them, and they shall stand afar off and tremble. And all nations shall be afraid because of the terror of the Lord, and the power of His might. Even so. Amen.
> (D&C 45:72-75)

The early saints did not heed the Lord's words of warning. Rather than keeping these prophecies from the inhabitants of Missouri, they tauntingly proclaimed them to them. Such proclamations enraged the residents and set them on edge. As such, they conspired together to rid themselves of the saints and, through atrocities and injustices, drove them from their lands at the point of the sword. Yet the prophecies of this revelation were not stopped or even delayed by the wicked. The God of heaven cannot be put off by humankind's puny arm. They will happen as soon as the sun rises in the east and sets in the west, according to the timing and wisdom of the Lord.
The days for the fulfillment of these prophecies are now upon us. As I have said above, I believe we will see these events occur within the next seven years or before the end of 2031.

The early saints lacked understanding of the Lord's timing in these things. The timing of the Lord was always going to be what it would be. True, the Lord did tell the Prophet

Joseph that if he lived to be 85 years old, he would see the coming of the Son of Man. Yet, Joseph only lived for 14 years after the restoration of the Church. Look how far the Church developed and grew over that time. Had Joseph presided over the Church for nearly another fifty years, the progress of the church would have been such that the timetable of the Lord's coming could have been accelerated. However, the Lord knew that Joseph would not live to be 85 years old, nor would he live to be half that age.

Thus, we see that one man's faith and leadership can tremendously influence the people. If one man can have such a great impact on the events and outcomes of the world, ought we not to labor diligently to influence our friends and family to prepare for the coming day? The Lord is merciful. He will aid us in our preparations.

Nevertheless, I believe that the Lord always knew that things would occur the way they did. Therefore, let us press on in the faith of the Lord, trusting in His timing and seeking to understand His will. He has given us the scriptures and more wisdom than we know, yet that wisdom is not found upon the surface but runs like veins of gold within the depths of its pages. We must seek to be taught by Him, and we will find. This chapter is evidence of this fact.

The Lord gave this revelation to Joseph Smith 193 years before publishing this book. It has taken us a long time to start catching up with him. Let us hasten the day of the Lord's coming by hastening our knowledge and understanding of His revealed truth. Such things have been given to us as tender mercy so we might be prepared for the incredible events now at our doorstep.

Chapter 19: Holy Men We Know Not Of – D&C 49

The premise of this section is that Jesus Christ used the title Son of Man as a marker for hidden knowledge in modern revelation, just as He did in ancient revelation. I postulated that the Book of Enoch is the key to deciphering such information. I began to test this theory in the prior chapter, which is the first chapter in the D&C to use the Enochian title Son of Man. That revelation was given only days after Joseph Smith had concluded the Book of Moses, which is replete with Enochian references.

The next chapter in the D&C, to mention the Son of Man, was revealed in May of 1831, approximately three months after the completion of the Book of Moses. The impetus for this revelation was a man named Leman Copley. Leman was a former member of a curious religious sect known as the United Society of Believers in Christ's Second Coming, more commonly known as the Shakers. While Leman was steadfast in his belief in the restored gospel, he was still concerned about some of the curious doctrines the Shakers professed. Based on Leman's discussion with Joseph Smith about his concerns, Joseph Smith inquired of the Lord and received this revelation.

While this revelation addresses some of the Shaker's erroneous beliefs that the Second Coming had already occurred, based on the premise of this section of this volume, I believe there is more to be understood. As such, let us consider the subject matter of this revelation in conjunction with the Book of Enoch. As we do so, you will see a layer of hidden knowledge within this chapter that is entirely consistent with the hidden secrets safeguarded by the Enochian Son of Man.

Consider the following revelation:

> Thus saith the Lord; for I am God, and have sent mine Only Begotten Son into the world for the redemption of the world, and have decreed that He that receiveth Him shall be saved, and He that receiveth Him not shall be damned—And they have done unto the **Son of Man** even as they listed; and He has taken His power on the right hand of His glory, and now reigneth in the heavens, and will reign till He descends on the earth to put all enemies under His feet, which time is nigh at hand— (D&C 49:5-6)

As we will learn in the final verse of this revelation, Jesus Christ is speaking, yet He is clearly quoting the Father, "I am God and have sent mine Only Begotten Son into the world." It is not rare that the Son refers to His Father; however, it is quite rare to have the Son bring a specific message from the Father. My experience with such messages is that they are essential. You will recall that Christ's message to the Nephites in 3rd Nephi was highly influenced by the Father, particularly the portion of his discourse regarding the Gentiles of America and the Remnant of Jacob. The Father's involvement with this revelation is an obvious clue that this will be about much more than the false doctrine of a defunct sect of Christianity that has long since disappeared.

The discerning reader will find that there is much more to this chapter than meets the eye. There is hidden knowledge in this chapter that will prepare those with eyes to see it for the events that will soon transpire – which, according to the timing of the Father, are night at hand. To illustrate this point, let's assume that Jesus Christ will return in the year 2034, two thousand years after His appearance to the Nephites. Let's then assume that the year 2034 represents midnight on the clock. According to the manner of the Lord's time, this current revelation would have been given at 7:36 PM, and today is now 11:52 PM. According to this calculation, we have approximately eight minutes left to midnight. Therefore, we ought to pay close attention to the Father's instruction as given in this chapter.

Whereas the Shaker's religion was based upon false ideas regarding the Second Coming, this revelation is about the true nature of the events leading up to the real thing. It is, therefore, significant that God, who knows all things, would begin such a revelation by drawing upon the Enochian title, Son of Man. As noted above, this is only the second time this title has been used within the D&C, and this is the forty-ninth section.

Furthermore, the Father's introduction to this revelation, as given by His Son, began by referencing the fact that the Son of Man was rejected by the Jews because they knew Him not. Recognizing the true nature of the Son of Man is one of the greatest challenges that we will face in mortality. It has been so. Consider the following passage from the Book of Enoch in which God the Father challenges the learned men of the Earth regarding their knowledge of His Son.

> **62.1.** And thus the Lord commanded the kings and the mighty and the exalted, and those who dwell on the earth, and said: 'Open your eyes and lift up your horns if ye are able to recognize the Elect One.'

> **62.2.** And the Lord of Spirits seated Him on the throne of His glory, and the spirit of righteousness was poured out upon

Him, and the word of His mouth slays all the sinners, and all the unrighteous are destroyed from before His face.

62.5. And one portion of them shall look on the other, and they shall be terrified, and they shall be downcast of countenance, and pain shall seize them, **when they see that Son of Man Sitting on the throne of His [*the Father's*] glory**.

62.6. And the kings and the mighty and all who possess the earth shall bless and glorify and extol Him who rules over all, who was hidden.

62.7. For from the beginning the Son of Man was hidden, and the Most High preserved Him in the presence of His might, and revealed Him to the elect.

This is an astounding passage from the Book of Enoch. It clearly demonstrates that very important knowledge is hidden from the world because of their wickedness and unbelief. Yet, at the same time, this knowledge is freely shared with those who seek to be taught by the Father Himself. This concept is explicitly stated within the D&C itself. Consider the following:

> And everyone that hearkeneth to the voice of the Spirit cometh unto God, even the Father. And the Father teacheth him of the covenant which He has renewed and confirmed upon you, which is confirmed upon you for your sakes, and not for your sakes only, but for the sake of the whole world. (D&C 84:47-48)

Those who listen to the voice of the Holy Ghost will be taught by the Father regarding His mysteries. His mysteries are not worthless mysteries like those possessed by the Watchers; they are vital mysteries to the salvation and preservation of humankind! Therefore, given that the Father is speaking to the world directly in this chapter, you can take it to the bank that this chapter will contain information that will be of paramount importance for the generation now living.

The Shakers were an influential group in their day. Not only is this chapter about them, but you will recall that Parley P. Pratt had his incredible experience of seeing flaming symbols drawn into the sky shortly after preaching to a congregation of Shakers. His experience is related to this series's twentieth chapter of Volume I.

We now return to this revelation wherein the Godhead reveals hidden things about the last days to those with eyes to see them. Consider the following:

> I, the Lord God, have spoken it; but the hour and the day no man knoweth, neither the angels in heaven, nor shall they know until He [*the Son of Man*] comes. Wherefore, I will that all men shall repent, for all are under sin, except those which I have reserved unto Myself, **holy men that ye know not of**.
> (D&C 49:8)

Jesus Christ has just dropped an incredible bombshell in the passage above, yet I have never heard this passage discussed. What are we to understand by the fact that ALL men need to repent EXCEPT for a race of holy people that the Father has reserved unto Himself that we, meaning the world at large, know not of? This is an astounding nugget of information, which once again is best understood in the context of the Book of Enoch. It is in the Book of Enoch that we learn of this group. Consider the following:

> **39.1**. [And it †shall come to pass in those days that elect and holy children †will descend from the high heaven, and their seed †will become one with the children of men.

I do not doubt that this passage from the Book of Enoch references the same group of holy men that the Father has reserved unto Himself as spoken above. The world does not know of these holy men, and yet the Father will teach those with eyes to see about them in great detail, as the content of my books can attest.

It should be noted that the above passage has nothing to do with the Shaker's religion, but it lies at the very heart of the actual events that will precede the coming of the Son of Man. I believe that this hidden group of righteous men of whom the Lord has spoken are the purifiers who will purge the Father's choicest vineyard before the coming of the Son of Man. These purifiers are members of a larger group. The Father speaks of them as men because they will be the warriors that preceded the main host that will come later. These warriors and the lagging host that will follow once America has been restored are discussed in the following passage:

> …take all the strength of mine house, which are my warriors, my young men, and they that are of middle age also among all my servants, who are the strength of mine house, save those only whom I have appointed to tarry; and go ye straightway unto the land of my vineyard, and redeem my vineyard… that by and by I may come with the residue of mine house and possess the land. (D&C 101:55-56, 58)

In the passage above, the Lord speaks of a group of mysterious warriors who will redeem the lands of His vineyard in the last days. The warriors will be comprised of both young and middle-aged men. Their women and children will come later. Note that the master of the vineyard, the Father, commanded these warriors to "unto the land of my vineyard," meaning that they were not already there. The world knows nothing of this host, nor will they believe such things even if a man declares it unto them. Consider Christ's words on this topic, which speak of the work that His Father will do in the last days:

> And when that day shall come, it shall come to pass that kings shall shut their mouths; for that which had not been told them shall they see; and that which they had not heard shall they consider. For in that day, for my sake shall the Father work a work, which shall be a great and a marvelous work among them; and there shall be among them those who will not believe it, although a man shall declare it unto them. (3 Nephi 21:8-9)

The Father is the Master of the vineyard, according to the allegory of the olive trees. He is the One who oversees grafting the tree's original branches. The Father's grafting represents the marvelous work and a wonder that will either destroy the wicked or the preservation and salvation of the righteous – see 1 Nephi 14:7. Wo to the spiritual blind that will not see these things because of their pride and their stiff-neckedness! Pride keeps many from learning the mysteries of God.

There are always reasons behind the Lord's actions. He is unparalleled in His understanding and in His power. All things are before Him; in time, we will all learn this for ourselves. Some of us will learn these things through the Spirit, and some will learn them through terrifying firsthand experiences. The fact that the world at large does not know of the righteous men that the Father has reserved unto Himself is of no consequence. Most ignorance is self-imposed. It is not that these things could not have been known; it is that the spiritual deafness and blindness of humankind prevented them from learning of them. It is clear that some people would understand these things, for Christ prophesied that a man would declare these things but that he would not be believed.

The Hopi prophecy, spoken of at length in volume I of this work, states that there will actually be two distinct groups of men that will come and purify the Americas. The first of these groups, we are told, will be a breakaway civilization that has joined forces with a remnant of repentant Nazis. I understand that this sounds absolutely unbelievable.

270

Yet, in volume I of this series, I reviewed numerous accounts attesting to the reality of thousands of Germany's top scientists disappearing along with their families, Maria Orsic, the entire Vril society, and a large portion of the German fleet of U-boats.

In volume I of this series, I shared accounts of survivors aboard two missing German Uboats that claimed that the secret Nazi base within Antarctica was taken over by a powerful nation of whom the world knows little. Yet, if the secret diary of Admiral Byrd is to be believed, in that case, he meet with the leader of this nation as part of Operation High Jump, a well-documented secret government military operation intended to root the Nazis out of Antarctica. According to Admiral Byrd, this nation possesses technology that is far more advanced than ours. The fact that Admiral Byrd's son was found dead under very mysterious circumstances after publishing his father's diary is alarming and suggests that someone did not want this information released.

As I consider these things, I think back to the ninth chapter of the book of Revelation. That chapter also describes two hosts under the command of the fifth angel, which, from D&C 77, we learn is John the Beloved, who will come and restore everything. The first of these two groups is described as rising from a hole in the earth and swarming humankind like stinging scorpions. This first group does not kill humankind but harasses those without the seal of God upon them. I conclude that this chastening serves as the Father's final wake-up call. We learn that this first group torments the wicked of humankind for five months. Interestingly, five months corresponds with the duration of the plagues leading up to the Egyptian exodus.

As I mentioned, the host rising from a hole in the earth is reminiscent of the strange account of Admiral Byrd's diary. It is also reminiscent of the account given in the book titled *The Smokey God*, as well as the account of the Green Children of Woolpit. If you are unfamiliar with these accounts, I encourage you to look into them. Then, peculiar scriptural passages suggest that people live within the earth itself. For example, consider the following passage:

> And this shall be the sound of his trump, saying to all people, both in heaven and in earth, **and that are under the earth**—for every ear shall hear it, and every knee shall bow, and every tongue shall confess, while they hear the sound of the trump, saying: Fear God, and give glory to Him who sitteth upon the throne, forever and ever; for the hour of His judgment is come. (D&C 88:104)

According to the book of Revelation, after the passage of five months, a different host of purifiers will arrive in the Americas. This last group is associated with the four angels under John's command. These come swiftly and according to the specific language of Revelation, by these "was the third part of men killed by the fire." What does it mean to kill the third part of men? After all, saying the third PART of men is quite different than saying that they will kill one-third of humankind. As I have considered this, my understanding has been clarified. I believe that "the third part of men" refers not to headcount but geography. The third part of the land occupied by the children of men will be purified by fire.

The nations of men have divided up the 51.8 million square miles of the earth's surface. This includes every continent except Antarctica, upon which no single nation exists. Of the total land occupied by humankind, 16.5 million square miles comprise territories of North and South America. Modern revelation defines North and South America as Zion. From a geographical perspective, North and South America represent the third part of the kingdoms of men, which will be purified by fire. The destruction in America will precede the destruction abroad—and represents one-third of the inhabitable surface area of the earth as defined above. I have come to believe that this is what is meant by the purge spoken of in the book of Revelation. The Lord has said that the purging of the last days will begin amongst the people of His House and then spread to the rest of His vineyard. We have also learned that the wicked will not be destroyed all at once but in stages, according to the prophecy of the Lord's vineyard as given in Jacob chapter five.

This brings us to the next part of the Father's incredible prophecy:

> Wherefore, I say unto you that I have sent unto you mine everlasting covenant, even that which was from the beginning. And that which I have promised I have so fulfilled, and the nations of the earth shall bow to it; and, if not of themselves, they shall come down, for that which is now exalted of itself shall be laid low of power.
>
> And again, verily I say unto you, that whoso forbiddeth to marry is not ordained of God, for marriage is ordained of God unto man. Wherefore, it is lawful that he should have one wife, and they twain shall be one flesh, and all this that the earth might answer the end of its creation; and that it might be filled with the measure of man, according to his creation before the world was made. (D&C 49:9-10, 15-17)

In the passages above, the Father refers to His everlasting covenant, which centers upon eternal marriage and the family. The plan of happiness that was put forward before the earth was made was contingent upon eternal marriage. Without eternal marriage, the earth could not fulfill the full measure of its creation. Nor could man obtain the full measure of his creation without his wife, nor the wife without her husband.

We learned previously that one of the signs that the day of the Gentiles had ended was their changing of this foundational ordinance upon which society is built. This has been done, and therefore, the everlasting covenant of marriage has been broken. Marriage redefined has become an institution of men and not of God. Therefore, the kingdoms of men that have exalted themselves shall be made low.

The kingdoms of Gentiles are about to be humbled to the dust. Their inheritances will be taken from them, and they will be given to another. Those who, in the pride of their hearts, stand against the Father and His covenants will find they will soon lack the strength to stand at all.

The revelation continues:

> And whoso forbiddeth to abstain from meats, that man should not eat the same, is not ordained of God; for, behold, the beasts of the field and the fowls of the air, and that which cometh of the earth, is ordained for the use of man for food and for raiment, and that he might have in abundance.
>
> But it is not given that one man should possess that which is above another, wherefore the world lieth in sin. And wo be unto man that sheddeth blood or that wasteth flesh and hath no need. (D&C 49:18-21)

In the passage above, the Lord states that it is not a sin to eat meat nor to wear clothing made from animals, for all things are given for the use of man. The Father has given such things that we might have in abundance. Nevertheless, the Lord stated that it is not good in His eyes that there are such large disparities among His children. He is speaking regarding food and clothing – the basic necessities of life.

In other words, the Father considers the feasting and fine clothing of the wealthy to be an affront to the poor and naked. The Father is not saying that all men should be equal in their possessions, for not all men are equal in their work ethic. Regarding talents, which symbolized wealth and prosperity, Christ taught that those who have magnified their talents shall be given more, and those who have not shall be taken away that which they had. The Father expects His people to be industrious and hard-working. Indeed, He has clearly stated that only slothful servants must be commanded in all things. Profitable servants are up and doing things of their own free will to further their Master's work.

Nevertheless, true religion is feeding the hungry, clothing the naked, and ministering to the widowed and the fatherless. The Lord will not hold the wealthy blameless if they have overlooked those lacking the bare necessities of life without looking for ways to use their blessings to lift and help those around them. Nor is the Father pleased with trophy hunters who spend great sums of money traveling to distant lands to shoot and kill beasts, not for food, but for trophies, while their fellow men quiver in their hovels, naked and hungry. The Father would have us open our eyes and look for ways to help eliminate the disparity that exists regarding the basic necessities of life.

It should be noted that while the Father does not condemn eating meat, He also introduced the Word of Wisdom within two years of this revelation. The word of wisdom promises that those who keep it will have access to hidden treasures of knowledge, such as those hinted at in this revelation. As such, there is a clear correlation between the Lord's law of health and spiritual communication, which should not be lost on the reader.

The Father's revelation continues:

> Verily I say unto you, that the Son of Man cometh not in the form of a woman, neither of a man traveling on the earth. Wherefore, be not deceived, but continue in steadfastness, looking forth for the heavens to be shaken, and the earth to tremble and to reel to and fro as a drunken man, and for the valleys to be exalted, and for the mountains to be made low, and for the rough places to become smooth—and all this when the angel shall sound his trumpet. (D&C 49:22-23)

The passage above is peculiar because it again uses the Enochian title, Son of Man. This time, he explicitly stated that He would not come in the form of a woman nor as a man traveling the earth. As I have said, I believe God's usage of this Enochian title places particular emphasis on the subject matter at hand and its relevance to the events of the last days. The Shakers believed Christ returned as Heavenly Mother in the form of Ann Lee. Yet, the Father adds to this warning a statement that Christ would not come as a messiah that would also broadly travel the earth. This last belief was not held by the Shakers; as such, there is clearly more to this warning for us to consider.

All things lay open before the Godhead. They see the beginning from the end. As such, at the time of this revelation, They knew that the Shaker movement would die out within a couple of decades. Therefore, this revelation speaks more to us than it ever did to the Shakers. The Father seems to be warning us that a Divine Feminine figure, together with a false Messiah who will broadly travel the earth in the last days, will deceive even the very elect according to the covenant.

Furthermore, God linked this deception with shaking the heavens and the earth. This is very important, for the heavens are not often shaken! Volume III of this series will include an incredible chapter titled The Heavens Will Shake, which should be read in the context of this chapter. These things speak of incredible events that are practically upon us!

However, without the context of that chapter, we have still hitherto learned that the terrible shaking of the earth will be related to the restoration of the main body of the tribes of Israel and, thus, the removal of the wicked from America. In the passage above, God the Father specifically linked the shaking of the earth with the Divine Feminine and a wondering false messiah. As such, we should consider these things carefully and not dismiss them as irrelevant revelations of a bygone era. Whoever dismissed a revelation in which God the Father Himself is involved does so at their own peril.

We are now given more contexts to this revelation:

> But before the great day of the Lord shall come, Jacob shall
> flourish in the wilderness, and the Lamanites shall blossom
> as the rose. Zion shall flourish upon the hills and rejoice upon
> the mountains, and shall be assembled together unto the place
> which I have appointed. (D&C 49:24-25)

This is an incredible prophecy because the church was less than a year old and had only a couple hundred members when it was received. Yet, in it, the Father demonstrates that He knows the end from the beginning. This will be discussed in greater detail as we look at these four critical prophecies contained in the passage above; each of these must occur before the Second Coming of Christ: 1) Jacob will flourish in the wilderness, 2) The Lamanites will blossom as the rose, 3) Zion will rejoice and flourish in the mountains, 4) Zion will be gathered to the place which God appointed.

It is important to understand that the first three of these prophecies involve three different groups of people. The fourth speaks of the day when these three groups will combine and become one people, of one heart and one mind, with no poor amongst them. I will discuss each of these four prophecies in turn.

1) Jacob will flourish in the wilderness.

In the twelfth chapter of the book of Revelation, we learn of an exceptional pregnant woman. This woman was described as wearing a crown of twelve stars, standing upon the moon, and clothed with the sun. She then gave birth to a manchild that was destined to rule the nations. The fact that woman is first seen from the perspective of the cosmos is crucial from the context of the writings of Enoch. As a people, despite our doctrine, most tend to believe that Earth has been cosmically isolated from the Father's other creations. As such, we tend to have an overly myopic interpretation of the Father's plan. We should seek to understand the symbolism behind this cosmic representation of the House of Israel with the other restoration scriptures. Why did the Lord provide us with such revelations so early on if we were not supposed to ponder upon them in this regard?

Many scripture passages often contain multiple layers of understanding. For instance, most consider the woman in this passage to simply be the Church, and they disregard her initial origins in space and focus exclusively on the Earth. This myopic perspective is limiting. The first time we are introduced to this pregnant woman, the earth is nowhere to be seen; instead, she is standing on the moon. This is particularly meaningful when you consider that scientific consensus states that the moon was once a part of this earth but was removed. Therefore, this woman stands upon a former fragment of the earth with a cosmic background. What is the meaning of this? Why are we shown that this woman is pregnant in space and not on earth? Do you not suppose that these details are important?

I believe that the reason for this is so that we could identify who this woman was. This cosmic woman gave birth to the Son of God. Therefore, this woman, first seen wearing a crown of stars upon a former fragment of the earth, represents the House of Israel. Her Son represents the Son of Man, the creator of heaven and earth and all things in them. Christ's mortal lineage was derived from the House of Israel. He is Jewish. Therefore, while the House of Israel can be described as the being of the Church, there is clearly more to it than this.

When we objectively evaluate this woman, we realize that her crown of twelve stars, the sun with which she was clothed, and the moon or fragment of earth upon which she stood are all symbols of the House of Israel. Such symbols were given in a dream to the birthright son of the House of Israel – Joseph. As such, the deeper meaning behind this passage is that the main body of the House of Israel would not dwell upon the earth but upon a form fragment of that earth and would have dealings with the cosmos, as is indicated by her crown of twelve stars. For those that can only see the woman as being the church, you must ask yourself which gave birth to Christ, the Church, or the House of Israel.

As we continue within the symbolism of Revelation chapter twelve, we read of a great dragon that was banished from the heavens to the Earth. Indeed, the first time we hear of the earth in this revelation is in conjunction with the third part of the hosts of heaven being banished there. The dragon, of course, represents Lucifer, and Earth represents his prison planet. We soon learn that that dragon is wroth for being imprisoned upon the earth and seeks to destroy the House of Israel and her favorite Son.

As such, during the revelation, the woman is given two wings of a giant eagle, with which she can flee into the wilderness beyond the dragon's reach. From the context of this revelation, the wilderness is clearly the immensity of space. The fact that John's vision opened up with Israel standing upon a former fragment of the earth while pregnant clearly indicates that the woman left the earth before Christ was even born.

Satan becomes wroth with the escaped woman and goes to make war with the remnant of her seed who remained upon his prison planet, Joseph and Judah. The dragon's war resulted in the annihilation of the two nation-states affiliated with both Judah and Joseph and the earth was plunged into apostasy.

However, while it is clear that Satan's prison planet descended into apostasy, we are told that the woman who flew into the wilderness both prospered and nourished there. According to the Father's prophecy above, this woman represents the portion of Jacob that has prospered in the wilderness. The Father is the God of the multiverse; all things are in His hand. He has taken grafts from His earthly vineyard and "planted the heavens with them" see Isaiah 51:16 & 2 Nephi 8:16. While Israel was in the heavens, they grew and prospered. By now, they will have become a host of nations and will return to the earth in our day in great power. Consider Jeremiah's teachings regarding this remnant.

> Behold, the whirlwind of the Lord goeth forth with fury, a continuing whirlwind: it shall fall with pain upon the head of the wicked. The fierce anger of the Lord shall not return, until He have done it, and until He have performed the intents of His heart: **in the latter days ye shall consider it**.
>
> At the same time, saith the Lord, will I be the God of all the families of Israel, and they shall be my people. **Thus saith the Lord, the people which were left of the sword found**

grace in the wilderness [*referring to the lost tribes of Israel who were delivered from their Assyrian captivity to find grace in the wilderness*]; even Israel, when I went to cause her to rest [*when he gave Israel the wings of a great eagle so that Israel might rest from the temptations of Satan until time, and times, and the dividing of time*].

The Lord hath appeared of old unto me, saying, Yea, I have loved thee with an everlasting love: therefore with lovingkindness have I drawn thee. Again I will build thee, and thou shalt be built, O virgin of Israel: thou shalt again be adorned with thy tabrets, and shalt go forth in the dances of them that make merry. Thou shalt yet plant vines upon the mountains of Samaria: the planters shall plant, and shall eat them as common things.

For there shall be a day, that the watchmen upon the mount Ephraim shall cry, Arise ye, and let us go up to Zion unto the Lord our God. For thus saith the Lord; Sing with gladness for Jacob, and shout among the chief of the nations: publish ye, praise ye, and say, O Lord, save thy people, the remnant of Israel.

Behold, I will bring them **from the north country**, and gather them from the coasts of the earth, and with them the blind and the lame, the woman with child and her that travaileth with child together: **a great company shall return thither**. They shall come with weeping, and with supplications will I lead them: I will cause them to walk by the rivers of waters in a straight way, wherein they shall not stumble: for I am a father to Israel, and Ephraim is my firstborn. (Jeremiah 30:23-33, 31:1-9)

These verses clearly speak of the last days' prophecies, for that is when Jeremiah stated that we would consider them perfectly. According to Jeremiah, the trials of those days will begin as a whirlwind. This whirlwind will start in North America, first among the Lord's people, those who professed to know His name but did not know Him. From there, they will spill out to all the nations of the earth. Yet the Lord will guide and protect His people in the coming days of darkness and trial. He will prepare the way for their delivery. The way of their deliverance will come in the form of two great purifiers who will purge the North American continent of wickedness, and nothing shall stand before them.

Israel will be restored in a single day when that great and glorious day occurs. She will emerge from the wilderness as a mighty host, as innumerable as the sands of the sea. According to the revelations found within section one hundred and one of the Doctrine and Covenants, the warriors of Israel's main host shall precede her. They will go forth first and purge the North American continent, making it safe for the main body, who will come next. The purifiers of Israel will destroy the wicked by fire. Then shall their watchmen see eye to eye with our watchmen, and we will rejoice with songs of gladness, singing, and dancing.

The return of the fragment of the earth upon which they now reside will cause the Earth to tremble and shake as it has never shaken before. The mountains will dissolve, and the valleys shall be exalted. The polar ice will be consumed with great heat and flow down as rivers return. The desolate lands of the Gentiles be repopulated by those willing to serve the Lord. Springs of living water will come forth in the uninhabitable regions of the earth, and they will come to life. When this mighty host of Israel first returns, they will come to the Children of Ephriam, who will still dwell in the shadow of the everlasting hills.

The following passage from the Doctrine and Covenants also speaks of this same event:

> And they who are in the North countries shall come in remembrance before the Lord; and their prophets shall hear his voice, and shall no longer stay themselves; and they shall smite the rocks, and the ice shall flow down at their presence. And an highway shall be cast up in the midst of the great deep.
>
> Their enemies shall become a prey unto them, and in the barren deserts there shall come forth pools of living water; and the parched ground shall no longer be a thirsty land.
>
> And they shall bring forth their rich treasures unto the children of Ephraim, my servants. And the boundaries of the everlasting hills shall tremble at their presence. And there shall they fall down and be crowned with glory, even in Zion, by the hands of the servants of the Lord, even the children of Ephraim.

And they shall be filled with songs of everlasting joy. Behold, this is the blessing of the everlasting God upon the tribes of Israel, and the richer blessing upon the head of Ephraim and his fellows. (D&C 133:26-34)

This is the portion of Jacob that is now flourishing in the wilderness. They will not remain in the wilderness much longer. Indeed, if you look into the skies on a dark, clear night, you just might see them looking back... waiting.

2) The Lamanites shall blossom as the rose.

Many in the church presume that the Lamanites are the remnants of Jacob. While it is true that all of us could be described as a remnant of Jacob, we are not THE remnant of Jacob of whom so many prophecies have been declared. While The Remnant of Jacob has prospered in the wilderness, the Lamanites have yet to prosper as the rose. By the term Lamanites, we are to understand the direct descendants of the Book of Mormon people - the Native Americans. To this day, the Lamanites are not thriving as they one day will.

The median income of the average Native American household in the United States is a full third lower than the country as a whole. As members of the House of Israel, they are living beneath their privileges. Although the gospel is more readily accepted among those of Lamanite ancestry than elsewhere on the planet, the blossoming of the Lamanites signifies much more than has been realized.

This prophecy is not just speaking of the select few Lamanites who have eyes to see; it is speaking of the entire race - wherever they are found throughout the Americas. However, before that day can come, they must be awakened from the deep slumber that fell upon their fathers. They must rise up like men and seize upon the covenants of the Lord, as did the people of Ammon.

The Lord has covenanted with their fathers that He will not forget them. He will prepare the way for their deliverance. As of yet, this day has not come, but it will! I suspect that the traditions of the Lamanites have prepared them for the coming day's events far more so than the average American. Their legends speak of the return of the star people. Their holy men have prophesied of these coming days. The Hopi prophecy discussed in Volume I of this series is a beautiful example of this. Yet the world mocks the traditions of the native Americans as foolish and barbaric, and many of their own rising generations doubt them as well.

However, that will soon change. When Jacob returns from the wilderness, we will learn that the Lamanites have had their own relationship with these scattered hosts of Israel, independent from Ephriam. In the coming day, the Lamanites will blossom as an energetic rose. The restoration of the star people among them will energize them, and they will remember the promises of the Lord unto their fathers. On that day, their young men will rise once more to the full measure of their creations, and they will take up the mantle of the priesthood with righteousness and fidelity. Their righteousness will become a thing of legend, just as it was in days past. This will be the glorious dawn of a bright new day for our Lamanite brothers and sisters across the land.

3) Zion will rejoice and flourish in the mountains.

When the Lord gave this amazing prophecy, the church was not yet a year old and had only a couple hundred members. Yet, even then, the Lord knew that the Church would be driven from place to place and would finally flee to the safety beyond the Rocky Mountains. He prophesied that they would flourish in the shadow of the everlasting hills. The word flourish is relative here. When the church crossed the plains, it did so in abject poverty. When they first arrived in the Salt Lake Valley, local mountain men told them that the land could not support them. Yet, when Brigham Young rolled into the valley, he said, this is the place! Against all odds, the barren sandy desert began to bring forth in abundance for the saints.

In time, the Salt Lake Valley transformed from a barren landscape to one of the most densely populated regions in the country. Today, approximately 2.6 million people live within six hundred square miles of sprawling residential area. The Salt Lake Valley remains one of the fastest-growing locations in the country. Since 1950, the population of the Salt Lake Valley has quintupled! The residential density of the Wasatch Front is nearly double that of the country's average urban density metrics. Once a massive empty space, the Salt Lake Valley has been filled to overflowing with new communities and has spilled up and over the mountains into adjacent valleys.

Alongside this massive population boom, the Church has risen from its early state of abject poverty to become one of the wealthiest organizations in the world. Next to the Federal Government, the Church is one of the largest landholders in the country. The treasuries of the church boast hundreds of billions, an astounding wealth accumulation! These resources allow the Church to spend billions of dollars in aid, helping the world's most vulnerable citizens and refugees. The Church's aid extends beyond the land of the living, with well over three hundred temples operating or announced worldwide. The Church has created the world's largest repository of family history resources. Since its formation, the ordinances of the temple have been made available to hundreds of millions within the Spirit World. These mind-boggling accomplishments are what flourishing upon the hills means.

4) Zion will be gathered to the place the Lord has appointed.

For all the growth the Church has seen amongst the everlasting hills, Utah has always been a temporary place of refuge. In the coming days, it will not be the Salt Lake Valley that will be the center place of Zion, but the land of our first inheritance – centered in Independence, MO. The New Jerusalem will literally descend from the heavens to rest atop the smoldering ruins of Independence, MO, which is currently one of the country's most crime-ridden cities.

As we learned in Volume I of this book, the main city center of New Jerusalem has already been built. Its descent from heaven will be numbered amongst the greatest miracles the world has ever seen and, indeed, that the Lord has ever performed. From this great and glorious city center, the entire North American continent will be rebuilt from the ashes of the incredible purge that will proceed with the Lord's coming. From the prophecies of Jesus Christ, the rebuilding of this nation will be overseen by the Remnant of Jacob, the first group mentioned by the Lord above. Consider the following passage that speaks of this process:

> But if they will repent [*the Gentiles of North America*] and hearken unto my words, and <u>harden</u> not their hearts, I will <u>establish</u> my church among them, and they shall come in unto the covenant and be <u>numbered</u> among this the remnant of Jacob, unto whom I have given this land for their <u>inheritance</u>; And they shall assist my <u>people</u>, the remnant of Jacob, and also as many of the house of Israel as shall come, that they may build a city, which shall be called the <u>New Jerusalem</u>. And then shall <u>they</u> assist my people that they may be gathered in, who are scattered upon all the face of the land, in unto the New Jerusalem And then shall the <u>power</u> of heaven come down among them; and <u>I</u> also will be in the midst. (3 Nephi 21:22-25)

The Gentiles that inhabit North America are Gentiles in the sense that they are not Jewish. This does not mean that the Gentiles of North America are not part of the House of Israel, for they certainly are. The Americans are the promised inheritance of the House of Joseph, see Ether 13:8. The pilgrims and early immigrants to this land were brought here by the hand of the Lord because they, too, were of the House of Joseph.

As I have laid out in volume I of this series, I believe there is ample evidence that the people of Hagoth made it to Europe and melded with the Germanic tribes of northern Europe. Those Germanic tribes were themselves the remnants of a larger body of the House of Israel that continued further north, beyond the lands of Scandinavia. That mysterious northern land, called Thule by the ancients, is lost to us. The Lord lifted it up into the cosmos, just as he had done in times past with other fragments of the earth. All Israel will be restored. This includes both our brothers and sisters among the Remnant of Jacob, as well as those among the Native Americans.

The work of gathering the House of Israel has been ongoing since the Lord started calling people forth from the old world to inhabit the new. When we spoke of gathering Israel on both sides of the veil, we spoke of a spiritual gathering. However, the days will soon come when this will no longer be a spiritual gathering but a physical gathering. The righteous, living, and dead will be physically gathered in New Jerusalem. Therefore, the time must soon come when the work and manner of gathering will take on a dramatic transformation. Jeremiah also prophesied of this change. Consider the following:

> Therefore, behold, the days come, saith the LORD, that it shall no more be said, The LORD liveth, that brought up the children of Israel out of the land of Egypt; but, The LORD liveth, that brought up the children of Israel from the land of the north, and from all the lands whither he had driven them: and I will bring them again into their land that I gave unto their fathers.
>
> Behold, [*first*] I will send for many fishers, saith the LORD, and they shall fish them; and after will I send for many hunters, and they shall hunt them from every mountain, and from every hill, and out of the holes of the rocks.
> (Jer 16:14-17)

Jeremiah stated that the restoration of Israel would rival the Exodus of Egypt. The only thing anyone will want to talk about is the miraculous manner in which Israel was both gathered and restored as the Egyptian Exodus took place due to a series of events over approximately five months, so the restoration of Israel will take place in a series of events and over a similar time frame.

The Lord has already sent forth His army of fishers. These have sought out the House of Israel. Ephriam and his fellows have been working or fishing for the Children of Men since 1830. My father, the first missionary in our family, fished in Texas. My brothers and I fished in Brazil, the Philippines, Chile, and Uruguay. Our children have, in turn, fished in Arizona, Canada, the Philippines, the East Coast, the Pacific Northwest, Denmark, Brazil, Utah, California, and beyond. As fishers of men, our methods were that of catch and release. Those who accepted the gospel were left to bloom in place.

However, the time soon approaches when the fishers will be recalled. When this happens, the Lord will replace them with hunters. No longer will the saints be left to bloom in place. Instead, they will be hunted and gathered by the Lord's special servants, called and set apart for this special purpose - 12,000 from every tribe. John taught that these 144,000 were among the first fruits of the resurrection. I take this to mean that these were righteous young men called by Jesus Christ and sealed to this work before the opening of the seventh seal by the hand of John the Beloved. As resurrected beings, nothing will stop these powerful young men from gathering the righteous into Zion.

We now return to the concluding passage of this singular revelation:

> Behold, I say unto you, go forth as I have commanded you;
> repent of all your sins; ask and ye shall receive; knock and it
> shall be opened unto you. Behold, I will go before you and
> be your rearward; and I will be in your midst, and you shall
> not be confounded. Behold, I am Jesus Christ, and I come
> quickly. Even so. Amen. (D&C 49:26-28)

Just as Christ invited the Nephites to pray unto the Father to help them understand His Father's message, He concludes this revelation with a similar invitation. There are things about this revelation that we must learn for ourselves. If we are not seeking, we will not find. If we do not knock, it will not be opened unto us. Great and terrible things lay at our door, but also marvelous things. It is 11:52 PM, and the Bridegroom comes at midnight. Let us put oil in our lamps now!

Chapter 20: Laying the Cornerstone – D&C 58

In the prior chapter, we reviewed an important message from the Father regarding the last few days' events. We learned that a great deception would involve a divine feminine figure and a false wondering Messiah. We also learned that before the actual coming of the Son of Man, four things must occur: 1) The Remnant of Jacob would prosper in the wilderness, becoming a mighty person capable of delivering the saints in the last days. 2) The Lamanites would prosper as an energetic rose, rising to the full measure of their creation. 3) The Saints would prosper in the mountains. 4) These three groups would have gathered in New Jerusalem in the last days.

This section of the Doctrine and Covenants discusses laying the cornerstone of the New Jerusalem. This revelation was given in August of 1831, five months after the revelation of the prior chapter. Large swaths of this revelation concern the administration of the Church. For purposes of continuity, our analysis of this chapter will focus on the relevant events of our day.

To the saints who received this revelation, it is clear that they believed that these events were at their door. Yet, it is clear from the revelation of the prior chapter that before the New Jerusalem would be established, the Saints would be driven from America to the unclaimed lands of the barren Salt Lake valley, where they would grow and prosper in the mountains. Therefore, this revelation can serve as a fascinating lab experiment for us to be able to analyze confirmation bias. By looking at all the Enochian chapters within the D&C that discuss the Son of Man, a clear pattern arises that reveals what was hidden. Yet, it would seem that few have done this experiment before. I believe that an analysis of this sort will be very beneficial as we consider how confirmation bias may have impacted how we read and understand the scriptures.

It is important to note that the saints had not forgotten about the revelations discussed in the prior chapters. Indeed, the whole reason they were now in Jackson County, MO, was because Joseph Smith, in his own words, had been contemplating the following questions raised from the revelation of the prior chapter.

> When will the wilderness blossom as the rose? When will
> Zion be built up in her glory, and where will Thy temple

stand, unto which all nations shall come in the last days? (D&C 52 chapter heading)

Joseph's questions clearly indicated he did not have all the answers. This highlights a crucial point. Good people do not understand the doctrines of the Kingdom just because they are good. Comprehension of such things takes time and effort. In time, Joseph Smith clearly came to understand more about these things than he was permitted to share with the Church. However, it became clear that he had learned that the Saints would need to relocate to a land beyond the Rocky Mountains. These questions clearly indicate that Joseph Smith was doing exactly what Jesus Christ asked him to do after the prior revelation. He pondered, sought, and knocked at heaven's door for answers. Yet, sometimes, even for prophets like Joseph Smith, answers can take years to find. If it can take years for such answers to come for those seeking to understand the mysteries of God, what chance do those not seeking have of learning them? The important takeaway from this is that Joseph Smith did not presume that he understood what the Lord meant; as such, he kept seeking answers.

Too many saints today presume that they know what everything means, and if they do not understand something, they presume that it is not important for them to understand. This is why the Lord stated that the Church is under condemnation for taking lightly the things which it has received. As members of the Church, we tend to overlook that knowledge of such things is limited to those who seek them. Thus, this is why the Lord so often spoke in parables to His people. Those who would ponder upon His parables would be taught by the Father, while those who did not would be taught by men.

Let us consider Joseph's questions. The way that Joseph phrased these questions is a clear indication of his confusion. The four prophetic elements of the coming days were jumbled in his mind. It was not the wilderness that would blossom as the rose, but the Lamanites. Jacob would flourish in the wilderness, and the Saints would relocate once again beyond the Rockies to build a temple amongst the tops of the mountains. In the coming day, all three of these groups would come to Jackson County, MO. Yet, these things were hidden from Joseph at this time. It is under the auspices of such confusion that Joseph went to the Lord the month before this present revelation, and the Lord told him to go with the Saints to Jackson County, MO. Knowing what we know today, let us consider the following revelation that the seeking Joseph receives along with his befuddled companions as they contemplate the mysteries of God.

This revelation begins as follows:

Hearken, O ye elders of my church, and give ear to my word, and learn of me what I will concerning you, and also concerning this land unto which I have sent you. For verily I say unto you, blessed is he that keepeth my commandments, whether in life or in death; and he that is faithful in tribulation, the reward of the same is greater in the kingdom of heaven. Ye cannot behold with your natural eyes, for the present time, the design of your God concerning those things which shall come hereafter, and the glory which shall follow after much tribulation. (D&C 58:1-3)

There are three cryptic statements given by the Lord in the passages above. The first of which is that the Lord would bless these righteous men if they continued to keep His commandment **"whether in life or in death."** Second, **the saints could not understand the Lord's current designs**. Third, the glory that would befall the saints who built up Zion in Jackson County, MO, **would come after much tribulation**. Those hearing this revelation for the first time would be hard-pressed to grasp its meaning. As such, like a drowning man, they grabbed on to the first thing to come within reach of their understanding – the physical location of Jackson County as the future location of Zion – the New Jerusalem.

Given the benefit of hindsight and from the comfort of our armchairs, let us evaluate their manner of thinking. Their underlying premise was very similar to ours – it is all about us. These men were engaged in the building up of the Kingdom of God on earth. Therefore, like every generation of saints, both before and after them, they assumed that the Lord's timetable aligned with their own lifespans. This leads us to the Lord's first cryptic point above that the righteous are blessed "whether in life or death." Curiously, the proper context from which to understand this passage is earmarked in the scriptures by the Enochian title, marking so many of the Lord's hidden mysteries.

Consider the following passage, which elucidates the meaning of the Lord's statements above. The passage I am about to share contains a brief conversation between Abraham and God. Abraham is now an older man. As discussed earlier in the book, Abraham began seeking the mysteries of God as a young man before he was married. He eventually obtained the same promise that his fathers had received before him, yet now he is nearing the end of his life and has not seen the covenants fulfilled in his lifetime. As such, the following precious and priceless conversation ensues:

And Abram said, Lord God, how wilt thou give me this land for an everlasting inheritance? And the Lord said, Though thou wast dead, yet am I not able to give it thee?

And if thou shalt die, yet thou shalt possess it, for the day cometh, that the Son of Man shall live; but how can He live if He be not dead? He must first be quickened. And it came to pass, that Abram looked forth and saw the days of the Son of Man, and was glad, and his soul found rest, and he believed in the Lord; and the Lord counted it unto him for righteousness." (JST, Genesis 15:9–12.)

The Lord spoke to Joseph and the saints like He spoke to Abraham and Sarah, his wife. Life does not end at death, and the righteous dead will inherit the earth every bit as much as the living. Yet, the fact that the Lord used this kind of language suggests that the saints of that day would not live to see these things fulfilled. You will recall that one of the keys from the prior chapter for understanding the timing of the Lord was the restoration of the Jews to their homeland. This had not occurred in the saint's day. Indeed, it occurred over a hundred years later, in 1948. The Lord said that there would be those living on the earth on that day who would live to see the great and terrible day of the Lord. None of these saints would live to see the homeland of the Jews restored. Yet, many among the saints believed that the Second Coming of Christ could happen any day. Confirmation bias gives us tunnel vision. We see what we want to see and disregard everything else. It is only by combining all of the breadcrumbs from the Lord that the picture of the last days begins to take shape.

As the Lord said, everything was so new to the saints that they were not yet in a position to be able to comprehend the Lord's designs. The Lord reveals His truths line upon line, precept upon precept. You can see those precepts embedded throughout both ancient and modern revelation. Yet, it is up to us to put them together. It is also clear from the passages above that the saints would inherit the New Jerusalem after a period of great trials. The saints did experience great trials. They would live to be driven from their homes many times before they would reach the refuge of the West. Yet, such trials were not all that uncommon in those days—similar things are happening to the other scattered remnants of Israel. The Lamanites were also repeatedly driven and scattered during this time, as were the Jews in Europe. Yet the persecution described as coming upon the world in the last days will be worse than any time since there was a nation – see Daniel 12:1. As such, the time of trials to which the Lord was referring also lays ahead.

The revelation continues:

For after much tribulation come the blessings. Wherefore the day cometh that ye shall be crowned with much glory; the hour is not yet, but is nigh at hand. Remember this, which I told you before, that you may lay it to heart, and receive that which is to follow. (D&C 58: 4-5)

In the passages above, the Lord tells the saints of that day, and our own, that they will be crowned with much glory if they endure the trial of mortality well. However, from the context of these passages, it is clear that the Lord indicates that a big event will occur before the establishment of Zion. That event will be the great and terrible day of the Lord. The Lord is telling us these things before they occur so we can be prepared for them. He warned us that this was coming; at least He warned those willing to hear His words and seek out their meaning.

> Behold, verily I say unto you, for this cause I have sent you— that you might be obedient, and that your hearts might be prepared to bear testimony of the things which are to come; and also that you might be honored in laying the foundation, and in bearing record of the land upon which the Zion of God shall stand. (D&C 58:6-7)

To me, it is clear that the Lord loved these people, and He wanted to honor their sacrifice. These men were the pioneers of the faith, the first to receive the testimony of the restored gospel. As such, He wanted to honor them by allowing them to be the first ones to see this land in modern times for what it would become. In retrospect, it is clear that none of these men would live to see the New Jerusalem descending from the heavens upon Independence, MO, while in the flesh - but we will. We will remember that these obedient elders were before us when we saw these things. These elders looked forward to our day, longing to see the fulfilment of what they would only glimpse in their mind's eye. The Lord knew that the New Jerusalem would not be built by these men, but that did not stop Him from letting them lay the proverbial cornerstones of that great city. I fully suspect that when that great city descends, there will be monuments to the faith of all those who participated in this event.

The Lord continues by linking their current actions to the parable that He gave the saints of His first coming:

> And also that a feast of fat things might be prepared for the poor; yea, a feast of fat things, of wine on the lees well refined, that the earth may know that the mouths of the prophets shall not fail; yea, a supper of the house of the Lord, well prepared, unto which all nations shall be invited.

First, the rich and the learned, the wise and the noble; and after that cometh the day of my power; then shall the poor, the lame, and the blind, and the deaf, come in unto the marriage of the Lamb, and partake of the supper of the Lord, prepared for the great day to come. Behold, I, the Lord, have spoken it. And that the testimony might go forth from Zion, yea, from the mouth of the city of the heritage of God— (D&C 58:8-13)

The Lord called the righteous and obedient elders of the land upon which the future city of the heritage of God would rest as a symbol that He knows the end for the beginning. It was also done in similitude of the events to come. In the coming day, the Remnant of Jacob and the righteous 144,000 will go forth from the New Jerusalem to gather the righteous unto Zion. However, before that day, the Lord called these men, the children of Ephriam, His servants, to do it first.

Even if the saints themselves did not understand what was happening at the time, the Captain of the Host of Israel most certainly did, for it is all laid before Him. In the very next verses, the Lord begins to call missionaries to go out from the location of the future city of God to gather in the righteous. These elders were to first take this invitation to the wise and noble ones. Like the wise men of old, these were seeking the Lord. The missionary force of the world is still extending this invitation for the inhabitants of the world to come and dine at the Lord's Table. The long night of apostasy is over, the Lord's Table is spread, and those with hears to hear, eyes to see, and hearts to feel will accept the Lord's invitation and come to His banquet.

Yet, the day is soon coming when the elders will be called home, and the testimony of thunder and lightning will come. Enoch has spoken of this coming storm in the earlier chapters of this volume. After the coming storm, according to the Lord, a different crowd will come – the poor, the lame, the blind, and the deaf. To whom is the Lord referring? He refers to those who love the Lord but are too deaf and blind to accept His invitation the first time around. Ezra saw this multitude of poor, bedraggled saints in his vision. His angelic guide explained the circumstances and timing of their gathering, and Ezra was astonished by it.

Consider the following extract from this vision of Ezra:

I dreamed a dream by night: and, lo, there arose a wind from the sea, that it moved all the waves thereof. And I beheld, and, lo, that man waxed strong with the thousands of heaven: and when he turned his countenance to look, all the things trembled that were seen under him. And whensoever the voice went out of his mouth, all they burned that heard his voice, like as the earth faileth when it feeleth the fire. (2 Esdras 13:1-4)

In the passages above, Ezra sees a mysterious man arise from the depths of the sea. Later in the vision, Ezra learns that as the depths of the sea are mysterious, so are the origins of this man and the mighty heavenly host that he gathered unto him -see verses 51 & 52. Later in the vision, we also learn that the Lord extended this man's life by a great season – see verse 26. We also learn that this heavenly multitude represents the lost ten tribes whom the Lord led away from the land to return in the last days; see verses 39-46. We learn that the earth's inhabitants are terrified by this man and flee from him as one flees the overwhelming heat of a flame. We will better understand why in a few verses.

And after this I beheld, and, lo, there was gathered together a multitude of men, out of number, from the four winds of the heaven, to subdue the man that came out of the sea but I beheld, and, lo, he had graved himself a great mountain, and flew up upon it. But I would have seen the region or place where out the hill was graven, and I could not. And after this I beheld, and, lo, all they which were gathered together to subdue him were sore afraid, and yet durst fight. And, lo, as he saw the violence of the multitude that came, he neither lifted up his hand, nor held sword, nor any instrument of war: But only I saw that he sent out of his mouth as it had been a blast of fire, and out of his lips a flaming breath, and out of his tongue he cast out sparks and tempests. And they were all mixed together; the blast of fire, the flaming breath, and the great tempest; and fell with violence upon the multitude which was prepared to fight, and burned them up every one, so that upon a sudden of an innumerable multitude nothing was to be perceived, but only dust and smell of smoke: when I saw this I was afraid. (2 Esdras 13:5-11)

Ezra saw that John and the tribes of Israel returned to the earth upon a great floating mountain. This great mountain represents the portion of the earth that was removed at the time of their leaving but restored with this host. Interestingly, Ezra saw people coming to destroy this man, and yet, in an instant, the armies of the wicked were consumed by fire. This is obviously referring to the purification of America by the incredible Remnant of Jacob. When Ezra tried to discover the location from whence these people came, he could not do so, for the distance they had traveled was too great.

> Afterward saw I the same man come down from the mountain, and call unto him another peaceable Multitude. And there came much people unto him, whereof some were glad, some were sorry, and some of them were bound, and other some brought of them that were offered: then was I sick through great fear, and I awaked, and said, "Thou hast shewed thy servant these wonders from the beginning, and hast counted me worthy that thou shouldest receive my prayer: "Shew me now yet the interpretation of this dream."
> (2 Esdras 13:12-15)

This is where Ezra's dream becomes relevant to our present conversation. Ezra is terrified by the vision that he saw. In the vision, he saw three different multitudes of people. The first John gathered in the heavens and was brought to the earth atop a flying mountain. The second host was wicked and was consumed with fire by the host flying upon the mountain. The last host represents the host of bedraggled saints to whom the Lord referenced in the last passages of D&C 58 that we read previously. We are to understand that the heavenly host that arrived atop the flying mountain mingled with the third host of bedraggled saints, becoming one body. In other words, Ezra saw the same thing Enoch saw in this passage:

> **39.1**. [And it †shall come to pass in those days that elect and holy children †will descend from the high heaven, and their seed †will become one with the children of men.

When Ezra asks for an explanation with regards to who these groups were, as mentioned previously, the heavenly group represents the lost ten tribes, and the group that they mingle is explained by Ezra's angelic guide as follows:

> But those that be left behind of thy people [*the house of Israel that remained upon the earth*] are they that are found within my borders [*meaning the confines of the Father's earthly vineyard*]. Now when he [*John and Remnant of Jacob*] destroyeth the multitude of the nations that are gathered together, he shall defend his people that remain.

And then shall he shew them great wonders. (2 Esdras 13:48-50)

Ezra is told that the earthly component of this peaceable multitude represented the bedraggled remnant of the House of Israel that was not given the wings of a great eagle to flee into the wilderness, unlike their cosmic brothers. We are also told that he was preserving the righteous by destroying the wicked multitude, even if it was by fire. The man representing John is clearly a dual symbol of the coming Son of Man as well. There will be a remnant of the righteous among all nations, kindreds, and tongues. The Father knows His children and will save them, regardless of how dire their circumstances become. All of these will be gathered in the city of Refuge, the sick, the lame, the blind, and the deaf, and they will be healed. Their healing is entirely due to the mercy of the Father, for these did not see clearly at the time but only afterwards saw things for how they really are.

Returning to the narrative of D&C 58, the Lord stated that there would be days of terrible trial before the gathering of the saints unto the City of Refuge or the New Jerusalem. Ezra saw these days in his dream, and his angelic guide explained these things to him. This explanation is particularly relevant to us, for I believe we will live to see them fulfilled. Consider the following regarding those who will experience the tribulations of the Great and Dreadful Day of the Lord:

> For as I conceive in mine understanding, woe unto them that shall be left in those days and much more woe unto them that are not left behind! For they that were not left were in heaviness. Now understand I the things that are laid up in the latter days, which shall happen unto them, and to those that are left behind. Therefore are they come into great perils and many necessities, like as these dreams declare. Yet is it easier for him that is in danger to come into these things, than to pass away as a cloud out of the world, and not to see the things that happen in the last days.
>
> [*The angel*] answered unto me, and said: The interpretation of the vision shall I shew thee, and I will open unto thee the thing that thou hast required. Whereas thou hast spoken of them that are left behind, this is the interpretation: He that shall endure the peril in that time hath kept himself: they that be fallen into danger are such as have works, and faith toward the Almighty. Know this therefore, that they which

be left behind are more blessed than they that be dead. (2 Esdras 13:16-24)

Ezra deduced by the Spirit, and the angel confirmed that those suffering during the last days placed their faith in the Almighty. Ezra also saw that those who survived to fulfill those days were far more blessed than those who did not. Another way to say this is that those who survive these days will be the most blessed generation ever. Why?

Consider what we have learned from the Book of Enoch thus far. Those who live during the millennium will experience a change in their mortal bodies, resulting in the incredible expansion of their lifespans. Some scriptures state that we will live to be the age of a tree, but Enoch clarifies that by stating men would live to be the age of their fathers. Enoch's fathers lived to be over nine hundred years old. That means the oldest among us could easily live another eight hundred years after the millennium begins! With the renewal of our bodies, the renewed ability to have children will come.

The children raised during the millennium will be righteous and very numerous. Yes, they will have an effectual struggle at the end of their lives when Satan returns with the hosts of heaven to attack the New Jerusalem, but I am confident that we can help them through that trial of faith. Furthermore, our children will have children and their children for generations. Our living posterity will number in the millions! Of this posterity, the vast majority will not be lost – see 3 Nephi 27:30

As such, these will enter the next life not with a handful of their posterity but with millions of them. Such will be able to rejoice and have joy and rejoice with their posterity like no other generation before them ever has. Consider, therefore, the tragedy for those who abandon the good ship Zion right before it reaches the silver shore. Let us hold fast!

We now return to the D&C 58 and the wise council that the Lord gave to those who aspire to help Him in His vineyard:

> Wherefore, let them bring their families to this land, **as they shall counsel between themselves and me**. For behold, it is not meet that I should command in all things; for he that is compelled in all things, the same is a slothful and not a wise servant; wherefore he receiveth no reward. Verily I say, men should be anxiously engaged in a good cause, and do many things of their own free will, and bring to pass much righteousness; for the power is in them, wherein they are agents unto themselves. And inasmuch as men do good they

shall in nowise lose their reward. But he that doeth not anything until he is commanded, and receiveth a commandment with doubtful heart, and keepeth it with slothfulness, the same is damned. (D&C 58:25-29)

The following passage of scripture is incredible. It is easy to fall into the trap of being a follower of men rather than followers of God. God did not ask Joseph Smith to command the people to assemble in Missouri. Instead, the Lord asked them to counsel with their families and Him, and together, they would figure out what they should do. From the context of the revelation, it was clear that the Lord did not want many people moving to Missouri; rather, he wanted the focus of this experience to serve as the epicenter from which the invitation to the world to accept the restored gospel would be sent.

The Lord followed up this novel concept by stating that He was not interested in servants who must be bossed around like mindless robots. He wants discerning disciples who will rise to the opportunity of mortality by exercising their agency and obeying the council and commandments that He has given us. This is what Abraham and the other great patriarchs before us did. Nobody commanded Abraham to find the Lord and make a covenant with Him. It is something that he did of his own volition. What are you doing with the Lord of your own volition? If the answer is nothing, you had better rethink your strategy.

When the Lord spoke of those that do nothing but the things that they are commanded to do being damned, what did He mean? What is damnation, if not the hindering of forward motion? Therefore, when the Lord says that such people are damned, He is stating that they have stopped their own spiritual growth and progression. Abraham was a force to be reckoned with. He did not let obstacles stop him; he went over, around, and through them to obtain the hope for which he had spent his whole life seeking, not by commandment but through the exercise of his own free will. As such, when he graduated from mortality, he was given a throne and sat upon it as a god, while a multitude of others will never come where he is because they have damned themselves in the way they exercised their own agency. The Lord stated that we have the power to bring to pass much righteousness of our own volition. Great things are born of small and simple ones. I suggest that we get to it!

The next passage from the Lord is also incredible:

> Who am I, saith the Lord, that have promised and have not fulfilled? I command and men obey not; I revoke and they receive not the blessing. Then they say in their hearts: This

is not the work of the Lord, for His promises are not fulfilled. But wo unto such, for their reward lurketh beneath, and not from above. (D&C 58:31-33)

Why do I think this passage is incredible? It is incredible because the saints have yet to move to Jackson County, MO, and the Lord is already warning them that if they disregard His council above, they will not have His protection. The laws of heaven are linked to obedience to the Lord's comments. If we follow His council, we are blessed. If we do not follow His council, as stated above, He can and will withdraw His support so that the buffeting of life will get us back on track. He will not limit our agency to act for ourselves. As we are learning in these chapters, it does not matter if we understand the Lord's mysteries or not; the consequences are the same.

A child who does not understand the laws of electricity will still get shocked if he inserts a key into an outlet. The shock becomes the teaching, and in this way, even an ignorant child will eventually understand. Some consider God unjust because of this. They think God should place tamper-proof covers over all of His outlets. This is not how He works. He teaches us correct principles, provides counsel, and lets us choose for ourselves. Life is a story of choosing your own adventure. The path forward becomes clear in retrospect, but it is not that way now. However, we can and should learn from our mistakes.

The Lord provided the council above before what He knew would happen. As such, before we get to the end of this chapter, we will review some uncomfortable realities. The purpose of doing so is not to condemn those who walked in darkness before us but to learn from their mistakes so that, hopefully, we do not repeat them. The Lord continues His attempt to teach the Saints that the time has not yet come for Zion to be built up in Missouri, nor will it be for many years in the future. Consider His words carefully:

> And now, verily, I say concerning the residue of the elders of my church [*which was the vast majority of them*], **the time has not yet come, for many years, for them to receive their inheritance in this land**, except they desire it through the prayer of faith, **only as it shall be appointed unto them of the Lord**. For, behold, they shall push the people together from the ends of the earth [*in reference to missionary work - the bulls of Ephriam are to gather the righteous in to the refuge of the gospel from the ends of the earth – Duet 33:17*]. Wherefore, assemble yourselves together; and they who are not appointed to stay in this land, let them preach the gospel

in the regions round about; and after that **let them return to their homes (i.e., don't come back to Missouri)**.

Let them preach by the way, and bear testimony of the truth in all places, and call upon the rich, the high and the low, and the poor to repent. And let them build up churches [*throughout the land – not in Missouri*], inasmuch as the inhabitants of the earth will repent. And let there be an agent appointed by the voice of the church, unto the church in Ohio, to receive moneys to purchase lands in Zion [*this was to be done discreetly to not upset the people of Missouri*].

For, verily, the sound must go forth from this place into all the world, and unto the uttermost parts of the earth—the gospel must be preached unto every creature, with signs following them that believe. And **behold the Son of Man cometh**. Amen.(D&C 58:44-49; 64-65)

In certain passages that have been excluded from the present analysis, the Lord asked a few people in Missouri to do specific things. However, for the balance of the Elders present, the Lord told them they would not receive inheritance in Jackson County for many years. It is highly unusual for the Lord to speak of things in the distant future. He more typically speaks of how soon they will occur, such as "I am Jesus Christ, and I come quickly." Therefore, if the Lord says that Missouri will not become Zion for many years to come, you can take it to the bank that Missouri will not become Zion for many years to come! It seems clear from the context of this chapter and D&C 45 that the Lord intended for the church to acquire the land of Zion for a future purpose, which purpose was to be kept from the local inhabitants. Consider the following, which speaks to how the Lord counseled that the whole Missouri affair be conducted:

And now I say unto you, keep these things from going abroad unto the world until it is expedient in me, that ye may accomplish this work in the eyes of the people, and in the eyes of your enemies, that they may not know your works until ye have accomplished the thing which I have commanded you; that when they shall know it, that they may consider these things. (D&C 45:42-43)

The Lord wanted everything that was to be done in Missouri regarding the amassing of lands to be done discreetly and by way of an agent to keep it down low. With that being said, when the Lord speaks, people often hear what they want to hear, and all they heard from this revelation was that Zion was to be in Missouri. As such, instead of obeying the Lord's council, saints started to drop everything and relocate to Jackson County, MO, in mass. They did not consult the Lord; they packed up their things because others were packing them. This mass migration stemmed from FOMO (fear of missing out) rather than revelation.

By the end of 1832, there were ten times more saints in Jackson County than in Kirtland, OH. The actions of the Saint did not reconcile with the Lord's council. It was not the Lord's intent for the Saints to gather in Missouri now. He had told the Saints in March of 1831 that before they would gather in Zion, they would first prosper in the mountains. Yet, it took time for the Saints to understand this. However nebulous it was to the general Church, by 1834, Joseph Smith clearly understood and communicated his understanding to the Saints in Kirtland. On April 26, 1834, Joseph spoke to the saints of Kirtland concerning this. Consider what he said:

> I want to say to you before the Lord, that you know no more concerning the destinies of this Church and Kingdom than a babe upon its mother's lap. You don't comprehend it. It is only a little handful of Priesthood you see here tonight, but this Church will fill North and South America – it will fill the world. It will fill the Rocky Mountains. There will be tens of thousands of Latter-day Saints who will be gathered in the Rocky Mountains and there they will open the door for the establishing of the Gospel among the Lamanites... This people will go into the Rocky Mountains; they will there build temples to the Most High. They will raise up a posterity there, and the Latter-day Saints who dwell in these mountains will stand in the flesh until the coming of the Son of Man. The Son of Man will come to them while in the Rocky Mountains. (Conference Report, April 8, 1898 p. 57)

If Joseph understood what would happen to the Saints, why did He not relocate them earlier? I can't answer this question; however, Brigham Young stated that Joseph would have gone but could not comprehend how to do it yet. As such, the people remained divided. Some were in Kirtland, many were moving to Missouri, and few were blooming where they were planted. The number of Saints in Missouri began to alarm the local residents, as did the stories circulating amongst the people regarding why they were there. Pressure began to build and bubbled over on October 27, 1838, when Governor Boggs issued the Mormon Extermination order. Three days later, mobs began to open fire upon the saints, slaughtering them like dogs. As such, in the death of winter in 1838, many of the Saints found themselves impoverished, homeless, and living in desperate circumstances. Between this debacle and the collapse of the Kirtland Safety Society, growth in the Church slowed the most in its history. The second lowest year of Church growth was 1832, when the Church began flooding into Missouri. By 1839, the membership of the church shrank by 8%. The warnings that the Lord had given the Church had come to pass. As a result, the church created its most bitter enemies, the apostates that once belonged to its ranks. Just as the Lord had warned, these now blamed both Joseph and the Lord for their failures, despite the Lord having counseled them not to do what they did.

With thousands of refugees under dire conditions, Joseph was placed under impossible circumstances. By this time, Joseph knew the Church would find no rest until it arrived in the Rocky Mountains. Yet, such a journey would be expensive, and after the collapse of its bank in Kirtland and their ejection from Missouri, financial resources were in short supply. Because of the choices that had been made, the saints were in no position to make the arduous journey across the plains.

As such, the Church secured the title to a swamp off the Mississippi River in Illinois – Nauvoo. As Heber C Kimball entered Nauvoo for the first time, he stated, "It is a beautiful place, but not a long abiding place for the Saints." So it would prove to be. The Church's westward expansion plan would continue solidifying in Joseph's mind. On August 6, 1842, Anson Call and other men accompanied Joseph Smith to a masonic hall across the Mississippi River in Montrose, Iowa. There, Anson described an incredible vision that Joseph had received in real-time. Anson had once seen the prophet Joseph in vision and was thrilled to be able to record this account. In Anson's own words, he described the experience as follows:

> While [Joseph] was talking his countenance changed to white; not the deadly white of a bloodless face, but a living brilliant white. He seemed absorbed in gazing at something at a great distance, and said: "I am gazing upon the valleys of those mountains." This was followed by a vivid description of the scenery of these mountains, as I have since become acquainted with it…There was a force and power in his exclamations of which the following is but a faint echo: Oh the beauty of those snow capped mountains! The cool refreshing streams that are running down through those mountain gorges! Then gazing in another direction, as if there was a change in locality: Oh the scenes that this people will pass through! The dead that will lay between here and there! Then, turning in another direction as if these scene had

again changed; "Oh the apostasy that will take place before my brethren reach that land! "But", he continued, "the priesthood shall prevail over all its enemies, triumph over the evil and be established upon the earth never more to be thrown down!" He then charges us with great force and power to be faithful in those things that had been and should be committed to our charge, with the promise of all the blessings that the priesthood could bestow. (Edward W. Tullidge, History of Northern Utah and southern Idaho: Biographical Supplement pp. 271-272)

In retrospect, and from the safety of our armchairs, it is clear that the Lord intended the Church's activities in Missouri to be akin to what they are now. Today, the Church owns many acres in Missouri, which are farmed and held in escrow for the coming day. The plan was never for the Saints to build out the New Jerusalem. The New Jerusalem will descend from the heavens. While we can see this clearly now, the saints could not see it clearly then. I believe most saints are just as blind to the future as the past saints. This is primarily because we have treated the things we received lightly. We read the revelations that the Lord gave to others, but we do not seek revelation for ourselves. By this, I mean to say that we do not seek to be taught by the power of the Holy Ghost as we should.

This is why when it comes to things like Jacob flourishing in the wilderness and the differences between gathering Israel and the restoration of the Lost Ten Tribes, most saints are just as ignorant as the early saints were. If this chapter of the Church's history has taught us anything, the Lord will let us do what we want. After all, we are choosing our own adventure. Nevertheless, things would go much more smoothly if we did the Lord's will instead of our own.

Persecution continued to grow. By 1844, Joseph had lived an insufferable life. He had been in and out of jail many times. He had been beaten, tarred, feathered, and chased from place to place. He had witnessed his own children die as a result of the aftereffects of this persecution. In addition, he had carried the burdens of leadership during the darkest times in the church's history. Things did not get much better in Nauvoo. In fact, in 1844, he fled Nauvoo to avoid being arrested again. He hoped finally to make the journey out West and meet up with the Saints in the Rocky Mountains. Yet, word reached him on the far bank of the Mississippi River that some of his friends were calling him a coward for running.

Upon hearing those words, Joseph replied, "If my life is of no value to my friends, it is of none to me." He returned to Nauvoo and presented himself to the authorities as a lamb to the slaughter. He was killed in custody on June 27, 1844. The Saints would remain in Nauvoo until the temple was completed so they could receive their endowments, after which, once again, they left everything behind once more and traveled West to the valleys of the Rocky Mountains. Finally, fifteen years after the Lord told the saints that they would rejoice and prosper in the Rocky Mountains, they were on their way. According to Joseph Smith, they will remain there until the coming of the Son of Man.

Chapter 21: The Destroyer – D&C 61

In the prior chapter, we reviewed a revelation given to a group of elders who had traveled to Missouri, where the Lord showed them where Zion would be established in the last days. In that revelation, the Lord told the Elders that Zion would not be established for many more years to come. The Lord used the meeting as an opportunity for the elders to lay the foundation of Zion by preaching the restored gospel to the world. This revelation was given only five days later on their return trip back to Kirtland, OH.

You will recall that the Lord instructed the Elders to preach the gospel to everyone they encountered on their return trip. However, up to this point, they had been traveling by Canoe up the Missouri River. On the day of this revelation, William Phelps saw in vision a powerful destroyer riding upon the water, and others heard strange sounds but did not see the vision that Phelps saw. During the commotion, one of their Canoes nearly capsized, and the group decided to stop for the day and camp on the Missouri River's banks. After this experience, they renamed the River Destruction and Misery River.

For the sake of brevity, I will focus on the doctrinal matters within this revelation and not on the individual assignments or chastisements specific to the men on this revelation. If you care to do so, you can study such things yourself. Remember, we are evaluating each of these chapters because of their reference to the Enochian title Son of Man. Therefore, this and the accompanying doctrines being highlighted are our primary focus. With this in mind, we begin our analysis of the following revelation.

> Behold, and hearken unto the voice of Him who has all power, who is from everlasting to everlasting, even Alpha and Omega, the beginning and the end. Behold, verily thus saith the Lord unto you, O ye elders of my church, who are assembled upon this spot, whose sins are now forgiven you, for I, the Lord, forgive sins, and am merciful unto those who confess their sins with humble hearts; but verily I say unto you, that it is not needful for this whole company of mine elders to be moving swiftly upon the waters, whilst the inhabitants on either side are perishing in unbelief. (D&C 61:1-3)

The revelation that Joseph received was something of an admonishment. The Lord had asked the Elders while they were at Independence to preach the gospel to those they encountered on their return trip. Five days into their trip, they had yet to preach the gospel to a single soul. The Lord reminds the Elders that people on both sides of the river desperately need the gospel.

The Lord knows and loves His sheep. He loves these Elders for their diligence in traveling to Missouri so that He could instruct them about the coming days and begin to roll back the curtain on what is to come. Yet, just as Jesus Christ knew that there would be a man carrying a jug of water that would lead his disciples to the upper room where they would hold the Passover, He also knew all the families on both sides of the river that these Elders were passing by. The Lord loves people. Certainly, not all of these people would have accepted the gospel had the Elders taken the time to speak with them; however, they would have had the opportunity to learn if they had wanted to. The Lord is very concerned about the families living in ignorance on both sides of the river in our lives as well. If the Kingdom of God is to roll forth, we should open our mouths more often.

The Lord now expounds upon the vision that Brother Phelps saw – the vision of the Destroyer riding upon the waters:

> Nevertheless, I suffered it that ye might bear record; behold, there are many dangers upon the waters, and more especially hereafter; for I, the Lord, have decreed in mine anger many destructions upon the waters; yea, and especially upon these waters. Nevertheless, all flesh is in mine hand, and he that is faithful among you shall not perish by the waters.

> Behold, I, the Lord, in the beginning blessed the waters; but in the last days, by the mouth of my servant John, I cursed the waters. Wherefore, the days will come that no flesh shall be safe upon the waters. And it shall be said in days to come that none is able to go up to the land of Zion upon the waters, but he that is upright in heart.

> And, as I, the Lord, in the beginning cursed the land, even so in the last days have I blessed it, in its time, for the use of my saints, that they may partake the fatness thereof. And now I give unto you a commandment that what I say unto one I say unto all, that you shall forewarn your brethren concerning these waters, that they come not in journeying upon them, lest their faith fail and they are caught in snares; I, the Lord,

have decreed, and the destroyer rideth upon the face thereof, and I revoke not the decree. D&C 61: 4-6;14-19)

We will recall that the whole purpose of this journey was to reveal to these Elders the future location of Zion and the city of refuge that would be established in the last days. In the passages above, the Lord stated that He suffered that the Elders might travel upon the river to provide them with another lesson regarding the latter-day Zion. As discussed in the prior chapters, the New Jerusalem will be established upon the North American continent in the last few days and will be cut off from the rest of the world. The waters themselves will prove to be impassable to the wicked.

Interestingly, the Lord states here that in the last days, the waters will be cursed by His servant John, who means John the Revelator, whose life He extended. In the last chapter, I reviewed a vision of Ezra wherein he saw John the Beloved riding upon a large mountain that had been removed from the earth. With John was a mighty heavenly host that had come with him to the earth from unknown regions above. Upon their arrival, they destroyed an innumerable host of the wicked, and they did so to protect the righteous remnants of Israel that remained upon these lands. I believe that it is to this same experience that the Lord is now referring to.

In the last days, after John returns with the Remnant of Jacob, Zion will be established and made absolutely secure. No unrighteous force on earth can breach the oceans to arrive at the American Zion except the honest in heart. This will be because of John's curse. Said another way, John and the Remnant of Jacob will serve as the Lord's destroying angels, and the wicked will burn as stubble before them.

Thus, we see that each chapter we have reviewed this far has been closely related. Indeed, this is the meaning behind the following passage from the first chapter in the D&C that spoke of the Son of Man:

> And with one heart and with one mind, gather up your riches that ye may purchase an inheritance which shall hereafter be appointed unto you. And it shall be called the New Jerusalem, a land of peace, a city of refuge, a place of safety for the saints of the Most High God; and the glory of the Lord shall be there, and the terror of the Lord also shall be there, insomuch that the wicked will not come unto it, and it shall be called Zion.
>
> And it shall come to pass among the wicked, that every man that will not take his sword against his neighbor must needs

flee unto Zion for safety. And there shall be gathered unto it out of every nation under heaven; and it shall be the only people that shall not be at war one with another. And it shall be said among the wicked: Let us not go up to battle against Zion, for the inhabitants of Zion are terrible; wherefore we cannot stand.

And it shall come to pass that the righteous shall be gathered out from among all nations, and shall come to Zion, singing with songs of everlasting joy. And now I say unto you, keep these things from going abroad unto the world until it is expedient in me, that ye may accomplish this work in the eyes of the people, and in the eyes of your enemies, that they may not know your works until ye have accomplished the thing which I have commanded you; That when they shall know it, that they may consider these things. (D&C 45:66-76)

Many have mocked this particular revelation as the foolish imaginations of superstitious men. However, it is clear to me that these things are not foolish superstitions but evidence of the Lord's consistent message to the Gentiles regarding the marvelous work and a wonder that is about to take place upon this continent. I hope you are beginning to understand that the Lord has spoken plainly of these things. Yet, to most, they have been dark mutterings that they have not understood. They have not seen the beautiful symmetry that exists through the Lord's messages about these things. Whether the Lord spoke anciently through the mouths of Jeremiah and Isaiah or modern prophets, the message is the same. The destroyer that will ride upon the waters is not Satan but the Remnant of Jacob!

And all thy children shall be taught of the Lord; and great shall be the peace of thy children. In righteousness shalt thou be established; thou shalt be far from oppression for thou shalt not fear, and from terror for it shall not come near thee.

Behold, they shall surely gather together against thee, not by me; whosoever shall gather together against thee shall fall for thy sake. Behold, I have created the smith that bloweth the coals in the fire, and that bringeth forth an instrument for his work; and **I have created the waster to destroy**. No weapon that is formed against thee shall prosper; and every tongue that shall revile against thee in judgment thou shalt condemn. This is the heritage of the servants of the Lord, and their righteousness is of me, saith the Lord. (3 Nephi 22:13-17)

The portion of Jacob [*the Remnant of Jacob*] is not like them; for He is the former of all things: and Israel is the rod of His inheritance: the Lord of hosts is His name. Thou [*John and the Remnant*] art my battle axe and weapons of war: for with thee will I break in pieces the nations, and with thee will I destroy kingdoms (Jeremiah 51:19-20).

The passages above speak of the same events the Lord refers to. This is the destroyer that will ride upon the waters at the commandment of John in the last days. This destroyer is not Satan but John the Beloved. I understand that this may be a strange thing to consider for some, but it is true. I will provide you with another example; however, before I do, I must provide some background. The passage I am about to share speaks of the 5th angel from the Book of Revelation. This angel commands the four other destroying angels that have come to the earth from the heavens to burn the wicked with fire.

If we are to understand the meaning behind these passages, we need to look at some divine supplements to understand who this fifth angel is. Consider the following passage:

Q. What are we to understand by the angel ascending from the east, Revelation 7th chapter and 2nd verse?

A. We are to understand that the angel ascending from the east is he to whom is given the seal of the living God over the twelve tribes of Israel; wherefore, he crieth unto the four angels having the everlasting gospel, saying: Hurt not the earth, neither the sea, nor the trees, till we have sealed the servants of our God in their foreheads. And, if you will receive it, this is Elias which was to come to gather together the tribes of Israel and restore all things. (D&C 77:9)

In the passage above, we learn that the fifth angel represents the latter-day Elias, who would identify the righteous from the wicked before the Second Coming, and that Elias would also gather the tribes of Israel and he would restore all things. If you were to ask most latter-day saints who this man was, they would immediately say that it was Joseph Smith. The problem is that he does not check any of these boxes. He was not the Elias that would pave the way before the Second Coming. John the Baptist was the Elias for Jesus Christ's first coming, and Christ and John were contemporaneous - not separated by two hundred years. Nor have all things been restored, including the House of Israel. If it is not Joseph Smith, then who is it?

Consider the next passage of supplemental information that helps us to understand this better:

> Q. What are we to understand by the little book which was eaten by John, as mentioned in the 10th chapter of Revelation?
>
> A. We are to understand that it was a mission, and an ordinance, for him to gather the tribes of Israel; behold, this is Elias, who, as it is written, must come and restore all things. (D&C 77:14)

Recall that Joseph Smith is asking the Lord this question about the book given to John. The Lord told Joseph the book represented a mission and ordinance that John would complete in the last days and that John would be the Elias of the last days. You will also recall from the book of Revelation that when John first ate this book, it was sweet as honey on his tongue but then became very bitter. This is very important. The book represented John's mission in life. John's mission would begin very sweetly, with him preaching the gospel and bringing joy to countless people throughout the Lord's vineyard. However, the latter end of his ministry would be bitter and result in the purging of the vineyard by fire. Consider the following passages from the Book of Revelation:

> And the four angels [Remnant of Jacob] were loosed, which were prepared for an hour, and a day, and a month, and a year, for to slay the third part of men. And the number of the army of the horsemen were two hundred thousand thousand: [*200,000,000*] and I heard the number of them.
>
> And thus I saw the horses in the vision, and them that sat on them, having breastplates of fire, and of jacinth, and brimstone: and the heads of the horses were as the heads of lions; and out of their mouths issued fire and smoke and brimstone. By these three was the third part of men killed, by the fire, and by the smoke, and by the brimstone, which issued out of their mouths. For their power is in their mouth,

and in their tails: for their tails were like unto serpents, and had heads, and with them they do hurt.

And the rest of the men which were not killed by these plagues yet repented not of the works of their hands, that they should not worship devils, and idols of gold, and silver, and brass, and stone, and of wood: which neither can see, nor hear, nor walk: neither repented they of their murders, nor of their sorceries, nor of their fornication, nor of their thefts. (Rev 9:15-21)

While John will oversee the restoration of all things, he will also oversee the purification of Zion and the destruction of the wicked in North and South America, constituting a third of humankind's geographical inhabitation as we presently understand it. After John had performed this terrible task, he would have made the Americas completely secure. One aspect of this security will be that John, who, as far as the Americas are concerned, will be the latter-day destroyer and command the waters to become an impassible barrier to the wicked.

According to D&C 61, water will play a very destructive role in the events of the last days, particularly in the context of the Americas. The Missouri River itself is specifically called out for the role it will play in this regard. Given America will be home to Zion and that Independence, MO, will be home to the center of the New Jerusalem, the fact that Independence is built upon the banks of the Missouri River is telling. In the Book of Mormon, water was a major cause of destruction in numerous cities. Water can drown, flood, erode, bury, and carry away. It would seem that a destructive event of this nature lies in store for many of the settlements along the Missouri River, including Independence and St Louis.

After John has purged the Americas and commanded the waters to become an impassible barrier, Zion will be made safe. Only then will the New Jerusalem descend from the heavens as a bride adorned for her husband. Yet, as the Book of Revelation stated, the rest of the world will remain unrepentant and will persist in their wickedness by seeking to destroy the Jews. Yet, Zion will be unassailable. This is the meaning of the Lord's instruction to these ten Elders on the banks of the Missouri River. Yet, despite the Lord revealing these things, it would be many more years to come until they began to be understood. I suspect that most people will not be understood until they have occurred.

Consider this next portion of the revelation, which I believe will be very important concerning the saints of the last days:

Behold, I, the Lord, have appointed a way for the journeying of my saints; and behold, this is the way—that after they leave the canal they shall journey by land, **inasmuch as they are commanded to journey and go up unto the land of Zion**; and they shall do like unto the children of Israel, pitching their tents by the way.

And, behold, this commandment you shall give unto all your brethren. Nevertheless, unto whom is given power to command the waters, unto him it is given by the Spirit to know all his ways; wherefore, let him do as the Spirit of the living God commandeth him, whether upon the land or upon the waters, as it remaineth with Me to do hereafter. (D&C 61:24-28)

The passages above are very curious. They speak of the Lord moving upon certain saints to move to Zion, by way of a tent, like unto the children of Israel through the wilderness. I believe that we will find that this passage of scripture above will be very relevant to the events of the last days. The Lord warns the saints that their actions must be done through the Spirit. Our own prophet has told us that we will not survive the coming days unless we, too, follow the voice of the Spirit.

Many have felt the spirit whispering to their hearts concerning these things. We must harken to these whisperings. We should not move to Missouri for fear of missing out or because others are doing so. This was disastrous to the early saints, and I suppose it would be disastrous to us again. Follow the promptings of the Holy Ghost. If you do, you can rest assured that just as the Lord was with the children of Israel, He will be with you, not just in spirit but in power. According to the passages above, those who can listen to and be led by the spirit to them will be added power over the elements themselves. Therefore, those who are on the Lord's mission and are moving under His commands will be strengthened by His power and will be able to do His works, even if those works require them to command the elements themselves. Indeed, I believe that in the last days, as the world's circumstances become direr, the power of God will be poured out upon the saints and covenant people of the Lord with greater measure than at any time in the earth's history.

This will be the outpouring that was contemplated by 1 Nephi 14:14. By this same power, many men and women of understanding shall perform exploits, save lives, and feed thousands. God is no respecter of men. Recall that it was at Deborah's hand that the Lord called the kings of heaven to fight Israel's battles for them. According to the

Egyptians, this deed rivaled that of the Egyptian Exodus, and they should know. According to the passages above, hearing Him is the key component to this power.

This incredible chapter concludes in the following manner:

> And now, verily I say unto you, and what I say unto one I say unto all, be of good cheer, little children; for I am in your midst, and I have not forsaken you; and <u>inasmuch as you have humbled yourselves before me, the blessings of the kingdom are yours</u>. Gird up your loins and be watchful and be sober, looking forth for **the coming of the Son of Man**, for He cometh in an hour you think not. Pray always that you enter not into temptation, that you may abide the day of his coming, **whether in life or in death**. Even so. Amen. (D&C 61:36-39)

The passage above includes the Enochian Easter egg that links this chapter with the others we have studied thus far – the Son of Man. The correlation between these chapters and the material in the Book of Enoch has been strong and lays the groundwork for things to come for those with eyes to see it. Interestingly, the passage above uses the curious phrase "whether in life or in death." This phrase is only used twice in scripture, and both occurrences have been associated with the usage of "the Son of Man." The first time we read this phrase was in D&C Section 58, which was used in conjunction with the salvation of those who will abide by the tribulations of the coming day. You will recall that in Ezra's vision, those who survived the trials of those days would be more blessed than any other generation in the earth's history.

This singular phrase suggests that there would be a significant time between the coming of the Son of Man and the day on which this revelation was given. Many of the saints believed that the coming of the Son of Man was imminent. Thus, the Lord told them that the Son of Man comes in an hour you think not. Just because you think something is true does not make it so. Nevertheless, the Lord told the saints that even if they died before the coming of the Son of Man, they would still need to hold fast to their faith in Him until He came into power. Therefore, faith is still an important component of the Spirit World. For those who keep the faith, whether in life or in death, it will be well with them. This reminds me very much of the Lord's conversation with Moroni regarding the latter-day Gentiles. Consider that conversation in this light:

> And I said unto Him: Lord, the Gentiles will mock at these things, because of our weakness in writing; for Lord Thou

hast made us mighty in word by faith, but Thou hast not made us mighty in writing; for Thou hast made all this people that they could speak much, because of the Holy Ghost which Thou hast given them; and Thou hast made us that we could write but little, because of the awkwardness of our hands. Behold, Thou hast not made us mighty in writing like unto the brother of Jared, for Thou madest him that the things which he wrote were mighty even as Thou art, unto the overpowering of man to read them.

And when I had said this, the Lord spake unto me, saying: Fools mock, but they shall mourn; and my grace is sufficient for the meek, that they shall take no advantage of your weakness; and if men come unto me I will show unto them their weakness. I give unto men weakness that they may be humble; and My grace is sufficient for all men that humble themselves before Me; for if they humble themselves before Me, and have faith in Me, then will I make weak things become strong unto them. Behold, I will show unto the Gentiles their weakness, and I will show unto them that faith, hope and charity bringeth unto me—the fountain of all righteousness.

And I, Moroni, having heard these words, was comforted, and said: O Lord, Thy righteous will be done, for I know that Thou workest unto the children of men according to their faith; for the brother of Jared said unto the mountain Zerin, Remove—and it was removed. And if he had not had faith it would not have moved; wherefore Thou workest after men have faith.

For thus didst Thou manifest Thyself unto thy disciples; for after they had faith, and did speak in Thy name, Thou didst show Thyself unto them in great power. And I also remember that Thou hast said that Thou hast prepared a house for man, yea, even among the mansions of Thy Father, in which man might have a more excellent hope; wherefore man must hope, or he cannot receive an inheritance in the place which Thou hast prepared.

And again, I remember that Thou hast said that Thou hast loved the world, even unto the laying down of Thy life for the world, that Thou mightest take it again to prepare a place for the children of men. And now I know that this love which Thou hast had for the children of men is charity; wherefore, except men shall have charity they cannot inherit that place which Thou hast prepared in the mansions of Thy Father.

Wherefore, I know by this thing which Thou hast said, that if the Gentiles have not charity, because of our weakness, that Thou wilt prove them, and take away their talent, yea, even that which they have received, and give unto them who shall have more abundantly. And it came to pass that I prayed unto the Lord that He would give unto the Gentiles grace, that they might have charity.

And it came to pass that the Lord said unto me: If they have not charity it mattereth not unto thee, thou hast been faithful; wherefore, thy garments shall be made clean. And because thou hast seen thy weakness thou shalt be made strong, even unto the sitting down in the place which I have prepared in the mansions of my Father.

And now I, Moroni, bid farewell unto the Gentiles, yea, and also unto my brethren whom I love, until we shall meet before the judgment-seat of Christ, where all men shall know that my garments are not spotted with your blood. And then shall ye know that I have seen Jesus, and that He hath talked with me face to face, and that He told me in plain humility, even as a man telleth another in mine own language, concerning these things; and only a few have I written, because of my weakness in writing.

And now, I would commend you to seek this Jesus of whom the prophets and apostles have written, that the grace of God the Father, and also the Lord Jesus Christ, and the Holy Ghost, which beareth record of Them, may be and abide in you forever. Amen. (Ether 12:23-24; 26-41)

The passages above are astounding and were clearly written for us to understand. In these passages, the Lord speaks of the importance of the Gentiles humbling themselves before Him. Christ explains that true humility leads to faith, hope, and charity. Moroni then provided a specific example of each of these three things. The Brother of Jared could control the elements through his faith in the name of Jesus Christ. Men should have hope for a better world in the kingdom of the Father amongst the mansions that have been prepared. You will recall that the original source document for heavenly mansions is the book of Enoch, which, like the passage above, was written for our benefit. Lastly, Moroni equated Christ's willingness to lay down His life for us to Charity. Above all things, Moroni prayed that the Gentiles of the last days would have charity.

Moroni concludes his writings with an incredible sermon that his father gave about faith, hope, and charity. He concluded that sermon by stating that all true disciples of Jesus Christ are charitable and that those found possessing charity at the Lord's coming will be saved. Therefore, my friends, given that we are the latter-day Gentiles to whom this message was addressed, we must humble ourselves before Almighty God. Yes, we are weak. However, we have been given the weaknesses that we have by design. Our weaknesses and shortcomings are intended to cause us to be humble. Our weaknesses show us that we cannot return to the Father except through His hidden Son. Therefore, we must seek out this Jesus, who came into the world, but the world received Him not.

If we are to find Jesus Christ, we must be led to Him by the Lord of Spirits. To be led, we must be humble. In our seeking Him, our Faith in Him will grow, and this Faith will lead us to hope. I hope that the things that He has said are true. He said that His grace really is sufficient to cover all our weaknesses and all of our sins. The culminating fruit of our faith and hope is that the hidden Son of God will transform our hearts and cause us to be filled with His love. True disciples of Jesus Christ love their fellow man. Rather than considering ourselves better than others because of what we will learn, we will reflect on Moroni's actions, praying that they, too, might find the Hidden Savior – the Son of Man.

If we are true disciples of Jesus Christ, we will not lash out at others from behind the anonymity of online posts and forums. True disciples pray for their enemies and do not return railing for railing. The world is becoming more polarized. Satan is not as interested in your current belief system as much as he is interested in getting you to project your beliefs with rage and hate. Doing so is a clear indication of how far we have to go. If we can turn to the Son of Man, learn of Him, and seek to walk in His ways through true humility, then regardless of what the coming day holds in store, we will meet it with faith, hope, and charity, and it will be well with our souls.

Chapter 22: Astounding - D&C 63

In the prior chapter, we learned of interesting information that Joseph and others learned regarding John's roles in the last days as the purifying destroyer that will prepare the Americans for the establishment of Zion. The revelation of the present chapter was received shortly after Joseph and these Elders returned to Kirtland, OH, from their trip to Missouri. The revelations of the Lord regarding the location of Zion and the signs of the times were weighing heavily upon the prophet's heart. He pondered upon them night and day as Nephi pondered upon his Father's messages and the teachings that the Spirit had laid upon his heart. As such, Joseph inquired of the Lord to provide him with further light and knowledge on the subject, and as a result, we received another revelation containing an Enochian easter egg.

The way that the subject matter of all of these revelations weaves together to confirm, enrich, and supplement the teachings of Enoch is incredible. You will see what I am talking about as this revelation unfolds. Consider the following:

> Hearken, O ye people, and open your hearts and give ear from afar; and listen, you that call yourselves the people of the Lord, and hear the word of the Lord and His will concerning you. Yea, verily, I say, hear the word of Him whose anger is kindled against the wicked and rebellious; who willeth to take even them whom He will take, and preserveth in life them whom He will preserve; who buildeth up at His own will and pleasure; and destroyeth when He pleases, and is able to cast the soul down to hell.
>
> Behold, I, the Lord, utter my voice, and it shall be obeyed. Wherefore, verily I say, let the wicked take heed, and let the rebellious fear and tremble; and let the unbelieving hold their lips, for the day of wrath shall come upon them as a whirlwind, and all flesh shall know that I am God. (D&C 63:1-6)

The Lord begins this revelation with powerful language. It is as if He came out swinging from the get-go. The question is, why? The Lord understands perfectly well what will occur in both Kirtland and Missouri. He understands the apostasy that is about to take place in Kirtland. He also knows that against His better council, the saints are about to migrate to Missouri in large numbers and lose everything they have once again. He knows that while their motivations are pure, they go off half-cocked and act upon things they do not yet understand. As such, the Lord emphasizes that His authority is absolute. As far as time and space are concerned, the word of God is the governing force of the multiverse, and yet man will do whatever man will do. The very agency that God gave them and so ardently protects will be how so many of heaven's sons and daughters will damn themselves.

It brings to mind the heavenly families that gather before the Throne of God, petitioning the Father on behalf of their posterity, both the wicked and the righteous alike. These knew that their sons and daughters would be deceived by the powerful emotions and deceptions common to all those who spend mortality upon Satan's prison planet. They advocated to the Father precisely because the Father is the supreme power in the multiverse. The mercy of God is evident in the plan of salvation, which is laid out in astounding detail throughout the chronicles of Enoch's writings. Yet the Father's primary motive is the exaltation of His children. He has so much that He can give them if they are willing to accept it. However, because of their own blindness and lack of spiritual inquisitiveness, seeking to be taught by men rather than God through the administration of the Holy Ghost, they will fall into harm's way time and time again.

The revelation continues:

> And he that seeketh signs shall see signs, but not unto salvation. Verily, I say unto you, there are those among you who seek signs, and there have been such even from the beginning; but, behold, faith cometh not by signs, but signs follow those that believe.

> Yea, signs come by faith, not by the will of men, nor as they please, but by the will of God. Yea, signs come by faith, unto mighty works, for without faith no man pleaseth God; and with whom God is angry He is not well pleased; wherefore, unto such He showeth no signs, only in wrath unto their condemnation.

> Wherefore, I, the Lord, am not pleased with those among you who have sought after signs and wonders for faith, and not for the good of men unto My glory. Nevertheless, I give commandments, and many have turned away from My commandments and have not kept them.

There were among you adulterers and adulteresses; some of whom have turned away from you, and others remain with you that hereafter shall be revealed. Let such beware and repent speedily, lest judgment shall come upon them as a snare, and their folly shall be made manifest, and their works shall follow them in the eyes of the people. And verily I say unto you, as I have said before, he that looketh on a woman to lust after her, or if any shall commit adultery in their hearts, they shall not have the Spirit, but shall deny the faith and shall fear. (D&C 63:7-16)

All things are before the Lord. As such, He is not only speaking to the Saints of Kirtland; He is speaking unto us, the Saints that will see the signs and prophecies of which He has spoken fulfilled. Specifically, the Lord calls out those who are sexually impure in deed or in thought. He reminds us once again of His teachings to the House of Israel that to look upon a woman to lust after her is to commit adultery in your heart. The Lord commands His sons to repent before the extent of their sins are made bare to the world. Repent and be made pure and clean before the Lord.

The Lord's disciples living upon the earth today are living in the most challenging era of sexual impurity the world has ever known. Never before has it been so easy to immerse yourself in lust than it is today. Yet, based upon the Lord's admonitions above, His expectations are unchanged. He expects that we will put these things aside and master ourselves. We understand from the prior chapter that the Lord has given all men everywhere weakness. These weaknesses are intended to cause us to become humble, repent, and turn to the Lord Jesus Christ. As such, the true disciple of Christ will constantly cross himself in all things. The disciple of Christ will not be a whited sepulcher, putting forward one face in public but delighting in carnality in secret. This council from the Lord could not be more relevant to us today.

The revelation continues:

> Wherefore, I, the Lord, have said that the fearful, and the unbelieving, and all liars, and whosoever loveth and maketh a lie, and the whoremonger, and the sorcerer, shall have their part in that lake which burneth with fire and brimstone, which is the second death. Verily I say, that they shall not have part in the first resurrection. And now behold, I, the Lord, say unto you that ye are not justified, because these things are among you.

> Nevertheless, he that endureth in faith and doeth My will, the same shall overcome, and shall receive an inheritance upon the earth when the day of transfiguration shall come; when the earth shall be transfigured, even according to the pattern which was shown unto mine apostles upon the mount; of which account the fulness ye have not yet received. (D&C 63:17-21)

In the passages above, the Lord refers to the torment of that burning mountain ridge at the end of all things, which overlooks the sons of perdition. Those who are consigned to such a place choose not to rely upon the merits of the Father's hidden Son. As such, they will not come forth in the morning of the first resurrection but will endure the refining torment of their burning consciences for ten thousand years until, at last, their dross has been consumed, and they are made pure and holy through their own sacrifice. Yet, as we have learned elsewhere, their sacrifice is an inferior substitute for the infinite and eternal sacrifice of the Father's hidden Son. As such, where the Father is, they cannot come; the world's without end.

Nevertheless, the Lord clearly states that those of His disciples who struggle with weaknesses but who do so humbly before Him, seeking His help and strength, will overcome those weaknesses in Him. To overcome our weaknesses, we must endure in faith. The coming trials will shake both heaven and earth. Every man, woman, and child on this planet is plagued with weaknesses, and we are all equally reliant upon the hidden Christ for our salvation. The coming days of the trial will shake our faith, and even many of the very elect, according to the covenant, will fall. Yet those whose faith in the hidden Lord does not fail will be made strong. Such will live to see the earth renewed in its paradisical glory.

Christ then spoke of the transfiguration of the earth and how there is an accounting of the transfiguration that we have not yet received. As such, we are to understand that there are mysteries on such things that the world has not yet received but that they will in the due time of the Lord. I suppose the Lord is likely referring to the process wherein the earth will be removed from the influence of lesser beings of glory and relocated into the highest realms of Celestial Glory. Only those beings that inhabit such worlds are capable of transversing the entirety of the multiverse; all others are damned to the orders of the glory of equal or lesser value to that which they were worthy of receiving. If there is more or less to the mystery of the earth's pending transfiguration, we will soon come to understand it. John, who was present with the Lord upon the Mount of Transfiguration, is coming, and he will restore all things, including this lost information.

The revelation continues:

And now, verily I say unto you, that as I said that I would make known my will unto you, behold I will make it known unto you, not by the way of commandment, for there are many who observe not to keep my commandments. But unto him that keepeth my commandments I will give the mysteries of my kingdom, and the same shall be in him a well of living water, springing up unto everlasting life. (D&C 63:22-23)

In the passage above, Jesus Christ reveals His will to the saints, not by way of commandment, but by way of council. Those who keep the council of the Lord will be able to understand the mysteries of Christ's kingdom – if they seek them. Christ states that these mysteries will become a spring of living water in their souls. That is to say that the mysteries of the Kingdom of God are both highly prized and highly motivational, yet only those who seek them will come to understand these things. Consider this passage from the Book of Enoch that reconciles perfectly with Christ's teachings above.

49. l. For wisdom is poured out like water, and glory faileth not before Him [*the Son of Man*] for evermore.

49.2. For He is mighty in all the secrets of righteousness, and unrighteousness shall disappear as a shadow, and have no continuance; because the Elect One standeth before the Lord of Spirits, and His glory is for ever and ever, and His might unto all generations.

51.3. And the Elect One shall in those days sit on My throne, and His mouth shall **pour** forth all the secrets of wisdom and counsel: for the Lord of Spirits hath given them to Him and hath glorified Him.

58.4. And they [*the premortal righteous*] shall seek the light and find righteousness with the Lord of Spirits: There shall be peace to the righteous in the name of the Eternal Lord.

58.5. And after this it shall be said to the holy in heaven that they [*the peers of the premortal righteous*] should seek out the secrets of righteousness, the heritage of faith: For it has become bright as the sun upon earth, and the darkness is past.

I have discussed within this book the sigma that the ignorant have placed upon seeking to understand the mysteries of God. Such a stigma causes great joy amongst the demonic hosts of Lucifer, who have worked very hard to put this stigma in place. Yet, at the end of the day, those who learn directly from the Lord, by way of the constant guiding influence of the Holy Spirit, will withstand the evil hour and none else.

The mysteries of God are not found upon the surface of His words but deep within them. When the Lord speaks, He speaks in patterns. Each revelation of the Lord builds upon the last. This revelation was literally given on the heels of the other revelations and related to them. Therefore, it should be looked at in conjunction with the revelations that came before – line upon line, precept upon precept. If the saints would have done this, they would have better understood the Lord's council to them. You will see the Lord's counsel to them very plainly. The fact that He sees things very clearly is absolutely evident in this revelation, as will be demonstrated.

As we delve further into these Enochian revelations, you may ask yourself why the Lord didn't just speak out and speak plainly. If you think this, you likely think of all of the pain and suffering that might have been avoided with a more direct approach. Yet, if the Lord's objective were the avoidance of suffering, He would not have sent us to spend mortality upon Satan's prison planet. We did not come to mortality to avoid pain. We came to mortality to learn and develop. Christ is teaching us to not stop at the surface level of His teachings but to dig deeper through the guidance of the Spirit. This is not new; it has been so. Remember the following passage from a prior chapter?

> Jesus' disciples came and said to Him, "Why do you use parables when you speak to the crowds?"
>
> Jesus replied, "Because they haven't received the secrets of the kingdom of heaven, but you have. For those who have will receive more and they will have more than enough. But as for those who don't have, even the little they have will be taken away from them. This is why I speak to the crowds in parables (Matt 13:10-13 Common English Translation)

There are layers to the Lord's teachings. The Enochian links between these various modern revelations we have been studying demonstrate the existence of these deeper layers. As my other books also demonstrate, there are many such patterns throughout all of scripture. Studying the scriptures in this manner is how we open the wellsprings of living water that will sustain us through the spiritual famines of the coming days.

We now return to Christ's council to the Saints. Let us be extra careful as we proceed to connect the dots in these coming verses to those of prior chapters.

And now, behold, this is the will of the Lord your God concerning His saints, that they should assemble themselves together unto the land of Zion, not in haste, lest there should be confusion, which bringeth pestilence. Behold, the land of Zion—I, the Lord, hold it in Mine own hands; nevertheless, I, the Lord, render unto Caesar the things which are Caesar's.

Wherefore, I the Lord will that you should purchase the lands, that you may have advantage of the world, that you may have claim on the world, that they may not be stirred up unto anger. For Satan putteth it into their hearts to anger against you, and to the shedding of blood. Wherefore, the land of Zion shall not be obtained but by purchase or by blood, otherwise there is none inheritance for you.

If by purchase, behold you are blessed; if by blood, as you are forbidden to shed blood, lo, your enemies are upon you, and ye shall be scourged from city to city, and from synagogue to synagogue, and but few shall stand to receive an inheritance. I, the Lord, am angry with the wicked; I am holding my Spirit from the inhabitants of the earth. I have sworn in my wrath, and decreed wars upon the face of the earth, and the wicked shall slay the wicked, and fear shall come upon every man; and the saints also shall hardly escape; nevertheless, I, the Lord, am with them, and will come down in heaven from the presence of my Father and consume the wicked with unquenchable fire. Behold, this is not yet, but by and by. (D&C 63:24-35)

A surface reading of the Lord's council above might cause one to think it was the Lord's will for the saints to gather in mass to Zion, which is what they did. However, this most certainly was not the council the Lord gave them, as a closer study of these verses will reveal. You will recall from the prior chapter that the Lord told the saints they would not receive their inheritances in Zion for many years. In the passages above, He advises the saints not to relocate to Zion in haste, but first to acquire and own lands. Based upon 678 surviving petitions for redress, the saints in Missouri had purchased a minimum of $2.3 million worth of property in Missouri, a staggering sum for the impoverished saints. Particularly considering that the United States acquired 827,000 square miles from France in 1803 for $15 Million through the Louisiana Purchase. However, much of the land upon which the saints settled was not purchased but rather was occupied under preemption rights. Such rights delayed payment for land until the United States government surveyed the land. While this seemed a great opportunity for the saints to occupy land in Missouri without paying for it, it was a disaster for them. Upon surveying the land, much of the land was sold to speculators, who then forced the saints from the land in 1838. However, as the hundreds of petitions for redress attest, the state forced many members of the Church to vacate legally purchased land under threat of extermination.

Thus, the Lord's warning that Zion could only be obtained in one of two ways: by purchase or by blood. From the context of the revelation, it is clearly evident that the Lord already knew that Zion would be obtained by the latter. He overtly stated that Zion would be redeemed when unquenchable fire consumed the wicked. The Lord told them that the time for the destruction of the wicked by fire was not yet, but by and by. They did not understand what the Lord meant then, but they could have known. The Isaiah chapters contained in the Book of Mormon, which the Lord commanded them to study, speak of these things explicitly.

> Lift ye up a banner upon the high mountain… I have commanded my sanctified ones… They come from a far country, from the end of heaven, yea, the Lord, and the weapons of His indignation, to destroy the whole land… Behold, the day of the Lord cometh, cruel both with wrath and fierce anger, to lay the land desolate; and He shall destroy the sinners thereof out of it. (2 Nephi 23)

When we take the words of Isaiah together in the context of the material we have covered in the last couple of chapters, we should see things much more clearly. The Great and Terrible Day of the Lord would only occur after the Saints had been established in the mountains. Once that occurred, the days would come when a highway would be cast out of the great deep, meaning the infinite sea of space-time. Upon this highway, the Holy Race will return from the ends of heaven to destroy the sinners out of Zion and claim it through the shedding of blood. In that day, no sinners shall remain in all the lands of Zion.

Furthermore, the Lord told the Saints exactly what would happen if they did not abide by His counsel. He explicitly told them that if they went up in haste, the people of Missouri would rise against them in anger, and the saints would be driven from place to place. The Lord then stated that the land would descend into war, a war from which the saints would be delivered, but just barely.

This revelation is astounding and ironclad proof that the Lord sees the end from the beginning. This is exactly what happened. The Saints moved to Missouri both in haste and in great numbers. As such, the people of Missouri became alarmed and rose up against them, driving them out settlement by settlement. They continued to be driven until finally, they entered the refuge of the Rocky Mountains in 1846. The United States would descend into chaos within fifteen years of their departure. Less than twenty saints would be slaughtered by mobs in Missouri, while 13,000 Missourians would be killed in the civil war.

As a side note, the only LDS casualty of the Civil War was an ancestor of mine, Henry Wells Jackson. A picture of his daughter hung above our family piano for much of my life. He was a US government mailman, carrying mail between Utah and California. However, due to the outbreak of the Civil War, the government stopped paying him. He decided to go to Washington to get paid. Along the way, he was captured by Confederate soldiers and held as a prisoner of war for three months. Upon his release, he was so angry with the South for his unjust imprisonment that he enlisted in the Union Army. He was killed shortly after his enlistment at the Battle of White Bridge, a needless death.

I believe that it is clear from the Lord's council above that the saints would escape the civil war and the chaos leading up to the Great and Terrible Day of the Lord. The violence of the mob turned out to deliver the saints from the blood bath of the Civil War, and the Remnant of Jacob will deliver the saints from the consuming fire that will devour the wicked. The Saints will be preserved because they will be identified as having the seal of God upon them by none other than John the Revelator.

The Revelation continues:

> Wherefore, seeing that I, the Lord, have decreed all these things upon the face of the earth, I will that my saints should be assembled upon the land of Zion; and that every man should take righteousness in his hands and faithfulness upon his loins, and lift a warning voice unto the inhabitants of the earth; and declare both by word and by flight that desolation shall come upon the wicked. (D&C 63:36-37)

The Lord wants His Saints to gather to Zion – for Zion will be their inheritance. However, that gathering will not take place until desolation has rained down upon the wicked in a terrible firestorm. You will recall that the Lord provided the sequence in which these things would occur in the second Enochian section of the Doctrine and Covenants that we covered. Reconsider that prophetic passage:

> But before the great day of the Lord shall come, Jacob shall flourish in the wilderness, and the Lamanites shall blossom as the rose. Zion shall flourish upon the hills and rejoice upon the mountains, and shall be assembled together unto the place which I have appointed [*Jackson County, MO*]. (D&C 49:24-25)

The foresight of the Lord is astounding!

The next passage is even more curious to me than those that have come before. Consider the following:

> Let all the moneys which can be spared, it mattereth not unto me whether it be little or much, be sent up unto the land of Zion, unto them whom I have appointed to receive. (D&C 63:40)

Earlier in the revelation, the Lord told the saints that Zion would be redeemed in one of two ways: purchase or blood. The fact that the Lord is not concerned with the amount of money the saints send to acquire lands in Zion is telling. It is also consistent with the passages above. Even if the saints do not yet know it, the Lord knows that the lands of Zion will be redeemed by the blood of the wicked and not with money. However, purchasing some lands in Zion was pleasing to the Lord. The Church presently has vast land holdings in Jackson County. However, the Lord can do His work. As He stated above, He will render unto Ceasar that which is Ceasar's until the day of the Gentiles has come to a full. Then, on that day, He will reclaim all the lands of Zion, for all the Earth is His. Land purchase in Jackson County, MO, was largely symbolic of the people's trust in the Lord.

The Church of Jesus Christ of Latter-day Saints literally has hundreds of billions of dollars in diversified investments. These funds are a direct result of the law of the tithe. Yet, it is not the hundreds of billions that the Lord cares about, but rather the faith of His people in principle and sacrifice. The days will come when the Lord will cause the heavens to shake for the good of the saints who have willingly subjected themselves to the Lord's law. Whose actions align with their faith and not just their words.

Consider this principle in light of what the Lord says next:

> He that is faithful and endureth shall overcome the world.
> He that sendeth up treasures unto the land of Zion shall

receive an inheritance in this world, and his works shall follow him, and also a reward in the world to come. Yea, and blessed are the dead that die in the Lord, from henceforth, when the Lord shall come, and old things shall pass away, and all things become new, they shall rise from the dead and shall not die after, and shall receive an inheritance before the Lord, in the holy city. (D&C 63:47-49)

From the passages above, it should have been very clear that the early Saints would not obtain the land of Zion in their lifetimes. However, the Lord would honor their faith with an inheritance in the New Jerusalem in the coming day. As such, society will change during the millennium, when all things have become new, the heavens and the earth. I mentioned previously in this book that societies where gods and mortals mix in incredible yet common ways surely exist throughout the cosmos. According to the Lord, the New Jerusalem will be just such a place. The righteous and faithful saints of Joseph's day will rise from their graves and will have inheritances among their righteous living posterity. Such resurrected beings will not be angels; like Abraham, they will be gods. Therefore, the Eternal City will be a city of Gods and men and will be the most sought-after inheritance in the multiverse. The righteous will come from worlds without number, seeking an inheritance in Zion. How can I possibly know such a thing? Because the Lord told Enoch that such would be the case, and I believe Him when the Lord says something.

> And the Lord said unto Enoch: Then shalt thou and all thy city meet them there, and WE will receive them into our bosom, and they shall see US; and WE will fall upon their necks, and they shall fall upon OUR necks, and WE will kiss each other; and there shall be MINE abode, and it shall be Zion, which shall come forth out of ALL THE CREATIONS which I have made; and for the space of a thousand years the earth shall rest. (Moses 7:63-64)

These things are mind-blowingly amazing! They are just as plain to me as the prophecies the Lord laid out to the early saints. They are right before us, yet some can see them while most do not. It does not need to be this way, but it is this way. It is this way because we as a people are overly impetuous. Too often, like Peter, we leap before we look. The Lord has asked us to ponder upon His words for a reason. When we do so, we begin to see the reality that exists embedded within the greater message – the message within the message. The Lord spoke in parables in antiquity, and He still does so, yet to those who seek to be taught by the Holy Ghost, the mysteries of God can and will be unfolded until they are fully comprehended. The mysteries of God are invigorating. They increase and sustain one's faith in ways the gospel's milk never could.

The Lord now speaks regarding the mortal contingent living amongst the righteous in Zion during the millennium.

> And he that liveth when the Lord shall come, and hath kept the faith, blessed is he; nevertheless, it is appointed to him to die at the age of man. Wherefore, children shall grow up until they become old; old men shall die; but they shall not sleep in the dust, but they shall be changed in the twinkling of an eye. Wherefore, for this cause preached the apostles unto the world the resurrection of the dead.
>
> These things are the things that ye must look for; and, speaking after the manner of the Lord, they are now nigh at hand, and in a time to come, even in the day of the coming of **the Son of Man**. (D&C 63:50-53)

During the Millennium, there will still be death, yet death will not sting. That person will be instantaneously resurrected once one has lived a full life. To what degree of glory would one living in the New Jerusalem be resurrected? Not a soul of this generation who dies during the Millennium will be lost. However, our life spans will be greatly lengthened. Many of our posterity will live to see the end of the Millennium while still in mortality. Then, they will see Satan released from his prison planet for a little season. His release will result in one final attempt to overthrow the God of heaven and His Eternal City, which I have spoken of in detail in volume I of this series.

The Lord now admonishes his saints in a significant way. Consider the following:

> And until that hour there will be foolish virgins among the wise; and at that hour cometh an entire separation of the righteous and the wicked; and in that day will I send mine angels [*the five angels of the Book of Revelation representing John and the hosts of Israel whom he will restore*] to pluck out the wicked and cast them into unquenchable fire. (D&C 63:54)

To me, the meaning of the Lord's words is crystal clear. There are too many members of the Church who can be likened to the foolish virgins of whom Christ spoke in a parable. These did not have sufficient oil in and of themselves but had to obtain that which they had from others. The wise virgins carried with them an unquenchable flame that burned from within. These wise virgins obtained their oil from the source. As such, they knew the Bridegroom, and He knew them. However, to the foolish virgins, the Lord responded to their panicked knocking upon his chamber door –"of a truth –ye know me not." In other words, the foolish virgins do not know the Lord's hidden Son, for they have not sought to know Him.

If we are to survive the coming day, we must personally know the Lord. Let me be very clear here. I am not saying that we must have personally seen and spoken with the Lord. We will know Him because of the teachings of the Holy Ghost – the mysteries of God. Jesus Christ is the Father's hidden Son. While many proclaim to know Him, they do not know Him. There is only one way to know the Hidden Son: through the Father, who teaches us through the Spirit. To those who seek to be taught by the Spirit of God, the mysteries of the scriptures are revealed.

Many have said that they cannot understand the words of Isaiah. Yet Nephi stated that the words of Isaiah are clear to all those filled with Christ's testimony. Not the testimony of Him that the world bears, but the testimony which the Father shares. If the Father has revealed to you His Hidden Son, why would He keep the words of Isaiah from you, or the words of John, Daniel, Jeremiah, Ezekiel, Joel, Zechariah, or any other prophet that has ever lived? If you have not found the meaning of these things, it is because you have sought them only passively. All those who seek to understand such things through the Spirit of God will come to understand them, for God is the same yesterday, today, and forever. If you do not believe this, then you have not yet met the Hidden Son. Seek Him.

Now, the Lord turns to those who have learned of the truthfulness of His words through the administration of the Holy Ghost.

> And again, verily I say unto you, those who desire in their hearts, in meekness, to warn sinners to repentance, let them be ordained unto this power. For this is a day of warning, and not a day of many words. For I, the Lord, am not to be mocked in the last days. Behold, I am from above, and my power lieth beneath. I am over all, and in all, and through all, and search all things, and the day cometh that all things shall be subject unto me. (D&C 63:57-59)

The Lord wants us to feed His sheep. There is nothing that will be of more benefit to us than doing so. However, the Lord wants us to do so under the direction of a prior revelation that He gave in D&C 11:21. According to this passage, the Lord counseled

His people that they should first seek to understand His word before proclaiming it to others. The Lord does not want us to proclaim His mysteries to the masses. Indeed, the Lord has commanded that we preach only repentance to these people. The mysteries are His to teach. We must learn His mysteries because, in so doing, we become truly converted to the gospel of Jesus Christ and obtain an unshakable faith in the Hidden Son. Until you have come to know the Hidden Son of God, the entirety of the gospel is purely theoretical. Only in and by Jesus Christ is truth discerned from error.

> Behold, I am Alpha and Omega, even Jesus Christ. Wherefore, let all men beware how they take my name in their lips— For behold, verily I say, that many there be who are under this condemnation, who use the name of the Lord, and use it in vain, having not authority. Wherefore, let the church repent of their sins, and I, the Lord, will own them; otherwise they shall be cut off. (D&C 63:60-63)

In the passage above, the Lord strips away all doubt as to His thoughts regarding hypocrisy and blind guides. Israel has a long and storied history of men proclaiming to know the Lord, yet they have been blind guides. According to the Lord, many were like this in the Church in Joseph's day. We can easily look back at the early saints and identify weaknesses. Many of Joseph's original twelve apostles left the church because their faith in the gospel could not withstand the collapse of the Kirtland Safety Society.

When the Lord speaks of taking His name in vain, He is not talking about swearing. His concern has always been with His people, binding themselves with sacred covenants in His name, which they subsequently treat lightly or cast aside altogether. This has been the default state of the House of Israel, and it persists in the Church today. Too often, the principles and ordinances of the gospel become cultural rather than spiritual. Indeed, elsewhere in the D&C, the Lord states that the calamities of the last days will start first among His people who have professed His name but have not known Him. This demonstrates that Christ is every bit the Hidden Son today as He ever has been. We must come to know the Lord for ourselves. Yet, few will do so, bringing us back to the parable of the ten virgins.

We return now to the conclusion of this incredible revelation:

> Remember that that which cometh from above is sacred, and must be spoken with care, and by constraint of the Spirit; and in this there is no condemnation, and ye receive the Spirit through prayer; wherefore, without this there remaineth condemnation.

Let my servants, Joseph Smith, Jun., and Sidney Rigdon, seek them a home, as they are taught through prayer by the Spirit. These things remain to overcome through patience, that such may receive a more exceeding and eternal weight of glory, otherwise, a greater condemnation. Amen. (D&C 63:64-66)

The Lord concludes this chapter with an admonition to consider His mysteries sacred and to not reveal them to the masses. You might wonder if I violated this principle by publishing this book. The fact of the matter is that the things written in this book are every bit as guarded from the world as the mysteries of God ever have been. For the world is disinterested in such things. If it takes effort to read them on a page, they will not know them. If those who have read them on a page try to share them with the world, the world will not receive them. Only the Spirit of God can teach these things.

This is why the Lord commanded Joseph Smith and Sidney Rigdon to continue to study these things through prayer and the Spirit. God will teach us of the truthfulness of all things. Those that seek will find, and in so finding will open the possibility of an exceeding and eternal weight of glory. I say possibility because it is up to us to work out our own salvation before the Throne of God. He who has ears to hear, let him hear.

Chapter 23: Three In One D&C 64, 65, and 68

In the prior chapter, I reviewed an astounding revelation from the Lord regarding His plans for Zion and her ultimate redemption through the shedding of blood. That revelation was received on August 30, 1831. From September to November of 1831, Joseph Smith received three additional revelations that continued to add line to the previously covered revelations. As such, rather than covering each of these subsequent sections in detail, for the sake of brevity, I will focus my remaining remarks exclusively on the Enochian references made with each of these three revelations.

The following is an excerpt taken from the first of these three revelations, received by Joseph on September 11, 1831.

> Behold, now it is called today until the coming of **the Son of Man,** and verily it is a day of sacrifice, and a day for the tithing of my people; for he that is tithed shall not be burned at His coming. For after today cometh the burning—this is speaking after the manner of the Lord—for verily I say, tomorrow all the proud and they that do wickedly shall be as stubble; and I will burn them up, for I am the Lord of Hosts; and I will not spare any that remain in Babylon. Wherefore, if ye believe me, ye will labor while it is called today.
>
> For, behold, I say unto you that Zion shall flourish, and the glory of the Lord shall be upon her; and she shall be an ensign unto the people, and there shall come unto her out of every nation under heaven. And the day shall come when the nations of the earth shall tremble because of her, and shall fear because of her terrible ones. The Lord hath spoken it. Amen. (D&C 64:23-25; 41-43)

The passages above are incredible. To begin, we are promised that those who are tithed of the Lord will not be burned as stubble. This is not the only time Jesus Christ has associated tithing with salvation from destruction in the last days. Within my writings, I have repeatedly referenced the Lord's magnificent sermon to the Nephites. This is perhaps the most important discourse on this subject matter in all scripture.

Upon concluding His discourse, the Lord first councils the people to study the words of Isaiah and then commands them to study His words. Then, the Lord quotes the people in the third chapter of the book of Malachi, a prophecy not included in the Brass Plates. Consider the language of that prophecy and the relevance to the passages above.

> Will a man rob God? Yet ye have robbed me. But ye say: Wherein have we robbed thee? In tithes and offerings. Ye are cursed with a curse, for ye have robbed me, even this whole nation. Bring ye all the tithes into the storehouse, that there may be meat in my house; and prove me now herewith, saith the Lord of Hosts, if I will not open you the windows of heaven, and pour you out a blessing that there shall not be room enough to receive it.
>
> And I will rebuke the devourer for your sakes, and he shall not destroy the fruits of your ground; neither shall your vine cast her fruit before the time in the fields, saith the Lord of Hosts. And all nations shall call you blessed, for ye shall be a delightsome land, saith the Lord of Hosts. (3 Nephi 24: 8-12)

The Lord will preserve the righteous from the hand of the devourer. In the context of these chapters, the devourer and the destroyer are the same – John and the Remnant of Jacob. These terrible inhabitants will redeem Zion by shedding blood and making it an unassailable refuge unto the righteous.

Curiously, in the passages above from D&C 64, the Lord stated that Zion will come forth from every nation under heaven. As we have come to understand, this is to be interpreted quite literally. The righteous from every creation of the Father's will flow unto Zion in the last days. Why will they come? They will come to receive the fullness of the gospel at the hands of the children of Ephraim, the servants of the Lord, whose inheritance Zion is.

The next passage comes from a revelation received on October 30, 1831. The revelation was very short, only six verses long. The first five of which read as follows:

> Hearken, and lo, a voice as of one sent down from on high, who is mighty and powerful, whose going forth is unto the ends of the earth, yea, whose voice is unto men—Prepare ye the way of the Lord, make His paths straight. The keys of the kingdom of God are committed unto man on the earth, and

from thence shall the gospel roll forth unto the ends of the earth, as the stone which is cut out of the mountain without hands shall roll forth, until it has filled the whole earth.

Yea, a voice crying—Prepare ye the way of the Lord, prepare ye the supper of the Lamb, make ready for the Bridegroom. Pray unto the Lord, call upon His holy name, make known His wonderful works among the people.

Call upon the Lord, that His kingdom may go forth upon the earth, that the inhabitants thereof may receive it, and be prepared for the days to come, in the **which the Son of Man shall come down in heaven**, clothed in the brightness of His glory, to meet the kingdom of God which is set up on the earth. (D&C 65:1-5)

The passage above is reminiscent of John the Baptist preparing the way before the Lord's first coming. John was the chosen Elias to prepare Israel for their coming King. Yet the Baptist was incarcerated and beheaded. Some listened to John, but many did not. One of those who listened to John the Baptist was John the Beloved, amongst the Baptist's first disciples. John the Beloved will be the latter-day Elias that will restore the Lost Tribes of Israel and will restore all else.

In the passages above, the Lord also refers to Himself as the Bridegroom once more, referring to the parable of the ten virgins, wherein half of the Church was depicted as being unprepared for His coming. Most of Judah would not receive John the Baptist's warnings to them. In like manner, I fear that most of the Church will also not receive John the Beloved's warnings of these things. In both cases, it was not that they were not aware of such warnings; they just expected others to do the heavy lifting of receiving any necessary personal revelation on their behalf. Those who would take such a cavalier approach to their own spiritual education are woefully unprepared for what is coming. The heavens are coming to the earth; what a day that will be! Much more regarding what the coming of the heavens to the earth will look like will be spoken of in the last chapter of this volume – buckle up!

This next passage comes from a revelation given by the Lord to Joseph Smith on November 1, 1831.

Be of good cheer, and do not fear, for I the Lord am with you, and will stand by you; and ye shall bear record of Me, even Jesus Christ, that I am the Son of the living God, that I was, that I am, and that I am to come. This is the word of the Lord unto you… the faithful elders of my church—

Go ye into all the world, preach the gospel to every creature, acting in the authority which I have given you, baptizing in the name of the Father, and of the Son, and of the Holy Ghost. And he that believeth and is baptized shall be saved, and he that believeth not shall be damned.

And he that believeth shall be blest with signs following, even as it is written. And unto you it shall be given to know the signs of the times, and the signs of the coming of **the Son of Man**; and of as many as the Father shall bear record, to you shall be given power to seal them up unto eternal life. Amen. (D&C 68:6-12)

I find it curious that in the passages above, the Lord commands His Elders to carry the gospel to every "creature." Why does the Lord use the term creature here and not man, as is typical? The root of the word creature is create. Thus, anything that has been created by God is a creature. God created the human family when He created the physical bodies of Adam and Eve. Yet, before humankind, He created beasts. At present, there are no beasts upon the earth, known to humanity at large, that are intelligent enough to be taught the gospel. Does that mean that none exist throughout the cosmos? When the scriptures speak of seraphim, which are magnificent, winged beasts of great intelligence that love and serve the Lord. Are we to consider them to be total fabrications because they do not exist on this Earth? Therefore, do not be too quick to presume you know the answer to this question.

We have discussed strange things within this book, and by the conclusion of the last chapter of this volume, we will still discuss strange things. At present, it is enough for you to place a pin on this topic. However, I will invite you now to reconsider this admonition of the Lord to preach His gospel to every creature after this volume. It may be more meaningful to you then than it is now.

In addition, the passages above state that signs will follow the faithful. What does this mean? I think that often, we interpret this as meaning miracles. However, signs are not limited to overt miracles. More commonly, signs are indicators that communicate important information, such as traffic signs. I had an interesting experience with "signs' while in Israel just before the start of the Hamas war. I was traveling there with my brothers and their wives. We happened to be in Jerusalem on the Islamic day of sacrifice, one of the holiest days in Islam. As such, whole sections of the Muslim quarter were sectioned off by heavily armed Israeli soldiers.

The soldiers stopped us and said Muslims only beyond this point. My brother asked him how he knew that we were not Muslims, and the soldiers laughed as if that was a funny joke. Then someone on the street called out, you are Mormons. We were stunned. Elsewhere in Jerusalem, shopkeepers would call to us, singling us out in the crown and say Mormons, come in; I have something for you. In their shops, they had statues of Joseph Smith, the temple, Liahona replicas, and other paraphernalia that would be of no interest to any other group. They could easily pick out members of the Church from the crowded streets filled with tourists worldwide. It was then that I realized that signs do follow the Lord's people. If the shopkeepers of Jerusalem can so easily discern the signs that indicate a person is LDS from a sea of Christian tourists, should we not be able to discern the signs of the coming of the Son of Man?

Chapter 24: Kingdoms of Glory – D&C 76

In this chapter, I will discuss Joseph Smith and Sidney Rigdon's joint vision of the Kingdoms of Glory. I am doing so because it is one of the twelve revelations in the Doctrine and Covenants with the Enochian marker - Son of Man. Before this revelation was received, Joseph and Sidney were engaged in translating the New Testament text. As they were doing so, they happened upon the following curious Enochian passage from the writings of John.

> Verily, verily, I say unto you, The hour is coming, and now is, when the dead shall hear the voice of the Son of God: and they that hear shall live. For as the Father hath life in Himself; so hath He given to the Son to have life in Himself; and hath given Him authority to execute judgment also, because He is the Son of Man.
>
> Marvel not at this: for the hour is coming, in the which all that are in the graves shall hear His voice, and shall come forth; they that have done good, unto the resurrection of life; and they that have done evil, unto the resurrection of damnation. (John 5:25-29)

From our studies thus far of the Book of Enoch, it is becoming easier to recognize the influence of Enoch's writings within Christ's teachings. Enoch foresaw long before Christ's birth that the Lord of Spirits would give the authority of judgement to the Son of Man. We also learned that the Spirit World is divided amongst the righteous and the wicked. We learned that hosts of heavenly families advocate before the Throne of God for their children. Specifically, they advocated that the Son of Man would go amongst their offspring and reclaim as many of them as they were willing so that they might become the servants of God.

While it is clear that Christ knew these things and that He had taught them to His apostles, for they too wrote of them, until the restoration, this information had been lost. Therefore, given the impetus of the revelation of this chapter, which can be traced back to Enoch's writings, it is from the perspective of Enoch's writings that it becomes most meaningful. We will consider these correlations to Enoch's writings as the chapter unfolds. Consider Joseph Smith's introduction to this revelation.

> Hear, O ye heavens, and give ear, O earth, and rejoice ye
> inhabitants thereof, for the Lord is God, and beside Him
> there is no Savior. (D&C 76:1)

In this passage, Joseph unequivocally announced that this revelation was not only for the inhabitants of the Earth but for all of the inhabitants of the heavens. Why would Joseph Smith be receiving a revelation from the cosmos? What does it mean? Taken at face value, we must understand that Christ is the only Savior of this iteration of the Father's plan of Salvation. In other words, there are not multiple Saviors at work elsewhere in the multiverse. Christ is it. If any will be saved, regardless of the world upon which they reside, in that case, they must believe in Jesus Christ and apply His atonement in their lives – the atonement that Christ wrought outside the city wall of Jerusalem some two thousand years ago.

The gospel of John, whose writings prompted this revelation, confirms Joseph's statement:

> In the beginning was the Word, and the Word was with God,
> and the Word was God. The same was in the beginning with
> God. All things were made by Him; and without Him was
> not anything made that was made. (John 1:1-3)

John's statement leaves no room for doubt. There was, however, one caveat, "all things that were made, were made by Christ". By this, we are to understand that there were things that predated this creation that Christ would not have made. The Plan of Salvation is as eternal as God Himself. It has happened before, and it will happen again. Therefore, I believe that by this, we are to understand these creations in terms of the present iterations of the Father's plan. Christ made all the mortal worlds of men, regardless of where they are, throughout the cosmos, and He and He alone will be their Savior.

John is the most qualified of all Christ's original apostles to make a statement like this. Why? Because John was taken up into the heavens, just like the three Nephites were. As such, John absolutely knew what He was talking about. Therefore, when John says that Christ made everything there is, I believe him. However, it seems to me that only the mortal realms of the cosmos would need to have been reorganized. There would be no need to reorganize the other kingdoms and realms of the multiverse. I believe that the mortal realms of the multiverse comprise all the visible matter that our telescopes can see and beyond. I do not believe that the Web telescope is at risk of stumbling upon a kingdom of a higher order than those known to mortals. That being said, what do I know of the cosmos?

Some have postulated that God is God only of the Milky Way galaxy and that all else lies beyond His purview. Let us, therefore, consider that Christ is an All-knowing Being. As such, He fully understood the incredible changes the Industrial Revolution was about to enact. Shortly after this revelation, he knew that humankind would begin to pierce the great veil of space. Soon, we would learn that there were worlds without numbers and galaxies without numbers! The concept is astounding and speaks to the grandeur of God on a scope and scale that is terrifying to contemplate. I fear that if we truly understood to whom we prayed, we might never again have the courage to kneel before the throne of God in light of our own comparative nothingness. Yet, He has masked Himself from us precisely so that we would not fear to come before Him and, with fear and trembling, work out our salvation before Him. In this, the Islamic world speaks the truth - God is great!

Joseph's introduction of this revelation continues:

> Great is His wisdom, marvelous are His ways, and the extent
> of His doings none can find out. (D&C 76:2)

It is imperative to note that Joseph Smith stated that he and Sidney Rigdon were not permitted to write but a hundredth part of what they saw. Therefore, it is from this perspective that Joseph is writing. He means what he says about the vastness of God's dealings throughout the multiverse. Enoch saw such things, and so did Joseph.

> His purposes fail not, neither are there any who can stay His hand. From eternity to eternity He is the same, and His years never fail. For thus saith the Lord—I, the Lord, am merciful and gracious unto those who fear Me, and delight to honor those who serve Me in righteousness and in truth unto the end. Great shall be their reward and eternal shall be their glory. And to them will I reveal all mysteries, yea, all the hidden mysteries of My kingdom from days of old, and for ages to come, will I make known unto them the good pleasure of My will concerning all things pertaining to My kingdom.
>
> Yea, even the wonders of eternity shall they know, and things to come will I show them, even the things of many generations. And their wisdom shall be great, and their understanding reach to heaven; and before them the wisdom of the wise shall perish, and the understanding of the prudent

shall come to naught. For by My Spirit will I enlighten them, and by My power will I make known unto them the secrets of my will—yea, even those things which eye has not seen, nor ear heard, nor yet entered into the heart of man. (D&C 76:3-10)

In the passages above, Joseph clearly speaks about portions of his revelation that he was not permitted to share. However, it seems that Joseph indicated that while he was not at liberty to disclose these mysteries, God would share them with those seeking to be taught by the Father directly. To me, this is a clear example of the following passage:

> It is given unto many to <u>know</u> the <u>mysteries</u> of God; nevertheless they are laid under a strict command that they shall not impart <u>only</u> according to the portion of His word which He doth grant unto the children of men, according to the heed and diligence which they give unto Him. (Alma 12:9)

Joseph learned of the mysteries of God, and many others have learned of them as well. Men put God in a box and limit His communications to men of great importance. However, God is no respecter of persons. If men will draw near unto Him, He will draw near unto them, and He will share the secrets of the Universe with king and popper alike. If anything in any of my books is true, it is a testament to this principle. If the Holy Ghost has born witness to you of any of the concepts and teachings within my writings, or anytime you yourself have pondered deeply upon His Word, then you know this is true. The more firsthand experience we obtain with this concept, the thinner the veil will become. There is a reason that the restoration of all things will soon be upon us, not the least of which is the fact that many of the Lord's saints are beginning to rend their personal veils of disbelief. Such are learning that God is as assessable to them as He has been to any man who has ever lived, so long as you learn to hear Him within the gifts and talents that He has bestowed upon you.

When God stated that He would reveal His mysteries regarding many generations, I cannot help but think of the book of Enoch and the hidden history of this world. There are clearly things regarding our history that have been hidden from mainstream academics but which those with eyes to see can readily discern. The wisdom of the world's wise men will perish for reasons like these. A poor, unlearned farm boy can know more of the true nature of the cosmos than a thousand PhDs from the best universities in the world.

We now return to Joseph's explanation of his vision:

We, Joseph Smith, Jun., and Sidney Rigdon, being in the Spirit on the sixteenth day of February, in the year of our Lord one thousand eight hundred and thirty-two— By the power of the Spirit our eyes were opened and our understandings were enlightened, so as to see and understand the things of God— even those things which were from the beginning before the world was, which were ordained of the Father, through His Only Begotten Son, who was in the bosom of the Father, even from the beginning; of whom we bear record; and the record which we bear is the fulness of the gospel of Jesus Christ, who is the Son, whom we saw and with whom we conversed in the heavenly vision.

For while we were doing the work of translation, which the Lord had appointed unto us, we came to the twenty-ninth verse of the fifth chapter of John, which was given unto us as follows— Speaking of the resurrection of the dead, concerning those who shall hear the voice of the Son of Man: And shall come forth; they who have done good, in the resurrection of the just; and they who have done evil, in the resurrection of the unjust.

Now this caused us to marvel, for it was given unto us of the Spirit. And while we meditated upon these things, the Lord touched the eyes of our understandings and they were opened, and the glory of the Lord shone round about. And we beheld the glory of the Son, on the right hand of the Father, and received of His fulness; and saw the holy angels, and them who are sanctified before His throne, worshiping God, and the Lamb, who worship Him forever and ever. (D&C 76:11-21)

The parallels between what Joseph and Sidney saw in their vision and what Enoch saw in their vision are uncanny. Both saw God the Father sitting upon His throne, with Christ standing at His side. Both saw the hosts of heaven gathered before the throne of God. While Joseph stated that these were worshiping the Father, Enoch explained that they advocated for their posterity upon the earth. Again, the usage of the term Son of Man is Enochian and provides the context from which I believe all such references should be deciphered.

> And now, after the many testimonies which have been given of Him, this is the testimony, last of all, which we give of Him: That He lives! For we saw Him, even on the right hand of God; and we heard the voice bearing record that He is the Only Begotten of the Father— That by Him, and through Him, and of Him, the worlds are and were created, and the inhabitants thereof are begotten sons and daughters unto God. (D&C 76:22-24)

Once again, we have the clearest possible statement that Jesus Christ is the Savior of the entire multiverse. He created every mortal world upon which the children of heaven now reside. They know of Him. They all must choose for themselves if they will follow Him. If they so choose, it is by Him and Him alone that they become begotten sons and daughters unto God. Once more, this speaks of the true manner in which we become the children of God, with a capital "G." Every one of us is a child of heavenly parents. Our parents became God's begotten sons and daughters in the same manner that now lies before us. They overcame the trials and challenges of mortality and did so through their Savior, and we will do so through ours. There is never more than one Savior, just as there is never more than one Supreme Father and one Holy Ghost, who together comprise the Godhead. I believe that this is the true meaning behind Joseph's astonishing proclamation.

We return to the revelation:

> And this we saw also, and bear record, that an angel of God who was in authority in the presence of God, who rebelled against the Only Begotten Son whom the Father loved and who was in the bosom of the Father, was thrust down from the presence of God and the Son, and was called Perdition, for the heavens wept over him—he was Lucifer, a son of the morning.

> And we beheld, and lo, he is fallen! is fallen, even a son of the morning! And while we were yet in the Spirit, the Lord commanded us that we should write the vision; for we beheld Satan, that old serpent, even the devil, who rebelled against God, and sought to take the kingdom of our God and his Christ—Wherefore, he maketh war with the saints of God, and encompasseth them round about.

And we saw a vision of the sufferings of those with whom he made war and overcame, for thus came the voice of the Lord unto us: Thus saith the Lord concerning all those who know my power, and have been made partakers thereof, and suffered themselves through the power of the devil to be overcome, and to deny the truth and defy My power—They are they who are the sons of perdition, of whom I say that it had been better for them never to have been born; for they are vessels of wrath, doomed to suffer the wrath of God, with the devil and his angels in eternity; concerning whom I have said there is no forgiveness in this world nor in the world to come—

Having denied the Holy Spirit after having received it, and having denied the Only Begotten Son of the Father, having crucified Him unto themselves and put Him to an open shame. These are they who shall go away into the lake of fire and brimstone, with the devil and his angels— And the only ones on whom the second death shall have any power; yea, verily, the only ones who shall not be redeemed in the due time of the Lord, after the sufferings of His wrath. For all the rest shall be brought forth by the resurrection of the dead, through the triumph and the glory of the Lamb, who was slain, who was in the bosom of the Father before the worlds were made.

And this is the gospel, the glad tidings, which the voice out of the heavens bore record unto us— That He came into the world, even Jesus, to be crucified for the world, and to bear the sins of the world, and to sanctify the world, and to cleanse it from all unrighteousness; that through Him all might be saved whom the Father had put into His power and made by Him; Who glorifies the Father, and saves all the works of His hands, except those sons of perdition who deny the Son after the Father has revealed Him.

Wherefore, He saves all except them—they shall go away into everlasting punishment, which is endless punishment, which is eternal punishment, to reign with the devil and his angels in eternity, where their worm dieth not, and the fire is not quenched, which is their torment— And the end thereof, neither the place thereof, nor their torment, no man knows; neither was it revealed, neither is, neither will be revealed unto man, except to them who are made partakers thereof; nevertheless, I, the Lord, show it by vision unto many, but straightway shut it up again; wherefore, the end, the width, the height, the depth, and the misery thereof, they understand not, neither any man except those who are ordained unto this condemnation. And we heard the voice, saying: Write the vision, for lo, this is the end of the vision of the sufferings of the ungodly. (D&C 76: 25-49)

The passage above is at complete odds with traditional Christianity. According to the doctrines of men, all who die without knowledge of Christ are destined to languish in Hell for all eternity. According to the vision of Joseph Smith and Sidney Rigdon, nothing could be further from the truth. Furthermore, Joseph and Sidney's words are validated by the teachings of the Book of Enoch, which profess that God will give His children every opportunity to repent. Even those who will rise up in open rebellion against Him, as Lucifer did, will have an opportunity to view the horror of the infernal pit of outer darkness at the burning edge of all things. There, they will languish for ten thousand years. Yet, there is a purpose in their suffering. These rejected their Savior and, like Satan, sought to supplant Him. Yet, God will listen to their heavenly parents, who love them, and sue for their children night and day before His throne so they are not cast off forever.

They will not be cast off. However, because they rebelled against Christ and sought His kingdom, as did Lucifer, they must pay the price of their own sins. As inconceivable as it may seem, a very small few will still choose the horrors of outer darkness over a kingdom of glory. These will be resurrected and will reign in outer darkness over Satan and his angels, for they will have resurrected bodies, and Satan and His minions will not. Therefore, those who were the worst amongst us will become the kings and queens of hell, and Satan and his followers will be subjected to them, whom they created through their own lies and deceptions. These will be the only ones who will be worse off for having opted into the Father's plan of salvation.

The prospect of this terrible fate caused the Lady and many others like her to opt out of the Father's Plan of Salvation. They knew who they were, and they would not risk mortality. As such, they will forever be above those in outer darkness. It is an astounding vision; if Joseph is to be believed, it is a fraction of what he truly witnessed. While this speaks to the abject darkness that has engulfed certain entities throughout the cosmos, it also speaks of God's incredible mercy and love. That God will reward the children of heaven to the utmost of His abilities, according to the works and laws they have been willing to abide. Beyond this, the Lord will not do, lest the multiverse be plagued by supervillains of unchained power and reckless abandon. Thus, we see that the ability to wield the true power of the cosmos is reserved for those who have proven that they will put the will of the Lord and their fellow man before their own. God the Father values the agency of the children of heaven far too much to enable dark and loathsome entities to subject others to their wills in perpetuity.

Joseph's vision continues:

> And again we bear record—for we saw and heard, and this is the testimony of the gospel of Christ concerning them who shall come forth in the resurrection of the just—They are they who received the testimony of Jesus, and believed on His name and were baptized after the manner of His burial, being buried in the water in His name, and this according to the commandment which He has given— That by keeping the commandments they might be washed and cleansed from all their sins, and receive the Holy Spirit by the laying on of the hands of him who is ordained and sealed unto this power; and who overcome by faith, and <u>are sealed by the Holy Spirit of promise,</u> **which the Father sheds forth** upon all those who are just and true. (D&C 76:50-53)

Joseph speaks of the polar opposites of those who become the Sons of Perdition. Those who inherit outer darkness are those who continue to rebel against the Godhead despite having witnessed the horrors of outer darkness. Those who will become Celestial beings, on the other hand, are those who receive the testimony of Jesus Christ. By this, we are to understand that these learned of the Father's Hidden Son by being taught by the Holy Ghost. As such, these dared to go against the grain and to be baptized and receive the Holy Spirit by the laying on of hand by one with authority to do so. These then overcome the world through their faith in Jesus Christ. Not the Christ whom the world teaches, but the Christ of whom the Father teaches.

This is a fundamental fact to understand. The Father is at the helm of the Plan of Salvation. While there are men with the authority to perform sacred ordinances on the earth today, those ordinances are of no effect until they have been ratified by the Father's seal. This seal is the Holy Spirit of Promise. When the scriptures speak of the seal of God being placed upon the righteous, they speak of this. This seal ratifies and seals the ordinances of the restoration. Without this seal, it is as if the ordinances were never performed. Many have received the ordinances of the gospel throughout time. Far fewer have had the Father seal those ordinances upon them.

There have been some who have speculated that the Father can place this seal upon His children through the medium of the Spirit and nothing more. I do not dare prescribe what God can and cannot do, for He is God, the Almighty, and for Him, nothing is impossible. That being said, there is a pattern within the scriptures that speaks of this seal being placed by the servants of God under His guidance and command. Consider three examples:

1) **Ezekiel 9:4-6**And the LORD said unto [*His servant*], Go through the midst of the city, through the midst of Jerusalem, and set a mark upon the <u>foreheads</u> of the men that sigh and that cry for all the abominations that be done in the midst thereof. And to the others He said in mine hearing, Go ye after him through the city, and smite: let not your eye spare, neither have ye pity: slay utterly old and young, both maids, and little children, and women: but come not near any man upon whom is the mark; and <u>begin</u> at my sanctuary.

In the example above, the Lord sent six angels to Jerusalem. One of these angels placed a mark, or seal, upon the righteous, who bemoaned the sins of Israel. The other five angels marked all others for destruction, every man, woman, and child. Whereas I do not believe that the passage above is speaking of a literal marking on the forehead with a physical inkhorn, it is clear that the subsequent salvation or destruction of the inhabitants of Jerusalem was quite literal. I find the fact that this event began at the Lord's House and spread out from there to be reminiscent of the destruction of the last days. We are told that this destruction will begin at the Lord's house amongst those who have professed to know Him but have blasphemed His name. This suggests a very similar marking will take place in our day.

2) **Revelation 7:2-3** And I saw another angel ascending from the east, having the seal of the living God: and he cried with a loud voice to the four angels, to whom it was given to hurt the earth and the sea, saying, Hurt not the earth, neither the sea, nor the trees, till we have sealed the servants of our God in their foreheads.

The passage above speaks of the sealing of the 144,000, which took place in the sixth seal of the book of Revelation. Whether literally or spiritually symbolic, it is clear that God knew and sealed specific individuals unto a specific ordinance pertaining to the last days' events.

3) D&C 132:19-20. And again, verily I say unto you, if a man marry a wife by my word, which is my law, and by the new and everlasting

covenant, and **it is sealed unto them by the Holy Spirit of promise, by him who is anointed, unto whom I have appointed this power and the keys of this priesthood**; and it shall be said unto them—Ye shall come forth in the first resurrection; and if it be after the first resurrection, in the next resurrection; and shall inherit thrones, kingdoms, principalities, and powers, dominions, all heights and depths—then shall it be written in the Lamb's Book of Life, that he shall commit no murder whereby to shed innocent blood, and if ye abide in my covenant, and commit no murder whereby to shed innocent blood, it shall be done unto them in all things whatsoever my servant hath put upon them, in time, and through all eternity; and shall be of full force when they are out of the world; and they shall pass by the angels, and the gods, which are set there, to their exaltation and glory in all things, as hath been sealed upon their heads, which glory shall be a fulness and a continuation of the seeds forever and ever. Then shall they be gods.

The passage above is the most explicit example of this sealing ordinance I have found in the scriptures. It speaks of an ordinance that takes place with both a man and a woman. The ordinance is performed by a physical servant of God with the authority to carry out the ordinance. This ordinance itself constitutes the Holy Spirit of Promise and is also called the Second Anointing. It is alluded to in the temples of God but is not explained there. The fact that such is the case clearly indicates that this ordinance is sacred. As such, those who would learn of such sacred things should learn of them from God not from men, particularly from apostates. Suffice it to say that I have come to believe that this ordinance is associated with the ordinance wherein Christ washed His disciples' feet, and most likely, those of their respective spouses as well, for one does not attain godhood alone.

We return now to this incredible revelation, where Joseph continues to expound upon those who will inherit the Celestial Kingdom.

> They are they who are the church of the Firstborn. They are they into whose hands the Father has given all things— They are they who are priests and kings, who have received of His fulness, and of His glory; and are priests of the Most High, after the order of Melchizedek, which was after the order of Enoch, which was after the order of the Only Begotten Son. Wherefore, as it is written, they are gods, even the sons of God— (D&C 76:54-58)

You will have undoubtedly made note of the reference to Enoch above. The Priesthood covenant was made with Enoch before it was made with Melchizedek. It was made with Melchizedek before it was made with Abraham. The priesthood bore and bore the name of these men because of how they treated the covenants they entered into with the Father. We speak of the Abrahamic covenant, but it is also the Covenant of all righteous men who have sought it at the hands of the Father. It is an active covenant, and not a passive one, as the description of these Celestial beings should attest to. These wanted nothing more than to become like the Father and received nothing less. It is ludicrous to believe that those who do not seek such things with their whole souls, as these men did, would receive such an outpouring.

Joseph's explanation of these men and women who attained godhood continues:

> Wherefore, all things are theirs, whether life or death, or things present, or things to come, all are theirs and they are Christ's, and Christ is God's. And they shall overcome all things. Wherefore, let no man glory in man, but rather let him glory in God, who shall subdue all enemies under His feet.
>
> These shall dwell in the presence of God and His Christ forever and ever. These are they whom He shall bring with Him, when he shall come in the clouds of heaven [*Enochian reference*] to reign on the earth over His people. These are they who shall have part in the first resurrection. These are they who shall come forth in the resurrection of the just.
>
> These are they who are come unto Mount Zion, and unto the city of the living God, the heavenly place, the holiest of all. These are they who have come to an innumerable company of angels, to the general assembly and church of Enoch, and of the Firstborn. (D&C 76:59-67)

Here, Joseph explains that those who become gods are those who will become part of the innumerable company of angels that surround the throne of God. This is that same multitude which Enoch saw and bore a record of petitioning the Lord on the behalf of their children, whether they were righteous or wicked. To this host, Joseph added the Church of Enoch. By this, we are to understand the assembly of Enoch or the people of Enoch. These are the hosts of translated beings that have sought and obtained the City of Enoch throughout this Earth's history. This includes Melchizedek, his people, and many of the souls that Abraham and his wife converted along the way. These obtained the city of Enoch, while Abraham and Sarah remained upon the Earth that we might descend from them. If we obtain the Celestial Kingdom, we will be there with people of this caliber.

> These are they whose names are written in heaven, where God and Christ are the judge of all. These are they who are just men made perfect through Jesus the mediator of the new covenant, who wrought out this perfect atonement through the shedding of His own blood. These are they whose bodies are celestial, whose glory is that of the sun, even the glory of God, the highest of all, whose glory the sun of the firmament is written of as being typical. (D&C 76:68-70)

Joseph concludes his description of the gods of the Celestial Kingdom by stating that their physical bodies were Celestialized. By this, we are to understand that there are differences between the physical bodies of resurrected beings themselves. A Celestial body is more capable than a terrestrial body, and a terrestrial body is more capable than a telestial body. Inherent within these bodies is the ability to transverse the kingdoms of the multiverse. Only Celestial bodies can enter the Kingdom of God unless they are brought there by the power of Himself – who can do everything.

As has already been discussed at length, these obtain their bodies from Jesus Christ and by the power of His atonement, wrought by the shedding of His own blood. As such, Christ becomes their Father, and they become His heir to His kingdom. Therefore, they are like Him in that they, too, are gods. This is the greatest potential that the human family can aspire to. For such mighty entities such as these, nothing will be impossible. To these, the multiverse is truly an open door, and to none else. To these, the elements will joyfully obey. At the word of these, worlds will form and dissolve. By these, the kingdoms of mortal men will be replenished for the next iteration of the Father's never-ending plan of happiness and every subsequent iteration after that.

Joseph now describes the inhabitants of the terrestrial world:

> And again, we saw the terrestrial world, and behold and lo, these are they who are of the terrestrial, whose glory differs from that of the church of the Firstborn who have received the fulness of the Father, even as that of the moon differs from the sun in the firmament. Behold, these are they who died without law; and also they who are the spirits of men kept in prison, whom the Son visited, and preached the gospel unto them, that they might be judged according to

men in the flesh [*an Enochian doctrine*]; who received not the testimony of Jesus in the flesh, but afterwards received it. These are they who are honorable men of the earth, who were blinded by the craftiness of men. (D&C 76:71-75)

This passage classifies those who died without the law or without receiving the testimony of Christ as being Terrestrial. By this, we are to understand that there is little difference between those who did not know of Christ at all and those who had an incorrect idea of Him. The only concept of Jesus Christ that matters is that which is taught by the Father via the administration of the Holy Ghost. The Father will testify to His children of His Hidden Son, but those who would be valiant in that testimony must go against the grain of society.

Therefore, in every generation of time, those who have accepted the Father's Hidden Son have done so to the shame and scorn of the world. It is the case today, and it has always been the case. The opinions of men keep many from accepting the gospel of Christ while in mortality. Yet, the conditions for accepting the Father's teaching concerning His Hidden Son are far greater in the Spirit World than they are on Earth.

As the Book of Enoch teaches, Christ went and administered to those in the Spirit World. As such, they know of Him. Other religions exist in the Spirit World. Many who have died believing in reincarnation will be even more convinced of their beliefs. It will still take faith for people to believe in the Hidden Son because He will still be hidden. If it were not so, there would be no need for faith. Yet, there is no doubt that many more will accept Jesus Christ for who He actually is in the Spirit World than upon the Earth. The true Church of Jesus Christ will be far more common there than here. The omnipresence of the church is one of the main things that will make it so much more acceptable to the masses. The many touch points people will have had with the Church in mortality will resonate more fully with them there.

Joseph's description of this classification of resurrected beings continues:

> These are they who receive of His glory, but not of His fulness. These are they who receive of the presence of the Son, but not of the fulness of the Father. Wherefore, they are bodies terrestrial, and not bodies celestial, and differ in glory as the moon differs from the sun. (D&C 76:76-78)

Note that once again, Joseph classifies the beings of the Terrestrial world by the class of resurrected bodies they have obtained. It is a lesser form than their Celestial counterparts. Nevertheless, they are incredible beings of light, power, and majesty.

Joseph further explains why these fell short of a higher kingdom of glory – that of the Celestial worlds.

> These are they who are not valiant in the testimony of Jesus; wherefore, they obtain not the crown over the kingdom of our God. And now this is the end of the vision which we saw of the terrestrial, that the Lord commanded us to write while we were yet in the Spirit. (D&C 76:79-80)

Those resurrected with terrestrial bodies were not valiant in their testimony of Christ. By this, we are to understand that when they had to choose between acting on the promptings of the Holy Ghost or the ways of men, they chose the world. If they did act upon the Holy Ghost, they did not do so consistently. Terrestrial beings were overcome by the cares and perceptions of men in mortality, while Celestial beings were willing to bear the world's cross for the truth's sake. I have seen this many times in my life: good men and women receiving confirmation of the truthfulness of the gospel and then rejecting it because of the opinions of their friends and family. Terrestrial beings would rather offend the Hidden Son than the visible world around them. They will stand for convenient truths, but they will wither under the mocking crowds in the great and spacious buildings of the world. This is what is meant to not be valiant in one's testimony of Christ.

This concludes Joseph's vision of the terrestrial world, yet we will receive more insights into this and other kingdoms as his vision progresses.

> And again, we saw the glory of the telestial, which glory is that of the lesser, even as the glory of the stars differs from that of the glory of the moon in the firmament. These are they who received not the gospel of Christ, neither the testimony of Jesus. These are they who deny not the Holy Spirit. These are they who are thrust down to hell. These are they who shall not be redeemed from the devil until the last resurrection, until the Lord, even Christ the Lamb, shall have finished His work.
>
> These are they who receive not of His fulness in the eternal world, but of the Holy Spirit through the ministration of the terrestrial; and the terrestrial through the ministration of the celestial. And also the telestial receive it of the administering of angels who are appointed to minister for them, or who are

appointed to be ministering spirits for them; for they shall be heirs of salvation. And thus we saw, in the heavenly vision, the glory of the telestial, which surpasses all understanding; and no man knows it except him to whom God has revealed it. (D&C 76:81-90)

In the passages above, we receive confirmation of many of the concepts put forward in this volume. We learn of the one-way separation between the kingdoms of glory. Beings of a higher kingdom can enter lower kingdoms of glory and minister to their inhabitants. However, Telestial beings cannot enter the Terrestrial plain, nor can Terrestrial beings enter the Celestial realm. I believe that this is because glory can be moderated or reduced on demand, but it cannot be increased beyond the level endowed upon the recipient by God. As such, while there are most definitely places where beings of lower orders cannot go, there are certainly common-ground worlds where Celestial, Terrestrial, and Telestial beings can interact together.

We also learn in the passages above that the beings of a Telestial order received not Jesus Christ. This means that they did not receive Him in life, nor did they receive Him in the Spirit World. As such, His atonement was of no effect in their lives. These are they who were cast down into Hell, meaning the burning mountain range at the edge of all things, where they atone for their own sins. Yet, after a great while, these will be purged of their impurities, become servants of the Most High, and be given an endowment of power. These beings and the kingdom they reside in will be glorious beyond description.

The beings of a Telestial order will excel in all aspects, the disembodied spirits of the lesser kingdoms inhabited by those who opted not to participate in the Father's plan of salvation. The only ones for whom it can truly say that it would have been better for them had they never been born are those who will become the Sons of Perdition. These will descend below all, including their premortal peers who opted not to participate in the Father's plan. Yet, with resurrected bodies, they will reign in Outer Darkness over Lucifer and the fallen, what little consolation that might be.

The vision continues:

> And thus we saw the glory of the Terrestrial which excels in all things the glory of the Telestial, even in glory, and in power, and in might, and in dominion. And thus we saw the glory of the Celestial, which excels in all things—where God, even the Father, reigns upon His throne forever and

ever; before whose throne all things bow in humble reverence, and give Him glory forever and ever.

They who dwell in His presence are the Church of the Firstborn; and they see as they are seen, and know as they are known, having received of His fulness and of His grace; and He makes them equal in power, and in might, and in dominion. (D&C 76:91-95)

This is an astounding concept! The God of heaven will magnify the faithful with such an exceedingly great endowment of power and glory that they will become as He is. That is to say, they will obtain the full measure of their creation and become gods. As such, these glorified men and women will desire the next generation. They will become Heavenly Fathers and Mothers. They will raise up posterity in blissful conditions over eons of time. They will rejoice and have a fullness of joy in their posterity. For while their children will be able to choose for themselves what kingdom of glory they will obtain, there is no place in the multiverse where heavenly children are beyond the reach of heavenly parents.

And the glory of the Celestial is one, even as the glory of the sun is one. And the glory of the Terrestrial is one, even as the glory of the moon is one. And the glory of the Telestial is one, even as the glory of the stars is one; for as one star differs from another star in glory, even so differs one from another in glory in the telestial world; for these are they who are of Paul, and of Apollos, and of Cephas.

These are they who say they are some of one and some of another—some of Christ and some of John, and some of Moses, and some of Elias, and some of Esaias, and some of Isaiah, and some of Enoch; but received not the gospel, neither the testimony of Jesus, neither the prophets, neither the everlasting covenant.

Last of all, these all are they who will not be gathered with the saints, to be caught up unto the Church of the Firstborn, and received into the cloud. These are they who are liars, and sorcerers, and adulterers, and whoremongers, and whosoever loves and makes a lie. These are they who suffer the wrath of God on earth. These are they who suffer the vengeance of eternal fire [*the burning mountain range at the edge of all things*]. These are they who are cast down to Hell and suffer the wrath of Almighty God, until the fulness of times, when Christ shall have subdued all enemies under His feet, and shall have perfected His work; when He shall deliver up the kingdom, and present it unto the Father, spotless, saying: I have overcome and have trodden the wine-press alone, even the wine-press of the fierceness of the wrath of Almighty God. (D&C 76:96-107)

Here again, we learn about the nature of the beings of the Telestial worlds. These are called liars, sorcerers, adulterers, and whoremongers because they did not repent of their sins but rather wrought their own atonements in forges of Eternal Fire at the burning edge of the great pit that houses perdition itself. These subscribed to the doctrines of men and would not be swayed from them in life or in death. Therefore, having never accepted the enabling atonement of Christ, these are damned in their progression to the manner of salvation that their own works could bring to pass. Therefore, they are called after the philosophies to which they subscribed; some follow the world's version of Christ rather than that of the Hidden Son. Some patterned their beliefs after the erroneous teachings of important men, Apollos, Enoch, Moses, etc. Yet, there has only ever been one way back to the presence of the Father, and that is the Son of Man.

The Vision now turns to the grand conclusion of the Father's plan of Salvation when all have received the portion they were willing to receive.

> Then shall [*Christ*] be crowned with the crown of His glory,
> to sit on the throne of His power to reign forever and ever.
> (D&C 76:108)

Now the Son, having completed all His Father entrusted to Him, takes His place on His Father's Throne. Now, the Son becomes the Father, and He will oversee the next iteration of the great Eternal Plan of Happiness. He will oversee the process of the redemption of our heavenly children. Thus, they will have the same opportunities we had, and everything will become new. Our Father will then ascend into the Mount of the Congregation, upon the sides of the North, where He will join His Father, and His Father's Father, in an unbroken line through time. These are the great Patriarchs, and they will always be before us, and we before them.

Now, Joseph and Sidney provide a fascinating census of the eternal worlds:

But behold, and lo, we saw the glory and the inhabitants of the telestial world, that they were as innumerable as the stars in the firmament of heaven, or as the sand upon the seashore; and heard the voice of the Lord saying: These all shall bow the knee, and every tongue shall confess to Him who sits upon the throne forever and ever; for they shall be judged according to their works, and every man shall receive according to his own works, his own dominion, in the mansions which are prepared; and they shall be servants of the Most High; but where God and Christ dwell they cannot come, worlds without end. (D&C 76:109)

Joseph and Sidney saw that those who would atone for their own sins were an innumerable host. These are those who traveled the broad and easy road. Yet, its destination was anything but easy. These bore the weight of their own sins, and in the end, they finally see things as they really are. In the end, these, too, will know the Hidden Son, for He will be hidden from them no longer.

However, the passage above states that the inhabitants of this kingdom will never be able to enter the Celestial Kingdom. Where God and Christ are, they cannot come. Yet, God and Christ can travel to them. Thus, we see that man can never make of himself what God can make of him. Therefore, the inhabitant of the heavens and of the Earth must turn to God and look to Him for redemption, for He is mighty to save.

You will note that no such proclamation was pronounced upon the beings of the Terrestrial world. I believe that this is because such beings were redeemed through the atonement. As such, it is my opinion that these, through the process of time and perhaps the passage of many future cycles, may eventually be able to advance into the Celestial Kingdom in the process of Eternal Progression. I suspect that the process whereby Terrestrial material is transformed into Celestial material is gradual and prolonged, such as when coal becomes a diamond. How much easier it is to undergo this transformation on this side of the veil by following the Holy Spirit's promptings and discarding man's opinions and concerns.

Now Joseph concludes his incredible Enochian vision:

This is the end of the vision which we saw, which we were commanded to write while we were yet in the Spirit. But great and marvelous are the works of the Lord, and the mysteries of his kingdom which He showed unto us, which surpass all understanding in glory, and in might, and in dominion; which He commanded us we should not write while we were yet in the Spirit, and are not lawful for man to utter; neither is man capable to make them known, for they are only to be seen and understood by the power of the Holy Spirit, which God bestows on those who love Him, and purify themselves before Him; to whom He grants this privilege of seeing and knowing for themselves; that through the power and manifestation of the Spirit, while in the flesh, they may be able to bear His presence in the world of glory. And to God and the Lamb be glory, and honor, and dominion forever and ever. Amen. (D&C 76:113-119)

Here, we learn that Joseph and Sidney saw things they were not permitted to write but that God had shown unto others. I believe Enoch was one of the men God showed these things to. Volumes I and II of this series have largely focused on this incredible vision that Enoch witnessed and recorded. Yet, Enoch's writings are nearly impossible to understand without the light of the restored gospel of Jesus Christ. Yet, in conjunction with the restoration and guidance of the Holy Ghost, they are understandable and astounding. They speak of God's kindness, mercy, and long suffering on a scale that is unfathomable to the Christian world. They speak of a God, and gods, who are for us and not against us. They are advocating on our behalf and will move both heaven and earth for the sake of our salvation. God will greatly magnify our efforts on this side of the veil when all we do is done through hope, faith, and personal revelation.

Chapter 25: The House of God D&C 109

In the prior chapter, we reviewed the Lord's incredible vision to Joseph Smith and Sidney Rigdon, which mirrored Enoch's own vision of the Father's great plan of salvation. That vision was given in 1832. The next modern revelation with the Enochian marker would not come for another four years and would correspond with the dedicatory prayer of the Kirtland temple. Just yesterday, the Church announced that it had purchased the Kirtland Temple from the Community of Christ. Therefore, for the first time since this revelation was given, the Kirtland Temple is back in the hands of the original Church.

The Kirtland Temple is a monument of faith and the legacy of our forefathers, who built it in their extreme poverty. As such, it symbolizes placing the Kingdom of God first. While this section comprises the dedicatory prayer for the Kirtland Temple, Joseph stated that he received this prayer by revelation. Therefore, the fact that the first Temple dedication bore the Enochian marker is significant. As such, consider the words of this revelation regarding your usage of the Lord's Holy Houses that now dot the land.

The dedicatory prayer begins as follows:

> Thanks be to thy name, O Lord God of Israel, who keepest covenant and showest mercy unto Thy servants who walk uprightly before Thee, with all their hearts— Thou who hast commanded Thy servants to build a house to Thy name in this place [Kirtland]. And now Thou beholdest, O Lord, that Thy servants have done according to Thy commandment.
>
> And now we ask Thee, Holy Father, in the name of Jesus Christ, the Son of Thy bosom, in whose name alone salvation can be administered to the children of men, we ask Thee, O Lord, to accept of this house, the workmanship of the hands of us, Thy servants, which Thou didst command us to build.
>
> For thou knowest that we have done this work through great tribulation; and out of our poverty we have given of our substance to build a house to Thy name, that the Son of Man might have a place to manifest Himself to His people. (D&C 109:1-5)

Through the law of tithing, the treasuries of the Church of Jesus Christ of Latter-day Saints have been magnified beyond belief. The Church now has hundreds of billions of dollars. Yet it was not always so. The early temples of the church were built from tremendous sacrifice, and the Kirtland was the first of these. According to this revelation, the primary purpose of the very first temple of the modern age was to facilitate the manifestation of the Father's Hidden Christ to His people. If we are to know the Son of Man, we must come to Him. The Houses of God facilitate this journey.

Yet, hundreds of thousands of Saints literally live within the eyesight of numerous temples and yet go months or even years without entering such magnificent structures. These have allowed the world to shape their views of what happens within these holy structures rather than seeking to be taught of them by the Lord. Temples have always been peculiar places, yet the Lord's people have always been peculiar people. God's ways are not the world's ways. Rather than condemning what is not understood, would it not be better to acknowledge your ignorance before the Lord? Only by doing so can you empty your glass of its preconceived worldly notions and allow the Father to fill it anew with His understanding.

There is the same hidden beauty within the Temples of God as there is within the Father's Hidden Son. Such is not obvious to the world, but temples are not part of this world, and nor should they be the mindsets of those who attend them. Those who seek to find the Father's Hidden Son within the Holy Temples will find Him—those who do not, will not. Most of the House of Israel traveled to the temple in Jerusalem for cultural purposes because of the traditions of their Fathers. Yet some traveled to the Temple because it was the House of God, and there the blind received sight, and the deaf learned to hear the Lord. Not much has changed in the last two thousand years in this regard.

The prayer continues:

> And as thou hast said in a revelation, given to us, calling us
> thy friends, saying—Call your solemn assembly, as I have
> commanded you; (D&C 109:6)

In the passage above, Joseph speaks concerning the Lord's command for the saints to call a solemn assembly from a prior revelation. The revelation to which Joseph was referring is D&C 88, and the context for the command to call a solemn assembly is the great and terrible day of the Lord. Consider the following:

> For not many days hence and the earth shall tremble and reel
> to and fro as a drunken man; and the sun shall hide his face,

and shall refuse to give light; and the moon shall be bathed in blood; and the stars shall become exceedingly angry, and shall cast themselves down as a fig that falleth from off a fig tree. And after your testimony cometh wrath and indignation upon the people. For after your testimony cometh the testimony of earthquakes, that shall cause groanings in the midst of her, and men shall fall upon the ground and shall not be able to stand. And also cometh the testimony of the voice of thundering, and the voice of lightnings, and the voice of tempests, and the voice of the waves of the sea heaving themselves beyond their bounds. And all things shall be in commotion; and surely, men's hearts shall fail them; for fear shall come upon all people.

Therefore, verily I say unto you, my friends, call your solemn assembly, as I have commanded you. And as all have not faith, seek ye diligently and teach one another words of wisdom; yea, seek ye out of the best books words of wisdom; seek learning, even by study and also by faith. Organize yourselves; prepare every needful thing; and establish a house, even a house of prayer, a house of fasting, a house of faith, a house of learning, a house of glory, a house of order, a house of God; That your incomings may be in the name of the Lord; that your outgoings may be in the name of the Lord; that all your salutations may be in the name of the Lord, with uplifted hands unto the Most High. (D&C 88:87-91; 117-120)

Clearly, the Lord's purpose for having the Saints call their solemn assemblies is due to the calamities that will befall the earth on the great and terrible day of the Lord. Curiously, because not all people have the same skills in faith, that is to say, the same kinds of spiritual gifts, the Lord commands His people to search the best books for words of wisdom. By this, we are to understand that there will be books written that might not be scriptural cannons but that will help even the weakest of saints understand the context of events around them. Yet, for the wisdom in these books to be beneficial, they must be sought out and read. By the understanding and knowledge found in such books, the Lord explains that His people will focus less on the world and more on Him. In the words of our prophet, we will think Celestial.

The context of our latter-day solemn assemblies is consistent with ancient practices. Solemn assemblies were first introduced in the Old Testament to unite the people in fasting and prayer for deliverance. Such assemblies were typically associated with temples. Joel, who uses the term more than another Old Testament prophet, associates solemn assemblies with his prophecies of the last days' events and with the deliverance of the saints from otherwise certain destruction.

Both the first and second chapters of Joel's writings speak of the day when the Lord will send His army to make an utter end to the wicked by fire. No weapon formed by men prospers against the Lord's host, and His army renders the cities of the Gentiles utterly desolate. In both Joel's revelations, the Lord's people have been cut off from their temples and are in a period of great distress. As such, Joel calls upon them to hold a solemn assembly that the Lord might have mercy upon them and spare them. Consider the desperate circumstances under which Joel calls the latter-day saints to hold their solemn assemblies:

> Gird yourselves, and lament, ye priests: howl, ye ministers of the altar: come, lie all night in sackcloth, ye ministers of my God: for the meat offering and the drink offering is withholden from the house of your God. Sanctify ye a fast, call a solemn assembly, gather the elders and all the inhabitants of the land into the house of the Lord your God, and cry unto the Lord, Alas for the day! for the day of the Lord is at hand, and as a destruction from the Almighty shall it come. (Joel 1:13-14)

And

> Blow the trumpet in Zion, sanctify a fast, call a solemn assembly: Gather the people, sanctify the congregation, assemble the elders, gather the children, and those that suck the breasts: let the bridegroom go forth of his chamber, and the bride out of her closet. Let the priests, the ministers of the Lord, weep between the porch and the altar, and let them say, Spare thy people, O Lord, and give not thine heritage to reproach, that the heathen should rule over them: wherefore should they say among the people, Where is their God? Then will the Lord be jealous for His land, and pity His people.

> And it shall come to pass afterward, that I will pour out my spirit upon all flesh; and your sons and your daughters shall prophesy, your old men shall dream dreams, your young men

shall see visions: and also upon the servants and upon the handmaids in those days will I pour out my spirit.

And I will shew wonders in the heavens and in the earth, blood, and fire, and pillars of smoke. The sun shall be turned into darkness, and the moon into blood, before the great and the terrible day of the Lord come. And it shall come to pass, that whosoever shall call on the name of the Lord shall be delivered: for in mount Zion and in Jerusalem shall be deliverance, as the Lord hath said, and in the remnant whom the Lord shall call. (Joel 2:15-18, 28-31)

In both of these prophecies, the people of the Lord are facing total destruction and have been cut off from their temples. As such, they join their faith together in a solemn assembly to call upon the Lord for deliverance. Curiously, the saints find their deliverance in the REMNANT WHOM THE LORD SHALL CALL. This is most certainly the Remnant of Jacob, whom the Lord said would come in His incredible sermon on the topic in 3rd Nephi.

As such, these events are clearly associated with the Great and Terrible Day of the Lord and the Second Coming of Jesus Christ. As such, there can be little doubt that great trials lay ahead of us. Elsewhere in prophecy, we learned that these trials will begin amongst the Lord's people in America. From America, they will spread throughout the whole world, where they will culminate in Jerusalem. Is there any wonder why the Lord commanded us to seek knowledge from the best books regarding this subject?

Indeed, as the Revelation continues, Joseph cites this commandment from the Lord once more.

And as all have not faith, seek ye diligently and teach one another words of wisdom; yea, seek ye out of the best books words of wisdom, seek learning even by study and also by faith; Organize yourselves; prepare every needful thing, and establish a house, even a house of prayer, a house of fasting, a house of faith, a house of learning, a house of glory, a house of order, a house of God; That your incomings may be in the name of the Lord, that your outgoings may be in the name of the Lord, that all your salutations may be in the name of the Lord, with uplifted hands unto the Most High— (D&C 109:7-9)

Clearly, the Lord intends us to take responsibility for our spiritual education by seeking out these books ourselves. Too many wish to hide behind the coattails of the prophets, relegating to them the responsibility for their own spiritual education. Yet this commandment was given to the Saints as individuals, not as a collective. Similarly, the Lord commanded His people to study the words of Isaiah. If you have considered the Come Follow Me manual on Isaiah, it is clear that if you are to understand Isaiah's words, it will not be from that manual. You must seek out knowledge from the best books yourself. How will you know what the best books are? The same way you know the truthfulness of all things through the promptings of the Holy Ghost. If you pick up a book on the words of Isaiah or any other subject for that matter, and it teaches things that do not reconcile with the scriptures, set it down and leave it. Don't waste time on books that are not accompanied by the Spirit.

The dedicatory prayer continues:

> And now, Holy Father, we ask Thee to assist us, Thy people, with Thy grace, in calling our solemn assembly, that it may be done to Thine honor and to Thy divine acceptance; and in a manner that we may be found worthy, in Thy sight, to secure a fulfilment of the promises which Thou hast made unto us, Thy people, in the revelations given unto us; that Thy glory may rest down upon Thy people, and upon this Thy house, which we now dedicate to Thee, that it may be sanctified and consecrated to be holy, and that Thy holy presence may be continually in this house; and that all people who shall enter upon the threshold of the Lord's house may feel Thy power, and feel constrained to acknowledge that thou hast sanctified it, and that it is Thy house, a place of Thy holiness.
>
> And do Thou grant, Holy Father, that all those who shall worship in this house **may be taught words of wisdom out of the best books**, and **that they may seek learning even by study**, and **also by faith**, as Thou hast said; and that they may grow up in Thee, and **receive a fulness of the Holy Ghost**, and be organized according to Thy laws, and **be prepared to obtain every needful thing**. (D&C 109:10-15)

In the passages above, Joseph Smith associated temple worship with the ability to be taught wisdom from the best books and seek learning by study and faith. I served as an ordinance working in the Draper, Utah, and Franklin, TN temples for ten years. Most of my books were written during this period of my life. One of the many highlights of this experience was talking with sealers in the temple. Unlike ordinance workers, sealers are actively encouraged to answer any gospel-related questions that folks attending the temple might have. As such, I would take every opportunity to speak with them.

I was amazed by the depth of knowledge many of these sealers had obtained regarding the covenants and promises the Lord had made with the House of Israel. Four of the sealers that I spoke with were also Patriarchs, and they were the most insightful. In these special discussions, one such man explained how to decipher the meaning behind the Nashville Temple's Celestial room windows. They symbolize the restoration of the House of Israel, coming together as three separate bodies, each with twelve of their own leaders at their head.

In a separate conversation with a different sealer, who was also a Patriarch, we spoke of the difference between the gathering of Israel and the restoration of the Lost Tribes. This man told me the latter would be much more like a Star Wars movie than people realized. Another sealer confirmed that there was much more to the restoration of the Lost Tribes than most members of the church were prepared or willing to accept. All of these men had come to the same level of understanding that I had. The only way that this could have happened was by learning from the same teacher.

As such, as Joseph noted above, there are numerous ways to obtain wisdom. This is now the third time we have been told to obtain wisdom from the best books. This is significant! It can also be gleaned by study, and it can be obtained by faith. I obtained my understanding of these things using all three of these methods. Many people will need to use only one. Regardless of the method employed, Joseph linked all three with the attendance of the temple. I have found that a diversity of subjects is beneficial in understanding the larger picture of how all truth can be circumscribed into one great whole.

Indeed, the last phrase of the passage above, "Prepared to Obtain Every Needful Thing" became the title of one of my favorite talks from Elder Bednar. In that talk, he states that it is not the Church's responsibility to teach the members everything they must know. Rather, it is the members' responsibility to learn everything they must know through the instruction of the Holy Ghost. If members are not seeking, they are not finding. If they are not finding, they are not being taught by the Spirit. Without the instruction of the Spirit, they are not prepared for what is about to take place on the earth today. According to the passages above, the temple can be a wellspring of revelation. It certainly has been for me!

The revelation continues:

> And that this house may be a house of prayer, a house of fasting, a house of faith, a house of glory and of God, even Thy house; that all the incomings of thy people, into this house, may be in the name of the Lord; that all their outgoings from this house may be in the name of the Lord; and that all their salutations may be in the name of the Lord, with holy hands, uplifted to the Most High; and that no unclean thing shall be permitted to come into Thy house to pollute it; and when Thy people transgress, any of them, they may speedily repent and return unto Thee, and find favor in Thy sight, and be restored to the blessings which thou hast ordained to be poured out upon those who shall reverence Thee in Thy house.
>
> And we ask Thee, Holy Father, that Thy servants may go forth from this house armed with Thy power, and that Thy name may be upon them, and Thy glory be round about them, and Thine angels have charge over them; and from this place they may bear exceedingly great and glorious tidings, in truth, unto the ends of the earth, that they may know that this is Thy work, and that Thou hast put forth Thy hand, to fulfil that which Thou hast spoken by the mouths of the prophets, concerning the last days. (D&C 109:19-23)

In the Kirtland Temple dedicatory prayer, Joseph petitioned the Lord that He would help both the saints and the world to understand the prophecies the Lord has made concerning the last days. Certainly, two of the foremost prophets in this respect are Isaiah and John the Revelator. Nephi explicitly stated that he included the Isaiah chapters that he did to bless the Gentiles in the last days. Nephi specifically stated the following:

> I know that [*his Isaiah chapters*] shall be of great worth unto [*the Gentiles – you and I*] in the last days: for in that day shall they understand them; wherefore, for their good have I written them. (2 Nephi 25:8)

Nephi transcribed the Isaiah chapters for our benefit, yet they have enriched too few of them. Why have they not been enriched by them? Because they do not seek to understand them as they ought. Christ commanded us to study Isaiah's words, and yet we don't. Instead, we look forward to the day when supplemental revelations will be given, such as the sealed visions of the Brother of Jared. Why would the Lord give us more when we have not received the original gift? If you understand the words of Isaiah, you already know what is in the sealed portion of the Book of Mormon. According to Jesus Christ, Isaiah spoke of ALL things. You do not need to wait if you seek to be taught by the Lord now, using the temple to augment and strengthen the Holy Ghost in your life. If this is true for the words of Isaiah, it is also true for the words of John the Revelator. Consider what the Lord told Moroni in conjunction with His command for him to seal up the Brother of Jared's writings:

> Come unto me, O ye Gentiles, and I will show unto you the greater things, the knowledge which is hid up because of unbelief. Come unto me, O ye house of Israel, and it shall be made manifest unto you how great things the Father hath laid up for you, from the foundation of the world; and it hath not come unto you, because of unbelief.
>
> Behold, when ye shall rend that veil of unbelief which doth cause you to remain in your awful state of wickedness, and hardness of heart, and blindness of mind, then shall the great and marvelous things which have been hid up from the foundation of the world from you—yea, when ye shall call upon the Father in My name, with a broken heart and a contrite spirit, then shall ye know that the Father hath remembered the covenant which He made unto your fathers, O house of Israel.
>
> And then shall My revelations which I have caused to be written by my servant John be unfolded in the eyes of all the people. Remember, when ye see these things, ye shall know that the time is at hand that they shall be made manifest in very deed. Therefore, when ye shall receive this record ye may know that the work of the Father has commenced upon all the face of the land. (Ether 4:13-17)

According to Jesus Christ, the Brother of Jared's writings have been held back from the Church because of the Church's own unbelief. What is it that we do not believe? We do not believe that the Lord can help us to understand the words of Isaiah. We do not believe the Lord can help us understand John's writings. We do not believe in the spectacular nature of the Father's covenants with the House of Israel! John's writings speak of these things, just as Isaiah's writings speak of these things, and the Brother of Jared's writings speak of these things. The difference between Mahonri's writings and

Isaiah's and John's is the simplicity in which they were written. Mohonri wrote so simply yet powerfully that it would be impossible not to understand his words. However, the Father held such things back because mortality is a test of the faithfulness of His people.

We can learn of these things just as easily through the writings of John and Isaiah as we can through the sealed portion of the Book of Mormon. We only put in the spiritual effort required to obtain such understanding. Many who now read this book have done just that and rejoice with me in the knowledge the Lord has revealed. Yet, just as with the true nature of His Hidden Son, these things have been held back from the world. If so many of the Saints of God will not receive these things, what chance does the world have of receiving them? In the coming days, God will rend the veil of our unbelief, and we will be forced to acknowledge the shocking reality of the world around us. This reality will cause men's hearts to fail them for fear, for that which they had not considered shall they see.

The Revelation continues:

> We ask Thee, Holy Father, to establish the people that shall worship, and honorably hold a name and standing in this Thy house, to all generations and for eternity; that no weapon formed against them shall prosper; that he who diggeth a pit for them shall fall into the same himself; that no combination of wickedness shall have power to rise up and prevail over Thy people upon whom Thy name shall be put in this house; and if any people shall rise against this people, that Thine anger be kindled against them; and if they shall smite this people Thou wilt smite them; Thou wilt fight for Thy people as thou didst in the day of battle, that they may be delivered from the hands of all their enemies. (D&C 109: 24-28)

In this astonishing plea, Joseph petitioned the Lord to protect the saints from their enemies and to fight for them as He did in antiquity. Some will look at this passage in the context of the saints being driven from Kirtland, Missouri, and Nauvoo, as the Lord ignoring this request. At the same time, we learned earlier that the Lord told the saints long ago that they would not prosper until they were in the mountains. He then said that they would be gathered subsequently to Zion.

In prior chapters, we learned Zion would be purchased with money or redeemed by blood. There will be much more opposition before the end comes. When that end does come, the Lord will answer Joseph's plea. One of the particular things that Joseph asked of the Lord was that no weapon formed against the saints would prosper. When the day of battle comes, the Lord has promised that such would, in fact, be the case. Consider Christ's prophecy concerning this fact:

> Behold, they shall surely gather together against thee, not by Me; whosoever shall gather together against thee shall fall for thy sake.
>
> Behold, I have created the smith that bloweth the coals in the fire, and that bringeth forth an instrument for his work; and I have created the waster to destroy. No weapon that is formed against thee shall prosper; and every tongue that shall revile against thee in judgment thou shalt condemn. This is the heritage of the servants of the Lord, and their righteousness is of me, saith the Lord. (3 Nephi 22:15-17)

This passage speaks of the day when the Remnant of Jacob will come to the assistance of the saints and deliver them from the hands of their oppressors. On that day, the Lord will fight our battles for us. However, until that day comes, He will allow our faith to be tried, and it will be tried sorely. The day will come when the Lord will hear and answer Joseph's prayer, but it is not yet. Joseph's prayer for intervention is very insightful into the coming day's events. Consider it as it continues:

> We ask thee, Holy Father, to confound, and astonish, and to bring to shame and confusion, all those who have spread lying reports abroad, over the world, against thy servant or servants, if they will not repent, when the everlasting gospel shall be proclaimed in their ears; and that all their works may be brought to naught, and be swept away by the hail, and by the judgments which thou wilt send upon them in thine anger, that there may be an end to lyings and slanders against Thy people. For thou knowest, O Lord, that Thy servants have been innocent before Thee in bearing record of Thy name, for which they have suffered these things.
>
> Therefore we plead before thee for a full and complete deliverance from under this yoke; break it off, O Lord; break it off from the necks of Thy servants, by Thy power, that we may rise up in the midst of this generation and do Thy work. (D&C 109:29-33)

Joseph pled for deliverance from the lies and slandering that had plagued him and the saints from the beginning. By this time, Joseph Smith was becoming a name of national reputation. Most of what was told of him was based upon slanderous half-truths. These lies and myths largely continue today. To Joseph, these lies weighed heavily upon him. It was like unto a yoke of bondage, which he earnestly prayed for the Lord to remove from him. The Lord did not do so. He has permitted this yoke to remain in place. Yet the day will come when this yoke will be broken off of the shoulders of the saints.

Today, the Church of Jesus Christ of Latter-day Saints is still mocked and derided by many. It is not seen for what it is. The respect it has garnered seems to stem from the wealth and industry of its members. By every metric I have seen, the Church's resources place it as the wealthiest religious organization on planet Earth. For comparison purposes, the Church of Jesus Christ of Latter-day Saints has some 17 million members today, which is against the Catholic Church's membership of 1.4 billion. As such, for every member of the Church, there are over eighty Catholics. That being said, the financial resources of the Church of Jesus Christ, after less than two hundred years, now exceed those of the Catholic Church.

Furthermore, according to the CIA, the Catholic Church operates at an annual deficit in the tens of millions. In contrast, the Church of Jesus Christ operates at an astounding surplus in the billions annually. The world has come to respect the Church for its resources, not for its doctrine. Yet, how could a church as young as ours have prospered so much in a space of less than two hundred years if not for the hand of the Lord? These resources enabled the Church to pay $192.5 million in cash to acquire the Kirtland Temple in March of 2024.

Yet the Church's financial independence has not removed the yoke of stigmatic bondage from the Church's shoulders nor redeemed Joseph's name. Saints everywhere still feel the stigma of membership and despise its shame. Yet, when the great and glorious day finally comes, this yoke will be broken, and the Church will be seen for what it actually is. On that day, the survivors from all nations under heaven will flow unto the Church as will say, let us learn of the God of Jacob, that we may walk in His ways.

> O Jehovah, have mercy upon this people, and as all men sin, forgive the transgressions of Thy people, and let them be blotted out forever. Let the anointing of thy ministers be sealed upon them with power from on high. (D&C 109:34-35)

Joseph claimed that he received this dedicatory prayer by revelation. This prayer now means removing a yoke and anointing the Lord's people. As we consider these things, our minds should turn to the passage regarding the latter-day deliverance of the Saints from the hand of their oppressor, which closely mirrors the language of this inspired prayer.

> O *A*ssyrian, the rod of mine anger, and the staff in their hand is mine indignation. I will send him against an *h*ypocritical nation, and against the people of my wrath will I give him a charge, to take the spoil, and to take the prey, and to tread them down like the mire of the streets.
>
> Therefore thus saith the Lord GOD of hosts, O my people that dwellest in Zion, be not afraid of the Assyrian: he shall smite thee with a rod, and shall lift up his staff against thee, after the manner of Egypt. For yet a very little while, and the indignation shall cease, and mine anger in their destruction. And the LORD of hosts shall stir up a scourge for him according to the slaughter of Midian at the rock of Oreb: and *as* his rod *was* upon the sea, so shall he lift it up after the manner of Egypt. And it shall come to pass in that day, *that* his burden shall be taken away from off thy shoulder, and his yoke from off thy neck, and the yoke shall be destroyed because of the anointinghttps://www.churchofjesuschrist.org/study/scriptures/ot/isa/10?lang=eng. (Isaiah 10:5-6, 24-27)

The Lord told Isaiah he would send the Assyrians against a hypocritical nation. That nation was destined to become Zion. The Assyrians would be sent to be a scourge unto the Lord's people and to cause the spiritually blind and deaf to believe a strong delusion. The Assyrians will be a major part of that deception. Yet the Assyrian will reign, but for a very little time, and then he will be defeated, and the yoke of his oppression will be removed from off of the saints because of their anointing. I strongly believe Joseph's inspired prayer links to this miraculous purging that will occur in the coming days.

> Let it [*the power that will descend upon the saints during these days of trial*] be fulfilled upon them, as upon those on the day of Pentecost; let the gift of tongues be poured out upon Thy people, even cloven tongues as of fire, and the interpretation thereof. And let Thy house be filled, as with a rushing mighty wind, with thy glory.

Put upon Thy servants the testimony of the covenant, that when they go out and proclaim Thy word they may seal up the law, and prepare the hearts of Thy saints for all those judgments thou art about to send, in thy wrath, upon the inhabitants of the earth, because of their transgressions, that Thy people may not faint in the day of trouble. (D&C 109:36-38)

The passages above are clearly associated with the prophesied outpouring of great power upon the saints when they are being attacked by the Assyrians. Consider Nephi's words:

And it came to pass that I beheld that the great mother of abominations did gather together multitudes upon the face of all the earth, among all the nations of the Gentiles, to fight against the Lamb of God. And it came to pass that I, Nephi, beheld the power of the Lamb of God, that it descended upon the saints of the church of the Lamb, and upon the covenant people of the Lord, who were scattered upon all the face of the earth; and they were armed with righteousness and with the power of God in great glory. (1 Nephi 14:13-14)

God will pour His power upon the saints and the covenant people of scattered Israel. This power endowment will save their lives and enable them to withstand the evils of the day until the great purge occurs at the hands of the Remnant of Jacob. America is liberated, and the yoke is smashed upon the everlasting hills. The Lord knows of the trouble that is in store for the saints of God who will live to see these days fulfilled. These days are our days. We are the saints who will see these things. We are the saints that will receive this great endowment. The yoke will be destroyed because of the anointing that we have received. We must endure it by faith in Israel's God, who made all these things known long before they happened.

And whatsoever city thy servants shall enter, and the people of that city receive their testimony, let Thy peace and Thy salvation be upon that city; that they may gather out of that city the righteous, that they may come forth to Zion, or to her stakes, the places of thine appointment, with songs of everlasting joy; and until this be accomplished, let not thy judgments fall upon that city. (D&C 109:39-40)

This passage speaks of the last and final harvest that will take place in all the earth. This speaks of the days when the Fisher of Men will have been replaced with the Lord Hunters. These will go into all nations right before cities and nations fall and will reap in the righteous, gathering them into the American Zion with miraculous exploits. This will be led by the hundred and forty-four thousand. Yet, something tells me that they will be joined by many others who will have been filled with the power of God unto the deliverance and gathering of many. This is how the righteous will gather into Zion from Europe, Asia, Russia, Africa, Oceania, and the sea islands. This miraculous gathering will be absolutely astounding.

Therefore, just as Isaiah's prophecy spoke of mirrored events that would take place amongst two separate generations, I believe that the prophetic words of Joseph's inspired prayer speak of events that would occur in the days of the earlier saints, at the beginning of the restoration, and again in our days, at its conclusion. Therefore, the history of the Church and its future is like a chiasma.

In the early days of the Church, the missionaries had tremendous success in Europe, and tens of thousands of saints fled their homelands to come to Zion. The same will happen once again in our days, but on a far grander scale, for Europe will be emptied of their righteous inhabitants, and none but the fully ripened gentiles will remain. It is of that day that the next passages speak:

> And whatsoever city thy servants shall enter, and the people of that city receive not the testimony of Thy servants, and Thy servants warn them to save themselves from this untoward generation, let it be upon that city according to that which thou hast spoken by the mouths of thy prophets. But deliver Thou, O Jehovah, we beseech Thee, Thy servants from their hands, and cleanse them from their blood.

> O Lord, we delight not in the destruction of our fellow men; their souls are precious before Thee; but Thy word must be fulfilled. Help Thy servants to say, with Thy grace assisting them: Thy will be done, O Lord, and not ours. We know that Thou hast spoken by the mouth of thy prophets terrible things concerning the wicked, in the last days—that Thou wilt pour out thy judgments, without measure; therefore, O Lord, deliver Thy people from the calamity of the wicked; enable Thy servants to seal up the law, and bind up the testimony, that they may be prepared against the day of burning. (D&C 109: 41-46)

Although the saints did not know it at the time, most of the words of the dedicatory prayer would not be fulfilled by their generation but by ours. Shortly after the saints were driven from Kirtland, the temple was sold to cover the Church's outstanding debts. It has been in the hands of other stewards for almost two hundred years. I find it very curious that right before the fulfillment of this prophetic prayer, the first temple of the original Saints has been restored to the original Church. I believe that this is a powerful sign that the things of this prophetic prayer are now at our door.

The dedicatory prayer continues:

> We ask thee, Holy Father, to remember those who have been driven by the inhabitants of Jackson county, Missouri, from the lands of their inheritance, and break off, O Lord, this yoke of affliction that has been put upon them. Thou knowest, O Lord, that they have been greatly oppressed and afflicted by wicked men; and our hearts flow out with sorrow because of their grievous burdens. O Lord, how long wilt thou suffer this people to bear this affliction, and the cries of their innocent ones to ascend up in thine ears, and their blood come up in testimony before Thee, and not make a display of thy testimony in their behalf? (D&C 109:47-49)

Joseph and the saints did not know the answers to the above questions. Nevertheless, as we have seen, the Lord provided answers to these questions before they had been asked - three years earlier. The Lord told the saints that they would prosper in the mountains, after which they would be gathered in Zion. Elsewhere, He told them they would not receive their inheritance in Zion for many years to come. That inheritance has been reserved for our generation. We will live to see a great exodus from the valleys of the Rocky Mountains. Hundreds of thousands of saints will leave to go to Zion. Yet, Utah will not be abandoned, for the nations will still flow to the mountain of the Lord's houses, wherever those houses are located. Thus, we see that the same persecution that brought the saints to tears so many times also led them to the refuge of the everlasting hills. So, sorrows and tears will drive many to the City of Refuge in the last few days. Yet, after the tears, there will come a fullness of joy.

The prayer now turns towards the oppressors themselves.

> Have mercy, O Lord, upon the wicked mob, who have driven
> Thy people, that they may cease to spoil, that they may
> repent of their sins if repentance is to be found; but if they

will not, make bare Thine arm, O Lord, and redeem that which thou didst appoint a Zion unto Thy people. And if it cannot be otherwise, that the cause of Thy people may not fail before Thee. May thine anger be kindled, and thine indignation fall upon them, that they may be wasted away, both root and branch, from under heaven; but inasmuch as they will repent, Thou art gracious and merciful, and wilt turn away Thy wrath when Thou lookest upon the face of thine Anointed.

Have mercy, O Lord, upon all the nations of the earth; have mercy upon the rulers of our land; may those principles, which were so honorably and nobly defended, namely, the Constitution of our land, by our fathers, be established forever. Remember the kings, the princes, the nobles, and the great ones of the earth, and all people, and the churches, all the poor, the needy, and afflicted ones of the earth; that their hearts may be softened when Thy servants shall go out from thy house, O Jehovah, to bear testimony of Thy name; that their prejudices may give way before the truth, and Thy people may obtain favor in the sight of all; that all the ends of the earth may know that we, Thy servants, have heard Thy voice, and that Thou hast sent us; that from among all these, Thy servants, the sons of Jacob, may gather out the righteous to build a holy city to thy name, as Thou hast commanded them. (D&C 109 50-58)

The passages above speak to the goodness of the early saints, who prayed on behalf of their enemies. These enemies would drive them repeatedly until they finally reached the mountains. We will have cause to consider such things ourselves. It will not be easy for us to pray for our enemies either. Yet, doing so will help us to maintain an eternal perspective. We must see beyond the here and now to what comes next. There is more joy in heaven over one repentant sinner than in a hundred just men. May the Lord enlarge our hearts in the coming day so that we might have such a vision.

We ask Thee to appoint unto Zion other stakes besides this one which thou hast appointed, that the gathering of thy people may roll on in great power and majesty, that Thy work may be cut short in righteousness. (D&C 109:59)

As has been seen, the Lord did not cut His work short. He is in no hurry to destroy the wicked before righteousness takes root. Today, some also pray for the hastening of the Lord's work. By this, we should be praying that the Lord hastens the gathering of Israel and softens the hearts of men. We should pray that the eyes of those around us open to the lateness of the hour so that they may see what is happening in the world around us. This is happening today. While many remain asleep, thousands and even millions are waking up to the awfulness of our situation. This is a sign that the Lord hastened His work in His time. If men wake up and keep themselves through these coming times, the day will come when they will join us soon.

> Now these words, O Lord, we have spoken before Thee, concerning the revelations and commandments which Thou hast given unto us, who are identified with the Gentiles. But Thou knowest that Thou hast a great love for the children of Jacob, who have been scattered upon the mountains for a long time, in a cloudy and dark day. We therefore ask Thee to have mercy upon the children of Jacob, that Jerusalem, from this hour, may begin to be redeemed; and the yoke of bondage may begin to be broken off from the house of David; and the children of Judah may begin to return to the lands which thou didst give to Abraham, their father. (D&C 109:60-64)

Joseph's prayer for the gathering of the Jews was not merely lip service. Within five years of the dedication of the Kirtland Temple, Joseph Smith sent Orson Hyde to Jerusalem to dedicate the land for the regathering of the Jews. At the time of Orson Hyde's dedication to the lands of Israel for the regathering of the Jews, there were less than 20,000 Jews in Israel, which constituted less than 10% of the total population. The first major influx of Jewish immigrants into Palestine began in 1881, which is now known as the first Aliyah. In 1886, the first round of LDS missionaries arrived in Haifa. By 1914, the Jewish population had quintupled in Israel. By 1948, the day the modern state of Israel was formed, the population of Israel had grown to 806,000, of which over 80% were Jewish. The Kirtland Dedicatory prayer was prophetic.

However, the prayer did not only speak to the gathering of the Jews, but also consider the following:

> And cause that the remnants of Jacob, who have been cursed and smitten because of their transgression, be converted from their wild and savage condition to the fulness of the

everlasting gospel; that they may lay down their weapons of
bloodshed, and cease their rebellions. (D&C 109:65)

The passage above has caused many to believe that The Remnant of Jacob is the American Indian. A closer inspection of this inspired dedicatory prayer shows it uses the plural form "Remnants." Meaning there are more than one. Then, the inspired language identifies that it refers to the remnants that have been cursed and smitten. The plural form remnants suggest that while SOME of the remnants were cursed and smitten, others were not. We are meant to understand this in terms of a prior Enochian-flagged chapter. Recall the following prophecy from a former revelation:

But before the great day of the Lord shall come, Jacob shall
flourish in the wilderness, AND the Lamanites shall blossom
as the rose. (D&C 49:24)

The passage above clearly identifies two distinct remnants of Jacob—one that will flourish in the wilderness and one that constitutes the Lamanites. You will recall that in the same revelation cited above, the Lord also spoke of a Holy civilization that we know not of – see D&C 49:8. I believe that that civilization is the body of Jacob that is flourishing in the wilderness, while the Lamanites we know. Joseph's inspired prayer now broadens from the Jews and Lamanites.

And may all the scattered remnants of Israel, who have been
driven to the ends of the earth, come to a knowledge of the
truth, believe in the Messiah, and be redeemed from
oppression, and rejoice before thee. (D&C 109:66)

From the passage above, we learn that scattered remnants of the House of Israel have been driven to the ends of the earth and have lost knowledge of the truth. I take this to mean that they have forgotten who they are. As such, I have come to believe that the House of Israel, in its current form, represents four distinct groups of people. 1) The remnants of Joseph that have been gathered into the bodies of both Ephraim and Manasseh. 2) The Remnants of Judah that have been gathered into bodies, whether in Israel or in separate communities. 3) The Hosts of Israel that have been gathered into bodies of whom we know not of. 4) Those that have lost their identity as belonging to the House of Israel and are scattered amongst all the nations of the earth. The Lord has been the driving force behind 1), 2), and 3), while the missionary efforts of the Church of Jesus Christ of Latter-day Saints have been the driving force behind 4). The restoration of the entire House of Israel will happen before the great and terrible day of the Lord, and when it does, the world will be both shocked and amazed.

> O Lord, remember thy servant, Joseph Smith, Jun., and all his afflictions and persecutions—how he has covenanted with Jehovah, and vowed to Thee, O Mighty God of Jacob— and the commandments which Thou hast given unto him, and that he hath sincerely striven to do Thy will. Have mercy, O Lord, upon his wife and children, that they may be exalted in thy presence, and preserved by Thy fostering hand. Have mercy upon all their immediate connections, that their prejudices may be broken up and swept away as with a flood; that they may be converted and redeemed with Israel, and know that thou art God. (D&C 109:68-70)

Joseph was inspired to ask the Lord that his faith and sacrifice might cover his wife and children in a shroud of mercy. Given that this prayer was received by revelation, this passage is a testament that the Father knows what we need to ask for before we ask it. Why would the Lord inspire Joseph to pray on behalf of his family as part of the Kirtland Temple dedication? I believe it is because the Lord knew Joseph's family would need his mercy.

Joseph's extended family largely joined the church. The notable exception was his uncle Jesse Smith, who was adamantly against the restored gospel. His other uncles, Asael, John, Silas, and George, embraced the restored gospel. The same was true of Joseph's siblings; however, many preceded him in death or joined him shortly after that. Hyrum was killed alongside him at Carthage jail; Don Carlos joined the church and died before Joseph. Samuel, Joseph's younger brother, suffered internal injuries when trying to get to Carthage to protect his brothers and died shortly after that.

There is no doubt that Joseph and Emma Smith loved one another. However, there is also no doubt that marriage is challenging under the best circumstances. Christ taught that a prophet is not without honor except in his hometown. The meaning behind this statement is that it tends to be harder for those closest to a prophet, such as his family, friends, and neighbors, to see past the prophet's mortality. This was most certainly true for Joseph and Emma's relationship.

The phenomenon can be exacerbated by the hardships of life, particularly when many believe that the Lord shields the righteous from bad things. When bad things happen to good people, particularly good people in prominent leadership positions, doubt begins to seep in. Unemployment, underemployment, sickness, or even death of family members can trigger such responses. Indeed, the death of a single child can produce enough stress on a marriage to break it. Therefore, consider the strain upon Joseph and Emma's family when six of their eleven children died prematurely.

Yet the loss of life was far from the greatest challenge facing Joseph and Emma. As challenging as the loss of a loved one is, life and death lay in the hands of God. Some of the revelations that Joseph received were harder for Emma than the death of her children. The Book of Mormon was easy for Emma to accept, although the plate's persecution of her fledgling family was not. On the other hand, restoring the doctrine of Polygamy in modern times was simply too much for Emma. Polygamy might have been easier for her to swallow if women dramatically outnumbered men; however, the ratio of men to women throughout time has been as nearly as perfectly balanced as it could have possibly been. Therefore, when Joseph received a revelation on the practice of plural marriage, it was the equivalent of a nuclear bomb being detonated in their marriage, and nuclear bombs bring nuclear fallout that lasts much longer than the bomb itself.

Hyrum could tell the principle was stressing Joseph's marriage to a dangerous breaking point. As such, Hyrum wanted to help in any way that he could. To this end, Hyrum asked Joseph to dictate the revelation to him, and he would share it with Emma on his behalf. He was sure that he could convince her of its truthfulness. Joseph said, "You don't know Emma like I do."

Still, Hyrum wanted to try. As such, the two of them sat down in Joseph's office in the red brick store, and Hyram wrote while Joseph dedicated what is now D&C 132. True to his word, Hyrum went to Joseph's house to read the revelation to Emma. A short while later, Hyrum returned to the red brick store with his tail between his legs. When Joseph asked him how it had gone, he said that he had never received such a scolding in his life. He said he was astonished by the bitterness, resentment, and anger that seemed to fill Emma. Joseph quietly remarked, "I told you, you didn't know Emma like I do."

Emma never supported the practice of polygamy, and the resulting nuclear fallout hung over the Smith household like a toxic cloud. Other prominent men of Nauvoo were also practicing polygamy; the most prominent was the president of the Quorum of the Twelve Apostles, Brigham Young. Emma and Brigham both had strong personalities and were never considered friendly to each other. This unfriendliness changed to hostility when, after Joseph's death, Emma and Brigham had a dispute about property holdings. As such, a deep and bitter divide was formed between them.

Despite Joseph's mortality, his family loved him very much. That love grew stronger in death. Joseph had one surviving brother, William Smith, and three surviving sisters, Katharine, Sophronia, and Lucy. William and his sisters loved Joseph, and together with Emma and his immediate family members, began to believe that the rights of the leadership of the Church he has restored should be transferred like royalty, from father to son. Furthermore, some claimed that Joseph Smith Jr. had blessed his son Joseph III to be his successor. Mark Hoffman, the murderous forger, forged a document to this end. The succession confusion was a source of major confusion for the saints of Nauvoo at the time.

For most, the leadership of the Church seemed to naturally fall upon the Quorum of the Twelve Apostles and upon Brigham Young, specifically as the Quorum's president. This opinion was greatly bolstered when the countenance of Joseph Smith fell upon Brigham Young while he was speaking to the saints in Nauvoo. Many in attendance described seeing Joseph Smith speaking instead of Brigham.

Yet the rift persisted; ultimately, 25% of the church rallied around Emma and Joseph's living posterity. Those who rallied around Joseph's posterity remained in Nauvoo, while the rest followed Brigham Young into the great beyond in search of the long-promised mountain refuge of the west. Those who remained looked to young Joseph Smith III to lead them, yet, at the time of his father's death, he was but 11 years old. Ultimately, Joseph Smith III did not want to form a new Church because he did not feel that bloodline was sufficient. He felt that he had to be called to the work by God, and he did not feel the call. This apparently changed when he was 27 years old, when on April 6, 1860, the Reorganized Church of Jesus Christ of Latter-day Saints was formed.

Joseph Smith III had three younger brothers, Frederick, Alexander, and David. Neither Frederick nor Alexander joined Joseph III's new church at the time of its formation despite being in their twenties. At the age of 25, Frederick got sick and died two years after the formation of the RLDS church. The shock of Frederick's death stunned Alexander into getting baptized. Alexander mourned for the loss of his brother and the fact that he died without baptism. He said that as he contemplated his brother's death, he felt peace, knowing that he would not be lost, though he did not know how that could be.

In 1863, members of the RLDS Church began to be unhappy with how Joseph III was leading the church and began to call for his replacement. They wanted David, the youngest of Smith's sons, to lead the Church. David was born five months after the martyrdom of his father. David sought to quell the growing dissent in his brother's fledgling Church with the following poem, which he titled, "A Word of Advice to Those Who Look for Me to Be the Prophet":

> Joseph is the Chosen Prophet,
> Well ordained in God's Clear sight;
> Should he lose it by transgression,

Alexander has the right.
Joseph, Alexander, David,
Three remaining pillars still;
Like the three remaining columns,
Of the Temple on the hill!
Joseph's star is full and shining,
Alexander's more than mine;
Mine is just below the mountain,
Bide its time and it will shine.

David's star would not shine, however. He suffered from debilitating depression. While he was serving in the RLDS's first presidency, he wrote a letter to his mother, Emma. The following is a heart-wrench extract of that letter.

Mother I must tell you… I feel very sad and the tears run out of my eyes all the time and I don't know why… strive as I will, my heart sinks like lead.

David's condition did not improve, and he left the first presidency for an insane asylum, where he spent the next 27 years of his life until he died at the age of 59. With the issue of succession resolved for the present, Joseph Smith III became known amongst the RLDS as the pragmatic prophet. By pragmatism, we understand that he de-emphasized many of his father's revelations. For example, he removed the Book of Abraham from the Cannon. He also discontinued all speaking of temple ordinances and vicarious works for the dead. He also edited the Doctrine and Covenants, removing every section referencing polygamy. Due to his mother's influence, Joseph III would teach that Joseph Smith had never practiced polygamy and that it was a doctrine that came from Brigham Young alone.

All of Joseph Smith's surviving children joined the RLDS church. Julia Murdock Smith, Joseph's adopted daughter who was 13 at the time of his death, would later leave the RLDS church in favor of the Catholic Church. She died at the age of 49.

Alexander Smith, who joined the RLDS church after his Brother Frederick's death, was six at the time of his father's martyrdom. After his baptism, he was called on multiple missions out west. He even went to Utah, where he publicly denounced Brigham Young and preached his family's reorganized gospel to little effect. He left Utah, stating that he did so in fear of his life.

True to its founding, the leadership of the RLDS church passed through Joseph Smith's bloodline until it came to Wallace B. Smith, who became prophet on April 5th, 1978.

Up until this point in the church's history, the prophet had chosen its successor. Wallace was appointed by his father, the first Church leader to resign from being a prophet. Wallace Smith went on to serve as a prophet for eighteen years and then resigned himself and declined to name a successor. This caused what was known as the succession crisis in the RLDS church. The crisis was resolved when W Grand McMurray was appointed as a prophet, which broke the chain of blood descendants of Joseph upon which the Church had been originally formed. As a result, other splinter factions broke off with their own blood descendent lines, many of which have also now failed.

Experiencing financial distress due to declining membership contributions, the RLDS church was forced to begin to sell its historic assets. The only organization with the means and interest in such assets was the Church of Jesus Christ of Latter-day Saints. Considering the blessings the Lord has poured out upon the Church of Jesus Christ of Latter-day Saints is amazing. As Joseph Prophesied, it has filled the Rocky Mountains and North and South America, spreading to every inhabited continent of the world.

So far as I can tell, the only members of Joseph's extended family who went with the saints out west were Hyrum's family. Later, one of William Smith's sons, Edson Don Carlos Smith, and one of Lucy Smith's daughters, Julia Amelia Millikin, would join the saints out west. All others remained behind. Joseph Smith's mother died in 1856, four years before the formation of the Reorganized Church of Jesus Christ of Latter-day Saints. According to the words of this prophetic prayer, I have no doubt whatsoever that the Lord will be merciful to Joseph's family. After all, Emma's dying words were: "Joseph!"

The vision continues

> Remember, O Lord, the presidents, even all the presidents of thy church, that thy right hand may exalt them, with all their families, and their immediate connections, that their names may be perpetuated and had in everlasting remembrance from generation to generation. Remember all thy church, O Lord, with all their families, and all their immediate connections, with all their sick and afflicted ones, with all the poor and meek of the earth; that the kingdom, which thou hast set up without hands, may become a great mountain and fill the whole earth; that thy church may come forth out of the wilderness of darkness, and shine forth fair as the moon, clear as the sun, and terrible as an army with banners; and be adorned as a bride for that day when thou shalt unveil the

heavens, and cause the mountains to flow down at thy presence, and the valleys to be exalted, the rough places made smooth; that thy glory may fill the earth; that when the trump shall sound for the dead, we shall be caught up in the cloud to meet thee, that we may ever be with the Lord; that our garments may be pure, that we may be clothed upon with robes of righteousness, with palms in our hands, and crowns of glory upon our heads, and reap eternal joy for all our sufferings.

O Lord God Almighty, hear us in these our petitions, and answer us from heaven, Thy holy habitation, where Thou sittest enthroned, with glory, honor, power, majesty, might, dominion, truth, justice, judgment, mercy, and an infinity of fulness, from everlasting to everlasting. O hear, O hear, O hear us, O Lord! And answer these petitions, and accept the dedication of this house unto thee, the work of our hands, which we have built unto Thy name; and also this church, to put upon it thy name. And help us by the power of Thy Spirit, that we may mingle our voices with those bright, shining seraphs around Thy throne, with acclamations of praise, singing Hosanna to God and the Lamb! And let these, thine anointed ones, be clothed with salvation, and thy saints shout aloud for joy. Amen, and Amen. (D&C 109: 71- 80)

A careful reading of the conclusion of this prayer shows a close alignment with the events of the last days. Of particular note is when the Lord's Church will come out of the wilderness as a bride adorned for her husband on the day that the Lord will reveal the heavens. On that day, Joseph stated that the mountains would melt at their presence. Given this description, he was certainly not talking about the Church he was then leading, but rather the portion of Jacob that was prospering in the wilderness, whose return would result in a new heaven and a new earth.

Therefore, the early saints, the saints in the wilderness, and the saints of the last days will all see eye to eye in the last days. On that day, we will all together be caught up in the clouds of heaven to witness the glorious and powerful return of the Son of Man and His incredible deliverance to the Jews. In this regard, the past, present, and future are one.

Chapter 26: There will be Trials

In the last chapter, we reviewed the inspired dedicatory prayer of the Kirtland temple. In that prayer, we once again were reminded of the far-piercing sight of the Lord, as He inspired Joseph to pray for things that he could not have known of at the time. In this chapter, we will review a revelation given to Joseph Smith while in the Liberty Jail, which contains the same Enochian marker as the previous chapters. As such, I believe that the events of this chapter will be relevant to us all.

Joseph, Hyrum, Siden Rigdon, Lyman Wight, Caleb Baldwin, and Alexander McRae were all arrested on charges of treason, a capital crime, on December 1, 1838, under the orders of Governor Boggs. They spent a bitter cold winter in jail under extremely adverse conditions. This revelation was written on March 20, 1839. Several weeks before their hearing was to take place. Joseph and the other prisoners were disheartened and were missing their friends and families, who had been forced to flee Missouri under the threat of the extermination order. These were the circumstances of the following revelation:

> The ends of the earth shall inquire after thy name, and fools shall have thee in derision, and hell shall rage against thee; while the pure in heart, and the wise, and the noble, and the virtuous, shall seek counsel, and authority, and blessings constantly from under thy hand. And thy people shall never be turned against thee by the testimony of traitors. And although their influence shall cast thee into trouble, and into bars and walls, thou shalt be had in honor; and but for a small moment and thy voice shall be more terrible in the midst of thine enemies than the fierce lion, because of thy righteousness; and thy God shall stand by thee forever and ever.

> If thou art called to pass through tribulation; if thou art in perils among false brethren; if thou art in perils among robbers; if thou art in perils by land or by sea; If thou art accused with all manner of false accusations; if thine enemies fall upon thee; if they tear thee from the society of thy father and mother and brethren and sisters; and if with a

drawn sword thine enemies tear thee from the bosom of thy wife, and of thine offspring, and thine elder son, although but six years of age, shall cling to thy garments, and shall say, My father, my father, why can't you stay with us? O, my father, what are the men going to do with you? And if then he shall be thrust from thee by the sword, and thou be dragged to prison, and thine enemies prowl around thee like wolves for the blood of the lamb; and if thou shouldst be cast into the pit, or into the hands of murderers, and the sentence of death passed upon thee; if thou be cast into the deep; if the billowing surge conspire against thee; if fierce winds become thine enemy; if the heavens gather blackness, and all the elements combine to hedge up the way; and above all, if the very jaws of Hell shall gape open the mouth wide after thee, know thou, my son, that all these things shall give thee experience, and shall be for thy good.

The Son of Man hath descended below them all. Art thou greater than He? Therefore, hold on thy way, and the priesthood shall remain with thee; for their bounds are set, they cannot pass. Thy days are known, and thy years shall not be numbered less; therefore, fear not what man can do, for God shall be with you forever and ever. (D&C 122:1-9)

The gist of this revelation is that with the Lord, all things will work together for your good, even if we cannot see it at the time. We should endure our trials knowing that our adversity will be for a small moment, but our reward will endure forever. Our enemies have a bond set upon them, and they cannot do more to us than the Lord will permit. We must trust that so long as we are righteous and in pursuit of the Father's will in our lives, He will enable us to fulfill the full measure of our creation. We have no such promise if we are not pursuing His will but our own.

However, all of these men were pursuing the Lord's will, and their missions were not yet fulfilled. On April 6th, 1839, Joseph and his companions were taken from this jail to Gallatin, MO, near Far West. When they arrived at Gallatin, they were greeted by a large and hostile crowd. In the confrontation between the saints and the community of Gallatin, some of the town's structures had been burned to the ground, including the courthouse. When the people saw Joseph and those with him, they cried out for their blood with threats of violence. Joseph calmed the crowd down but assured them they were in their hands and would abide by their laws, whatever the outcome.

This was not the response the people expected, but it calmed them down. Joseph continued to be very friendly to the town's people, which disarmed them. Indeed, many of the townspeople, including two ministers of other faiths, became very curious about Joseph and visited him through the night.

As Joseph's kind and welcoming demeanor broke down walls of hostility, his guards began to be friendlier to them. They had heard that Joseph was a powerful man, and they wanted to match their strongest man against him in a contest of pulling sticks. The man the guards put forward was John Brassfield, who was known to be the strongest man in the county. At first, Joseph did not accept the challenge because he was a gospel minister. However, he conceded when the guards promised they would not bet on the outcome and that it would all be done in good sport. To the crowd's delight, Joseph threw John Brassfield several times in succession, and Joseph's popularity with the men increased.

Nevertheless, not all were softening to Joseph and his men, and during the proceeding, there were some heated arguments. One of the witnesses for Joseph and the other leaders of the Church was accosted by multiple men and was forced to spend the night with the prisoners for his own safety, leaving early in the morning. Because of the outbreak and other factors, Joseph's lawyers petitioned for a change of venue, believing they could not obtain a fair trial in Gallatin.

A change of venue was granted to Boone County, located a hundred miles away in the state's center. The guards assigned to escort the men to Boone County consisted of five men, one of whom was John Brassfield, the man Joseph had pulled sticks with in front of the townspeople. Curiously, rather than traveling directly to the new venue, the guards detoured Adam-ondi-Ahman, to the former house of Lyman Wight, one of the party's prisoners. This took the group five miles in the opposite direction. From there, they set out for Boone.

On Sunday night, April 14th, 1839, the party spent the night at Judge Josiah Morin's house, who was present at Joseph's legal proceedings. We do not have many details of Joseph's interaction with Judge Morin, but the judge was impressed with him and felt inspired to advocate for his release. Unbeknownst to Joseph and his fellows at the time, the judge told the sheriff overseeing their transfer to let the men go as soon as they were clear of the Mormon eaters.

The next day, Joseph and the men with him bought their guards a jug of whiskey, which further ingratiated them with the men. That day, they traveled almost twenty miles. By Tuesday night, they had reached Yellow Creek, near Chariton County. On this night, the men began to drink liberally from the jug. When all had fallen asleep, Sheriff

Morgan told the prisoners that he would take a good drink and then go to bed and that they could do as they pleased but that he was not of a disposition to continue to Boone County. As such, Joseph and his men escaped to Illinois on the night of April 16, 1839. They were again received with open arms by the saints in Quincy, who were overjoyed to have them back again.

Thus, we see that the Lord is mindful of His Saints, even if He does allow them to be persecuted and harassed for His name's sake. We do not understand how the Lord works for our good in everything, but we must believe He does. It is estimated that ten thousand saints were forced to leave Missouri under threat of violence. However, only twenty-one saints were killed during this time as a result of mob violence, and most of those at Hawn's Mill. This is a mortality rate of 0.2%. For comparison purposes, the mortality rate of saints crossing the plains was 3.25%, significantly higher. Yet the estimated mortality rate for those traveling the Oregon trail was almost double this, at 6%.

This suggests that while the Lord will not shelter His saints from trials, He will preserve them. The vast majority of the saints who lived through the persecutions of those days and remained faithful to their covenants entered the Salt Lake Valley alive and well. Therefore, regardless of the future, I believe that if we hold on to our faith, as the early saints held on to theirs, we will enjoy the same protection and deliverance as the saints. Yes, we will see hardship. Yes, we will see death. Yes, we will see violent persecution. Yet, if we endure it well, our persecutions will be but for a small moment, and the vast majority of the faith will enter the New Jerusalem, just as our fathers entered the Salt Lake Valley so many years ago. I believe this is the message of the Enochian marker in this chapter. Therefore, let us hold fast to our Faith in the Lord, regardless of what the adversary throws at us, and it will be well with us.

Chapter 27: The Saints of Ramus, IL D&C 130 & 131

This is the last of the Enochian-flagged sections of the D&C, which we will review in this book. The information contained within this chapter was given to the Saints in Ramus, IL. This little town was a special place for Joseph Smith to visit. His sisters Sophronia and Kathrine both lived in Ramus and for a time, his uncle John Smith presided over the congregation of saints there. Joseph was also an excellent friend of the Johnson family and stayed with them often.

Ramus, IL, was located approximately twenty miles east of Nauvoo, about two miles east of Carthage. The name was changed several times to Macedonia and then to present-day Webster, IL. As you will soon see, when Joseph was with the saints in Ramus, possibly because of his familiarity and closeness with them, he spoke more freely about the mysteries of God than elsewhere. You will know what I am talking about by the end of this chapter, and you will be grateful that he did.

You will note that the sections of the D&C that we are about to cover are unique. They represent notes on teachings Joseph gave the people of Ramus rather than complete discourses or revelations. Therefore, to some, it might seem discombobulated, while to others, it demonstrates just how much more Joseph Smith had obtained from the Lord than he shared with the general church, except for snippets such as these. However, in light of the overarching doctrines found within the Book of Enoch, these snippets become beautiful points of light in a vast interconnected tapestry that is vast enough to engulf the entire cosmos. Therefore, we will jump into Joseph's teachings to the saints, a Ramos, without further ado.

> When the Savior shall appear we shall see Him as He is. We
> shall see that He is a man like ourselves. (D&C 130:1)

Joseph clearly states that Jesus Christ is not an incorporeal force of the cosmos but a tangible, physical man like us. However, this is not all that we learn from this verse. Jesus Christ resides in the Celestial realm with God the Father. However, Celestial beings are not confined to the Celestial Kingdom. This world is a fallen world. It is the most wicked of all the Lord's creations, yet Christ can and will come here. If He can come here, He can go anywhere, for all things are below the Celestial Kingdom.

> And that same sociality which exists among us here will
> exist among us there, only it will be coupled with eternal
> glory, which glory we do not now enjoy. (D&C 130:2)

Here, Joseph teaches us that the same society that exists on earth exists throughout the cosmos. Yet, many such societies in the multiverse are infused with eternal glory, which will make them far more enjoyable than any with which we are now familiar. Given the veil and the nature or mortal societies we are familiar with, we cannot comprehend what this means. For now, we must be content to know that there is something far greater out there than we can presently imagine. The multiverse is incomprehensibly large. I believe that the lyrics to the following hymn hint at the wonders that such societies hold:

> If you could hie to Kolob In the twinkling of an eye,
> And then continue onward With that same speed to fly,
> Do you think that you could ever, Through all eternity,
> Find out the generation Where Gods began to be?
>
> Or see the grand beginning, Where space did not extend?
> Or view the last creation, Where Gods and matter end?
> Me thinks the Spirit whispers, "No man has found 'pure space,'
> Nor seen the outside curtains, Where nothing has a place."
>
> The works of God continue, And worlds and lives abound;
> Improvement and progression Have one eternal round.
> There is no end to matter; There is no end to space;
> There is no end to spirit; There is no end to race.
> There is no end to virtue; There is no end to might;
> There is no end to wisdom; There is no end to light.
> There is no end to union; There is no end to youth;
> There is no end to priesthood; There is no end to truth.
> There is no end to glory; There is no end to love;
> There is no end to being; There is no death above.
> (If you could hie to Kolob – LDS Hymnal)

The notes on Joseph's teachings to the saints in Ramus, IL, continue:

> John 14:23—The appearing of the Father and the Son, in that
> verse, is a personal appearance; and the idea that the Father
> and the Son dwell in a man's heart is an old sectarian notion,
> and is false. (D&C 130:3)

Here, Joseph clarifies that God the Father and His Son, Jesus Christ, are two separate and distinct beings. Both are men. Both are tangible. Both have lived distinct and separate lives, although both have spent their lives engaged in the family business of bringing men's immortality and eternal life to pass. However, as Joseph Smith states, the context of this verse is a personal visitation by the Father and the Son to the individual. This personal visitation will occur to all those who are heirs of salvation and is sometimes referred to in scripture as the more sure word of prophecy. It is also referred to as having one's calling and election ensured. More will be spoken of before the conclusion of this chapter; therefore, this is sufficient for the present discussion.

> In answer to the question—Is not the reckoning of God's time, angel's time, prophet's time, and man's time, according to the planet on which they reside? I answer, Yes. But there are no angels who minister to this earth but those who do belong or have belonged to it. (D&C 130:4-5)

Without the context of this book, the statement above seems to come out of left field. However, within the context of this book, it makes perfect sense. According to the book of Abraham, all mortal worlds orbit suns like our own and govern their time based upon their respective orbits – see Abraham 3:5-16. Joseph then teaches that the inhabitants of other worlds are not permitted to minister to the inhabitants of this world unless they have lived here. This is an inquisitive thing to say.

Furthermore, we have learned that the inverse of this doctrine is not true. Joseph taught that the primary reason for which people from this earth are translated is to enable them to administer the gospel to other worlds' inhabitants, as discussed in Volume I of this series. The doctrines being discussed with the saints in Ramus, IL, are to be understood from this perspective.

Joseph continues dropping spiritual bombshell after bombshell:

> The angels do not reside on a planet like this earth; but they reside in the presence of God, on a globe like a sea of glass and fire, where all things for their glory are manifest, past, present, and future, and are continually before the Lord. (D&C 130:6-7)

Like all the verses discussed thus far in this chapter, we are to understand the concept of angels from the context of the Book of Enoch. An angel is either a premortal spirit that has not opted out of the plan of salvation and is living in a Celestial world alongside their heavenly parents, awaiting their opportunity to be tested. Or it is a post-mortal being that has qualified themselves to return to live with their heavenly parents in the presence of God the Father and His Son Jesus Christ. Celestial worlds are not like mortal worlds. Joseph Smith explains that Celestial worlds are like a sea of glass and fire. The book of Revelation describes the Earth's future state of being to become a sea of glass. This is a function of the glory in the Celestial realms. There is a reason for such case, given in the next verse.

> The place where God resides is a great Urim and Thummim. This earth, in its sanctified and immortal state, will be made like unto crystal and will be a Urim and Thummim to the inhabitants who dwell thereon, whereby all things pertaining to an inferior kingdom, or all kingdoms of a lower order, will be manifest to those who dwell on it; and this earth will be Christ's. (D&C 130:8-9)

The Celestial worlds are seas of glass because they are great Urim and Thummims, which enable the inhabitants of the Celestial orders to see everything that is happening within the cosmos within kingdoms of equal or lesser glory. This goes hand in hand with the concept that beings of a Celestial order can transverse the cosmos to any kingdom of an inferior order and that all things are before them. Nothing is hidden from such beings. Kingdoms of lessor orders hold no mysteries to those of the Celestial Kingdom.

Also inherent within the passage above is that authority will be transferred from the Father to the Son. This is to say that Jesus Christ will now take upon Himself the role of the great sovereign of the multiverse, and His Father will take His symbolic seat upon the northern face of the Mount of the Congregation with His Fathers. Thus, we learn that Eternal progression is just as real for Gods as it is for men. Each subsequent iteration of the plan of salvation brings with it an outpouring of glory and advancement that can be achieved in no other way.

Joseph's doctrinal whirlwind to the saints at Ramus continues:

> Then the white stone mentioned in Revelation 2:17, will become a Urim and Thummim to each individual who receives one, whereby things pertaining to a higher order of kingdoms will be made known; and a white stone is given to each of those who come into the celestial kingdom, whereon is a new name written, which no man knoweth save he that receiveth it. The new name is the key word. (D&C 130:10-11)

Whereas the earth itself will be transformed into a great Urim and Thummim that will enable all its inhabitants to gaze into all the lesser kingdoms of the multiverse, the earth will not be able to view kingdoms of a higher order. The principle of lesser kingdoms enables beings to freely move within all kingdoms of equal lesser glory to that of the physical form of the traveler. The scriptures teach that there are at least three orders of glory within the Celestial Kingdom itself. By the law of lesser kingdoms, the highest of the three realms within the Celestial Kingdom itself would be barred to those of the first or second Celestial order. However, it appears that these white stones are not only Urim and Thummims that grant views of the comings and goings of higher orders but have engraved upon their surface a new name. This new name is unique to the stone's owner. By this, we must understand that white stones only work for their intended owners. They are not transferable. Furthermore, we learn that these white stones act as key words.

We are to understand this in conjunction with the instruction of the temple. There, we learn that keywords enable one to pass by the angels who stand as sentinels between the realms. Therefore, while the law of lesser kingdoms should prohibit a tier one Celestial being from accessing higher realms of glory, this token and keyword enable the entrance of lower beings into higher orders. The scriptures only speak of Celestial beings receiving these stones. They are not mentioned in conjunction with any other kingdom. Yet, the fact that they exist at all suggests that there is a way to circumnavigate the principle of lesser kingdoms, even if it is a highly regulated and personally encrypted method. Such things suggest that the multiverse is far more than we can comprehend now.

The prophetic notes on Joseph's instruction to the saints at Ramus now take a decidedly different tone, one regarding the events that will precede the Second Coming.

> I prophesy, in the name of the Lord God, that the commencement of the difficulties which will cause much bloodshed **previous** to the coming of the Son of Man will be in South Carolina. It may probably arise through the slave question. This a voice declared to me, while I was praying earnestly on the subject, December 25th, 1832. (D&C 130:12-13)

The passage above shows us that the Lord spoke to Joseph Smith about the Civil War that would ravish the United States of America. The Civil War began at 4:30 AM on April 12, 1861, when Abraham Lincoln ordered supply ships to reinforce Fort Sumpter, which the newly formed Confederate States of America expressly prohibited. The result was Confederate troops opening fire on Fort Sumter. In 1832, nobody was talking about the Civil War. It was not until the collapse of the 1850 Compromise that the potential for a Civil War became a real possibility. That compromise did five things: 1) admitted

California as a free state, 2) Recognized the Utah and South West territories as part of the United States, both without interests in slavery, and 3) Defined the western border of Texas – shrinking an existing slave state. 4) Abolished the slave trade in Washington DC 5) Enacted the Federal Fugitive Slave Act.

The Fugitive Slave Act was the big compromise that was granted for the permanent toppling of the balance of power that had existed between enslaved persons and Free states since the Missouri Compromise of 1820. The Fugitive Slave Act created much stricter laws for those harboring enslaved people or facilitating their escape via the Underground Railroad. These laws were to be enforced at the Federal level.

While the idea of stronger federal laws protecting southern rights looked good on paper, in practice, it was a façade. In practice, northern states largely ignored these laws, which enraged the South. This led many in the South to the conclusion that their ability to keep slaves and remain part of the United States was impossible. In the eyes of the South, the failed federal enforcement of the Fugitive Slave Act justified their articles of succession, making the Civil War all but inevitable.

Joseph's prophecy above stated that the Civil War would precede the Lord's Second Coming. The Lord did not tell Joseph how long it would proceed. As such, understanding the timing of such things became a topic of grave concern for the prophet, as attested to in the next point, which contains the Enochian marker – Son of Man. Consider the following:

> I was once praying very earnestly to know the time of the coming of the Son of Man, when I heard a voice repeat the following: Joseph, My son, if thou livest until thou art eighty-five years old, thou shalt see the face of the Son of Man; therefore let this suffice, and trouble me no more on this matter.

> I was left thus, without being able to decide whether this coming referred to the beginning of the millennium or to some previous appearing, or whether I should die and thus see his face. I believe the coming of the Son of Man will not be any sooner than that time. (D&C 130:12-17)

The Lord told Joseph that if he lived until 1890, he would see the coming of the Son of Man. It is clear from Joseph's remarks that he did not understand this prophecy. Joseph clearly did not live to be eighty-five. Joseph was murdered the following year, a couple of miles away from Ramus in Carthage, IL, at the age of 38. I am astounded as I contemplate what Joseph Smith accomplished in the fourteen years since founding the Church of Jesus Christ of Latter-day Saints. What might he have accomplished if he lived another 47 years?

He would have led the saints out west if Joseph had not been killed. While we sustain and honor all living prophets, there can be absolutely no doubt that Joseph Smith was a man apart. No other modern prophet has come remotely close to receiving the volume of revelation that Joseph received. He brought forth the Book of Mormon, the Pearl of Great Price, the Doctrine and Covenants, and the translation of the Bible. What other additional truths would we now have had Joseph lived another 47 years?

I believe that the following scripture applies to Joseph Smith – the Seer:

> …a seer is a revelator and a prophet also; and a gift which is greater can no man have, except he should possess the power of God, which no man can; yet a man may have great power given him from God.
>
> But a seer can know of things which are past, and also of things which are to come, and by them shall all things be revealed, or, rather, shall secret things be made manifest, and hidden things shall come to light, and things which are not known shall be made known by them, and also things shall be made known by them which otherwise could not be known. Thus God has provided a means that man, through faith, might work mighty miracles; therefore he becometh a great benefit to his fellow beings. (Mosiah 8:16-18)

In my opinion, Joseph Smith is the greatest Seer the world has seen since the days of Enoch. I believe that if Joseph had been permitted to live until the age of 85, he would have accelerated the progress of the Kingdom of God on Earth to such a degree that the timetable of the coming of the Son of Man would have been accelerated. Yet this was not to be, and God, the Greatest of All, knew this was not to be when He gave this answer to Joseph.

I believe God does not intend to have one man perform all the spiritual labor for His people. Yes, Christ performed the infinite atonement for every living creature in the multiverse, but it is still up to the individual to utilize it. It is the same thing with personal revelation. It is not for the general saint to receive revelation on the administration of the Church. The Church will administer the ordinances of salvation, but it is up to us to understand them. Far more has been revealed regarding the doctrines of the kingdom than most realize.

It is up to us to put these principles together and apply them in our lives. According to the passage above, had Joseph lived another 47 years, he could have greatly accelerated things because one man could have an incredible impact on the spiritual development of the masses. Yet, even so, the Church was condemned in Joseph's day for treating the revelations and spiritual knowledge as lightly as it was. We remain under that condemnation today. As individuals, we must collectively start moving the needle of spiritual knowledge and enlightenment in our own lives.

For some, this is a radical notion, bordering upon apostasy. Yet, this damming idea that we must spoon-feed everything we must know is what has always slowed the progress of the Lord's people. I think this principle is illustrated very well in the Book of Numbers. Consider how the people's philosophy of spiritual knowledge varied from that of Moses.

> A young man ran and reported to Moses, "Eldad and Medad are prophesying in the camp."Joshua son of Nun, assistant to Moses since his youth, responded, "Moses, my lord, stop them! "But Moses asked him, "Are you jealous on my account? If only all the Lord's people were prophets and the Lord would place His Spirit on them! (Numbers 11:27-29 – Christian Standard Bible)

In the above passage, Moses clearly indicated a desire that all God's people should be prophets. By this, we understand that Moses did not want to be the bottleneck in the people's spiritual progress. If the people wanted to understand the Lord's word, he wanted them to obtain that word from the Lord through personal revelation. Consider our own prophet's teachings on this same subject.

> The Prophet Joseph Smith set a pattern for us to follow in resolving our questions… In like manner, what will your seeking open for you? What wisdom do you lack? What do you feel an urgent need to know or understand? Follow the example of the Prophet Joseph…
>
> I urge you to stretch beyond your current spiritual ability to receive personal revelation, for the Lord has promised that "if thou shalt [seek], thou shalt receive revelation upon revelation, knowledge upon knowledge, that thou mayest

know the mysteries and peaceable things—that which bringeth joy, that which bringeth life eternal."

Oh, there is so much more that your Father in Heaven wants you to know. As Elder Neal A. Maxwell taught, "To those who have eyes to see and ears to hear, it is clear that the Father and the Son are giving away the secrets of the universe!" (Revelation for the Church, Revelation for Our Lives)

If we as a people had been collectively living this standard, the world would be a very different place. If Joseph Smith, with his spiritual gifts, could have accelerated things so dramatically, how might the world be if we all followed his example, as President Nelson implores us to do? This powerful concept has been a constant recurring subtheme in Enoch's writings. There is a crucial reason for this. We must take responsibility for our spiritual education and do so with urgency! The hour is very late for us to only now start opening our eyes and looking into the cosmos.

I fear that before most have gone to the cosmos in contemplation, the cosmos will have come to us. How will we survive that coming day without the spiritual infrastructure required to penetrate the coming deceptions? Our need is dire. Time is running far shorter than you know. The Lord's people are as unprepared for what is about to happen as the Jews were for the Lord's first coming. May the Lord have mercy on us in our blind and foolish state!

Joseph's pearls of wisdom continue:

Whatever principle of intelligence we attain unto in this life, it will rise with us in the resurrection. And if a person gains more knowledge and intelligence in this life through his diligence and obedience than another, he will have so much the advantage in the world to come. (D&C 130:18-19)

This is an astounding statement! I believe this statement addressed the resurrection and our lives in the spirit world. It is up to us to rend our veils of doubt and disbelief and learn how to be taught by God the Father. We will have so much advantage in the next stage of our lives to the degree that we do so. The same veil that is upon us now will be upon us in the Spirit World. Yet, the knowledge we acquire here through the Spirit will greatly accelerate our progress there. I believe that one of the reasons that there will be no death during the millennium is because knowledge will have flooded the earth to such a degree that the Spirit World is not needed for our eternal progression because of the knowledge we have obtained while in the flesh. This is why I believe we can be resurrected in the blink of an eye during the millennium. I firmly belief that those who died with great knowledge of the Father's mysteries are put to work in far more meaningful ways in the Spirit World than those who knew little to nothing of the Father's mysteries while in mortality.

Joseph continues:

> There is a law, irrevocably decreed in heaven before the foundations of this world, upon which all blessings are predicated— And when we obtain any blessing from God, it is by obedience to that law upon which it is predicated. (D&C 130:20-21)

There are laws of a celestial order, laws of a terrestrial order, and laws of telestial order. For every kingdom in the multiverse, there is a law, including Outer Darkness. We obtain the kingdom of glory that we do by aligning our lives with the laws of that kingdom. The law of the Celestial Kingdom is rooted in personal revelation. The law of the Celestial Kingdom is simply this: to fulfill the measure of one's creation and to keep the commandments of the Lord. It is impossible to fulfill the measure of one's creation without receiving personal revelation. Therefore, one might say that the law of the Celestial Kingdom is the law of personal revelation. Those who do not receive personal revelation are not living the celestial law and cannot abide by its glory. To receive true and pure revelation from God is to show true valiance in one's testimony of Christ.

Many will accept the gospel truths that the world has previously deemed worthy of acceptance. Yet, such shy away from greater light and knowledge because it threatens to overturn their spiritual status quo. Many turn away from such divine revelation because of the fear of men and only receive it in the Spirit World when the collective consciousness of the masses has been elevated enough to permit them to accept such truths without bearing the shame of it. Such have not been valiant in the testimonies they received but instead opted for the law of the telestial world.

Yet most will receive the revelation of the Lord neither here nor there. These look to the philosophies of men for their salvation. This is the law of the Telestial world. This law must lead to redemption in the fiery burning mountains at the end of everything. In contrast, those in outer darkness have followed the law of their own kingdom. These sought to be a law unto themselves. Their only law was the fulfilment of their own lust and carnal urges. These do what they will, when they will, and enforce their own will by shedding innocent blood. Nothing stops them from worshiping themselves. Such people live hollow, empty lives, ever chasing the substance of eternal things yet finding only the incorporeal dream of it. Choose wisely the law you live by; nobody else can choose it for you.

This Enochian section of the D&C ends with the following passage:

> The Father has a body of flesh and bones as tangible as man's; the Son also; but the Holy Ghost has not a body of flesh and bones, but is a personage of Spirit. Were it not so, the Holy Ghost could not dwell in us. A man may receive the Holy Ghost, and it may descend upon him and not tarry with him. (D&C 130:22-23)

In the passage above, Joseph lays out the nature of the Godhead. God the Father is a glorified and perfected Man with a physical body. His Son, Jesus Christ, began this cycle without a body. Still, he lived and died and rose from the dead during this cycle to obtain a physically glorified body just like that of the Father – who we understand obtained His body similarly. The Holy Ghost does not have a body, nor will He obtain one in this cycle. Instead, He, like Christ before Him, witnessed all things that the Godhead has done and testifies of the truthfulness of those things to us if we will listen.

If we harken to His teachings, our ability to hear and recognize His instruction will grow and develop. If we do not listen to His voice, He will not tarry with us but will leave us to our own devices. The Gods have prepared the path for us and will cause all those seeking to understand it to walk it, though it is straight and narrow. By seeking Them, we can learn and grow far more than we know. Alternatively, we can bumble through life without substantial spiritual objectives or goals. If we do this, there will be weeping and wailing and gnashing of teeth, for mortality is precious, and our time here is of a limited duration.

This concludes D&C 130. However, D&C 131 also stems from Joseph's visit to the saints at Ramus and is very similar. Therefore, even though it does not include the Enochian marker "Son of Man" upon which this last section of this book has been based, given its similar nature, to me, it is the same as if the marker was there. You will see what I mean as we continue. Consider the gems that are found in this brief section.

> In the celestial glory there are three heavens or degrees; and in order to obtain the highest, a man must enter into this order of the priesthood - meaning the new and everlasting covenant of marriage; and if he does not, he cannot obtain it. He may enter into the other, but that is the end of his kingdom; he cannot have an increase. (D&C 131:1-4)

Earlier in this chapter, I discussed the white stones that serve as keywords that enable celestial beings to visit kingdoms of a higher order than their own. Here, we learn that the highest order of the Celestial Kingdom is reserved for Kings and Queens, Priests and Priestesses—those that have been joined in the new and everlasting covenant of marriage. Those that reside in the highest order of the Celestial Kingdom are gods, for they have no end. They participate in the family business, raising the spiritual offspring for the next great cycle of the Father's great plan of happiness. Those not members of the Highest Order of the Celestial Kingdom are not gods but servants of the Most High. These facilitate the Father's great plan but are unlike the Father, for they do not have sons and daughters. Thus, we see that in heaven, no parent is single.

If you would obtain the highest order of the Celestial Kingdom, you cannot do so alone, for the children of heaven are raised in nuclear families by the Father's choicest disciples. Only those that lived by the highest order of the Celestial law will be worth to sire the next generation. It is so because the Father wants these precious sons and daughters of heaven to have the best possible chance of returning to His presence. As such, only those who have learned to hear and follow Him with their spouse will be considered worthy to participate with Him in the process as joint heirs. Your spouse is of far greater value to you than you understand. The need to nurture and foster each other's spiritual development is paramount.

Still, the Lord will not hold back any worthy person who has proven themselves equal to the task. God is boundless. While men and women can only be sealed for time and eternity in holy temples by those with proper authority, God is God, and His word is the Law. David, the King of Israel, fell from his exaltation when he shed Uriah's innocent blood to hide his own sins. As a result, Joseph Smith taught that his wives were taken from him and given to another who was worthy of them – see D&C 132:39.

Thus, we learn that while on earth, men and women can only be sealed to one another in the temples of God. However, the Father can seal in heaven, and nothing can break. As such, it is important to remember that the keys that the prophet holds are not his own; they are God's. Men can wield the power of God only as God sees fit. God can wield His power as He wills, for He is God, the greatest of all. This leads us to the next point.

> The more sure word of prophecy means a man's knowing
> that he is sealed up unto eternal life, by revelation and the
> spirit of prophecy, through the power of the Holy Priesthood.
> (D&C 131:5)

Receiving the more sure word of prophecy is the same thing as having one's calling an election made sure. Joseph touched upon this doctrine with the saints of Ramus earlier in this chapter (D&C 130:3). From the passage above, we are to understand that this process is comprised of three separate things: 1) revelation, 2) the spirit of prophecy, and 3) the power of the Holy Priesthood. First, we need to understand that revelation is a vital component of the process of salvation. Indeed, the Bible Dictionary states that the principle of revelation is the principle of salvation. If you are not receiving personal revelation, something is amiss in your life and must be corrected. Those who do not receive personal revelation will not receive the more sure word of prophecy.

Secondly, we should understand that the same John referenced in D&C 130:3 also taught that the spirit of prophecy is nothing less than the testimony of Jesus Christ, see Rev 19:10. When understood in conjunction with John 14:21-23, we must realize that the spirit of prophecy transcends revelation through the Holy Ghost. It is a physical manifestation of the Father and the Son to the individual. All those who would be heirs of Salvation will have this experience. For most, this experience will happen before the Judgement Bar of God. For some, it will happen in mortality, which brings us to the next point.

The more sure word of prophecy is a priesthood ordinance. It is administered by one having the authority to do so. Just as a person cannot baptize himself in the privacy of his own house, neither can this ordinance be received by oneself in seclusion. Furthermore, just as one cannot enter into the higher degree of the Celestial Kingdom by oneself, this ordinance, like the everlasting covenant, involves a man and a woman. According to Joseph Smith above, the ordinance is performed by one with proper authority. Going through the genealogy of my fathers, I came across a letter wherein one of my ancestors and his spouse were invited by the First Presidency to come to the temple on a certain date to have this ordinance performed. I believe that while some people have this ordinance performed in mortality, most will have it performed by the Lord Jesus Christ before the Judgement Bar of God. I believe this ordinance has to do with washing one's feet.

I believe that this is the context for Joseph's next statement:

> It is impossible for a man to be saved in ignorance. (D&C 131:6)

A man can't be saved in ignorance because salvation is an active endeavor. The ignorant man will not happily awake on the other side to find that he has been saved by his good fortune. Men and women must work out their salvation with fear and trembling before the throne of God. Salvation in the Celestial Kingdom is a very active, hands-on process. If you are not working with God regarding your salvation, do not presume that someone else is doing it for you. This is why no man will be saved in ignorance. Just as the atonement was not a passive endeavor for Christ, neither should you expect your salvation to be passive.

Joseph concludes his discussion with the following statement on the matter:

> There is no such thing as immaterial matter. All spirit is matter, but it is more fine or pure, and can only be discerned by purer eyes; we cannot see it; but when our bodies are purified we shall see that it is all matter. (D&C 131:7-8)

This last statement is amazing. According to Joseph Smith, spirits are comprised of matter, just as our physical bodies are comprised of matter. Elsewhere, Joseph taught that one can prove spirits by shaking their hands. Joseph stated that evil spirits will always try to deceive you but that you will not be able to feel their hand. From the passage above, this is not because their hand is not comprised of matter; rather, the matter from which it is comprised is purer.

Physical matter, as we understand it, is comprised of atoms. Atoms, in turn, are comprised of quantum particles bound to a center nucleus at a comparatively great distance. This anchoring of subatomic particles to a nucleus makes atoms appear solid. If it were not so, we could not see them, for quantum particles are smaller than visible light, and as such they cannot be observed with physical light as we know it. When quantum particles are bound to a nucleus, they act something like a spinning fan blade. When a fan is on, the blades move so quickly that they appear to be everywhere all at once - solid. Furthermore, the spinning fan blades create a barrier miming a solid surface. Despite not being solid, the spinning blades prohibit objects from passing through them like a solid surface.

We do not understand how spiritual matters are organized. However, spiritual matter may comprise quantum particles organized by different quantum forces we have yet to understand. Without being bound to a nucleus, spiritual matter would be invisible to our eyes. We would also be unable to discern it through physical touch. Nevertheless, similarly organized material would be just as tangible as we are. Therefore, when we say that spirits do not have bodies, we must understand that this is not really true. They do have bodies, but those bodies are organized differently from our own.

Joseph taught that a fullness of joy can only be achieved when the spirit, or quantum entity, is inseparably connected to a physical body. Why is this the case? We do not fully comprehend it. Surely, there is a synergistic relationship that would blow our minds if not for the veil. After all, quantum bodies surely have capabilities beyond our physical bodies alone. For example, we know that quantum matter follows a completely different set of rules than Newtonian physics. While physical matter cannot be in two places simultaneously, as strange as it seems, quantum matter can. Physical matter is bound by the speed of light, and quantum matter is not. Entangled quantum particles communicate faster than light. We have not yet begun to scratch the surface of the quantum realm. Nevertheless, herein lies a mystery that caused the premortal heavens to ring with shouts of joy and acclamation. Time will reveal this incredible mystery to us.

This concludes the portion of Joseph's words included in the Doctrine and Covenants to the Saints in Ramus, IL. However, it does not conclude his message to them. There were other things the prophet taught to the saints at Ramus that were more incredible than anything covered in this chapter. I can't say why they were not selected to be included in the Doctrine and Covenants. I guess that they were too strange. Some truths are too hard to hear, and you will receive a sampling of such in the concluding chapter of this book.

Chapter 28: The Ramifications of Ramus

In the prior chapter, we reviewed excerpts from the teachings of the Prophet Joseph Smith to the saints at Ramus, IL. I do not know who selected the information from Joseph's teachings to be included in those chapters, but based on the context, they are snippets from a larger conversation. In this chapter, we will touch upon one other point that Joseph Smith taught to the saints in Ramus that was not included in the Doctrine and Covenants, but that is particularly relevant to the subject matter of the last days, and this is the beast spoken of in the Book of Revelation. Joseph Smith taught some incredible doctrines about these things that, as far as I have learned, are only ever discussed in a discourse that was recorded in *Teachings of the Prophet Joseph Smith*.

After we have discussed the material in his discourse, you will understand why you have likely never heard of this before. It is highly unusual. This is how Joseph begins this most peculiar of sermons:

> The subject I intend to speak upon this morning is one that I have seldom touched upon since I commenced my ministry in the Church. It is a subject of great speculation, as well amongst the elders of this Church, as among the divines of the day: it is in relation to the beasts spoken of by John the Revelator. I have seldom spoken from the revelations; but as my subject is a constant source of speculation amongst the elders, causing a division of sentiment and opinion in relation to it, I now do it in order that division and differences of opinion may be done away with, and not that correct knowledge on the subject is so much needed at the present time. (*Teachings of the Prophet Joseph Smith page 287*)

In Joseph's opening remarks, he stated that it was rare for him to speak about the meaning of the things in the Book of Revelation. He emphasized that he was doing so now to stifle contentions that had arisen amongst them on the subject and not because the saints of Joseph's day needed to understand these things. For context, Pelatiah Brown, who Joseph described as one of the wisest men among the saints, was called in by his stake high council and censured for teaching the subject. Elder Brown had been teaching that the beasts in the book of Daniel referred to kingdoms. Joseph Smith then told the saints that Brother Brown was correct in this teaching. I have written of the beast of Daniel in my other writings and do not intend to rehash those teachings here, but I have come to the same conclusion as Brother Brown.

We will get into what Joseph Smith taught regarding the Beast of Revelation, but before we do, I now want to jump to the conclusion of Joseph's talk after he had finished teaching the saints about the Beast of Revelation. Consider the following:

> I have said more than I ever did before, except once at Ramus, and then up starts the little fellow (Charles Thompson) and stuffed me like a cock-turkey with the prophecies of Daniel, and crammed it down my throat with his finger. (April 1843.)

Joseph Smith concluded his remarks by stating that the only time he ever shared more than he would share in the discourse I am about to review was with the saints at Ramus, IL, in April 1843. His reference to being stuffed like a cock-turkey was clearly an indication that he felt comfortable with the saints with whom he was speaking. This is probably the only reason he spoke about them in the first place. As you will soon learn, what he talks about is bonkers. You will recall that D&C 130, which we reviewed in the prior chapter, was taken from Joseph's April 1843 visit to Ramus, IL. Therefore, Joseph spoke to the saints of the Beast in the context of the prior chapter of this book.

For the sake of brevity, I will not review Joseph's entire discourse, for he also spends a lot of time speaking of Daniel's beasts. Therefore, I will focus on the parts of his discourse that, while not overly important for the saints of his day to understand, will be of life-saving importance for you and me.

In this discourse, Joseph makes a key distinction between the Beast that John saw would destroy the saints and the beasts that Daniel spoke of. Consider his explanation on the subject:

> There is a grand difference and distinction between the visions and figures spoken of by the ancient prophets, and those spoken of in the revelations of John. The things which John saw had no allusion to the scenes of the days of Adam, Enoch, Abraham or Jesus, only so far as is plainly represented by John, and clearly set forth by him. John saw that only which was lying in futurity… (TPJS pg 287-294)

Again, the context of Joseph's teaching pertains specifically to the Beast. The Beast represents something that will happen in the future and not something that occurred in the past, as with many of Daniel's beasts. This does not mean that John did not speak of past things. For example, most of the seven seals covered events that took place in the past, although I believe they foreshadow future events as well. Joseph felt that this was important for us to understand.

Now, there are many beasts spoken of in the Book of Revelation. Therefore, the following explanation of Joseph Smith is very curious. Consider the following:

> John saw beasts that had to do with things on the earth, but
> not in past ages. The beasts which John saw had to devour
> the inhabitants of the earth in days to come. (TPJS 287-294)

Joseph Smith stated that the beasts spoken of by John would devour the earth's inhabitants in the last days. Note his plural usage of the term beasts. By this, we must understand that multiple beasts will devour the earth's inhabitants in the last days. Four of these beasts, with wings, eyes, and the faces of a lion, ox, eagle, and man, represent the Lost Tribes of Israel. We know that these will come to devour the wicked by fire. However, according to John, all the beasts described in Revelation will devour humankind in the last days. Therefore, consider the following passage from the book of Revelation, which describes two other beasts in which we should be particularly interested.

> And I saw another sign, in the likeness of the kingdoms of
> the earth; [an image of] a beast rise up out of the sea, and he
> stood upon the sand of the sea, having seven heads and ten
> horns, and upon his horns ten crowns, and upon his heads
> the name of blasphemy. And the [image of the] beast which
> I saw was like unto a leopard, and his feet were as the feet of
> a bear, and his mouth as the mouth of a lion: and **the dragon
> gave him his power, and his seat, and great authority.**
> (Rev 13:1-2 JST)

The passage above is augmented with the Joseph Smith translation. In that translation, Joseph noted that the beast rising out of the sea was representative of the degenerate kingdoms of the earth. You will note that I added the phrase "an image of" before the phrase "a beast." This was not included in our Joseph Smith Translation of this verse, but as you will soon see, Joseph Smith explicitly stated that this phase should be included here, which I will discuss in short order. This may seem trivial, but I assure you it is most profound. You will also note that the "image of the beast" that rises from the sea is an amalgamated creature comprised of various parts of the four beasts of Daniel's vision. Joseph also taught that Daniel's vision of beasts pertained to earthly kingdoms. The fact that this beast is comprised of an amalgamation of those same beasts suggests that this beast will have power over the kingdoms of the earth. With this in mind, we must review Joseph's precise teaching regarding the "image of the beast" which rose up out of the sea.

> The beast that rose up out of the sea should be translated "the image of a beast", as I have referred to it in Daniel's vision…
>
> The prophets do not declare that they saw a beast or beasts, but that they saw the image or figure of a beast. Daniel did not see an actual bear or a lion, but the images or figures of those beasts. The translation should have been rendered "image" instead of "beast" in every instance where beasts are mentioned by the prophets. But John saw the actual Beast in heaven, showing to John that beasts did actually exist there, and not to represent figures of things on the earth. When the prophets speak of seeing beasts in their visions, they mean that they saw the images, they being types to represent certain things. At the same time they received the interpretation as to what those images or types were designed to represent. (TPJS p287-294)

Joseph Smith distinguishes between the prophets' and John's visions in the passage above. He stated that an "image of a beast" is not an actual creature but rather a symbol of a beast that represents something else. He stated that John the Revelator saw actual beasts that dwelt in the heavens, which are not to be confused with the "images of beasts" that other prophets saw. To this end, Joseph Smith stated that John's writings should have included the phrase "image of a beast" about the image he saw rising up out of the sea, for it was not an actual beast but the representation of the earthly kingdom that would be formed by the terrible machinations of the secret combinations of the last days – the product of Ezra's Eagle.

Joseph further explained why this distinction is KEY to understanding John's writings. Consider the following:

> The beasts which John saw and speaks of being in heaven, were actually living in heaven, and were actually to have power given to them over the inhabitants of the earth, precisely according to the plain reading of the revelations. **I**

give this as a key to the elders of Israel. The independent beast is a beast that dwells in heaven, abstract [apart] from the human family. (TPJS p287-294)

According to Joseph Smith, we must understand that the "image of a beast" rising up from the sea was just a symbol because the other references to Beasts in John's writings refer to literal Beasts! Let me be obvious. As shocking as this may sound, Joseph Smith taught that highly intelligent non-human entities will come to Earth in the last days and subject humanity to their rule. He explicitly stated that these creatures live apart from the human family and exist independently from us.

As shocking as this teaching is, let us now continue in the book of Revelation with this perspective in mind.

> And I saw one of the heads [*the leaders of the Kingdom produced by the events of Ezra's Eagle*] as it were wounded to death; and his deadly wound was healed: and all the world wondered after the Beast. And they worshipped the Dragon which gave power unto the Beast: and they worshipped the Beast, saying, Who is like unto the Beast? who is able to make war with him? And there was given unto him a mouth speaking great things and blasphemies; and power was given unto him to continue forty and two months. (Rev 13:3-5 JST)

The passage above introduces us to three specific characters: 1) a literal Beast that will receive a deadly headwound. 2) A Dragon that will empower an actual Beast with great power and then give the kingdoms of the Earth to him. The Dragon is clearly Satan and is defined as such in Revelation 12:9. The kingdom which the Dragon gives to the Beast is the Kingdom of Ezra's Eagle 3) A mouth speaking great things. This is the latter-day antichrist that will rise.

The idea that the Beast that receives a deadly head wound could have been an actual creature from the Cosmos would never have occurred to me. It is simply too crazy. I have always assumed that this Beast represented either Russia or communism. However, according to Joseph Smith, it is an actual Beast from the cosmos. The world will look at this creature with shock, wonder at it, and be terrified by it. "Who is like the Beast?" "Who can make war with him?" Now, these questions have very different meanings for me. Joseph Smith removes all doubt about this Beast being a country with the following definitive statement:

All the world wondered after the Beast… if the beast was all the world [*meaning the kingdoms of the world*], how could the world wonder after the beast?... Suppose we admit that it means the kingdoms of the world, what propriety would there be in saying, Who is able to make war with my great big self? If these spiritualized interpretations are true, the book contradicts itself in almost every verse. But they are not true. (TPJS pg 287 -294)

In the passages above, Joseph is removing all doubt that the Beast will not represent a kingdom but rather an actual entity. I know this sounds wild, and as you read this, you are saying, "Oh my, Rush has lost his mind!" Perhaps I have lost my mind; who on earth would want to publish a book like this with their name on the front cover? Yet, these are not my teachings; they are Joseph Smith's Teachings. I love Joseph Smith and honor him as one of the greatest men ever. Therefore, I cannot cherry-pick from his teachings. Either he was a prophet, or he was not. All his fruits bear witness to the fact that he was a prophet. Therefore, as strange, frightening, and crazy as these things sound, I cannot dismiss them, for I cannot dismiss Joseph Smith. Still, some might believe that I am twisting the prophet's words, taking things out of context. This is why I must reference his entire discourse on the subject when I reference his teachings, not just cherry-picked passages. Yet, Joseph Smith removed all doubt that he was actually talking about Beasts coming to the Earth from outer space in the following passages. Consider them very carefully:

I suppose John saw beings [*in space*] of a thousand forms, that had been saved from ten thousand times ten thousand earths like this,--strange beasts of which we have no conception: all might be seen in heaven. **The grand secret was to show John what there was in heaven**. John learned that God glorified Himself by saving all that His hands had made, whether beasts, fowls, fishes or men; and He will glorify Himself with them.

Says one, "I cannot believe in the salvation of beasts." Any man who would tell you that this could not be, would tell you that the revelations are not true. (TPJS 287-294)

When Joseph Smith talks about creatures worthy of salvation, he talks about sentient beings who possess great intelligence and free will. Without intelligence and free will, there can be no sin, for there can be no comprehension of good and evil. Therefore,

Joseph states that the "GRAND SECRET" is that the cosmos are filled with such life forms and that many of these life forms were not created in the image of God. Indeed, Joseph implied that we have no concept of what some of these creatures are like. The Book of Enoch likewise suggests that the multiverse is far more diverse and vibrant than we could have expected. Yes, there are mortals, and yes, the Sons and Daughters of God will rule the Cosmos, but this fact does not preclude the existence of other intelligent beings in all their varieties.

As such, we must conclude that some of these creatures are benevolent, and some are not, just as some humans are good and some are evil. According to Joseph Smith, some of these creatures will seek to enslave and subject the human race as part of the events described in the book of Revelation. In our lifetimes, we will see all things restored. Apparently, this restoration will include the true nature of the Cosmos. Such things are truly astounding to contemplate. We live within the most epic story ever told, with a cast of characters beyond comprehension or boundaries: giants, angels, demons, monsters, and men.

As we consider such things, I would call to mind the curious radio interview with General Jeremiah from Chapter 8. In that interview, General Jeremiah claimed to command a Galactic Federation starship called the Alliance and stated that he had captured and interviewed a large "reptilian" creature of vast intelligence and grace. Such a creature would be a beast to us. The creature's name was General Gail-Kah-Tray, and he stood about seven feet tall and spoke perfect English. General Jeremiah stated that this creature had as solid an understanding of our scripture as any being he had ever encountered.

Furthermore, the creature claimed to have prophets in his home world that warned them of the spread of Christianity. They were told that they should seek to inhibit the belief in Christ on planet Earth at all costs. Fifteen years ago, General Gail-Kah-Tray's people believed that the second coming of Christ would occur within the next 30 years or by the year 2039. I believe that it will occur before that date as well.

Again, I did not introduce this account expecting you to believe it outright but to consider it in light of the other teachings in this book. What does this all mean? If any of this is true, what hope do the spiritually lackadaisical have of seeing through the great deceptions when the paradigm of everything they ever thought they knew has collapsed around them?

With this in mind, I present another curious data point for your consideration. This data point comes from Dr. Steven Greer's presentation in Arizona in May of 2018. Dr. Greer has accumulated an astonishing network of whistleblower contacts and resources. I believe Greer is at his best when he cites these resources rather than pontificating their meaning. I do not believe it is possible to comprehend such things in any context other than the fullness of the Gospel of the Lord Jesus Christ. The following is a transcript that I made of the relevant parts of his presentation. I word-smithed it a bit to make more sense without the context of his larger presentation, which was several hours long. Consider the following:

> There is a group [*within the United States*] that is racing forward towards disclosure. This group is a breakaway group from the Mormon Corporate Empire [*in other words they have the religious context to understand these things*] This breakaway group has reached full functionality on an antigravity interdimensional devise as of a few weeks ago. Based on their discoveries, the intelligence community just had a meeting in Cheyeanne Mountain between April 28 and May 5th to discuss the Mormon group's achievements. The purpose of the meeting was to determine a go/ no-go on disclosing their system as part of a broader disclosure. Here is the problem. There are powerful people that want to use this technology to stage an eschatological end of the world scenario.

> One of the things that happened in the labin Salt Lake City, was that a device, about the size of a basketball, was being tested. When the device was hit with a certain frequency it began to levitate and exhibit free energy. It then opened a portal into a lower dimension. When the portal opened, all kinds of monstrous creatures started coming through the portal into the lab. The Mormon's filmed it. As soon as this happened, I was notified by senior officials from both the NSA, and the CIA.

> You have to understand that this type of eschatological disclosure has been authorized. Now I am speaking about this subject at great peril, meaning I am taking a great personal risk in sharing this information with you today. You have to understand that if this rolls out the way the Cheyeanne Mountain Group wants it to, they will present it as the end of the world. The return of Christ.

Here is the problem. It was confirmed to me that the Cheyeanne Mountain Group has now weaponized these portals into other dimensions. The weaponization of this kind of technology is an absolute threat to the structure of space-time, earth, and humanity. Furthermore, the CIA and NSA told me that this technology is now in the hands of a man who claims to be the Messiah of this galaxy. I am quoting the NSA and CIA. This is the scariest [expletive] thing I've encountered in 28 years of doing this. You ignore what I am telling you at your peril. (Dr. Steven Greer – May 12th 2018 Part II Close Encounters of the 5th Kind Youtube video, min 52:30 to 57:00)

Dr. Steven Greer is many things, but a liar is not one of them. I believe he did if he said that he had these conversations. The implication of such things is truly astounding! I once heard Dr. Greer give a separate three-hour presentation regarding government black site projects that he had direct knowledge of. He stated that an underground base in Dugway, Utah, is the most advanced base on the planet. He also stated that a breakaway group from the Mormon Corporate Empire has more authority in that facility than the President of the United States. I asked him if he would clarify what he meant by a breakaway group of the Mormon Corporate Empires, and he said that he could not talk about it.

As such, I am left to wonder what it all means. The church does support universities in and around Salt Lake City. These universities are heavily involved in scientific research. I do not know whether the breakthrough described is coming through these programs or facilities affiliated with the Dugway facility. I know that according to Dr. Greer, people with access to incredible technology also know the restored gospel of Jesus Christ. It causes me to ponder upon a passage of scripture in Daniel 11 that speaks of both the antichrist and members of the Church of Jesus Christ of Latter-day Saints. Consider the following:

> For the ships of Chittim shall come against him: therefore he shall be grieved, and return, and have indignation against the holy covenant: so shall he do; he shall even return, and have intelligence with them that forsake the holy covenant. (Dan 11:30)

To me, this passage suggests that some of the LDS scientists who are affiliated with these projects will fall away. Presumably, some of them will not. It is an inquisitive thing to contemplate. Dr. Greer refers to them as a breakaway group, which suggests they are not operating under the Church's direct oversight. However, by associating them with the Mormon Corporate Empire, one is led to believe that, somehow, this group has access to the tremendous resources of the Church to fund their research. When you are dealing with tremendous sums in the hundreds of billions, it is entirely possible that funds can be redirected without the knowledge of the Church. After all, the Pentagon is on record stating they cannot account for trillions of dollars in funding they have received over the years. We will all understand what Dr. Greer meant one day, but we can only ponder and speculate for now.

When I hear such things from sources that I deem credible, I look for substantiating evidence to support the claim. Therefore, consider my surprise when, on January 1, 2024, social media began to go wild with stories of portals and monstrous creatures at a mall in Miami, FL. Videos showed literally hundreds of police surrounding the mall. Independent people posted firsthand accounts of eight to ten-foot alien creatures opening portals and stepping through them inside the mall. Social media was filled with footage and people describing their firsthand accounts.

All mainstream news sources were quick to debunk the story, saying that the unprecedented police presence was due to a group of teenagers fighting each other with sticks. If you are unfamiliar with the incident, I encourage you to use your Google and Thummim to look into it. One interesting thing that came out of my looking into this story further was a curious correlation with the global coordinates of the Miami Mall where these portals were opening up. Those coordinates are 25°46' 42.2N 80°11'12.5"W. However, if you accidentally inverted these coordinates, rather than ending up in the middle of a mall in Miami, Florida, you would end up in the middle of

Antarctica. Given the interesting history of Antarctica discussed in Volume I of this book, I find this correlation to be fascinating. What does it mean, hopefully, nothing. I present it simply as another data point in a very curious string of events. This is not 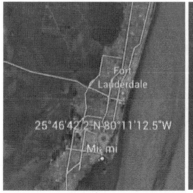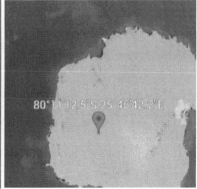 proof of anything. Indeed, one of the things that will make the coming days so challenging will be all the "proof" that will contradict the testimonies of the faithful. When things are being turned upside down, and the nature of the reality that we thought we lived in is stripped away, it will be nearly impossible to hang on to the truths we knew before the cataclysmic events changed everything.

With these bizarre data points in mind, we will continue exploring the passages in the book of Revelation that speak of this Beast. In light of Joseph's grand keys, I think they seem very different from before.

> And there was given unto him[*meaning the Beast that will rule the great nation of Ezra's Eagle*] a mouth speaking great things and blasphemies; and power was given unto him to continue forty *and* two months [*meaning the antichrist would survive the collapse of the American empire by forty-two months*]
>
> And he opened his mouth in blasphemy against God, to blaspheme his name, and his tabernacle, and them that dwell in heaven. And it was given unto him to make war with the saints, and to overcome them: and power was given him over all kindreds, and tongues, and nations.
>
> And all that dwell upon the earth shall worship him, whose names are not written in the book of life of the Lamb slain from the foundation of the world. If any man have an ear, let him hear. He that leadeth into captivity shall go into captivity: he that killeth with the sword must be killed with the sword. Here is the patience and the faith of the saints.
>
> And I beheld **another Beast** coming up out of the earth; and he had two horns like a lamb, and he spake as a dragon. And he exerciseth all the power of the **first Beast** before him, and causeth the earth and them which dwell therein to worship the **first Beast, whose deadly wound was healed**. (Rev 13:5-12)

The last passage above was always a little confusing to me. Given that I had associated the wounded Beast with communism, it did not seem to fit that people would worship a form of governance. However, as Joseph Smith stated, the Beast that received a deadly head wound is not a country but an actual living creature that will come to this earth from the ends of heaven. This Beast will rule in America with the antichrist for a time. However, given the context of the scriptures, I must presume that the Beast will be injured by the unstoppable Remnant of Jacob. The restoration of the Lost Ten Tribes will blindside the Beast and the Antichrist, resulting in their expulsion from the Americas.

After the Beast is wounded and expelled, he is whisked away, presumably by the antichrist, to a place of refuge, which I believe will be the continent of Europe. There, we learn that the antichrist will seek intelligence from those who have forsaken the covenant. By this, we must assume he is seeking intelligence from members of the Church of Jesus Christ of Latter-day Saints, the only ones whose doctrines can make sense of world events. From John's writings, it would appear that while the first Beast is convalescing from his head wound, another independent two-horned Beast rises to power. Given that Joseph Smith stated that these Beasts are literal creatures, I presume that this last horned Beast will literally have two horns. John stated that this second Beast would speak like the Dragon, meaning Lucifer himself. With this in mind, we must consider the implications of the following passage:

> And [the antichrist] doeth great wonders, so that he maketh fire come down from heaven on the earth in the sight of men, and deceiveth them that dwell on the earth by *the means of* those miracles which he had power to do in the sight of the Beast; saying to them that dwell on the earth, that they should make an image to the Beast, which had the wound by a sword, and did live.
>
> And he [*the antichrist*] had power to give life unto the image of the Beast, that the image of the Beast should both speak, and cause that as many as would not worship the image of the beast should be killed. (Rev 13:13-15)

There are three entities at play in the passages above: 1) the antichrist, 2) the first Beast, and 3) an image of the Beast that the entire world worshiped. Curiously absent from these passages is any reference to the second Beast that spoke like the Dragon. I believe the reason for this is that the Second Beast and the image of the Beast are the same. Throughout the whole of Revelation, there is no further reference to the Second Beast; rather, from this point forward, it speaks only of the antichrist, the original Beast, and either the image of the original Beast or the Dragon. Consider the following example of the next passage that speaks of these entities:

> And I saw three unclean spirits like frogs come out of the mouth of the dragon, and out of the mouth of the Beast, and out of the mouth of the false prophet [the antichrist]. For they are the spirits of devils, working miracles, which go forth

unto the kings of the earth and of the whole world, to gather them to the battle of that great day of God Almighty. And he gathered them together into a place called in the Hebrew tongue Armageddon. (Rev 16:13-14; 16)

Here, we have the unholy trinity listed in order of supremacy. First is the Dragon, which is now physically presented to the world. Next is the Beast, who received the deadly head wound but was healed. Third is the antichrist. From a prior passage, you will recall this curious description regarding the antichrist and the miracles that he could perform: "which he had the power to do in the sight of the Beast." By this, we understand that the antichrist is subservient to the Beast, which is subservient to the Dragon, aka the Image of the Beast.

Furthermore, in this passage, John associates the power of all three of these entities with demonic possession. Since the beginning of time, Lucifer has never had a physical body. However, according to John's vision, the Beast and the Antichrist will create an image and give the image life. I do not understand how this could be possible, yet Joseph's grand key is that these things are literal.

We are, therefore, left to contemplate the terrible. If the Beast represents an actual physical creature that will come to the Earth from the depths of space, it stands to reason that he will not come alone. Many believe that the Earth is now inhabited by non-human entities, yet such claims are relegated to the realm of crazed conspiracy theories. Yet, whatever the truth is, when these things spoken of in this chapter occur, they will happen in broad daylight. Their open presence will be one of the things that turns the world upside down.

Therefore, given that such creatures will be openly observed and possibly found in mass upon the earth, is it possible that the Second Beast might be an actual creature that offers himself up as a host for Satan to possess? Might this explain the cryptic description of the Second Beast speaking in the voice of the Dragon? These things are strange and dark, yet that does not make them untrue.

It is a well-documented fact that spirits can possess physical bodies that are not their own. Indeed, often, more than one spirit can inhabit a possessed being. Indeed, in the fifth chapter of Mark, we learn of an account where one man is possessed by a legion of demons. These demons can break any bond, be they strong cords or heavy chains. Such an exhibition of strength is clearly supernatural. Yet, these days, the supernatural will become the norm. However it happens, the fact that Satan obtains a body seems a given.

However, if there is a silver lining here, it is that Satan does not receive his body until after the Remnant of Jacob has returned. Indeed, while these things are spoken of in Revelation 13, Revelation 14 is dedicated to the 144,000 and the harvesting of the earth. In other words, before Satan obtains his apex of power, the 144,000 will gather in the righteous to the incredible City of Refuge that will now be established upon the American continent. Thus, we see that the tremendous evil Satan will be permitted to unleash upon the Earth will be counterbalanced with a tremendous outpouring of righteousness.

According to the passages above, the first thing on this wicked trio's agenda is the destruction of the State of Israel, or the battle of Armageddon as it has been called. These will deceive all the remaining nations of the earth to rally with them in the fulfillment of the Lady's final solution, which Hitler failed to carry out – the eradication of the Jews. Consider the following:

> And I saw the Beast, and the kings of the earth, and their armies, gathered together to make war against Him [Jesus Christ] that sat on the horse, and against His army. And the Beast was taken, and with him the false prophet that wrought miracles before [*the Beast*], with which he deceived them that had received the mark of the Beast, and them that worshipped his Image [Satan]. These both were cast alive into a lake of fire burning with brimstone. (Rev 19:19-20)

The destruction of the Jews does not go according to their plan. The Jewish Messiah will descend from the Heavens in righteous indignation the likes of which planet Earth has never before witnessed. He will eradicate the host of the wicked. He will take the Beast and the Antichrist and banish them to outer darkness in the flesh. Lucifer, the terrible son of the Morning, will be bound, and his influence will not be felt for a thousand years. Yet, the day will come when he is released from his prison planet, and he will rally the cosmos against the Son of Man one last time. The cosmos will burn in that last great epic battle, and the Father's great Plan of Salvation will come to its epic conclusion. Whether in life or in death, all those who make it to the millennium will witness these events firsthand. The might and power of God will become legendary, imprinted within the very fabric of the multiverse itself. Finally, God's greatest adversary will be definitely conquered and will be relegated to the lowest realm in the cosmos – Outer Darkness, which will be his prison forever more.

We will then join the gods who raised us and prepared us for all of these events. We will take our place amongst the most valiant of God's sons and daughters. There, we will rest from all the toils and cares of this iteration of the Plan of Salvation. Our purpose will be to raise the next generation. The cosmos will be an open door to us and our posterity. The wonders and joys of an unfathomable multiverse will lay before us, and we will take great delight in exploring it with our posterity. Based upon our instructions, our posterity will choose for themselves, as we did before them. We will take great joy in the fact that there is nothing that our posterity can do that will cut them off from our presence, for all things will be open before us, even if they are not open before them. And so it will continue, the great turning of the cosmic wheel, with its affiliated kingdoms, thrones, powers, principalities, dominions, exaltations, and eternal lives. Oh, my Great and Glorious God, how Thy works are both wonderful and beyond reckoning!

Chapter 29: Supernatural

As I consider the events of the last days, I have often pondered what the most challenging aspects for the faithful will be. We know these will be times of trial unlike anything the world has ever experienced. Yet, trials and persecution have a way of galvanizing faith rather than destroying it. Consider all of the terrible things that have happened to the saints of God throughout world history. The righteous have been stoned, burned alive, sawn asunder, fed to wild animals, and killed for sport in the arenas of Rome. Even in the modern age, saints were driven from their homes. Yet, the saints weathered such trials both anciently and in modern times with their faith intact.

If overcoming the saints will not lead to the collapse of their faith, what will? I believe that Jesus Christ gave us the answer to this important question when He prophesied to His disciples upon the Mount of Olives in Jerusalem two thousand years ago. Consider His prophetic warning:

> For in those days there shall also arise false Christs, and false
> prophets, and shall show great signs and wonders, insomuch,
> that, if possible, they shall deceive the very elect, who are
> the elect according to the covenant. Behold, I speak these
> things unto you for the elect's sake(JSM 1:22-23)

According to Jesus Christ, events of a supernatural order will challenge the elect's faith more than anything else. Note that Christ is not generally referring to Christians here, but rather the elect according to the covenant. The covenant refers to the New and Everlasting Covenant of the restored Gospel of Jesus Christ. Therefore, these supernatural events will be particularly trying for the members of the Church of Jesus Christ of Latter-day Saints. Why?

I think the answer is that complacency towards the supernatural has crept into our cultural and religious practices. Many refuse to believe that there will even be an antichrist. Others do not believe the Lord would permit visitors from other worlds to come here and interact with us, even though transmedium craft are already flying in our skies and oceans with impunity. I worry that such religious paradigms create dangerous baby-and-the-bath-water-type scenarios wherein the whole gospel will be rejected because their doctrinal paradigms will have no place for these pending supernatural events.

The question then becomes, are saints such as these really elect according to the covenant? What does it mean to be elected? I think that this is an important question. Consider the following passage from Modern Revelation that addresses this very question:

> And ye are called to bring to pass the gathering of mine elect; **for mine elect hear my voice and harden not their hearts**; wherefore the decree hath gone forth from **the Father** that they **(the elect)** shall be gathered in unto one place upon the face of this land (the city of refuge, the New Jerusalem), to prepare their hearts and be prepared in all things against the day when tribulation and desolation are sent forth upon the wicked. For the hour is nigh and the day soon at hand when the earth is ripe; and all the proud and they that do wickedly shall be as stubble; and I will burn them up, saith the Lord of Hosts, that wickedness shall not be upon the earth (D&C 29:7-9).

The elect are those who hear the Lord's voice and do not harden their hearts against it. Many in the Church today refuse to listen to anything about this subject matter. As President Nelson has said, if you have eyes to see, it is clear that the Lord is giving away the secrets of the Universe. The context of this statement was President Nelson's encouragement for us to expand our present ability to receive personal revelation. Yet, while personal revelation is a core tenant of the gospel, not as many people believe in this concept as they should; they believe that ordinary members of the Church cannot learn extraordinary things through personal revelation. They believe extraordinary learning is limited to the prophet.

Case in point: Consider the following comment posted on my YouTube channel. I do not know who this person is, but for the sake of this narrative, let's assume that this is a righteous young man. Consider his comment.

> Let's say for a moment that what you're saying is true, and it very well could be. But this would be undeclared, or unrevealed doctrine. And when I say unrevealed, I mean to the prophet of the church who is the only one who holds the keys and has the authority to declare doctrine. Who knows, maybe it has been revealed to modern day prophets, but it has not been declared to the body of the church. **Therefore, before these things can be ratified by the spirit to me personally, it would first have to go through the prophet**

of the church, and to the 12 as well. Then revealed to the world. There is a line of authority and a process to these things. What you teach is very interesting and I love listening and learning. BUT, until the brethren declare it, these things should only be discussed as theories for now, and not taught as doctrine in Sunday School.

To many, a cursory reading of this comment sounds spot on. However, what this well-meaning young man has written goes to the heart of the matter. He has very eloquently summarized most of the Church members' reasoning regarding personal revelation. According to this young man, the prophet is the ultimate gatekeeper for all understanding and learning. All we need do is turn on the conference and listen to what He says. If he does not talk about something, we need not concern ourselves with it, for it is unknowable.

Whether this young man realizes it or not, he has created his own creed. A creed is a religious paradigm from which a person views the world. This is what Joseph Smith taught regarding the perils of such creeds.

> I want to come up into the presence of God and learn all things; but the creeds set up stakes [limits], and say, "Hitherto shalt thou come, and no further"; which I cannot subscribe to. (History of the Church 6:57)

Essentially, this young man has created a creed whereby only certain individuals can be taught of the Lord and that all others are dependent on them to know what the Lord would have them know. This is not only false but perilous! Yes, there is an order in the heavens. The prophet of God, the First Presidency, and the Quorum of the Twelve are the princes of the covenant. They hold all the keys for the administration of the priesthood ordinances of the gospel and the administration of the Church. Yet personal revelation is the gift of God to every man, woman, and child living on this planet.

President Nelson clearly teaches us that this young man's creed is wrong. Consider the following teaching from President Nelson:

> I urge you to stretch beyond your current spiritual ability to receive personal revelation, for the Lord has promised that "if thou shalt [seek], thou shalt receive revelation upon revelation, knowledge upon knowledge, that thou mayest know the mysteries and peaceable things—that which bringeth joy, that which bringeth life eternal."

Oh, there is so much more that your Father in Heaven wants you to know. As Elder Neal A. Maxwell taught, "To those who have eyes to see and ears to hear, it is clear that the Father and the Son are giving away the secrets of the universe!" (Pres Nelson – Revelation for the Church, Revelation for our lives)

President Nelson is clearly teaching something very different from what this young man has understood. The prophet has clearly debunked the idea that all revelation regarding the last days must be bottlenecked through himself or the quorum of the twelve. The Lord has limited these men in what they can teach – "preach nothing but repentance unto this generation." This is why the prophet is URGING us to stretch beyond our current spiritual abilities to receive personal revelation for ourselves. He has stated in no uncertain terms that we will not survive the coming day without personal revelation. If the prophet admires us and seeks to learn from the Spirit, how is it that so many of us are so willfully ignorant of these things?

One of the primary themes of this book has been the Father's Hidden Son. The world does not really know Jesus Christ. His true nature is hidden and has been from the beginning. Now we see that it is hidden because too few people are truly interested in learning of Him from the Father. Think back to the fifth chapter of this book, wherein I shared President Taylor's letter to the Church. That letter was about the incredible supernatural events that will take place in the last few days. Reconsider this portion of his letter:

> Who shall be able to withstand? Do you think that your great sagacity and the compass of your profound, philosophical turn of mind will enable you to detect the error and delusion of these arts? Oh, man, this is a vain hope. Your mind will not be competent to detect the delusion. God Himself will allow Satan to ply your scrutinizing eye with powers and sophistications far beyond your capacity to detect…

> Don't tell me about Popes and Prelates sitting in the Temple of God as God. One far greater than any Pope or Prelate is soon to be revealed, and he will claim to be worshipped as God…

> The Devil in the last stage of desperation, will take such a pre-eminent lead in literature, politics, philosophy, and religion; in wars, famines, pestilences, earthquakes,

thunderings and lightnings, setting cities in conflagration, etc., that mighty kings and powerful nations will be constrained to fall down and worship him. And they will marvel at his great power, and wonder after him with great astonishment. For His signs and wonders will be among all nations. [Satan will be worshiped as God for the world will not know God.]

You cannot know God without present revelation. Did you ever think of this most solemn and essential truth before? You may have been accustomed to pray, all your life time, and as yet you, even you, do not know God. You may have heard many thousand sermons, with a sincere desire both to remember and practice them, and yet you do not know God. But it has been decided in the court of heaven, that no man can know the Father but the Son, and he to whom theSon REVEALETH Him. Now, has Jesus Christ ever revealed God the Father to you, dear reader?

Be honest with yourself, and do not err in your answer to this most important question. However much the Son may have revealed the Father to Prophets, Patriarchs, and Apostles of old, the question still remains in full force — has He revealed the Father to YOU? A revelation to another man is by no means a revelation to YOU! (Millennial Star, April 30, 1853 Vol 15, page 273)

This is a powerful statement by a prophet of the Lord, and it, too, debunks our young YouTube poster's creed. We have a responsibility to seek revelation. The Father will teach us directly. Now, let me be clear. The Lord has already revealed what will transpire upon the earth in the last days through His prophets, for He doth nothing without revealing it first. Therefore, it is not that the Lord is revealing new groundbreaking doctrines to us personally; rather, He is opening the eyes of our understanding regarding the meaning of what has already been given to the world. There is no greater starting point for this subject matter than the Book of Mormon and the portions of that book that Jesus Christ specifically called out and commanded us to study. To this end, those writings were transcribed upon gold plates and preserved miraculously. It is our responsibility to understand them so that we might be better prepared as a result. This is why President Nelson has said: "Oh, there is so much more that your Father in Heaven wants you to know." God can and will teach us if we will open our hearts and minds to the experience. Everything that He will teach us will reconcile with the restored gospel perfectly. If not, your understanding of the revelation is off and not the gospel.

The philosophy of this young man is not that different from the false premise of Laman and Lemuel. Lamen and Lemuel had questions. They asked Nephi for answers. Nephi insightfully asked them in return, "Have ye inquired of the Lord?" Their response was essentially the same as the young man's: the Lord makes no such things known unto us. Laman and Lemuel believed their prophet's father could receive answers, but the Lord would not speak to them. In reality, they were unwilling to expend the spiritual energy required to obtain the answers to their questions, but Nephi was willing to.

Our prophet has asked us to study these things. He talks about these things generally, but he does not teach us in detail about them. There is a reason for this. The last days are intended to be a test. We have been invited multiple times to study these things; it is our choice whether to do so or not. One of the Church's biggest problems at the moment is that we listen to the Prophet, but we do not follow his admonitions as we ought. If we acted on his council as a Church, we would not be as woefully ignorant of these things as we are.

We are not spiritually prepared for supernatural events that are about to occur on Earth. These supernatural events will try our faith more than any generation that has ever lived. The saints, in general, do not even believe in an antichrist. This incredible ignorance comes from a lack of study and personal interaction with the scriptural texts themselves. People seek to understand the scriptures via YouTube rather than through the Spirit of God. As such, how will the faith of these endure when antichrists descend from the heavens and perform great miracles and wonders in the eyes of all people? How will faith endure when strange, intelligent, and powerful creatures descend from the heavens and begin to wreak havoc upon the earth alongside these powerful antichrists? How will faith endure when the strange gods of the ancient world step out of history and into our lives? How will faith endure when Satan transforms himself from a nebulous boogie man into a tangible entity that is known and worshiped the world over?

I am convinced that supernatural aspects such as these will obliterate the faith of the saints more than anything else. It should not be this way, but it will be. After all, the fundamental tenets upon which our faith is built are supernatural. We suppress the supernatural because it is strange. It is far easier to believe these things in theory than in practice. Yet, God is, first and foremost, a Supernatural Being.

Every ancient account that we have of the creation is based upon the supernatural principle of Divine Utterance - God speaks, and the elements obey. The scriptural account depicts this process as transpiring instantaneously. Yet, such concepts are too much for our church-own schools and universities. They consider such concepts to be symbolic at best. Darwinism is the doctrine of the day.

Yet, the principle of Divine Utterance cannot be separated from the life and ministry of Jesus Christ. He spoke the Word, and water became wine. He spoke the Word, and the terrible tempest abated into calm seas. At His command, the dead rose from the grave, the leprous became whole, the deaf could hear, the blind could see, and the lame could walk. Why do we believe these last things can be the product of Divine Utterance but not the world's creation? Either God is all-powerful, or He is not. What is the difference between commanding the dead to rise and commanding the waters to separate from the dry land? Why wouldn't the elements do the same if the dead rise instantaneously at His command?

I do not know everything. However, I have learned that there is far more to the multiverse than we have ever been taught in school. The Newtonian world around us would have us believe that science restricts God and that God is somehow bound by its laws. Yet, what if the laws of science are what they are because God has dictated them to be so? I have come to believe that God is the most powerful force in the Multiverse. By Divine Utterance, the laws of science can be manipulated and changed.

His Word and promises are the cosmos's only true and immutable laws. We must prepare ourselves for this reality. After all, the word supernatural is a misnomer in that it is thought to exceed the powers or laws of nature. In reality, the supernatural is the norm, and the Newtonian world in which we place so much trust and confidence is nothing more than a facade that keeps us from seeing things as they are. Prepare for the façade of the normal world to come crashing down shortly. When that happens, I pray we might all be guided by the constant influence of the Holy Ghost; if not, we will not survive. May God be with us!

Made in the USA
Columbia, SC
02 September 2024

41431512R00230